PeopleSoft HRMS Reporting

Adam T. Bromwich

Prentice Hall PTR
Upper Saddle River, NJ 07458
http://www.phptr.com

Editorial/Production Supervision: *MetroVoice Publishing Services*
Acquisitions Editor: *Tim Moore*
Editorial Assistant: *Julie Okulicz*
Manufacturing Manager: *Alexis R. Heydt*
Marketing Manager: *Bryan Gambrel*
Art Director: *Gail Cocker-Bogusz*
Interior Series Design: *Meg VanArsdale*
Cover Design Director: *Jerry Votta*
Cover Design: *Anthony Gemmellaro*
Project Coordinator: *Anne Trowbridge*

Prentice Hall books are widely used by corporation and government agencies for training, marketing, and resale.

The publisher offers discounts on this book when ordered in bulk quantities. For more information, contact

Corporate Sales Department,
Prentice Hall PTR
One Lake Street
Upper Saddle River, NJ 07458
Phone: 800-382-3419; FAX: 201-236-7141
E-mail (Internet): corpsales@prenhall.com

Printed in the United States of America

10 9 8 7 6 5 4 3 2 1

ISBN 0-13-021612-7

Prentice-Hall International (UK) Limited, *London*
Prentice-Hall of Australia Pty. Limited, *Sydney*
Prentice-Hall Canada Inc., *Toronto*
Prentice-Hall Hispanoamericana, S.A., *Mexico*
Prentice-Hall of India Private Limited, *New Delhi*
Prentice-Hall of Japan, Inc., *Tokyo*
Prentice-Hall (Singapore) Pte. Ltd., *Singapore*
Editora Prentice-Hall do Brasil, Ltda., *Rio de Janeiro*

Contents

Part 2

Human Resources   67

6

Personal Information   69

7

The Job Table   89

8

Status   *107*

9

Compensation History   *123*

10

Position/Job History

11

Corporate Hierarchy

12

Employment Information

13

Background Information   *159*

Part 3

Payroll   165

14

Working with Payroll Data   *167*

15

The Paycheck   191

Part 4
Benefits   265

23

Dependents and Beneficiaries *317*

24

Rates *329*

Part 5

Query and SQR Tools   *335*

Series Foreword

In 1999, the enterprise software industry hit the wall. Or did it? After a cycle of explosive growth, the leaders of the enterprise software pack, including PeopleSoft (www.peoplesoft.com), Oracle (www.oracle.com), Baan (www.baan.com), JDEdwards (www.jde.com), and SAP (www.sap.com), came crashing to earth. Stock market gurus and financial mavens flinched, but the growing army of consultants and enterprise software users hardly even noticed. There were many clever explanations about why software sales stalled, including the impact of Y2K, the Euro, low ROI, high TCO, and even the Internet. In spite of these speculations, the fact remains that years of impressive sales have created a surfeit of business engineering and implementation projects. In *PeopleSoft HRMS Reporting*, Adam Bromwich speaks to those resolute implementers charged with making the investment in enterprise software pay off. In the process, he imparts his wisdom about setting up a PeopleSoft system in the working world. There are far too few books on the market today that capture real-world experience and reveal the inner secrets of complex enterprise software products. This is one.

The market for enterprise applications is estimated to be about 12 billion dollars. For every dollar of software revenue, another five to seven dollars is spent on implementing the software solution. That adds up to between 60 and 84 billion dollars spent in 1999 on enterprise software related implementation services. Increasing global competition, customer demands and changing markets are driving more and more companies to take on business process engineering. With the help of PeopleSoft, companies can build a technological platform that supports continuous process change, not just one-time efforts. New developments in software such as extensibility, interoperability, and scalability are matched with business goals such as improved customer service, lower costs, and more efficient production to create an ideal enterprise application software product. This book examines the ways to deliver a system that supports the overall engineering effort.

Ease of use and the potential to customize a standard software solution continue to draw companies to PeopleSoft. One leading retailer in the US, Sears Roebuck (www.sears.com) of Chicago, Illinois, was impressed with the flexibility and implementation tools available for PeopleSoft's application suite, and it was a key point in their buying decision. Sears expects a 46 percent decrease in operating expenses by installing PeopleSoft.

Arthur Martinez, CEO of Sears Roebuck, acknowledges that "PeopleSoft helps provide information for making faster, better decisions, which ultimately makes Sears a compelling place to shop." But how will his customers shop in the future? The Internet has had such a profound impact on enterprise computing that a new generation of application software is needed to address the dramatic and fundamental shift in the way companies work. The Internet, combined with the core elements of client/server technology, such as scalability, messaging, application partitioning, and distribution, and the technological possibilities now available to facilitate large-scale application components, are fueling a revolution in the way business and technology interact.

Application Software Providers (ASPs) provide a hosted and managed solution platform for enterprise software. For a monthly fee, ASPs offer enterprise application software and a range of implementation services. Instead of implementing an application solution in their own facility, customers rent application usage in a managed Internet environment. Some pioneering ASPs offer their customers services and application functionality based on PeopleSoft. Companies who are considering an ASP as an alternative to implementing PeopleSoft on site will find that Adam's book provides a very useful basis for conducting discussions with the ASP implementation team.

At SAP AG in Germany, I was repeatedly charged with preparing competitor information and positioning against PeopleSoft. SAP's sales force was often baffled by PeopleSoft's ability to create neat prototype applications that would succeed on the fly. There are many legends about how PeopleSoft's flexible front end and user-friendly interface impressed the client. In 1996, when Siemens AG, one of Germany's largest electronic companies and a loyal SAP partner, decided to use PeopleSoft for its human resource solution, it was a rude awakening for SAP. PeopleSoft, a fierce competitor with a world-class product, beat SAP in their own back yard. One of the core competencies of PeopleSoft is information management and reporting; this book explains how to harness this strength to the benefit of every project.

As the name implies, PeopleSoft, founded by Dave Duffield in 1987, began as software for people—software that automated all human resource processes in a company. The Pleasanton, California company rapidly expanded its product line to include finance, sales, and manufacturing so that it became a full-blown ERP solution. Along with this growth in functionality grew an interest in extending applications. PeopleTools, the application development and product extension platform for PeopleSoft's application suite, earned high marks with programmers. Even though the hallmark of enterprise software is standard business functionality in the box, as Adam deftly describes in this book, there are many ways to use PeopleTools to make the product a better fit with the company.

Whether you need to streamline human resources, set up payroll and benefits, or simply get a report, this book is an important reference for anyone involved with implementing a PeopleSoft solution. Project managers will discover useful product information that will help them judge the resource requirements for an implementation. Programmers will find useful tips about querying and reporting. Consultants will find a broad base of information about the business blueprint contained in the PeopleSoft application that will help them answer questions about business practices. While teaching computer science to undergraduate students, I was at a loss to find books with real-world examples and material. Students and teachers alike will appreciate this book's practical approach to its subject, including its many insights into using the product.

Adam has brought a wealth of knowledge about implementing PeopleSoft to this project. His precise but effortless prose and his obvious experience with the product make reading this book an enjoyable learning experience.

—Thomas Curran
Cambridge, MA
July, 1999

Foreword

PeopleSoft is widely regarded as the leading vendor for enterprise-wide human resources (HR) software. Over the past decade, major corporations have consistently selected PeopleSoft over the competition. Although PeopleSoft has released several other applications, including a financials and manufacturing package, none has the market dominance that the human resources package currently and historically has.

Why is PeopleSoft HR so popular? First, PeopleSoft HR is written and maintained by human resources professionals who have strong backgrounds in both custom and package human resources solutions. The organization of the application and the overall design of the user interface reflect an understanding of what human resources departments do, and how they do it best. It is not by accident that most companies fit fairly well into the PeopleSoft package mold.

PeopleSoft is designed from an idealist perspective, reflecting a "best-practices" mentality. Each function is carefully designed with attention paid to how human resources departments will maintain and augment the application. Although not entirely consistent, most PeopleSoft functions are easy to use and understand. When human resources users compare their current methods with PeopleSoft's design, they often choose PeopleSoft as the ideal way to go.

UNDERSTANDING THE BASICS: PEOPLETOOLS VS. THE APPLICATION

PeopleSoft is also favored because it provides the applications necessary for making customizations. There is an understanding that no two human resources departments are alike, and that customization is a requirement, not an afterthought. PeopleSoft provides tools to modify the application and provides the source code for complex functions, allowing you to customize almost anything.

When you purchase the PeopleSoft HR package, there are two main components:

1. **PeopleTools** form the basis of the application. They are the tools that write, compile, and read the "language" that PeopleSoft is written in.

2. **The Human Resources** application is the actual program that is used to manage human resources functions. All of the panels, fields, and programs for the application are written using PeopleTools.

It is difficult to distinguish PeopleTools from the rest of the application, since they are so integrated. One easy way to determine what is a PeopleTool and what was designed and built with a PeopleTool is to look at the menu structure of the Go menu in PeopleSoft (Figure 1).

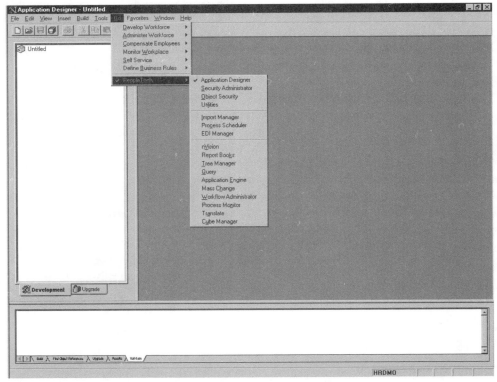

▶ **Figure 1**   PeopleSoft 'Go' menu

All of the functions of the HR application are listed at the top of the Go menu, and the PeopleTools are under a sub-menu.

The majority of the PeopleTools are meant for programmers or those actually modifying the system. PeopleSoft Query and nVision are for end-users (see Chapter 25 for more information about Query). The remaining tools are specific to certain functions, such as the setup of security, establishing the necessary organizational trees, and coordinating the execution of batch (automatic) processes.

Also, PeopleTools are not specific to the PeopleSoft HR package. They are delivered with every application package sold by PeopleSoft. The items in the Go menu before the PeopleTools sub-menu are the only items that are HR-related and delivered uniquely with PeopleSoft HR.

Application Designer

The first item on the PeopleTools sub-menu, the Application Designer, is the principal tool for modifying the PeopleSoft delivered package (it is shown in the background of Figure 1). In the Application Designer a programmer can add, modify, delete, or just view tables, panels, fields, and menus. The Application Designer is a robust tool that can easily customize the PeopleSoft package.

> Since the Application Designer is provided with all PeopleSoft packages, there is a great deal of documentation on its use. It is a simple application, operating much like a word processor, where you can open items, create new items, and make changes. We do not go into the workings of the Application Designer in this book, but it is a good idea to become familiar with the basic components. Let's look at the basic items that can be accessed in the Application Designer and what they do.

Panel

Panels are the windows that users interact with. They contain fields, which can be viewed or edited online. When a user clicks save, the data in these fields is typically evaluated and saved to the database. A panel is simply a way to interact with one or more tables in the database. It does not contain any code—it simply groups fields from various tables onto a single screen for data entry.

Record

A record is a group of fields. A record definition explains which fields are included. In this book, we call records *tables*, which is the traditional database terminology. All of the information in the PeopleSoft database is stored in different tables. For example, pay checks are stored in a table called PS_PAY_CHECK. The 'PS' identifies the table as a PeopleSoft table. In this table, there are many fields, such as employee ID, date, and dollar amount. Each check in this table represents one row in the table—each row has a different employee ID, date, and dollar amount.

The definition of a table occurs at the database level, but is mirrored in the Application Designer. If you open a table in the Application Designer, you will see a list of the fields that make up the table. You can double click these fields to get the field definitions. In other words, a table definition is made up of many field definitions.

PeopleSoft does not use the "record" terminology often to describe a table, but you will find it when you open a table in the Application Designer. Instead of selecting "table," you will need to select "record" in order to open a table.

Field

A field is an individual piece of data. Since the same field definition is often found on many tables, it is defined only once in PeopleSoft and then applied to each table. Only the size, type, and description of a field are stored in the field definition.

PeopleCode

Custom code can be attached to a particular field on a table (record) definition. This code can operate when a field is looked at, changed, saved, etc. Depending on the action taken regarding the field, a particular piece of code will always execute, no matter what panel was used to access the field. For example, every time an employee ID is entered, PeopleSoft checks to make sure it is valid. This occurs in one piece of PeopleCode attached to the employee ID field.

> PeopleCode is based at the record definition level (table level). If a piece of code is actually the same across tables (such as the verification of an employee ID), it is typically stored in a function library table, and called from each table that needs it. Function library tables are prefixed with FUNCLIB (i.e., FUNCLIB_HR).

We discuss some of the more advanced reference features of the Application Designer in Section 1. The actual creation and modification of items in the Application Designer, however, is not discussed, since these items usually occur once and are handled by one person on an implementation. For information regarding these uses, refer to PeopleSoft documentation.

THINKING VANILLA

PeopleSoft is designed to be customized. It is easy to open an existing panel, choose a field, and add it. Creating a table can take ten minutes, with no programming knowledge required. PeopleSoft takes great pride in this feature.

The result, though, is a tendency for companies to over-customize. This issue is not unique to PeopleSoft. Any package software implementation faces the question of whether to customize or make changes to the organization itself. PeopleSoft tries to make modifications easier because many times they are inevitable.

The vanilla concept is vital to the success of any implementation. The fact that PeopleSoft can be customized with a few clicks often works against the vanilla philosophy. It is too easy to make a simple modification—and it is too easy to ignore the long-term implications of such customizations.

First, consider the immediate effects of a customization. Does changing the value in a delivered field have a ripple effect downstream in the processes that perform payroll calculation or benefits eligibility determination? Changing a table definition can impact numerous delivered programs that contain a copy of the definition. Analyzing, modifying, and testing these customizations to avoid potential downstream issues can be a significant cost.

Furthermore, the maintenance of a single customization is a burden. New users who have PeopleSoft experience must be trained to understand customizations. And every time PeopleSoft sends an upgrade to be installed, every customization must be manually re-applied and tested. The costs of making this change over and over again can add up. Hence even a simple change of nomenclature can generate long-term costs.

Although users tend to resist changes, many of the differences PeopleSoft brings are minor and are easily adjusted to. If groups of people in your company are called "organizations," it will not be very difficult to start calling them departments. The change many appear significant, but since PeopleSoft looks for departments and employees will be referring to organizations, it makes sense to adapt. Similar situations occur with nearly every aspect of PeopleSoft, from the types of benefit plans offered, to the calculation of earnings and taxes, to the use of an employee ID versus a Social Security number.

PeopleSoft means change, period. Embrace it and you will reap the awards of low maintenance costs that package software can bring. If you make many small modifications, no matter how small, you will be defeating the purpose of the package.

The vanilla philosophy pertains to all aspects of a PeopleSoft implementation. Let's look at the different types of changes that can be made to PeopleSoft and the impact of each.

Online modifications

Changing a panel or table means that the change must be applied every time the application is upgraded. Adding a custom table also requires the creation of a new table definition for each upgrade. Any PeopleCode that is added to a table definition must be copied from one version to the next, and inserted in the appropriate place. Customizations to menus must also be made; if you added or subtracted many items to the menus, each modification must be made the upgraded version.

Process modifications (COBOL)

Modifying the COBOL programs that perform payroll and benefits administration processes can have significant repercussions. You should coordinate all modifications to COBOL with your PeopleSoft representative. In most cases, COBOL should not be modified except to expand sizes of arrays to accommodate larger implementations. Unfortunately this modification must be made for each upgrade until PeopleSoft makes the change permanent.

Interfaces and Reports

PeopleSoft comes delivered with hundreds of reports and files that support human resources functions. Adapting to these standards in lieu of coding a custom program to perform a similar function can save significant implementation and maintenance time. Going to users and presenting the delivered report output is often not enough. A user is likely to ask for a different sort order, or an additional field or subtotal. Such a minor modification can mean high costs. A programmer would need to understand the program and code, test, and maintain the modification through every subsequent upgrade. Often users of reports are not aware of how the PeopleSoft online panels operate, and what other delivered reports they will receive. Minor items like sorting and extra data may be necessary to fulfill an existing process that will change anyway. An extra field may only be needed twice a year, and could be looked up online. Managing the process of converting existing files and reports to a PeopleSoft environment is a critical part of an implementation.

REALIZING THE TRUE SAVINGS OF A PEOPLESOFT IMPLEMENTATION

PeopleSoft is not a piece of cake to implement. At most companies, it requires a significant investment in software, hardware, and people. The return on this investment is an expected reduction in programming and maintenance costs.

PeopleSoft will also deliver updates to tax information and other features to accommodate new trends and laws in benefits and payroll. Many implementations begin by considering the value of these upgrades and their implication that fewer people will be required to run and maintain PeopleSoft. Soon it becomes clear that the additional functionality PeopleSoft provides can actually require more people—as well as training. Advanced functions like benefits administration are difficult to understand. The resources required to implement, maintain, and use PeopleSoft are rarely fewer in number than before PeopleSoft is implemented.

The true savings of a PeopleSoft implementation comes from the chance to openly question existing functional processes. In order to fit PeopleSoft into an organization, it is necessary to ask what happens in a human resources area, and how transactions are processed. What are the volumes of different transactions—is offering a benefit plan with five participants cost effective when it requires a special report and an interface file to a vendor? These questions are rarely asked in the daily course of business. Customizing PeopleSoft to accommodate these items, though, begins to force the question and at least encourages exploration.

Implementing PeopleSoft requires a careful look into what data is needed, how often it is used, and most importantly, why? These questions can be difficult to ask, but are the most essential. Too many times a PeopleSoft implementation goes live, and a custom report that took 200 hours to design, code, and test goes unread, because it reflects a former process, not the new PeopleSoft way of doing things. The more you analyze and design, the less you need to code, test, and ultimately maintain.

Preface

All too often individuals are not aware of what is going on at the other end of an implementation. Programmers do not understand the reasons behind requirements, and human resources professionals (the users) do not understand the limitations of the application. When PeopleSoft users and programmers understand each other's concerns, a better product results every time. This book bridges this gap. The material in the chapters that follow answers questions related to specific human resources issues, and then goes on to explain how to implement real solutions. The philosophy is simple—technical and functional individuals should be exposed to as much of the other's viewpoint as possible. You cannot separate the two without generating greater confusion.

As a result, this book is organized by function: human resources, payroll, and benefits. Within each function the structure, features and pitfalls of the PeopleSoft database are explained in detail.

There are many items that are not covered in depth. The online application, where users enter transactions and process data, is better left to PeopleSoft's documentation and online PeopleBooks literature. The PeopleTools, which assist in one-time tasks such as modifying a panel or uploading converted data, are also well-documented elsewhere.

Why are these items not covered in this book? Because they have little to do with the issues that truly make or break an implementation. The PeopleSoft online application and tools are important skills, but they do not reveal the underlying data structure—if anything, they conceal it. And this creates misunderstandings between those who interact every day with the online application, and those who report on the data directly.

This book also does not provide detailed explanations of standard reporting languages. You will note, however, that examples of reporting code are often shown to clarify an important issue or provide a solution. These examples assume a basic knowledge of how a relational database is organized. A rudimentary understanding of Structured Query Language (SQL) is also useful, even if it is limited to the basic meanings of the SELECT/FROM/WHERE terminology.

Knowledge of basic Structured Query Reporting (SQR) language, a language provided with PeopleSoft, is only necessary for the final chapter, Chapter 26. This final chapter demonstrates some advanced SQR techniques and also details many of the advantages and pitfalls of using SQR.

In sum, this book contains a great deal of information, much of it garnered from experience. It does not contain everything—to do so would occupy volumes and volumes. Instead, this book is a detailed guide to the PeopleSoft database, concentrating only on the areas you will encounter the most. It explains how the underlying database relates to the core PeopleSoft functions, such as payroll calculation and benefits administration. It explains each table and field, and how they relate to one another. This book is not simply a reference tool—it is a critical guide to how PeopleSoft works behind the scenes.

To help you derive benefits from this book long after you've purchased and read it, go to the Prentice Hall PTR ERP Series Companion Website. This website is designed to keep you up-to-date with the latest tools, techniques, information, and data on Enterprise Resource Planning technologies. You'll find this Companion Website to be a great information kiosk, one that you may go back to again and again and again. So go to: http://www.phptr/erp.

Acknowledgments

his book required the involvement of an extensive group of supporters who deserve much recognition.

I must first thank my group of core advisors, who reviewed this manuscript and greatly assisted with their own unique (and many years combined) experience with PeopleSoft HR. Erin Bertelsen (benefits), Jonathan Golner (HR and reporting), Jim Knoop (HR and reporting), and Lynn Sardonia (payroll) played critical roles in the compilation of this book. They also encouraged my organization of the book and greatly influenced my editorial decisions regarding what would be most valuable to PeopleSoft HR users.

The second group of individuals is not as easy to recognize because they are so numerous. My coworkers on PeopleSoft projects have provided me with countless experiences and tidbits of knowledge that have made their way into the manuscript. There are also several individuals who supported this endeavor that ultimately allowed me to write and publish this book, who are both close friends and co-workers. Thank you for supporting and encouraging me through these many months. I hope you enjoy the results.

PART 1

401K

PAY ✓

PeopleSoft Basics

PeopleSoft HRMS: The Basics

The PeopleSoft HRMS database has over 5,000 tables. Trying to navigate through this vast system takes both time and patience—and a basic understanding of where to begin. This chapter covers the basic rules of the PeopleSoft database, enabling you to obtain accurate results. Successive chapters go into each table in detail.

If you have worked with PeopleSoft before, chances are you used the online application, with menus and panels for data entry. The online system lets the user search for existing data and insert new data into the database. We will avoid panels in this book (except for references to panels as a resource), since they mask the data and make it difficult to retrieve results.

Instead, this book looks at the underlying database tables. Our goal is to retrieve accurate data from PeopleSoft by hitting the database directly using SQL. This chapter is an introduction to the PeopleSoft database and its unique requirements. It will introduce you to the database and provide the basic rules of the road.

We will look at how the database is organized, functionally and technically. We will look at the tools provided by PeopleSoft for finding the appropriate table, and review the core PeopleSoft tables. We will consider the common requirements that pertain to database queries, such as keys, table links, and required fields. All of this information is technical in nature, but essential if you want to understand how data is stored and processed in PeopleSoft.

AN INTRODUCTION TO THE PEOPLESOFT HRMS DATABASE

All PeopleSoft products attempt a balance between functional requirements (what works best for humans) and relational database requirements (what works best for computers).

This issue is especially relevant to human resources requirements. Human resources professionals must be customer-oriented, and this requires extraordinary flexibility. Casual statements such as "We have to cut 5,000 checks by tomorrow morning!" or "We just bought XYZ corporation and need to add 30,000 employees to our system!" can bring an entire human resources department to tears. PeopleSoft's role is to simplify these seemingly drastic changes in company structure. Functional flexibility, the ability to perform human resources feats in a single click, is a cornerstone of the PeopleSoft product.

On the other hand, PeopleSoft is a software product with many programmers behind it. These programmers work together, writing separate components and improving technical benchmarks, like access time and storage capabilities. The companies who purchase PeopleSoft also typically employ programmers who modify and maintain the product. The "user," then, could be a programmer or a VP of human resources. The computer and human effort required to maintain an infinitely flexible system becomes overwhelming.

To prevent a tangled web of data, PeopleSoft stores data using a database organizational concept called "data integrity." The philosophy of data integrity is simple: a database stores data efficiently by storing it once, and only once. Duplication equals inefficiency and creates a chance that data will be changed in one place and not another. The efficient storage of data assures its integrity. It is a mantra followed by database programmers, and PeopleSoft is no exception.

Data integrity keeps the database happy and allows it to grow as functionality is added to PeopleSoft. Yet it divides the human resources data we need into over 5,611 tables. With each new PeopleSoft release, data is spread thinner and thinner, to more and more tables. For version 7.5, for example, PeopleSoft took the Social Security Number and made three new tables to store it. Now PeopleSoft can store different forms of the SSN for different countries with different validations. As the functional flexibility of the program grows, so does the size of the database.

Yet for a user trying to look up information in a database, a larger database has the opposite effect. Users need to find data when and where they need it. Human time is more expensive than computer time.

The fact is that most queries against the database require at least a 7-table join—for basic information on an employee like Social Security Number, name, hire date and department name. Knowing where to find each element and how to link them together is not common knowledge, and is difficult to derive. It is critical to understand which tables are the core sources of information.

This book is a guide to a subset of about 75 tables that contain the most commonly used data in PeopleSoft HRMS. These tables are not all essential, but they are accessed often and provide the foundation for the database. By exploring these central tables, we can get a better idea of how the PeopleSoft database is organized.

TYPES OF TABLES

There are six basic types of tables that we will discuss. As an overview, let's look at each type of table. You can even perform a quick SQL statement to look at the contents of the example table names provided. Simply type (for example):

```
SELECT * FROM PS_PERSONAL_DATA
```

Each table type is explained in detail in a separate chapter, except for application tables, which are not used in reporting.

Base Table (i.e., PS_PERSONAL_DATA, PS_JOB)

A base table is the place where nearly every query starts. These tables store information about an employee and contain data about the employee. A base table stores live data that is continually changing. The table could store information about employees, their dependents, their earnings, taxes, deductions, or benefits. In short, these tables hold the real data, the non-static data. Base tables are not distinguished with a prefix or suffix; they are named according to their function. See sections 2, 3 and 4 for specific table information.

Control Table (i.e., PS_EARNINGS_TBL)

A control table contains a short list of values that classify and categorize. For example, a table that contains all of the possible earnings codes (regular, bonus, overtime, etc.) is a control table, whereas the table that contains the actual earning amounts is a base table. A table listing all department codes or state names is a control table. Each control table has a key (the code) which ties to a field on a base table. Some control tables are larger than others. Often the department and jobcode tables are thousands of rows long, and change often. Control tables are usually identified by a suffix of '_TBL'. See Chapter 3 for more information on control tables.

Control tables are also commonly known as 'lookup' or 'prompt' tables.

Views (i.e., PS_BENEFITS_VW)

Views are timesavers; they are the result set of an SQL statement. For example, the benefits view table takes fields from several tables, links them together correctly, and presents the result as a new table. Views link to original tables (base or control), so no data is duplicated or out of sync. Views are usually identified by a suffix of '_VW'. See Chapter 4 for more extensive information on views.

Reporting Tables (i.e., PS_EMPLOYEES)

In an attempt to appease those toiling away, searching for the location of basic employee data, PeopleSoft created three tables that contain the most-often-used human resources fields. These tables are similar to views, but are not dynamic. Their data is only current after a program is executed every night. Their chief benefit is performance. Instead of joining 10 tables every time you look something up, the tables are joined once at night and then used throughout the next day as a single table. PS_EMPLOYEES, PS_BEN_PER_DATA, and PS_BEN_PLAN_DATA are reporting tables. See Chapter 4 for more information on reporting tables.

Application Tables (i.e., PSTREENODE)

The PeopleSoft application stores application rules and definitions in application tables. Occasionally these tables temporarily store data in the middle of a process. With few exceptions, these tables store data that is not relevant to the organization. Most of these tables are not discussed in this book since they contain application data, not HR data. System tables often do not include an underscore after the 'PS' prefix.

The Non-Table: Sub-Records

PeopleSoft is intent on making sure no data or effort is ever duplicated. For this reason, they created sub-records. Sub-records are like a mini-table, since they are a definition of a group of fields. A useful example is the address sub-record (ADDRESS_SBR) shown in Table 1-1.

▶ **Table 1-1** Example sub-record: ADDRESS_SBR

Column number	Field name
1	Country
2	Address Line 1
3	Address Line 2
4	Address Line 3
5	Address Line 4
6	City
7	Number 1
8	Number 2
9	House Type
10	County
11	State
12	Postal Code
13	Geographical Code
14	In City Limit

This is the definition of an address in PeopleSoft. Addresses, however, are used all over the place. There is the address of the employee, the work address, the building address, the paycheck address, and so on.

The sub-record is a single definition that is used in many different records. Addresses are consistently stored, and if a change is required, such as an extra digit added to the postal code definition, that change needs to be made in only one place—that is, from an application standpoint. From the perspective of the database, the sub-record does not exist (that's why you can't find it). As far as the database is concerned, the actual fields from the sub-record reside on the table. So when PeopleSoft's definition of a table contains ADDRESS_SBR as one of the fields, there will be 14 separate fields on the database definition and no mention of ADDRESS_SBR.

As a rule, consider the sub-record as part of the table it is found on. To get the city, you can't query the ADDRESS_SBR. You must query the table the sub-record is on.

THE CORE BASE TABLES

Now that we have looked at the different table types, let's look at the major base tables in PeopleSoft. These are the core tables in the database. Almost all PeopleSoft processes touch one of these tables, and chances are you'll need to do the same in nearly every query. Since you will almost always be starting with one of these tables, learn their differences in order to choose the correct one. Each table contains every employee no matter what their status (active, inactive, on leave, etc.).

The relationship between these three tables is simple (Figure 1-1). The PS_PERSONAL_DATA table has one row per employee—it is *the* parent table. Next in line is the PS_EMPLOYMENT table, which stores one row per employee job (if employees can have more than one job at a time in your organization). Finally, the PS_JOB table stores all of the status, compensation, and position history for the employee on many rows.

- **PS_PERSONAL DATA**. Stores current and historical information on the employee's home address, SSN, and personal history such as birth date. Choose this table when you need personal (and sometimes confidential) data. Remember, everyone in the database (actives, terminated employees, and retirees) is on this table. Each person has exactly one row. See Chapter 6 for information on keys and field definitions.

- **PS_EMPLOYMENT.** Contains a general record of the employee's employment, with information such as hire date, years of service, and EEO categories. Choose this table when you're looking for a

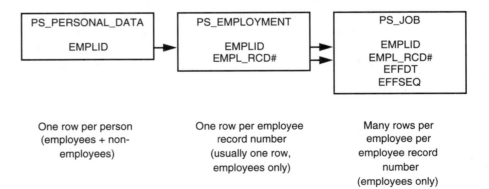

▶ **Figure 1-1**   Relationships between PeopleSoft HRMS core tables particular date. All "set-in-stone" dates, like hire date and rehire date are stored here. Just like PS_PERSONAL_DATA, everyone in the database is on this table. See Chapter 12 for information on the specific fields found on PS_EMPLOYMENT.

- **PS_JOB**. Stores current and historical information about an employee's job, such as status, compensation, promotions, and company categories. All history for this information is stored here, too. Choose this table when you need a list of employees who have a certain status. Typically users look for employees who are "A, L, P," or Active, On Leave, or On Paid Leave. Each employee will have several rows. See Chapters 7 through 10 for information on querying the PS_JOB table for different kinds of information.

USING THE APPLICATION DESIGNER TO FIND TABLE DEFINITIONS

Although data is rarely duplicated in PeopleSoft, if you look for a single field such as deduction code, thousands of references will appear. Which is the "real" field?

It depends on what you are looking for. Are you looking for a list of possible deductions, a list of deductions an employee receives, or a list of deductions that were taken from a paycheck? Each of these is in a different location, but they all share the same field name. There is no foolproof way to tell—even educated guesses are difficult.

Once you have a good idea of the piece of data you want, you must find where it is truly stored. The application designer is useful for tracking down a piece of data in PeopleSoft. You can open up tables, explore the definitions of fields, and trace the links between panels and database tables.

Querying Tables

The Application Designer can help you in your search for the perfect table. Not only does it provide an easy way to view table definitions, it also lets you quickly scan through the table names and cross-reference the occurrences of a field.

Before looking at how the Application Designer can assist, there are critical terminology changes to be aware of. First, in the Application Designer, database tables are called "records." This can be confusing, since to a database, a record is a row on a table. When PeopleSoft talks about records in the Application Designer, however, they are speaking of tables. In PeopleSoft, a record = a table.

Second, tables in PeopleSoft are referred to without the 'PS_' prefix. This prefix is masked from the user of Application Designer. Type it in, and you will find nothing.

Let's say Karen is looking for tax data. She isn't sure what tables tax data is stored on. Where to start? First, she opens the Application Designer, and goes to "Open." She picks "Records," places her cursor in the Name field, and types "TAX" (Figure 1-2).

A list of 28 tables is returned:

TAXFORM_BOX	Taxform Box Definition
TAXFORM_BX_LANG	Related Lang for TAXFORM_BOX
TAXFORM_DED	Taxform Deductions
TAXFORM_ERN	Taxform Earnings
TAXFORM_FORM	Tax Form Form Parameters
etc.	

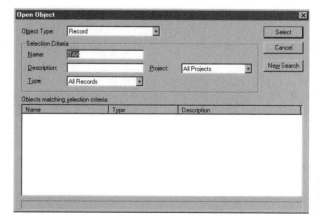

▶ **Figure 1-2**   Finding a table using the Application Designer.

Essentially, PeopleSoft takes what Karen has typed and appends a wildcard to it. Application Designer sends the database a query that looks for all tables with the name "TAX%" where the "%" is the wildcard.

You can use this wildcard to your advantage. There are, for example, several tables in the database that have the phrase "TAX" in the middle of their table name. So STATE_TAX_DATA won't appear in Karen's original search. She now types "%TAX" and gets a dazzling array—127 tables.

Cross-Referencing Fields

Another method that can quickly locate the data you need is to use the Application Designer's cross-referencing tool. For example, let's say Karen is looking for the number of withholding allowances an employee has in a particular state. She can search for the actual field name. First, she goes to "Open" and picks "Field." She types "%ALLOWANCE" and the following is returned:

ALLOWANCE_AMT	Allowance Amount
ALLOWANCE_DESCR	Allowance Description
ALLOWANCE_FLAG	Allowance Flag
FWT_ALLOWANCES	FWT Allowances
LWT_ALLOWANCES	Local Withholding Allowances
SWT_ALLOWANCES	Withholding Allowances
SWT_ALLOWANCE_MSG1	SWT Allowance Message 1
SWT_ALLOWANCE_MSG2	SWT Allowance Message 2

Opening SWT_ALLOWANCES brings up the right field. Now, to find where this field is located, Karen right-clicks the definition and chooses "Find Object References." Voilá—a list of locations appears in Figure 1-3.

The list that is returned contains tables (records), panels, and other elements in PeopleSoft. Karen can then double-click on these items to open them and continue to cross-reference.

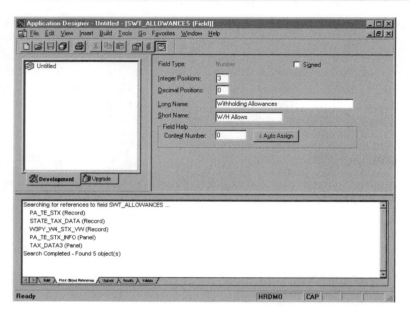

▶ Figure 1-3   Cross-referencing results

Cross-Referencing Panels and Tables

PeopleSoft's suggested technique for finding tables is to explore the structure of a functional process. To find the location of a field, you should look at the panel that contains the field and work your way back to the underlying table. For example, we can see the original hire date field on the Go ➤ Administer Workforce ➤ Administer Workforce (U.S.) ➤ Use ➤ Personal Data panel. Let's find out where it is actually stored:

1. Obtain the panel name. Pull down the View menu and choose Panel Name. A check will appear next to Panel Name and the name will appear at the bottom of the panel. The name of the panel is PER-SONAL_DATA1.

2. In the Application Designer, pull down the File menu and select Open. Choose "Panel" and type in PERSONAL_DATA1.

3. The panel is listed. Select it to open it. Then find the original hire date and right click on it. Choose View Definition. (Figure 1-4).

4. The table definition appears. The field is on PS_PERSONAL_DATA.

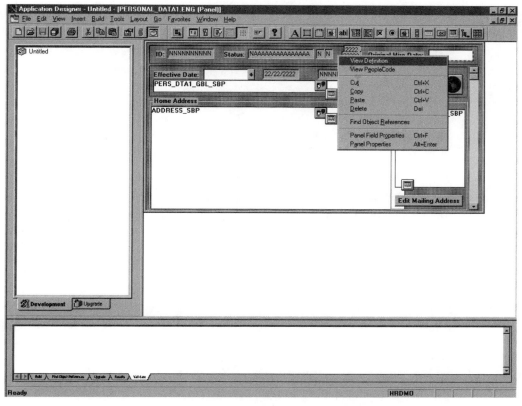

▶ **Figure 1-4**   Cross-referencing a field in the application designer.

This method is accurate and straightforward. There are times, however, that the cross-referencing gets crazy, since panels can contain sub-panels which contain records with sub-records, and so on. You could be cross-referencing for quite some time, but eventually you will arrive at an answer.

One drawback of this method is that you must know which panel the field is on. If you have not used the online application, it could be more difficult to find the panel than to find the corresponding table. Additionally, you could choose the wrong panel. Some panels summarize many tables, and connecting these tables to the base tables can require looking at delivered PeopleSoft programs (SQR, COBOL, PeopleCode). In brief, the cross-referencing method does not provide a complete picture of what is going on and what the possible tables are. A combination of different researching methods is best.

Looking for Comments

One useful resource is the comments in the Application Designer that explain each table. A one or two-sentence description of a table can really help. Unfortunately, not all of the tables have comments. And sometimes the comments aren't very descriptive.

To view the comment in the Application Designer, open the table and choose Object Properties from the File menu. The description is under the General tab. You can see if the table is a table or a view of other tables by looking at the Type tab.

Searching the Code

Another technique for figuring out what a field or table is used for is to look at how PeopleSoft uses it in places outside of the Application Designer. There are hundreds of reporting programs that PeopleSoft delivers, written in Structured Query Reporting (SQR) language. A quick search of these programs often reveals not only the meaning of a field, but also the appropriate way to retrieve its contents.

To search through SQR, first use Windows to view the directory where delivered SQR is stored. This is typically a folder called 'sqr' (for example, g:\psoft\sqr, if your drive is 'g' and PeopleSoft is in the 'psoft' folder). Once in this folder, perform a find file (control-F, or choose 'Find...Files or Folders' from the 'Start' menu and type in the SQR directory manually). In the Find dialog box, choose the 'Advanced' tab. In 'Containing text:', type the name of the field or table you are searching for. All of the SQR programs that use this field will be located for you (Figure 1-5).

While the Application Designer contains a great deal of information, there are other techniques to consider when searching for data. It is important to consider the type of data you are searching for. Data can also be found in other areas, such as SQR or COBOL programs.

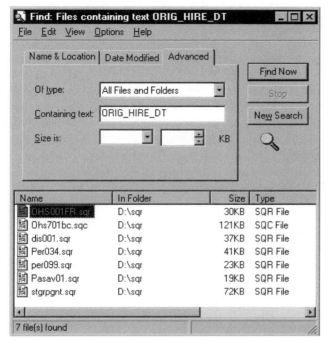

▶ **Figure 1-5**   Searching through SQR code for a data element.

PEOPLESOFT PROCESSES

Many of the techniques described here are technical research methods. Using the PeopleSoft delivered tools enables us to find tables and fields, but each requires some knowledge of what we are looking for. What if we have no idea what the field is, or where the panel is?

Most of this book is dedicated to assisting with this issue—describing a functional process and providing the table and field names associated with it. For example, suppose you need a report of the flexible spending account (FSA) deductions for employees. It is difficult to determine what the field or table names would be. Where are deductions recorded? Are FSA deductions found in the benefits or payroll section of the application?

This book will provide the answers to questions like this, but it is important to understand that PeopleSoft operates with distinct functional processes. There is a payroll process, a benefits administration process, and several processes for hiring and maintaining the status and other data of employees. Corresponding to these processes, there are base benefit tables and benefit administration tables. There are earnings tables and payroll tables.

It is important to distinguish between the tables that come before a functional process, the tables used during the process, and the tables that are populated with the results of the process. When looking for the right table, knowing what step of the process you're looking for makes a huge difference.

The two major processes in PeopleSoft are Payroll and Benefits Administration. Depending on the implementation, these processes are executed on a regular schedule. Each process is basically a series of COBOL programs that takes data from certain tables, applies calculations based on data in other tables, and writes the result to output tables. Payroll, for example, looks at the earnings, deductions, garnishments, and taxes defined for a specific employee. Depending on the rules for each of these elements, dollars are added and subtracted from the employee's gross pay. The result is more than just a check—the other elements are output as well. The deductions actually taken, the garnishments applied and the taxes paid could all fluctuate based on the gross pay and the rule definitions. This output is stored in output tables beginning with the 'PAY' prefix (see Figure 1-6).

Hence, to find deductions taken from a paycheck, you would look at PS_PAY_DEDUCTION. To find the deductions that *should* be taken from a pay-

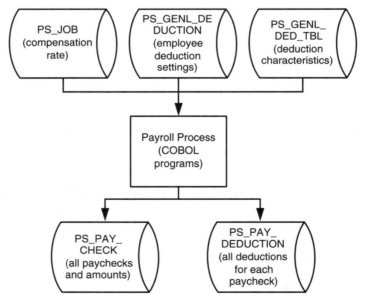

▶ **Figure 1-6**   Example tables used in the payroll process. The output tables have a 'PAY' prefix, and the control table PS_GEN_DED_TBL has a 'TBL' suffix.

check (i.e., before the process), you'd look at PS_GENL_DEDUCTION. And to find the definition of the deduction, the control table PS_GEN_DED_TBL is the appropriate place to search.

Always consider the process, not just the name of the field, when you are looking for data.

DISSECTING A PEOPLESOFT TABLE

The best way to get a good look at a PeopleSoft table is to open up the definition in PeopleSoft's Application Designer.

Identifying the Elements: A Look at a Table

Once we find the table we're looking for, there are several ways to look at it. Most people find it quicker and more convenient to print out the table. PeopleSoft prints the table with the record name, field names, definitions, formats, descriptions, and other technical information. This information will help in the construction of your query. Looking at Figure 1-7, we can see the result of an Application Designer printout.

```
Printed: 12/25/98 10.25.35

Field Name          Type  Length  Format  Long Name                        Short Name      Key  Req TblEdt AU Dt PC Aud Prompt Table      Default Value
Record Description:  EE U.S. State Tax Data
         This record is used to define an employee's status for state tax purposes.  If an employee works in multiple states or lives in a state other than the st.
         employment, a record for each state must be maintained.

         A view W3PY_W4_STX_VW based on this record has been created for the purpose of WEB-enabled W4 update.  Changes made to the record  STATE_TAX_DATA would  :
         be analyzed and made to W3PY_W4_STX_VW, if necessary.

Parent Record Name:  FED_TAX_DATA
Last Updated Date/Time:  03/09/1998  9.58.53am
Last Updated by Operator:  PPLSOFT

EMPLID              Char  11      Upper   EmplID                           ID              KALS Yes Prompt      Y     PERSONAL_DATA
COMPANY             Char  3       Upper   Company                          Co              KALS Yes Prompt            COMPANY_TBL
EFFDT               Date  10              Effective Date                   Eff Date        KD   Yes                                        $date
STATE               Char  6       Upper   State                            St              KALS Yes Prompt      Y     CO_STATETAX_TBL
RESIDENT            Char  1       Upper   Resident                         Resident             Yes Y/N         Y                         'Y'
NON_RES_DECLARED    Char  1       Upper   Non-Residency Statement Filed    NR Decld             Yes Y/N                                   'N'
SPECIAL_SWT_STATUS  Char  1       Upper   Special Tax Status               Spec Stat            Yes Xlat                                   'N'
         Values: E         Active  01/01/00  Exempt                        Exempt          09/05/1997 12.00.00am        PPLSOFT
                 G         Active  01/01/00  Maintain gross                Maintn Grs      09/05/1997 12.00.00am        PPLSOFT
                 N         Active  01/01/00  None                          None            09/05/1997 12.00.00am        PPLSOFT
SWT_MAR_STATUS      Char  1       Upper   SWT Marital/Tax Status           SWT Mar St           Yes Prompt      Y     SWT_MARSTAT_TBL
SWT_ALLOWANCES      Nbr   3               Withholding Allowances           W/H Allow            Yes              Y
SWT_ADDL_ALLOWANCES Nbr   3               Additional Allowances            Addl Allow           Yes              Y
WAGE_PLAN_CD        Char  1       Upper   Wage Plan Code                   Wage Plan            Yes Xlat                                   'S'
         Values: A         Active  01/01/00  None/State                    None            09/05/1997 12.00.00am        PPLSOFT
                 J         Active  01/01/00  State/Exempt                  State           09/05/1997 12.00.00am        PPLSOFT
                 L         Active  01/01/00  Voluntary/Exempt              Voluntary       09/05/1997 12.00.00am        PPLSOFT
                 P         Active  01/01/00  None/None                     PIT Only        09/05/1997 12.00.00am        PPLSOFT
                 R         Active  01/01/00  DI Exempt/State               DI Exempt       09/05/1997 12.00.00am        PPLSOFT
                 S         Active  01/01/00  State/State                   State           09/05/1997 12.00.00am        PPLSOFT
                 U         Active  01/01/00  Voluntary/State               Voluntary       09/05/1997 12.00.00am        PPLSOFT
ANNL_EXEMPTION_AMT  Nbr   5               Annual Exemption Amount          Exemp Amt            Yes              Y
PERCENT_OF_FWT      Nbr   2.3             % of Federal Withholding         % of FedWH           Yes              Y
SWT_ADDL_AMT        Sign  5.2             SWT Additional Amount            Amount               Yes              Y
SWT_ADDL_PCT        Nbr   2.3             SWT Additional Percentage        Percentage           Yes              Y
SDI_STATUS          Char  1       Upper   SDI Status                       SDI Status           Yes Xlat        Y
         Values: E         Active  01/01/00  Exempt                        Exempt          09/05/1997 12.00.00am        PPLSOFT
                 N         Active  01/01/00  Not Applicable                N/A             09/05/1997 12.00.00am        PPLSOFT
                 V         Active  01/01/00  Voluntary Disability Plan     Vol Dis         09/07/1997 12.00.00am        PPLSOFT
                 Y         Active  01/01/00  Subject                       Subject         09/05/1997 12.00.00am        PPLSOFT
SUT_EXEMPT          Char  1       Upper   Exempt From SUT                  SUT Exempt           Yes Y/N                                   COMPANY_TBL.SUT_EXEMPT
UI_JURISDICTION     Char  1       Upper   UI Jurisdiction                  UI                   Yes Y/N         Y                         'N'
ADDL_AMT_ADJ        Char  1       Upper   Additional Amount Adjustment     Addl Adjst           Yes Xlat                                   'I'
         Values: D         Active  01/01/00  Decrease Additional Amount    Decrease        09/07/1997 12.00.00am        PPLSOFT
                 I         Active  01/01/00  Increase Additional Amount    Increase        09/07/1997 12.00.00am        PPLSOFT
LOCK_IN_RECVD       Char  1       Upper   Lock-In Letter Received          Letter Received      Y/N              Y                         'N'
LOCK_IN_LIMIT       Nbr   3               Limit On Allowances              Limit On Alwncs      Yes              Y
```

▶ **Figure 1-7**   Printout of a PeopleSoft table

To get a simple printout, turn off the PeopleCode that by default appears on printouts of tables. You can find the check box to turn off PeopleCode by looking at Page Setup under the File menu in the Application Designer.

Along the top are the column names: Field Name, Type, Length, Format, Long Name, Short Name. These are self-explanatory. Let's look carefully at some of the remaining elements of this printout, which are critical for understanding how the table functions.

Keys

Identifying the keys in a table is a critical step to retrieving accurate data. Keys are the unique identifiers of a row in the table. Sometimes there is one key, such as employee ID, but more often there are several. When there is more than one key, the values in a certain key could be duplicated, but there are never two rows with the same values in every key. In other words, the *combination* of the key fields must be unique. In the STATE_TAX_DATA table, the following situation is likely:

```
EMPLID      COMPANY      EFFDT            STATE
-------     --------     ------------     ------
8121        CCB          01-JAN-1991      CA
8121        CCB          01-JAN-1991      PA
8200        PST          01-OCT-1993      CT
8200        PST          01-JAN-1991      CA
```

Each row is unique based on these four keys. You will *never* find the following when all four fields are keys:

```
EMPLID      COMPANY      EFFDT            STATE
-------     --------     ------------     ------
8121        CCB          01-JAN-1991      CA
8121        CCB          01-JAN-1991      CA
```

When selecting data, *always consider every key*. To retrieve the appropriate row, each key must be limited to exactly the values you are looking for. For example, to find the allowances for employee ID 8121 in California, you will need to look at four different fields (Table 1-2).

▶ **Table 1-2**   Considering keys (finding allowances for employee 8121 in CA)

Key	Criteria
Employee ID	This is '8121' and can be hard-coded into the query. This value never changes.
Company	This is the company the employee belongs to. Since it could change at any time, the current company should be obtained from another table. The core table that stores company is JOB.
Effective date	Choose the most recent effective date (more information on effective dates can be found in Chapter 2) to get current information.
State	This is 'CA' and can be hard-coded into the query. This value never changes.

If you neglect one of the keys, such as effective date, you will probably get several rows back (one for each effective date). A key like 'company' is ignored more often—after all, it is rare that an employee works for two companies. Be careful: PeopleSoft allows people to work for more than one company. Also, consider what happens if an employee changes companies. There may be two records with the same effective date, for the same state, for the same employee— one with the old company and one with the new.

Often a table has many keys, but when you look at the data in it, only one or two keys are used. The other key fields all have the same value. Don't be fooled—there are two good reasons to still include those keys in your criteria. First, just because the data looks like this now doesn't mean it isn't going to change. If the ability to change is there, it will probably happen. Second, database engines (i.e., Oracle, DB2, Sybase) usually return data faster when all of the keys are specified in the criteria. The database does not know what the data looks like—it assumes that all of the keys are necessary. As soon as you leave a key out of the criteria, the database may ignore an index it has created and take longer to retrieve the data.

Another tip: Be sure to distinguish among types of keys. The first letter of the "Key" column in the Application Designer is the important one. It is either "K" for key or "A" for alternate key. Keep in mind that an alternate key is not a key. The database does not recognize this as a key—*an alternate key does not distinguish a row.* An alternate key is used by the PeopleSoft application for looking up information. An example is the PS_PERSONAL_DATA table, which has a key of employee ID. The alternate key is name. Although in the PeopleSoft application you can look people up by name, you may retrieve more than one person with the same name. Hence it is not a key; it is just an alternative way to look up rows. It is best not to use it for a direct database query, especially if you want to retrieve only one distinct row.

Required Fields

The column labeled "Req" tells you whether PeopleSoft requires a field. A required field, from an application perspective, must be filled in. If you are typing information into the state tax data panel (which updates the PS_STATE_TAX_DATA table when you click "Save"), the SWT_MAR_STATUS field will be required.

This is not the case from the database perspective. When inserting data into PS_STATE_TAX_DATA using a SQL statement, you can leave SWT_MAR_STATUS blank. The chance of this occurring is usually slim depending on the company and the environment.

At best, the required flag tells you whether to expect blanks in the data returned. If it isn't required, there is a good chance some fields will be blank. If it is required, there is a slim chance that the field will be blank.

Translation Values

Many fields have only a few possible values. These values are stored in a common table, the XLATTABLE (see Chapter 3).

The table printout provides a nice way to look at the possible values for certain fields, since they are selected straight from the XLATTABLE for the printout. The SPECIAL_SWT_STATUS field, for example, can only have three possibilities: E, G, or N. Hard-coding the criteria of 'E' for exempt into your query would return employees who are exempt from state taxes.

Never assume that translate values are set to the PeopleSoft standards. Sometimes companies customize translate values to resemble the values they are familiar with. If someone changes exempt to be an 'X,' it is an important change. Always print out the table before constructing a query to check the translate values.

Prompt Tables

The prompt table column lists the tables that provide values for a certain field. Often this is a control table, such as PS_COMPANY_TBL. In PeopleSoft, when typing state tax data into a panel, you can prompt for a list of possible companies from the PS_COMPANY_TBL. Although this is a convenience built for the application, it also indicates a link in the database.

Notice, for instance, that the SWT_MAR_STATUS field does not have translate values. Instead, the prompt table PS_SWT_MARSTAT_TBL is shown. The PS_SWT_MARSTAT_TBL contains a list of possible state marital status values. For the description of a value, it would be necessary to link to this control table.

PEOPLESOFT HRMS BASICS: A REVIEW

The first step in any query is to find where the data is located. Since the PeopleSoft HRMS database is so large, the tools described in this chapter are useful for taking this first step at a smaller scale. Research tools like cross-referencing, looking for comments, and thinking about the functional process allow us to link the online PeopleSoft panel functions to database tables and fields. The basic tables we discussed, PS_PERSONAL_DATA, PS_JOB, and PS_EMPLOYMENT, provide a starting point for understanding the structure of the database. And the knowledge of the elements of a table, such as how keys and required fields affect the storage of data, help us as we start linking tables together, searching for data and connecting PeopleSoft online with the PeopleSoft database. These guidelines pertain to all users—those who are looking at the online panels, those who are setting up the database for the first time, and those who are extracting data for reports.

2 *Effective Dating*

One of the key concepts in PeopleSoft is effective dating. It is one of the unique features of a PeopleSoft database and is a critical item for understanding how HR data history is stored. Nearly every piece of data has an effective date value. This chapter will introduce effective dating, and will point out some of the things to look out for when working with effective dates. It is important not only to see how effective dates are used in the database, but also to consider the SQL code required to use effective dates accurately.

THE EFFECTIVE DATE DEFINED

Effective dates allow the storage of data for many points in time. With an effective date, data from the past, the present, and the future are stored together, in the same database table. All payroll, benefits, and human resources processing depends on effective dates as triggers to major events. Effective dates form the foundation of the PeopleSoft database.

Don't worry, because effective dating is much simpler in PeopleSoft than it is in real life(!). An effective-dated table is identified by the presence of the EFFDT field. This field allows numerous rows with different information to refer to a single employee on a single table.

Often users see an effective date and immediately think that it is a timestamp. This is a mistake—the effective date field is definitely *not* a timestamp. In many HR systems, a timestamp identifies when a row of data is entered into the database. An effective date is the date the row became or will become effective. The effective date field has nothing to do with when the row was entered into the database. (If you love your timestamps in your current system, it is time to start letting go. PeopleSoft does not have any timestamps. We discuss this issue in greater detail in Chapter 7).

To get an idea of how an effective date looks and feels in PeopleSoft, we will look at some queries against the job table, PS_JOB. This table is the most common source of effective dated information. And we will go through some "dating tips" that will demonstrate how to avoid the pitfalls of effective dated information (Table 2-1 shows how the effective date is used in the PS_JOB table).

Although PeopleSoft's applications provide extensive effective date functionality, it is critical to understand what is going on behind the scenes. Most applications construct elaborate SQL code when the user requests effective dated data. This reduces the flexibility of a query, and for an unaware end-user, inaccurate data can result. Even when using PeopleSoft applications to work with effective dates, it is critical to understand how the data is really being accessed.

▶ **Table 2-1**   Retrieving the contents of the PS_JOB table

The query	`SELECT  JO.EMPLID,`
	`         JO.EFFDT,`
	`         JO.ACTION`
	`FROM PS_JOB JO`

	EMPLID	EFFDT	ACTION
Returns the data set	------	----------	------
	8001	01/01/2000	HIR
	8001	02/01/2000	TER
	8001	03/01/2000	REH
Employee 8001 ➤	8001	04/10/2001	LOA
	8001	05/26/2002	DTA
	8001	07/01/2002	RFL
	8002	10/21/1979	HIR
	8002	12/01/1985	PAY
Employee 8002 ➤	8002	12/02/1985	LTO
	8002	01/01/2001	TER

CONSIDERING THE DESIRED RESULTS WHEN USING EFFECTIVE DATES

First and foremost, decide which row you are really looking for. Ninety-nine percent of the time, we want the maximum effective date as of a certain date. For example, we may want to determine the current employee status. This would be the most recent effective date as of today. Or we may be interested in any past changes in status. This would be the effective dates that are less than (before) today's date. Keep in mind that PeopleSoft also stores future-dated information (i.e., what the employee's status in the future may be). Before starting to construct a query, consider the following questions and look through the examples that follow to see the myriad of possibilities for selecting effective dated data.

1. How many changes in the data (i.e., how many different effective dates) should be returned for each employee, payroll department code, etc.?

2. What kind of change does the effective date represent? Does it represent a status change, a department change, or a name change?

3. What happens when two or more changes are made in a single day? Will the same effective date appear in the table twice?

4. Is all of the historical information desired or just the current information?

5. If there is a future-dated transaction, should it be selected instead of the current information?

6. If the current (most recent) information is desired, as of what date is the information current?

7. Is a mixture of historical, future, and current information required? Are there limits on the extent of desired historical and future information?

These questions will provide a better idea of exactly what the query must retrieve and how the effective dated data relates. Again, the majority of queries simply retrieve one row, the most recent row. But be sure to ask these questions to ensure that you are retrieving the correct data. You will find that they can uncover several important issues.

For one, these questions address the timeframe that you are retrieving. In a timestamped system, you can retrieve all of the data that changed since the last time you performed a query. PeopleSoft is different—there is no timestamp. Without an indicator that a record has changed, queries must retrieve the correct timeframe using effective dates.

Retroactive transactions are especially difficult to track. If an employee terminates, but the termination is entered into the system months later, the effective date will be accurate. If you need to query a list of terminated employees, you could miss this termination since the effective date is entered retroactively. To obtain this information, you need to query the history of each employee and decide how far back you wish to look.

Another issue is that many effective dated tables, such as PS_JOB, store different kinds of information together using the same effective date field. A recent row may not be the appropriate row if it is associated with the wrong type of data. You may need to add criteria to narrow an effective dated search. Chapter 7 elaborates on the intricacies of PS_JOB; we look at effective dates with additional criteria later in this chapter.

THE BASIC EFFECTIVE-DATE SUB-QUERY

Note in Table 2-1 that each employee has several rows. The most common request of an effective dated table is for one row per employee. If we want just the row with the greatest date, we need to pick the maximum date (Table 2-2). Our first thought is to use the MAX function to retrieve the maximum date.

▶ **Table 2-2** Retrieving the maximum effective date

The query	`SELECT MAX(JO.EFFDT)`
	`FROM PS_JOB JO`
	`WHERE EMPLID = '8001'`

Returns the
data set
	`EFFDT`
	`----------`
	`07/01/2002`

But what happened to the other employee? Just because the effective date for employee 8002 isn't the greatest doesn't mean the employee should be excluded. The solution to this dilemma requires a sub-query.

Sub-queries are considered an offbeat SQL topic. They aren't used often, but in PeopleSoft, they are everywhere. Now is the time to get comfortable with sub-queries, whether you are writing SQL or using the PeopleSoft application.

A sub-query is a query embedded within a query. The sub-query executes first, and joins to the main query according to its result. An effective date sub-query for the PS_JOB table executes for each employee to retrieve the maximum effective date for a given employee. Since the sub-query is joined to the main query by the effective date, and the sub-query only returns the maximum effective date, the whole query returns the maximum effective date for each employee.

▶ **Table 2-3**   The effective date sub-query on the PS_JOB table

The query	SELECT JO.EMPLID,
	          JO.EFFDT,
	          JO.ACTION
	FROM PS_JOB JO
	WHERE JO.EFFDT =
	          (SELECT MAX(JO1.EFFDT)
	          FROM PS_JOB JO1
	          WHERE JO1.EMPLID = JO.EMPLID)		

Returns the data set	EMPLID ------ 8001 8002	EFFDT ---------- 07/01/2002 01/01/2001	ACTION ------ RFL TER

Table 2-3 demonstrates the effective date sub-query. The effective date is set equal to a 'mini query' that selects the maximum date from the same table, for the current employee. Since the sub-query is in the WHERE clause, it is used as criteria for selecting a row. The maximum effective date for an employee is selected.

This is a good time to look at the common SQL mistakes users make when writing a sub-query:

1. Make sure you are using table aliases (in this case JO and JO1).
2. You must select the MAX of the sub-table (JO1) effective date and link it back.
3. A sub-query requires parentheses, starting before SELECT and ending after the last sub-query WHERE clause.
4. Consider the criteria used in the WHERE clause of the sub-query. Most of the time, you should link every single key of the table. If you forget a key, you will get strange stuff back.
5. Although it doesn't matter which order you use for your WHERE clause (it could be JO1 = JO or JO = JO1), it reads better to keep the sub-query alias on the left, or at least keep it consistent.

Some of these mistakes result in inaccurate data, and often these inaccuracies can be difficult to detect. It is important to go over sub-queries carefully and ensure that the correct terms and aliases are used. A sub-query is an advanced SQL procedure; although it is common in PeopleSoft, it requires careful attention to detail.

Using an As-Of Date To Exclude Future Rows

The query in Table 2-3 brings back the correct number of rows, one per employee. It does not retrieve the most current row—it retrieves the maximum row. This effective date could be years from now; it is the maximum. Most of the time, though, data must be retrieved as of the current date. If today's date is June 1, 2001, we do not want to know that an employee will be terminated three years from now. We want the employee's current status. We need to ignore any future-dated rows that might change an employee's status.

▶ **Table 2-4** The effective date sub-query with an as-of date

The query	
| | ```
SELECT  JO.EMPLID,
        JO.EFFDT,
        JO.ACTION
FROM PS_JOB JO
WHERE JO.EFFDT =
        (SELECT MAX(JO1.EFFDT)
           FROM PS_JOB JO1
          WHERE JO1.EMPLID = JO.EMPLID
            AND JO1.EFFDT <= 'JUN-01-2001')
``` |

Returns the data set	EMPLID	EFFDT	ACTION
	------	----------	------
	8001	04/10/2001	LOA
	8002	01/01/2001	TER

The effective date must be less than or equal to the as-of date, which is usually the current date (Table 2-4). All dates after the current date are appropriately ignored. This is a much more typical result. It is rare that a user would like to see a future-dated transaction.

If future dates are desired, it is advisable just to select historical data without an effective date sub-query at all. In the example above, without an as-of date to eliminate future-dated data, an active employee could appear terminated due to a future-dated row. It is safer to query the entire data set and look at the effective dates when dealing with future-dated items.
```

USING ADDITIONAL CRITERIA WITH A SUB-QUERY

You may be wondering why we put the current date criteria in the sub-query. Table 2-5 shows what happens if the current date criteria is used in the main query instead.

▶ **Table 2-5** Incorrectly using an as-of date

| The query | ```
SELECT   JO.EMPLID,
         JO.EFFDT,
         JO.ACTION
FROM PS_JOB JO
WHERE JO.EFFDT =
         (SELECT MAX(JO1.EFFDT)
          FROM PS_JOB JO1
          WHERE JO1.EMPLID = JO.EMPLID)
          AND JO.EFFDT <= 'JUN-01-2001'
``` |
| Returns the data set | EMPLID   EFFDT   ACTION
------   ----------   ------
8002   01/01/2001   TER |

Employee 8001 has disappeared. This is because the sub-query executes first. For each employee, it retrieves the maximum effective date without boundaries. For employee 8001, this date is 07/01/2002. Then the database applies the current date criteria outside of the sub-query. Since 07/01/2002 is not less than or equal to 06/01/2001, the employee is not returned. For employee 8002, it just happens that the maximum date occurs before the current date. There is no future-dated row for 8002. Hence when effective date criteria are placed outside of the sub-query, a future-dated row could cause an employee to be dropped from the results.

A similar rule applies to any additional criteria we apply (Table 2-6). For example, if we desire a list of employees who are terminated as of the current date, we must limit the ACTION field to the termination code of 'TER.' Only employee 8002 is currently terminated. This is the expected desired result, and yet the termination criteria are *outside* of the sub-query. Look at what happens when the criteria are placed inside the sub-query in Table 2-7.
```

▶ **Table 2-6** Using additional criteria for an as-of date

| The query | ```
SELECT    JO.EMPLID,
          JO.EFFDT,
          JO.ACTION
FROM PS_JOB JO
WHERE JO.EFFDT =
          (SELECT MAX(JO1.EFFDT)
            FROM PS_JOB JO1
          WHERE JO1.EMPLID = JO.EMPLID
            AND JO1.EFFDT <= 'JUN-01-2001')
AND JO.ACTION = 'TER'
``` |
| Returns the data set | ```
EMPLID    EFFDT          ACTION
------    ----------     ------
8002      01/01/2001     TER
``` |

▶ **Table 2-7** The effective date sub-query

| The query | ```
SELECT    JO.EMPLID,
          JO.EFFDT,
          JO.ACTION
FROM PS_JOB JO
WHERE JO.EFFDT =
          (SELECT MAX(JO1.EFFDT)
            FROM PS_JOB JO1
            AND JO1.EFFDT <= 'JUN-01-2001'
            AND JO1.ACTION = 'TER')
``` |
| Returns the data set | ```
EMPLID    EFFDT          ACTION
------    ----------     ------
8001      02/01/2000     TER
8002      01/01/2001     TER
``` |

This is a list of the termination dates of all employees who at one time were terminated. Although employee 8001 is currently active, at one point a termination occurred.

In Tables 2-3 through 2-7, we have discovered that:

- **When using an effective dated table, all *date* criteria should go in the effective date sub-query** (i.e., less than or equal to the current date).

- **Criteria should go outside of the effective date sub-query if it does not depend on the date.** If we want a list of currently terminated employees, the date of termination doesn't matter. The current status matters.

- **Criteria should go inside the effective date sub-query if it depends on the date**. If we want all terminated employees, regardless of whether they are currently terminated, the date matters. We no longer want the maximum date, we want the maximum termination date.

Every query request requires a different effective date and criteria use. There is no all-encompassing foolproof rule for placing criteria. In every case, it is important to independently consider the implications of each piece of criteria. Experiment, and add criteria piece by piece. Look at the data without any criteria, and see how the placement of each WHERE clause affects the results.

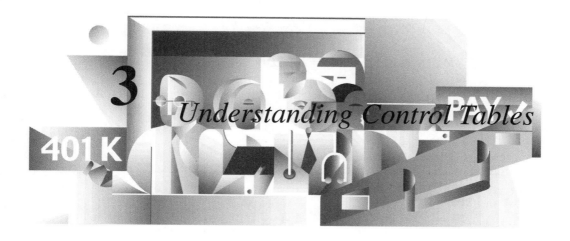

C ontrol tables store lists of standard values. In PeopleSoft, 376 different control tables store everything from department numbers to military status options. There is even a table that lists types of animals (for accident reporting). Most of the time control tables are used to find a description or particular attribute of a code. Rather than store the full name of every department on every table that has the department field (you'll find it on over 300 tables), PeopleSoft stores it in one place—the department table.

Control tables are also referred to as "lookup" or "prompt" tables, since PeopleSoft continually prompts users for and looks up values to ensure they are accurate. This lookup prevents inaccurate data from entering the system. If you try to place someone in the 'BOZO' department, PeopleSoft will look up 'BOZO'—and if it isn't there, PeopleSoft will not let you choose it.

The PeopleSoft application is responsible for performing this verification. The database, on the other hand, has no responsibility for accuracy. To the database, 'BOZO' is a perfectly fine department—the database will not check values against control tables.

Because the database is oblivious to control tables, it is important to include control tables when accessing the database directly (without using the PeopleSoft application). If you are extracting data for another system, it is wise to weed out the 'BOZO' by using SQL to look up each department on the department table. Similarly, if you are loading new data into the PeopleSoft database, it is critical to verify the accuracy of control values.

STRUCTURE OF A CONTROL TABLE

Although all control tables are unique, there is a common format that pervades the majority of control tables. Let's look at the first few fields of the department table as a typical example (Table 3-1).

▶ **Table 3-1** Sample data from the department table: PS_DEPT_TBL

SetID (key)	DeptID (key)	Eff. Date (key)	Status	Description	Short Description
SETID	DEPTID	EFFDT	EFF_ STATUS	DESCR	DESCR SHORT
USA	20001	01/01/1985	A	Human Resources	HumanRes
USA	90874	01/01/1990	A	Quality Control	QualCntrl
USA	90874	11/08/1998	I	Quality Control	QualCntrl
USA	00001	01/01/1988	A	Headquarters	HQ
USA	00001	01/01/1990	A	Headquarters – CA	HQ-CA
USA	00002	01/01/2050	A	Office of the President	President

SETID   The setID field is a high-level control value. It is the control value of the control values. In other words, PeopleSoft allows you to store different sets of control values according to setID. Although the departments listed above are associated with the USA setID, they could also be associated with another setID. See Chapter 5 for information on using the setID field.

DEPTID   Department ID is the major key of the table. This is the department table, and it lists information about departments according to department ID. Each control table has a unique value field— it could be earning code, state code, or location code.

EFFDT   An effective date is used to track historical information. It is provided for two reasons:

1. The effective date provides the capability to store changes in departments. For example, department ID 00001 above changed its description in 1990 because the department moved to California and is now identified as HQ-CA. This change is recorded, and the old description can be accessed as well.

2. PeopleSoft uses the effective date to determine when a department is effective. Department 00002 above, for instance, is not effective

until January 1, 2050. When a PeopleSoft user hires a new employee, department 00002 will not appear as a possible choice until the hire date is in 2050.

EFF_STATUS The effective status is not a key. This means that a department cannot be active and inactive at the same time.

The effective status indicates the status of the department as of the effective date. The status can be either (A)ctive or (I)nactive. In the example above, as of November 8, 1998 department 90874 is no longer an active department. In the PeopleSoft application, this means that an individual cannot belong to this department after 11/8/98. It is possible that employees will continue to exist in this department after 11/8/98; a terminated employee, for example, may still appear in department 90874 even though the department is inactive. New employees, however, cannot be assigned to this department. Keep in mind that these rules apply to the application, not the database. The database does not apply these rules, so it is technically possible to have an active employee in an inactive department.

DESCR The description field contains a long description of the code. For a department, this is the department name. For an earnings code, this is the earnings code name.

For a jobcode, the description field is the title of the job.

DESCRSHORT The short description is a ten-character abbreviation of the full description.

ADDING A CONTROL TABLE TO A QUERY

This section demonstrates the basic combination of a base table, PS_JOB, and a control table, PS_DEPT_TBL. The contents of the PS_DEPT_TBL are shown in Table 3-1 above and the contents of the PS_JOB table are in Table 3-2.

A query such as this is necessary if you need to list employees and their department name. A department ID is stored on PS_JOB, but the department name is on PS_DEPT_TBL. In order to combine these sets of data, the tables must be joined. The most recent effective date for the employee on PS_JOB must be linked to the most recent effective date for the employee's department on PS_DEPT_TBL.

▶ **Table 3-2** Sample data from PS_JOB

The query	SELECT JO.EMPLID,
	         JO.EFFDT,
	         JO.EMPL_STATUS,
	         JO.DEPTID
	  FROM PS_JOB JO

Returns the data set	EMPLID	EFFDT	EMPL_STATUS	DEPTID
	8001	01/01/1985	A	20001
	8001	01/01/1990	A	90874
	8001	01/01/2050	A	00002
	8002	01/01/1992	A	90874
	8002	01/01/1993	L	90874
	8002	01/01/1998	T	90874
	8003	02/01/1988	A	00001
	8003	01/01/1990	L	00001

First we need to limit the query to only one job table row per employee, so we add an effective date sub-query, as shown in Table 3-3.

▶ **Table 3-3** Employee department codes on PS_JOB

The query	SELECT JO.EMPLID,
	         JO.DEPTID
	  FROM PS_JOB JO
	  WHERE **JO.EFFDT =**
	         (SELECT MAX(JO1.EFFDT)
	          FROM PS_JOB JO1
	          WHERE JO1.EMPLID = JO.EMPLID
	          AND JO1.EFFDT <= [today])

Returns the data set	EMPLID	DEPTID
	8001	20001
	8002	90874
	8003	00001

Then we add the department table and link the tables together. We want the department with the most recent effective date, so a sub-query is used on the department table (Table 3-4) as well.

▶ **Table 3-4**   Control table join

| The query | ```
SELECT  JO.EMPLID,
        JO.DEPTID,
        DT.DESCR,
        DT.EFFDT,
        DT.EFF_STATUS
FROM PS_JOB JO,
     PS_DEPT_TBL DT
WHERE DT.DEPTID = JO.DEPTID
  AND JO.EFFDT =
      (SELECT MAX(JO1.EFFDT)
        FROM PS_JOB JO1
       WHERE JO1.EMPLID = JO.EMPLID
         AND JO1.EFFDT <= [today])
  AND DT.EFFDT =
      (SELECT MAX(DT1.EFFDT)
        FROM PS_DEPT_TBL DT1
       WHERE DT1.DEPTID = DT.DEPTID
         AND DT1.EFFDT <= [today])
``` |

Returns the data set	EMPLID	DEPTID	DT.DESR	DT.EFFDT	DT.EFF_STATUS
	------	------	-----------------	----------	-------------
	8001	20001	Human Resources	01/01/1985	A
	8002	90874	Quality Control	11/08/1998	I
	8003	00001	Headquarters - CA	01/01/1990	A

We successfully return a single row for each employee based on the most recent effective date from both tables.

USING EFFECTIVE STATUS

The example query in Table 3-4 is the standard way to accurately link to a control table. Note, however, that the return data set includes departments that are inactive.

Typically this is what we want to return. Whether an employee is in an *active* department is not important to most people in an organization. If the department exists, it was valid at one point. If an employee is in an invalid department, they probably were in it when it was valid before.

Take note, however, that there are two potential traps found in nearly all control tables:
```

1. When a user marks a department inactive, information may also change on other fields. For instance, perhaps every time a department is made inactive, the manager ID for that department is set to a default value. Or maybe the description is set to all asterisks. Although this is unlikely, the possibility does exist.

   To limit a query to return the *most recent active* department, place effective status criteria inside the sub-query, as in Table 3-5.

▶ **Table 3-5** Employee department codes on PS_JOB

| The query | ```
SELECT JO.EMPLID,
       JO.DEPTID
FROM PS_JOB JO,
     PS_DEPT_TBL DT
WHERE DT.DEPTID = JO.DEPTID
  AND JO.EFFDT =
          (SELECT MAX(JO1.EFFDT)
             FROM PS_JOB JO1
            WHERE JO1.EMPLID = JO.EMPLID)
  AND DT.EFFDT =
          (SELECT MAX(DT1.EFFDT)
             FROM PS_DEPT_TBL DT1
            WHERE DT1.DEPTID = DT.DEPTID
              AND DT1.EFF_STATUS = 'A')
``` |

Returns the data set	EMPLID	DEPTID	DESR	EFFDT	EFF_STATUS
	------	------	-----------------	----------	----------
	8001	20001	Human Resources	01/01/1985	A
	8002	90874	Quality Control	**01/01/1990**	**A**
	8003	00001	Headquarters - CA	01/01/1990	A

2. Depending on the control table and the function of the query, inactive codes sometimes need to be identified. Maybe you're loading in deductions for employees using a SQL query, and if an employee is in an inactive department, you want to make sure they don't get a deduction. Or you're generating a list of all valid departments, active or inactive. In both cases, the effective status field is a valuable piece of information and should be included in the criteria of the query. In Table 3-6 the selection is limited to only active departments.
```

▶ **Table 3-6** Employee department codes on PS_JOB

The query	```SELECT JO.EMPLID,```

```
SELECT JO.EMPLID,
       JO.DEPTID
FROM PS_JOB JO,
     PS_DEPT_TBL DT
WHERE DT.DEPTID = JO.DEPTID
  AND JO.EFFDT =
      (SELECT MAX(JO1.EFFDT)
        FROM PS_JOB JO1
        WHERE JO1.EMPLID = JO.EMPLID)
  AND DT.EFFDT =
      (SELECT MAX(DT1.EFFDT)
       FROM PS_DEPT_TBL DT1
       WHERE DT1.DEPTID = DT.DEPTID)
  AND DT.EFF_STATUS = 'A'
```

Returns the
data set

EMPLID	DEPTID	DESR	EFFDT	EFF_STATUS
------	------	-----------------	----------	----------8001
20001		Human Resources	01/01/1985	A
8003	00001	Headquarters - CA	01/01/1990	A

Employee 8002 drops out of the result set in Table 3-6. The difference between the query for Table 3-5 and the query for Table 3-6 is the location of the effective status criteria. When the criteria are inside the sub-query, the sub-query will always return an active row for every department. If a department is inactive, the active row preceding it is used. When the criteria are outside the sub-query, if the most recent row is not active, the row is dropped completely, as is the case for 8002.

MERGING EFFECTIVE DATED DATA ACROSS TABLES (POINT-IN-TIME QUERIES)

What if we want a list of all employees and their department descriptions, but for a historical point in time? Employees change departments, and departments change as well. How do we link the history of an employee with the history of a department?

The examples shown in Tables 3-4 through 3-6 assist in determining if a department is inactive or active. The following examples in Tables 3-7, 3-8, and 3-9 demonstrate how to link a control table to a base table at a historical point in time. This method considers that we are looking for information from one table that is effective at the same time as information at another.

The first rule is that the effective date on one table is unrelated to that on another. For example, Susan's most recent job effective date could be December 1, 1960, but she could be in a department that was last updated on May 12, 1965. If we look for Susan's department information as of January 1, 1970, we should get the 1960 job information and the 1965 department information. We certainly don't want 1960 job information with 1960 department information, since our point-in-time is 1970.

In the example below our goal is to get a snapshot of which employees and departments were active on January 1, 1989. Look again at the data in Table 3-2. If we use January 1, 1989 for the as-of date, we should retrieve 2 rows (employee 8002 did not exist in 1989).

▶ **Table 3-7** PS_JOB with an as-of date

The query	SELECT JO.EMPLID,
	        JO.EFFDT,
	        JO.EMPL_STATUS,
	        JO.DEPTID
	FROM PS_JOB JO
	WHERE JO.EFFDT =
	        (SELECT MAX(JO1.EFFDT)
	          FROM PS_JOB JO1
	         WHERE JO1.EMPLID = JO.EMPLID
	           AND JO1.EFFDT <= '01/01/1989')

Returns the data set	EMPLID	EFFDT	EMPL_STATUS	DEPTID
	------	----------	-----------	------
	8001	1985-01-01	A	20001
	8003	1988-02-01	A	00001

Now consider the extract of the DEPT_TBL table in Table 3-8.

▶ **Table 3-8** PS_DEPT_TBL

The query	SELECT DT.DEPTID,
	        DT.EFFDT,
	        DT.EFF_STATUS,
	        DT.MANAGER_ID
	FROM PS_DEPT_TBL DT

Returns the data set	DEPTID	EFFDT	EFF_STATUS	MANAGER_ID
	------	----------	----------	----------20001
		1985-01-01	A	8234
	90874	1990-01-01	A	8655

▶ **Table 3-8** continued

Returns the data set				
	90874	1998-11-08	I	8655
	00001	1988-01-01	A	7942
	00001	1988-06-15	A	8006
	00001	1990-01-01	A	8006
	00002	2050-01-01	A	8500

In order to get back accurate department descriptions, we need to link each employee row retrieved to the department table *using the same maximum effective date.* This type of query is common, especially when searching for historical information. For example, there could be a legal case pending where it is essential to know who managed a particular employee on a specific day. Linking the job table effective date with the department table effective date is the only way to achieve an accurate result. Table 3-9 demonstrates this link and the result set.

▶ **Table 3-9** Control table merged with base table

The query
```
SELECT  JO.EMPLID,
        JO.DEPTID,
        DT.MANAGER_ID,
        DT.EFFDT,
        DT.EFF_STATUS
FROM PS_JOB JO,
     PS_DEPT_TBL DT
WHERE JO.EFFDT =
        (SELECT  MAX(JO1.EFFDT)
            FROM PS_JOB JO1
            WHERE JO1.EMPLID = JO.EMPLID
              AND JO1.EFFDT <= '01/01/1989')
    AND DT.EFFDT =
        (SELECT  MAX(DT1.EFFDT)
            FROM PS_DEPT_TBL DT1
            WHERE DT1.DEPTID = DT.DEPTID
              AND DT1.EFFDT <= '01/01/1989')
```

Returns the data set	EMPLID	DEPTID	MANAGER_ID	EFFDT
	------	------	----------	----------
	8001	20001	8234	1985-01-01
	8003	20001	8006	1988-06-15

Because we used the same job table effective date and the department table effective date, employee 8003 is shown in department 20001 when employee ID 8006 managed that department. If the job table effective date were used instead, the department would appear to be managed by employee ID 7942, since this employee used to manage it.

FINDING TRANSLATE VALUES

PeopleSoft places data on a control table when the control values need to be associated with additional data. If there is no additional data to store, the value is usually placed on the "translate table" (Table 3-10). This table holds the majority of translate values for fields in PeopleSoft.

> The translate table does not have a PS_ prefix. The table is referred to as 'XLATTABLE' both in the PeopleSoft application and in the database.

▶ **Table 3-10**   Translate table: XLATTABLE

Field Name (key)	Lang. Code (key)	Value (key)	Effective Date (key)	Version	Status	Long Name
FIELDNAME	LAN-GUAGE_CD	FIELD VALUE	EFFDT	VERSION	EFF_STATUS	XLATLONGNAME
EMPL_STATUS	ENG	A	1900-01-01	66,418	A	Active
EMPL_STATUS	ENG	D	1900-01-01	66,418	A	Deceased
EMPL_STATUS	ENG	L	1900-01-01	66,418	A	Leave of Absence
EMPL_STATUS	ENG	P	1900-01-01	66,418	A	Leave With Pay
EMPL_STATUS	ENG	Q	1900-01-01	66,418	A	Retired With Pay
EMPL_STATUS	ENG	R	1900-01-01	66,418	A	Retired
EMPL_STATUS	ENG	S	1900-01-01	66,418	A	Suspended
EMPL_STATUS	ENG	T	1900-01-01	66,418	A	Terminated
EMPL_STATUS	ENG	U	1900-01-01	66,418	A	Terminated With Pay
EMPL_STATUS	ENG	V	1900-01-01	66,418	A	Terminated Pension Pay Out
EMPL_STATUS	ENG	X	1900-01-01	66,418	A	Retired-Pension Administration
FULL_PART_TIME	ENG	F	1900-01-01	60,022	A	Full-Time
FULL_PART_TIME	ENG	P	1900-01-01	60,022	A	Part-Time

The translate table is set up exactly like a typical control table. The effective date and effective status are present and follow the same rules. Yet there are several differences to pay attention to:

1. Many fields are on the translate table. To get the appropriate translate value, we must specify the field name we are looking for in the criteria. The FIELDNAME field is a permanent part of the query.

2. The field values of the field you are looking up are stored in a single generic field, FIELDVALUE. In the criteria you must set FIELDVALUE equal to the value of the field from the base table.

3. The translate table is language-dependent. Deciding what criteria to use here is discussed further in chapter 5. Often this field is hard coded to 'ENG' for English.

Table 3-11 shows an example query that retrieves the employee status description for each employee.

▶ **Table 3-11**   Translate table query

| The query | ```
SELECT   JO.EMPLID,
         JO.EMPL_STATUS,
         XT.XLATLONGNAME
FROM PS_JOB JO,
     XLATTABLE XT
WHERE XT.FIELDNAME    = 'EMPL_STATUS'
  AND XT.FIELDVALUE = JO.EMPL_STATUS
  AND XT.LANGUAGE_CD = 'ENG'
  AND XT.EFFDT      =
    (SELECT MAX(XT1.EFFDT)
       FROM XLATTABLE XT1
      WHERE XT1.FIELDNAME   = XT.FIELDNAME
        AND XT1.FIELDVALUE = XT.FIELDVALUE
        AND XT1.LANGUAGE_CD = XT.LANGUAGE_CD
        AND XT1.EFFDT      <= '01/01/2000')
``` |
| Returns the data set | ```
EMPLID EMPL_STATUS   XLATLONGNAME
------ -----------   ------------
8001   A        Active
8002   T        Terminated
8003   X        Retired-Pension
8004   A        Active
``` |

To quickly determine translate values, the simplest query is to just select all from the table for the appropriate field name. For example, to get all the possible employee status values, type:

```
SELECT * FROM XLATTABLE WHERE FIELDNAME = 'EMPL_STATUS'
```

4 Reporting Tables— An Overview

One of the reasons companies install PeopleSoft is to clean up their data and make information more accessible to end-users. The philosophy of the delivered reporting tools, PeopleSoft Query and SQR, is that the user should be able to get to the data quickly and easily.

PeopleSoft also provides special views and tables to assist users with reporting. These devices bring together elements from different parts of the database—pieces of data that are stored separately for efficiency. There are advantages and disadvantages to using these devices, and each implementation will follow a different strategy. This chapter explains each device in detail to give database managers and end-users an understanding of what these tables and views have to offer.

REPORTING TABLES—AN OVERVIEW

With all of the confusing tables and concepts, it becomes difficult to teach an entire organization how to get some of the simplest information onto a report. Instead of explaining each key field of the major tables (as we do in subsequent chapters), PeopleSoft provides a few tables, which we will call reporting tables, that shelter the user from the way data is stored and provide just the raw data.

Reporting tables are similar to views, in database jargon, but there are important differences. A view links two or more tables together to make data easier to access. A reporting table also links tables together—but performs this link usually only once a day. A view, on the other hand, performs a link whenever you select data from it.

The principal advantage of a reporting table is performance. Each table added to a query increases the time for processing. The database must search through all of the rows in one table to link them to another table. When we're dealing with tables like PS_JOB and PS_PERSONAL_DATA, the number of rows involved grows. This means that getting simple information, such as a list of employee names and statuses for a single department, can take an awfully long time.

A view would not increase performance, since it is performing the same table link behind the scenes. Therefore, PeopleSoft created programs that perform this link once (usually overnight, although the program can be executed as frequently or as seldom as you like) and save the resulting set into a reporting table.

We summarize the three reporting tables provided by PeopleSoft (one for HR data and two for benefits data) below. At first glance, it looks like heaven—everything *is* in one place after all! That enthusiasm is valid but may be short-lived. Be aware that there are several important things to watch out for when using a reporting table.

The Employees Table (PS_EMPLOYEES)

Populated by: PER099.SQR program

Major tables: PS_EMPLOYMENT, PS_JOB, PS_PERSONAL_DATA

Minor tables: PS_DEPT_TBL, PS_DISABILITY, PS_DIVERSITY,
                  PS_JOBCODE_TBL, PS_JOB_LABOR, PS_NAMES, PS_PERS_NID

- Includes only the most recent record from the PS_JOB table.
- Employee ID, employee department, and employee jobcode link the tables at the employee level. All control table values are linked with the PS_JOB effective date (see Chapter 3) to get values that were valid as of the historic point-in-time.
- Includes all employees who have an employee status on the PS_JOB table of A, P, L, or S (active, on leave, on paid leave, suspended). Excludes non-employees that may be stored on PS_PERSONAL_DATA with a personnel status other than 'E.'

Used for: Reporting employee human resources information, employee counts. Provides convenient one-stop shopping for hidden information such as:

- manager ID
- jobcode detail information (including job title)
- EEO codes
- disabled indicator
- ethnic group

- union information
- preferred name
- national ID (Social Security Number)

The Benefits Plan Data Table (PS_BEN_PLAN_DATA)

Populated by: BEN100.SQR program, using the following common modules:

- BENOTR.SQC selects all minor table fields.
- BENDEPS.SQC selects all dependent data.
- BENPERS.SQC selects all major tables for populating PS_BEN_PERS_DATA (see below).

Major tables: PS_JOB, PS_BEN_PROG_PARTIC, PS_HEALTH_BENEFIT, PS_DISABILITY_BEN, PS_LIFE_ADD_BEN, PS_FSA_BENEFIT, PS_SAVINGS_PLAN, PS_VACATION_BEN, PS_DED_CALC, PS_DEPENDENT_BENEF, PS_HEALTH_DEPENDNT, PS_LIFE_ADD_BENEFC, PS_SAVINGS_BENEFC

Minor tables: PS_BEN_PLAN_TBL, PS_PROVIDR_TBL, PS_PROV_POLICY_TBL, XLATTABLE, PS_BEN_DEFN_PGM, PS_COMPANY_TBL, PS_PAYGROUP_TBL

- Includes all employees who do not have an employee status of T or D (terminated or deceased).
- Includes only the most recent elected and waived plans (not terminated plans) for each plan type of the elected benefit program.

Used for: Retrieving information on all benefit plans for all employees, dependents and beneficiaries. Consolidates benefit program, plan, participation and deduction information:

- vacation hours
- savings plan deductions
- FSA deductions and pledge
- disability plan elections
- health plan elections
- COBRA participation
- calculated original enrollment date for each plan (see chapter 22) for both employees *and* dependents
- plan deduction taken and calculated base for the most recent pay period

The Benefits Personal Data Table (PS_BEN_PER_DATA)

Populated by: Like PS_BEN_PLAN_DATA, populated by the BEN100.SQR program.

Major tables: PS_BEN_PLAN_DATA, PS_PERSONAL_DATA, PS_PERS_NID, PS_DEPENDENT_BENEF, PS_DEP_BENEF_NID

Minor tables: XLATTABLE

> • The selection criteria are identical to the PS_BEN_PLAN_DATA table.

Used for: Includes personal data for every employee, beneficiary, and dependent found in the PS_BEN_PLAN_DATA table. Contains personal information such as:

> • name, address
> • relationship (for dependents and beneficiaries)
> • birth date, gender

Let's look in detail at each of the reporting tables to get a better idea of their utility. Each table has features and drawbacks that should be clearly understood before the table is used in a query, no matter how simple.

THE EMPLOYEES TABLE

The best-looking table in PeopleSoft is, beyond a doubt, the PS_EMPLOYEES table. This table appears to have everything in one convenient place. For many, the PS_EMPLOYEES table provides a one-stop, organized and appropriate place to handle most major HR reporting requirements.

PeopleSoft encourages the use of the PS_EMPLOYEES table because of its performance. By constructing queries that use the PS_EMPLOYEES table in lieu of huge tables like PS_JOB, a query returns data faster. PeopleSoft recognizes this fact by using the PS_EMPLOYEES table in at least 15 delivered SQR programs.

It is important to understand just what the PS_EMPLOYEES table contains, and what its limitations are. Often users try to include the employees table and get inaccurate results. Before creating queries with PS_EMPLOYEES, be sure to understand the following limitations… or inaccurate data could result:

1. **The data is not always current.** The data in the PS_EMPLOYEES table must be manually refreshed, usually on a daily basis. This creates four important considerations:

   • *Queries and programs created with the PS_EMPLOYEES table will be dependent on the refresh program PER099.SQR.* If PER099.SQR does not run, the PS_EMPLOYEES table will not return the most current row for each employee.

   • *The PS_EMPLOYEES table is not an up-to-the-minute reflection of the data.* It will not, for example, reflect the name of an employee that was hired this morning until it is refreshed, usually that night. All queries are at least one day behind.

   • *Consider whether you will need to run the query or program for a date in history.* Since the PS_EMPLOYEES table is refreshed often, the results of a query run today cannot be returned at a later date. For example, an interface file that may get damaged en route and needs to be rerun for the original date should not use the PS_EMPLOYEES table.

- *The PS_EMPLOYEES table is not easy to populate.* Although it creates an overall performance gain, the PER099.SQR program that creates the PS_EMPLOYEES table can occupy a large chunk of a nightly batch window. Since many delivered SQRs also depend on the PS_EMPLOYEES table, PER099.SQR must be run first. Some organizations may not run the refresh program as often as once a day. This further reduces the effectiveness of the table.

2. **Not all of the employees are there.** The PS_EMPLOYEES table only contains active, on leave, on paid leave, and suspended employees. Any time you need to include terminated or retired employees, or non-employees, forget about it. You'll have to go back to the original tables (PS_JOB, PS_PERSONAL_DATA, etc.).

3. **Some of the fields are missing.** PeopleSoft conveniently left off 1% of the fields. The JOB table, for example, is included in its entirety (50+ fields), except for the EMPL_CLASS field. If you need this field you're out of luck. For control tables like the PS_DEPT_TBL table and the PS_JOBCODE_TBL table, only a fraction of the fields are on PS_EMPLOYEES. PeopleSoft made the call—certain fields are more frequently needed than others.

4. **Customizations to base tables must be duplicated.** Consider any custom fields your organization is adding to the base tables. Adding a field to the PS_JOB table means that it should be added to the PS_EMPLOYEES table as well so end-users can easily obtain it. This requires additional modification to the PeopleSoft system.

5. **Certain statuses, like long-term disability, cannot be detected.** Since the PS_EMPLOYEES table only contains the most recent PS_JOB table row (the most recent effective date), it cannot distinguish between status, compensation, and position changes, which are stored in the ACTION and ACTION_REASON fields. This topic is discussed in Chapter 8. The most serious impact of this issue is on queries that need to know if an employee is on long-term disability. The only field that indicates long-term disability is the ACTION field on the PS_JOB table, which is an inaccurate field on the PS_EMPLOYEES table.

6. **The effective date is misleading.** Users are accustomed to effective dates, and assume that the PS_EMPLOYEES table is an effective-dated table. It is not; the effective date is populated with the

effective date of the PS_JOB table row. Only one row is included in the PS_EMPLOYEES table (as delivered), making the effective date an 'information only' field.

But don't forget the positive facts about the PS_EMPLOYEES table:

1. Programs that use PS_EMPLOYEES can execute many times faster than those that hit all of the base tables.
2. Using the PS_EMPLOYEES table makes PeopleSoft much easier to understand for a new user.

> Tip: Database detectives can use the PS_EMPLOYEES process to see where things are stored and how to accurately retrieve them. The PER099.SQR program, usually inside the SQR directory of a PeopleSoft installation, contains the field names and criteria used to create the PS_EMPLOYEES table.

Improving the PS_EMPLOYEES table

Many improvements can be easily made to the PS_EMPLOYEES table. Certain fields can be added, and the exclusions of portions of the employee population can be removed. Since modifications to PeopleSoft eventually cause headaches with every upgrade, it may be best to consider creating a parallel PS_EMPLOYEES table. Many organizations create such a table. Treated like a custom table, this version of the PS_EMPLOYEES table could contain the entire employee population and could be fine-tuned for your organization.

Issues surrounding obtaining status from the PS_EMPLOYEES table can also be solved through modifications. Refer to Chapter 8 for more information on possible solutions to these issues.

THE BENEFITS TABLES

The two benefits reporting tables that PeopleSoft provides bring together information from many different benefits areas. These reporting tables are a feat of consolidation.

All employee and dependent personal information relative to benefits, such as birth date, are on PS_BEN_PER_DATA. The storage of information on PS_BEN_PER_DATA is straightforward—by employee ID and dependent/benefit number.

All employee and dependent elections, coverage, and deduction information are on PS_BEN_PLAN_DATA. Let's look at it extensively since it contains not only employees and dependents/beneficiaries, but also data for each benefits plan.

Looking at PS_BEN_PLAN_DATA

The benefits plan table contains all of the plans from an employee's elected benefit program. Health, disability, life, savings, FSA plans, and vacation balances are found on PS_BEN_PLAN_DATA. Health, life, and savings plans are included for dependents and beneficiaries as well.

How rows are organized

As with all benefits tables, we need to know the organization of the rows to effectively retrieve data. On PS_BEN_PLAN_DATA, one row represents a single plan type for a single person. For example, Bob is enrolled in a health plan and a life plan, and he has an FSA account. Three rows will be on the PS_BEN_PLAN_DATA table for Bob, one for each of these items. Each row will show his coverage level, the provider name, a description of the plan, and the dollar amount being deducted. Bob's dependents will have their own rows. His two children are enrolled only in the health plan. Hence the five rows have Bob's employee ID as a key.

To distinguish employee rows from dependent rows, we look at the DEPENDENT_BENEF field. If it is blank, this is a row for the employee. If it has a value, this is the number assigned to the dependent or beneficiary (more information on this field is available in Chapter 23), and indicates a dependent row.

Included plan types

Although information is stored by plan type, not all plan types will be present in the PS_BEN_PLAN_DATA table. Unless the table is customized by your organization, only the plan types listed in Table 4-1 should appear. Table 4-2 lists plan types not found on the table.

▶ **Table 4-1** Plan types on the benefits data table: PS_BEN_PLAN_DATA

Value	Description	Base Table
1x	Health plans	PS_HEALTH_BENEFIT
2x	Life plans	PS_LIFE_ADD_BEN
3x	Disability plans	PS_DISABILITY_BEN
4x	Savings plans	PS_SAVINGS_PLAN
4A	Employee stock purchase plans	PS_SAVINGS_PLAN
6x	Flexible Spending Account plans	PS_FSA_BENEFIT
9x	Vacation buy/sell plans	PS_VACATION_BEN

▶ **Table 4-2** Plan types *not* on the benefits data table: PS_BEN_PLAN_DATA

Value	Description
5x	Leave plans
7x	Retirement plans
8x	Pension plans

Effective date selection

The coverage end date and effective date are both used as criteria to select the appropriate row for each employee plan. The maximum effective date as of a provided date (usually the current date) is considered the current row. If this current row has a coverage end date that is greater than the current date, it is excluded.

For example, if Bob's health coverage end date is set for 01/01/2005, when the PS_BEN_PLAN_DATA table is populated on 01/02/2005, his health coverage will no longer appear. The most recent plan information is used only if the coverage has not ended. The current date is used as criteria.

Also keep in mind that the PS_BEN_PLAN_DATA table only contains election or waived elections, known as 'E' or 'W' records. No termination 'T' records are included. To determine the termination from a plan or termination information such as the date of termination, we must look at the base table for each plan. More information on benefit plan elections can be found in Chapter 22.

USING THE BENEFITS TABLES TOGETHER: *PS_BENEFITS_DATA*

Both the PS_BEN_PLAN_DATA and PS_BEN_PER_DATA tables are often used in conjunction. These two tables are similar because they take employee, dependent, and beneficiary information and place them in one consolidated table. The PS_BEN_PLAN_DATA table also consolidates information from a wide array of benefit election tables. The PS_BEN_PER_DATA table is not as extensive, but it is useful because it pulls the necessary personal data, including national ID (Social Security number) for each employee/dependent/beneficiary.

The data in these two tables is consolidated in a PeopleSoft view, PS_BENEFITS_DATA. This view takes all of the data from both tables and combines it into a single place. The data is joined on the common keys: employee ID, COBRA record ID, and dependent/beneficiary ID.

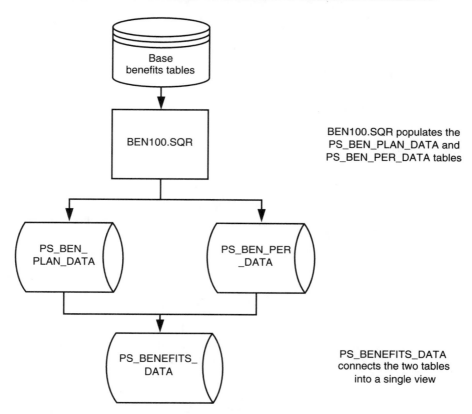

Base
benefits tables

BEN100.SQR

BEN100.SQR populates the
PS_BEN_PLAN_DATA and
PS_BEN_PER_DATA tables

PS_BEN_
PLAN_DATA

PS_BEN_PER
_DATA

PS_BENEFITS_
DATA

PS_BENEFITS_DATA
connects the two tables
into a single view

▶ **Figure 4-1**   Relationships among benefits reporting tables

Essentially, the link takes all of the rows from the PS_BEN_PLAN_DATA table, which has a row for each person in each plan, and at the end of each row places general personal data about the person. An employee row for the health plan type will contain the employee's name, address, birth date, etc. A dependent/beneficiary row will contain the dependent/beneficiary's name, address, birth date, and relationship to the employee.

Although the combination of data in PS_BENEFITS_DATA creates some duplication, the result is an extremely comprehensive set of benefits information.

Enrollment Date

Appendix A contains a chart showing where each field on the PS_BENEFITS_DATA table comes from. Each field comes from a particular benefits table. Note, however, that one field is calculated. This field, ENROLLMENT_DT, is not found on any other table in PeopleSoft. The enrollment date field provides the original enrollment date for a plan. Since the base benefits tables are arranged by effective date, a special query must go through each historical record to retrieve the initial enrollment date. This query is explained in detail in Chapter 22, but it is much easier to just select it from PS_BEN_PLAN_DATA or PS_BENEFITS_DATA.

VIEWS

The benefits data table is actually a view, not a reporting table. Views are the most overlooked feature for extracting data from PeopleSoft. Over 1,500 views come delivered with PeopleSoft. No matter what your query, there is probably a view that could at least come close to providing the same information.

"My problems are solved!" you exclaim. Not so fast. Views do not have all of the answers. It is important to focus on both the advantages and limitations of views.

Keeping a Level Head: Positives and Negatives

Part of the reason why views are overlooked is that they offer no real technical advantage. That is, when they are at their most versatile, linking all of the fields from large tables, they degrade performance by retrieving data you do not need. On the other hand, when they are customized to pick just a couple of fields, there can be a performance advantage.

This performance advantage explains the principal reason why most views exist—to support a piece of the PeopleSoft delivered application. From the application standpoint, a view takes only certain fields from certain tables and allows the result set to be displayed on a panel. Since the application requires views, they are widely used. Other delivered programs, such as SQRs, also use views, but only if the view already exists to support the application.

Very few views exist to consolidate data in a way that can be utilized outside of a pop-up window on a panel. A few out of 1,500, though, isn't bad. Views have a great deal of potential when used correctly.

There are several advantages to using views:

1. **Views simplify the database.** Instead of linking three payroll tables to determine earnings from a recent paycheck, a view allows you to look at one convenient table. The view provides the antidote to the growing relational database.

2. **Views take care of the table links**. Since all of the tables in a view are linked by that view, the chance for programmer error is

decreased. Users can concentrate on using the data rather than on extracting it.

3. **No modifications are necessary** to the delivered application objects in order to create a view. A view is just a link between delivered objects, not a modification to them.

There are also several disadvantages:

1. **Views hide the user from the underlying data.** Sometimes a user could better understand what is going on if he or she could see what the data actually looks like. A view is just another layer the user needs to cut through.

2. **Often table links vary.** In certain circumstances, you may want to link two tables according to only one key, or according to two keys. This is unlikely to happen within a view.

3. **Although views make the database easier, they do not decrease the processing time.** Just because you can't see it doesn't mean it isn't there. For this reason, use caution with ambitious views. Using a huge view that links 6 tables probably isn't the best way to extract just employee ID, name, and status. The advantage of simplification can be quickly eliminated by the retrieval of tons of useless data... data that takes extra processing time.

Views You Can Use

Some basic views can help you access data quickly. The following descriptions of different views is a short sampling of useful views delivered by PeopleSoft. The list is not comprehensive—the way to incorporate views into your PeopleSoft lifestyle is to get in the habit of looking for one whenever you begin a query. For example, a simple look in the Application Designer for "EARN%VW" or "ERN%VW" will bring up most of the views that contain earnings information.

Benefits views

PS_BENEFITS_VW   The benefits view contains the most recent actual deduction and calculated base for any employee benefit plan. Information comes from the PS_PAY_CHECK and PS_PAY_DEDUCTION tables. The plan type must be greater than or equal to 10, which returns only benefit plan deductions. Only the minimum deduction class is selected for each benefit deduction, in the following order: (A)fter tax is first, (B)efore tax is next, and (T)axable benefit is last.

PS_BENEFITS_DED_VW The benefits deduction view is the same as the benefits view (PS_BENEFITS_VW), but it returns the deduction calculation results. These results do not represent the confirmed paycheck results.

PS_FSA_VW, PS_HEALTH_VW, PS_LIFE_VW The Flexible Spending Account (FSA), health, and life views retrieve the current elections for their respective plans (FSA, health, or life plans). Information comes from the PS_FSA_BENEFIT, PS_HEALTH_BENEFIT, and PS_LIFE_ADD_BEN tables for the most recent effective date.

PS_IMMEDIATE_FAMILY_EE The immediate family view contains the name and birth date of the employee's spouse, and children. Information from the PS_DEPENDENT_BENEF table is used for these relationships if the dependent is not on COBRA.

HR views

PS_CAREER_SUMM_VW The career summary view contains a summary of all career changes for an employee. One row is stored for each career change. The minimum effective dated row for each distinct department and jobcode is retrieved from the PS_JOB table. This returns a row for every time the employee changed to a new jobcode, department, position number, grade, or business unit.

PS_COMPSUMMRPT_VW The compensation summary reporting view contains one row for every change to an employee's salary. Information is taken from the PS_JOB table for all rows that have a change amount greater than or less than zero. Only employees who are currently active, on leave, on paid leave, or suspended are included. The hire or rehire row is included as the first compensation change for the employee.

PS_DEPT_POSN_COUNT The department position count view provides a summary count of approved and actual positions in each department. This view can only be used if position management is turned on (see Chapter 10). The counts are taken of the PS_POSITION_DATA and PS_DEPT_TBL tables.

PS_HISTORY The history view is the same as the PS_EMPLOYEES reporting table, except that it contains history information as well as current information for all employee statuses. All effective dates that are between the two dates found on the PSASOFDATE table are found on the PS_HISTORY view. The FROMDATE field is the from date, and the ASOFDATE field is the through date. The dates in this table may need to be manually updated before using the PS_HISTORY view.

Like the employees table, information comes from the PS_JOB, PS_PERSONAL_DATA, PS_EMPLOYMENT, PS_JOBCODE_TBL, PS_DEPT_TBL, PS_PERS_NID, PS_DIVERSITY, and PS_DISABILITY tables. The person status (PER_STATUS) must be 'E' for employee.

PS_PERSONNEL The personnel view is the view version of the PS_EMPLOYEES reporting table, but it contains all employee statuses. The ASOFDATE field on the PSASOFDATE table provides an as of date for selection, and may need to be manually updated before using the PS_PERSONNEL view. Information comes from the PS_JOB, PS_PERSONAL_DATA, PS_EMPLOY-MENT, PS_JOBCODE_TBL, PS_DEPT_TBL, and PS_PERS_NID tables. The person status (PER_STATUS) must be 'E' for employee.

PS_PERSONNEL_HIST The personnel history view is the same as the personnel view PS_PERSONNEL, but with no effective date criteria. It contains all of the rows in the PS_JOB table, and contains the PS_DIVERSITY and PS_DISABILITY tables as well. This view is extremely large and should be used with caution.

PS_POSN_HEADCOUNT The position headcount view provides a head-count by position number. The view returns one row per distinct position number with a count of the employees with that position. Information comes from PS_JOB and considers only employees who are active, on leave, on paid leave, or suspended. Employees with blank position numbers are excluded.

PS_POSN_HISTORY The position history view contains the initial position information for an employee. Information comes from PS_JOB table. The initial position is obtained retrieving the row where the effective date equals the position entry date, and selecting the minimum effective sequence for that date.

PS_POSN_HISTORY The position history view shows when an employee changed position. Information comes form the PS_JOB and PS_POSN_HISTORY tables. It retrieves the first row in the PS_JOB table that has an effective date occurring after the position entry date and a position different from the current position. It also chooses a row where the employee status is no longer active, leave, paid leave, or suspended. The minimum effective sequence number is selected for that date in order to retrieve the first PS_JOB record for the new position.

PS_STATE_NAMES_VW The state names view retrieves the state description and numeric code for a state code from the PS_STATE_NAMES_TBL. The country code is ignored.

Security-free views

Unlike most tables, security-free tables do not have PeopleSoft security turned on. When these tables are included in a query program that uses PeopleSoft security, such as PS Query, the overall query will perform much faster. For obvious reasons, very few tables have security turned off. In the two views listed here, PeopleSoft determined that no one should be restricted from looking up an employee ID and retrieving a name. Similarly, no one should be restricted from looking up an employee ID and retrieving a position number. By creating a view that limits the data to just two fields, security can be disabled on certain pieces of a table.

Views are also an integral part of PeopleSoft security. Special views quickly determine if a user is allowed to see particular information. The views are described in Section 5 along with more information on security and PS Query security.

PS_JOB_POSN_CURR   The current job position view retrieves the current position number for an employee ID. Only active, on leave, on paid leave, or suspended employees are retrieved. The most recent row is taken from the PS_JOB table. This view does not use a PeopleSoft security view.

PS_PERSONAL_DTA_VW   The personal data view returns the employee name for an employee ID. Information is from the PS_PERSONAL_DATA table. This view does not use a PeopleSoft security view (the PS_PERSON-AL_VW has the same definition with security turned on).

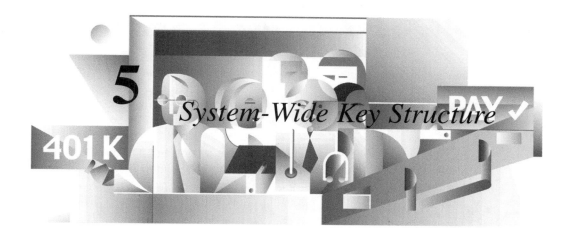

Several fields organize the PeopleSoft HR database at a high level. These fields appear as keys on certain tables, and drive most of the functionality of the system. They are provided to help companies migrate to PeopleSoft and organize their data according to arbitrary groupings. A business unit, region, territory, country, or language could form the highest level of organization for an installation. These keys affect downstream panels, reports, interfaces, and processes.

The two principal keys that organize the PeopleSoft database are SETID and BUSINESS_UNIT. These two keys are found on tables throughout the database, and it can be difficult to determine what they mean or how they are used. Each implementation is different—that is the whole purpose of these fields. Some companies may use SETID religiously; others may just default it to a single value.

PeopleSoft is constructed to group data according to company and department, since these are the groups required by agencies of the U.S. government. Tax reporting and EEO reporting, for example, must occur according to company and department. By adding two additional keys, setID and business unit, PeopleSoft provides two *additional* ways to organize your data. Companies and departments are still maintained separately. The new keys are not at a higher level than company or department—they are simply auxiliary.

THE PEOPLESOFT BUSINESS UNIT

The business unit field has virtually no real function. It is purely for classification. For this reason, many users default it to a single value. PeopleSoft didn't create it for fun, though. Here are some reasons why you may want to use the business unit field:

1. **Create groups of people that exist today but don't fit into PeopleSoft.** Perhaps 10 of your departments are considered "A" departments and the other ten are considered "B" departments. Call "A" and "B" business units. Headcount reports and other analyses can now be grouped by a new category.

2. **Define processing rules according to business unit.** Maybe the people in the "B" business unit need to be paid in lira. Set up business unit "B" with a new currency, and you're all set. PeopleSoft allows you to specify default values by business unit. Default values are the values that pop up when you first open a panel and stay there if you do not change them. PeopleSoft also lets you define benefits eligibility according to business unit.

3. **Share business units across applications.** This is a good way to make friends with the folks in finance. If you're using PeopleSoft applications such as Financials or Manufacturing, the business units can carry over.

4. **Use business units with setIDs for flexibility.** Since these two keys work together, they eliminate the duplication of data. An eligibility rule for one business unit can be used for another without typing it in twice. PeopleSoft uses setIDs to group different values or rules. Business units can then selectively link to these sets, combining sets to achieve the values and rules desired. A set can be used by many different business units. We'll discuss setIDs in greater detail below.

5. **Process employees in multiple countries.** Storing values according to country and then setting up particular business units for each set of values allows you to keep employees in the same companies and departments, but organized by country as well. The business unit works across these existing divisions. SetIDs and business units are virtually essential for setting up employees in different countries and processing different payrolls for each country.

If none of these reasons add any value to your implementation, there is no need to establish a group of business ID values. Simply set up a single setID and a single business unit, and assign it to all employees.

USING BUSINESS UNITS WITH SETIDS

The Set ID

The setID field is the label for what PeopleSoft calls TableSets. The general principle of a TableSet is simple:

A TableSet is a group of rows in a single table. A TableSet lets you categorize control values into separate groups of values.

Most control tables have the setID field as a key. This key allows you to do two things: define a value twice within a single table, or further separate different values from one another in a table.

You define a value twice if you want a single object to have two different definitions. For example, you may have a department that spans two countries (Table 5-1).

▶ **Table 5-1** Sample setID use in the department table

SETID	DEPTID	DESCR	LOCATION
USA	0001	Popsicle Department	012 (New York)
FRA	0001	Popsicle Department	036 (Paris)

There is really only one department 0001, but there are two definitions of it. If you're producing a list of everyone in department 0001, you can group by DEPTID. But since the departments need to be defined differently within PeopleSoft, the setID allows more than one occurrence of the same department ID.

The second use of the setID is to further separate already distinct values. For example, you may only want certain locations to exist for certain departments. A location with a setID of 'USA' can only be used in conjunction with a department ID with a setID of 'USA,' and so on. Even though there are other locations in the location table, they cannot be accessed.

There is a performance issue regarding the length of the setID codes used in PeopleSoft. With ID codes under 5 characters in length, PeopleSoft sometimes takes a long time to bring back lists of employees in online dialog boxes. By changing your setID values to 5 characters, this performance issue should not occur.

Business units and setIDs are meant for each other. Their relationship provides additional flexibility. For example, a business unit of 'USA' for an employee might mean to PeopleSoft that:

- For departments, the setID will be 'GLOBAL'
- For locations, the setID will be 'USA'
- For jobcodes, the setID will be 'CORP'

When an employee is hired they are placed in a business unit (on their PS_JOB record). Once this business unit is defined, only control values that are valid for the specified setIDs within the business unit definition will appear. For the situation described above, only 'GLOBAL' departments can be chosen, and only 'USA' locations.

By specifying business units to include different groupings of setID values, data duplication is kept to a minimum.

Relational Requirements

Although setID is a commonly used key, it may be different for a single employee depending on where you are looking. PeopleSoft stores different setIDs in different locations.

The PS_JOB table is a perfect example. Just looking at the DEPTID field and the SETID field is not sufficient for looking up the correct department. Since an employee can be bound by different setID values, the department could use an entirely different setID than the job table setID. There is a special field called SETID_DEPT.

And on the PS_DEPT_TBL, where the departments are listed, there is a location field. Since the locations an employee can work in could be under yet another setID, there is a SETID_LOCATION field. You can see that there is some serious cross-table activity going on. And there is a potential for setID conflicts.

PeopleSoft follows a general rule when storing setID field values. The employee's business unit overrides the setID of the control table. In other words, if an employee is in a business unit that specifies only locations with setID 'USA,' this setting will override the fact that the department setID is 'GLOBAL.'

From the database perspective, conflicts should not occur. The processing that populates the setID fields is performed by the PeopleSoft application. The application edits and validates the values before setting up an employee, guarding against conflicts.

Determining the Appropriate SETID in a Query

With all of these setID values floating around, we need to know which setID is appropriate for a given situation. If we are looking at a table and do not have a setID, we need to look up the appropriate setID for the employee's business unit. The business unit is always on the employee job record (PS_JOB).

To look up the setID, we look at the PS_SET_CNTRL_REC table (Table 5-2). In this table each business unit is connected to a setID field.

▶ **Table 5-2** Set control record: PS_SET_CNTRL_REC

Set Control Value (key) SETCNTRLVALUE	Record Group ID (key) REC_GROUP_ID	Record Name (key) RECNAME	SetID SETID
USA	HR_01	DEPT_TBL	GLOBAL
USA	HR_02	JOBCODE_TBL	CORP
USA	HR_03	LOCATION_TBL	USA
USA	HR_03	LOCATION_TBL_LANG	USA
EURO	HR_01	DEPT_TBL	GLOBAL
EURO	HR_02	JOBCODE_TBL	CORP
EURO	HR_03	LOCATION_TBL	EURO
GLOBAL	HR_01	DEPT_TBL	GLOBAL
GLOBAL	HR_03	LOCATION_TBL	GLOBAL

Note that the organization of this table follows the relationship between business units and setIDs. A business unit (SETCNTRLVALUE) is linked to a record group (REC_GROUP_ID), which contains different tables (RECNAME). These three fields form the key that is linked to a specific setID. In Table 5-2, employees in the 'USA' business unit have departments under the 'GLOBAL' setID. They have locations under 'USA.' And those in the 'EURO' business unit also have 'GLOBAL' for departments, but 'EURO' for locations.

Remember that PeopleSoft calls tables records (i.e., recname, rec_group_id).

The values in Table 5-2 seem confusing, since the same exact codes are used for setID and business unit. Although this is not necessary, companies tend to use the same codes. In fact, PeopleSoft's sample data uses similar sets of codes. Of course, it is always important to stop and think about whether we are using a business unit or a setID.

The query that hits this table is simple. Table 5-3 shows an example where we want to retrieve the department and jobcode descriptions for each employee. Each control table has a typical effective date sub-query (covered in Chapter 2) and the PS_JOB table has two required sub-queries for effective date and effective sequence (these sub-queries are covered in Chapter 7). The sub-queries to note are the ones in bold. These two sub-queries retrieve the appropriate setID.

▶ **Table 5-3** Query using set control record

| The query | ```
SELECT JO.EMPLID,
       JO.DEPTID,
       DT.DESCRSHORT,
       JO.JOBCODE,
       JT.DESCRSHORT
FROM PS_JOB JO,
     PS_DEPT_TBL DT,
     PS_JOBCODE_TBL JT
WHERE JO.EFFDT =
        (SELECT MAX(JO1.EFFDT)
           FROM PS_JOB JO1
          WHERE JO1.EMPLID = JO.EMPLID
            AND JO1.EMPL_RCD# = JO.EMPL_RCD#
            AND JO1.EFFDT <= [current date])
    AND JO.EFFSEQ =
        (SELECT MAX(JO2.EFFSEQ)
           FROM PS_JOB JO2
          WHERE JO2.EMPLID = JO.EMPLID
            AND JO2.EMPL_RCD# = JO.EMPL_RCD#
            AND JO2.EFFDT = JO.EFFDT)
    AND JO.JOBCODE = JT.JOBCODE

    AND JT.SETID =
    (SELECT CR.SETID
      FROM PS_SET_CNTRL_REC CR
     WHERE CR.RECNAME = 'JOBCODE_TBL'
       AND CR.SETCNTRLVALUE = JO.BUSINESS_UNIT)

      AND JT.EFFDT =
        (SELECT MAX(JT1.EFFDT)
           FROM PS_JOBCODE_TBL JT1
          WHERE JT1.JOBCODE = JT.JOBCODE
            AND JT1.SETID = JT.SETID
            AND JT1.EFFDT <= JO.EFFDT)
      AND JO.DEPTID = DT.DEPTID
``` |
```

▶ **Table 5-3** continued

```
            AND DT.SETID =
        (SELECT CR1.SETID
           FROM PS_SET_CNTRL_REC CR1
          WHERE CR1.RECNAME = 'DEPT_TBL'
            AND CR1.SETCNTRLVALUE = JO.BUSINESS_UNIT)

            AND DT.EFFDT =
              (SELECT MAX(DT1.EFFDT)
                 FROM PS_DEPT_TBL DT1
                WHERE DT1.DEPTID = DT.DEPTID
                  AND DT1.SETID = DT.SETID
                  AND DT1.EFEDT <= DT.EFFDT)
```

Returns the data set	EMPLID	DEPTID	DESCRSHORT	JOBCODE	DESCRSHORT
	------	------	----------	-------	----------
	8002	10110	HR-PAYROLL	Q006	MANAGER
	8006	12004	POPSICLES	G003	FRZR MNGR

These sub-queries use the value of the employee's business unit to look up the appropriate setID value on the PS_SET_CNTRL_REC table. The result is a set of data that accurately retrieves information using the employee's appropriate setID settings.

PART 2

Human Resources

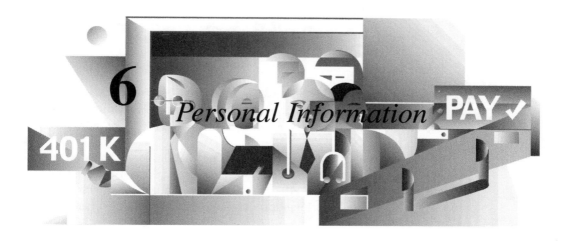

6

Personal Information

What is personal information? In most cases, it is private information about a person (employee or non-employee). Things like name, home address, birth date, and Social Security number are stored in PeopleSoft. This information has little or nothing to do with the job being performed. But it is necessary for processing checks, assigning benefits, and filing taxes. The principal personal data tables are shown in Table 6-1. These are the tables we will review in this chapter.

▶ **Table 6-1** Tables reviewed in this chapter

Table	Description
PS_PERSONAL_DATA	Core personal data table
PS_PERS_DATA_EFFDT	Effective-dated personal data
PS_PERS_NID	Personal national ID table

The information located in the personal data tables is usually highly sensitive. Depending on the organization, the release of a home address, a home phone number, or a birth date can be a breach of employee privacy. PeopleSoft places most of the sensitive information about an employee on these tables. Use caution when deciding to include it in a query, interface, or report.

PERSONAL DATA

Let's look first at the PS_PERSONAL_DATA table (Table 6-2). This is the table where most of the personal data about an employee is stored—things like name, address, and birth date. The personal data table is one of the core records of the PeopleSoft HR database.

PeopleSoft stores a great deal of personal information, for all types of people. Employees, trainees, recruits, consultants, temporary employees, and even dependents and beneficiaries all have records in the database with personal information. This allows tracking of different populations and facilitates the hiring process.

▶ **Table 6-2** Personal data table: PS_PERSONAL_DATA

Structure	Only one row per person.
Keys	Employee ID
Alternate keys	Full name or last name only
Sub-records included	Home address
	Mailing address, used for sending out letters (COBRA, benefit summary, etc.)
	Home phone
	Non-employee trainee information
	USA-specific personal data
	Canada-specific personal data
	Germany-specific personal data
	France-specific personal data
	Japan-specific personal data
	UK-specific personal data
Panels to look at	Go ➤ Administer Workforce ➤ Administer Workforce U.S. ➤ Use ➤ Personal Data

Identifying Employees: The Employee ID

The employee ID field stores the unique identifier of a person. This field is the principal key of the table. Each row on the PS_PERSONAL_DATA table is identified by a unique employee ID value. An employee ID identifies a person, not necessarily an employee.

Choosing how you want to identify employees in your organization is no simple task. PeopleSoft recommends the use of the employee ID field as the single key that can uniquely identify an employee. Why?

Many organizations rely on Social Security number to identify employees. Technically, no two people should have the same SSN. In reality, however, duplicate SSNs occur. Often when new employees are entered into the system, and an SSN is not available, users will type in a dummy SSN. This can cause duplication. In addition, with PeopleSoft going global, not every employee has a SSN. Creating unique SSNs becomes increasingly difficult.

Other keys, of course, suffer from greater duplication. Names are often the same, especially in large organizations. Birth dates, or combinations of dates and SSN are also vulnerable and cumbersome.

Plus, there are significant privacy issues surrounding the SSN. Employees are hesitant to supply an SSN, especially when calling an HR desk to ask a simple question. If SSN were used as the main PeopleSoft key, PeopleSoft users would be typing in SSNs before accessing every panel.

PeopleSoft's employee ID is designed *always* to be unique. New numbers are assigned to new employees automatically. And the employee ID identifies a person everywhere in PeopleSoft:

1. Most panels ask for an employee ID.
2. Most delivered reports print out the employee ID.
3. The pay check and advice contain the employee ID.
4. All employee-level tables are linked by employee ID.

This doesn't mean that it is impossible to identify an employee by SSN or name. Often a panel will allow you to specify a name or SSN, and then it will pop up a list box to let you choose between duplicates. And many delivered reports, such as tax reports, include the SSN as well as the employee ID.

The employee ID exists to make your life easier. Encourage its use in your organization. When employees call up and provide an employee ID instead of an SSN, every process runs that much smoother.

> PeopleSoft is delivered to accommodate employee IDs up to 4 characters in length. Although the field can be 11 characters in the database, some internal program routines expect the ID to be 4 or fewer characters long. This setting can be changed, but PeopleCode must be modified. This PeopleCode is stored in the human resources functional library (PS_FUNCLIB_HR, the EMPLID field).

The PeopleSoft Name Format

The name field stores the employee name in a special PeopleSoft format. Names are formatted as "Smith,John H". Employee name is not a required field in the database, but it cannot be left blank on the PeopleSoft entry panel.

Often when users look at the personal data table, they see two additional fields that split the name up into first and last pieces. The FIRST_NAME_SRCH and LAST_NAME_SRCH fields do split the name at the comma. These fields are not meant for queries, however. They are formatted for database searches in all capital letters with no accents or special characters.

Storing a name

At first glance, PeopleSoft's name formatting looks strange. Every new user, when typing a name into a panel, gets the red box and a stern warning, "Name Field Format Error. Please reenter using the PeopleSoft standard name format. (15,35)." I still get it once and a while.

Okay, what are they looking for? PeopleSoft accepts names in the following format:

```
<last name><optionalspace+suffix><comma><optionalprefix+space>
<first name><optionalspace+middle name or initial>
```

In other words:

"Dostevesky,Fyodor" is good.

But "Dostevesky, Fyodor" is not good. Notice the space after the comma.

And "Dostevesky Jr.,Mr. Fyodor Dimitri" is good (last name, suffix, prefix, first name, middle name).

But: "Dostevesky,Jr.,Mr. Fyodor Dimitri" is not good. Commas confuse PeopleSoft; it expects a prefix or first name.

Acceptable characters are A–Z, spaces, periods, hyphens, and apostrophes. For anything else, one option is to use the alternate character name. When enabled, you can click on a box and specify a name with special characters like 'ï'. This name is stored in the NAME_AC field on PS_PERSONAL_DATA.

Also, the case that you enter the name in is the case the name is saved in. Enter it like "dOSTEVESKY,fYODOR" and that's how it'll look on his COBRA letter. Be careful!

Retrieving a name

Retrieving the name from PeopleSoft is simple—look at the NAME field on PS_PERSONAL_DATA. There are also prefix, suffix, first and last name fields. And in SQR, PeopleSoft provides several common modules (all begin with ROTNAME) to extract and reconfigure the name according to your needs.

Keep in mind, however, that extracting pieces of a name is not an exact science. PeopleSoft provides independent fields for information like prefix. If you type a prefix in the name field, and then specify a separate prefix, they conflict. Consider the following entries and what the delivered PeopleSoft routines come up with.

In the PeopleSoft panel, if we enter the following, we get the results in Table 6-3:

```
Name = 'Clown IV,Mr. Bozo The'
Initials = 'ABB'
Prefix = 'Dr.'
```

▶ **Table 6-3** Name formatting

The query	`SELECT PD.NAME,`
	`        PD.NAME_PREFIX,`
	`        PD.NAME_SUFFIX,`
	`        PD.LAST_NAME,`
	`        PD.FIRST_NAME,`
	`        PD.MIDDLE_NAME,`
	`        PD.NAME_INITIALS`
	`FROM PS_PERS_DATA_EFFDT PD`
	`WHERE PD.EMPLID = 'BOZO'`
	`   AND PD.EFFDT = (SELECT MAX(PD1.EFFDT)`
	`                    FROM PS_PERS_DATA_EFFDT PD1`
	`                    WHERE PD1.EMPLID = PD.EMPLID)`

Returns the data set	NAME		NAME_PREFIX	NAME_SUFFIX
	----------------------------		-----------	-----------
	Clown IV,Mr. Bozo The		Dr	
	LAST_NAME	FIRST_NAME	MIDDLE_NAME	NAME_INITIALS
	---------	-----------------	-----------	-------------
	Clown IV	Mr. Bozo The		ABB

Note how the name is parsed out:

1. The name contains the prefix and suffix.
2. The prefix and suffix specified in the name field are not placed in the NAME_PREFIX or NAME_SUFFIX fields.
3. The NAME_INITIALS field takes what was typed in, not the actual initials.
4. The last name includes the suffix.
5. The first name includes the prefix and the middle name.
6. The middle name is not retrieved.

The SQR routine has even more trouble, returning the following:

```
Last name = Clown IV
First name = Mr.
Middle initial = B
```

The moral of the story is to avoid using the NAME field to enter prefixes. If you use the drop-down prefix list instead, the prefix is accurately recorded in NAME_PREFIX. Suffixes are up to you; PeopleSoft provides no way of recording the suffix in the NAME_SUFFIX field on PS_PERS_DATA_EFFDT. This field will always remain blank unless data is entered into it using a custom program or an SQL statement. It may be wise, then, to enter suffixes in the NAME field. No great tragedies will occur; the last name will just always contain the suffix field.

The Resident Address and Phone

Some basic fields store the home address of the employee on PS_PERSON-AL_DATA. These fields are located on the ADDRESS_SBR and are used often. On PS_PERSONAL_DATA, these fields represent home address. Table 6-4 lists each field that is part of the address sub-record, its definition, and any additional tips.

▶ **Table 6-4** Address sub-record fields

Field	Description/Notes
COUNTRY	The country field stores the country of residence.
ADDRESS1, 2, 3, 4	The address lines store the street address lines of the employee's residence. It is always wise to check with your organization to see which address lines will be utilized, since few organizations use all four lines.
CITY	The city field stores the resident city of the employee.
NUM1, NUM2	The number fields store additional numbers for the employee's home address. These fields are optional.
HOUSE_TYPE	The house type field indicates if the employee lives in a house boat or a house trailer. This field is optional.
COUNTY	The county field stores the resident county. It is optional and not used often.
STATE	The state field stores the resident state.
POSTAL	The Postal Code field stores the home postal code (in U.S., zip code). Although this is not a required field, benefits processing uses the home zip code to determine eligibility. Depending on how paycheck distribution is set up, the zip code may be used as the sort criteria for sorting paychecks.
GEO_CODE	The tax vendor geographical code functionality is not delivered. This field is not on any panel and is not used by any delivered processes.
IN_CITY_LIMIT	The In City Limit field functionality is not delivered. This field is not on any panel and is not used by any delivered processes. It is a yes/no value.

The personal data table also has other 'home' identifiers. There is a set of address fields marked '_OTHER' that are identical to the address fields except they have an "other" appended at the end. PeopleSoft uses this second address as a mailing address. Letters that go to an employee's home (such as COBRA) automatically use this address when it is populated.

Phone number is also stored on the PS_PERSONAL_DATA table, along with a country code when necessary. This is the home telephone number.

Non-Employees on PS_PERSONAL_DATA

The personnel status field indicates whether the current record contains information for an employee ('E') or a non-employee ('N') such as a consultant or trainee. Organizations may choose to store personal information about non-employees, but these people are usually ignored by most of the PeopleSoft system processes. Many delivered processes make a point of excluding non-employees. If you are using personal data and want to exclude non-employees, use the personnel status field to distinguish them. Several delivered programs use this field as criteria.

Non-employees, notably instructors, sometimes have data stored in several other fields on the personal data table. The business title field (BUSINESS_TITLE) does not store the business title for each employee (see Chapter 10 for job title). Similarly, the EMPLOYER, BUSINESS_UNIT, DEPTID, and SUPERVISOR_ID fields are not employee fields either. The employer field stores the name of the instructor's real employer. The business unit and department fields store where the instructor is assigned in the organization, for headcount and accounting purposes. The supervisor ID field stores the employee ID of the instructor's supervisor.

Original Hire Date

The original hire date field stores the date the employee was first hired. If the employee has a hire record on the PS_JOB table (action = 'HIR'), the effective date for that record will equal the ORIG_HIRE_DT. Note that only an effective date of a hire record is used; a rehire record is not used. This means that the original hire date is the first hire date for the employee.

The original hire date is different from the HIRE_DT and REHIRE_DT fields on the PS_EMPLOYMENT table, which we look at later in Chapter 12. Both of these fields on the employment table are overwritten automatically. The original hire date, on the other hand, can only be manually entered and changed.

Birth Information

The date of birth field (BIRTHDATE) stores the employee's birth date. Birth date is not a required field, but a warning message will appear in the panel if it is not entered. Many payroll and benefits processes rely on this date to calculate age and other important dates. If it is not provided here, processes down the line will fail.

The birth country field stores the country of birth. Values are verified against the PS_COUNTRY_TBL. The birth state field stores the state in which the employee was born. Values are verified against the PS_BIRTHSTATE_VW, which selects all rows from the PS_STATE_NAMES_TBL.

Education Status

The highest education level field (HIGHEST_EDUC_LVL) stores an indicator of the highest level of education the employee has achieved. Values are verified against the translate table. The value of this field does not relate to the education information stored in the PS_ACCOMPLISHMENTS table. The value of this field must be changed manually if accomplishments are added since it does not automatically reflect new accomplishment records.

Referrals

Employee referrals are when an employee refers someone for a position at the company. The personal data table can track the links between employees and provide a data source for reporting on referrals.

The referral source field (REFERRAL_SOURCE) stores an indicator of how the employee was referred to the company. Values are verified against the translate table. This field is automatically filled in when you are using PeopleSoft for applicant data, but can also be manually entered through the personal data panels.

The employee referral ID (EMPL_REFERRAL_ID) field stores the employee ID of the referring party if an employee referred the individual. This value is filled in and checked against valid employee IDs only when PeopleSoft is used for applicant data. The field cannot be manually entered via a panel; it is typically provided by the applicant data function of PeopleSoft. This field ties each referred employee back to his or her referring employee.

There is also a general text field, specific referral source, that is provided for recording a source name, such as a publication or agency.

Citizenship Status

The citizenship status field stores whether the employee has citizenship status for the installation country. Official citizenship information is stored elsewhere; this field indicates whether a person is native, naturalized, etc. of the local country. A report, PER033.SQR, identifies discrepancies among the value of this field, the defaulted local country, and the records on the PS_CITIZENSHIP table. Values are verified against the translate table.

Strange, but Important Fields

QDRO

The *employee has QDRO* indicator (QDRO_IND_YN) is used by the Pension Administration module. The field is a yes/no value. Qualified Domestic Relations Order indicator is set to yes if an employee's pension is to be divided among different people.

Person Type

The *person type* field identifies certain non-employees such as applicants, COBRA recipients, pension payees, or contractors. Typically employees who are no longer employed but receive payments from the payroll system have a person type indicated.

Date Entitled to Medicare

The *date entitled to medicare* field (MEDICARE_ENTLD_DT) stores the date the employee is entitled to medicare. This date is used to process employees under COBRA.

On Demand EM DoSaveNow

The *on-demand event maintenance do save now* field is an indicator used by on-demand event maintenance (see Chapter 21). It is a yes/no value.

Personal Data for Other Countries

Many fields on the PS_PERSONAL_DATA table look like they could contain valuable data, but are really meant for processing employees in other countries. These fields are required by their respective countries and are not used for United States employees. Table 6-5 lists each field and its description.

▶ **Table 6-5** Personal data in countries other than the United States

Field	Description/Notes
Bilingualism Code, Health Care Number, Health Care Province	The bilingualism code indicates if the employee is bilingual, for Canadian records. Values are verified against the translate table. The health care number and province fields store the Canadian health care number and province. Values for the province are verified against the PS_STATE_NAMES_TBL.
Military Status, Expected Military Date	The military status field stores the Germany military status. Values are verified against the translate table. The expected military date field is populated for German employees if the employee has not yet served with the German Armed Forces.
HR Responsible ID	The HR responsible ID field identifies an HR employee who is responsible for the employee. It is used for German record processing. Values are verified against the PS_PERSONAL_DATA table.
Name Royal Prefix, Name Royal Suffix	The royal prefix/suffix fields store the German prefix and suffix for German employees. Values are verified against the PS_NM_ROYSUFF_GER table and PS_NM_ROYPREF_GER table.

▶ **Table 6-5** continued

Field	Description/Notes
Date of First Entry in France	The date of first entry in France field is used to track foreign employees in France.
Military Status	The military status field stores the French military status. Values are verified against the translate table.
Honseki Prefecture	The Honseki Prefecture field is used in Japan to track where an employee's family comes from. Values are verified against the PS_STATE_MC_JPN_VW, which selects rows with a country = 'JPN' from the PS_STATE_NAMES_TBL.
Tax Code, Tax Basis	The tax code and tax basis fields are used by the European payroll process. Values for the tax basis are verified against the translate table.
Alternate Character Name, Address 1, Address 2, Address 3	The alternate character name and address fields store the name and address of an employee if it contains characters other than English characters. The alternate character functionality must be enabled to use these fields.
Language Code	The language code field indicates the person's preferred language. This field is not used for processing in PeopleSoft. It is an informational field and appears on reports. Values are verified against the translate table.

UNDERSTANDING EFFECTIVE-DATED PERSONAL DATA

PeopleSoft began effective-dating certain personal data items with version 7.5. Previously, no history was stored for any personal data items. If a name changed, then it changed permanently, and no record of the former name could be obtained.

Only a small portion of the fields on PS_PERSONAL_DATA are now effective-dated. Rather than effective-date the entire table, which is sizable already, PeopleSoft made a new table just for the history of certain fields. The new table, PS_PERS_DATA_EFFDT, stores the current and historical values of the employee name, address, marital status, and smoker status.

The remaining non-effective-dated fields are housed only on PS_PERSONAL_DATA. Keeping the old PS_PERSONAL_DATA table around is certainly worth the extra effort, since nearly all programs that look at the PeopleSoft database inevitably look at PS_PERSONAL_DATA. Changing these programs would be a nightmare. So, in order to keep all of the fields in one place, both effective-dated and non-effective-dated fields are stored on PS_PERSONAL_DATA.

To keep the PS_PERSONAL_DATA table intact, a nightly batch job must execute to keep it in sync with PS_PERS_DATA_EFFDT.

Here's how the process works. First a user changes an employee's name and address in the PERSONAL_DATA1 panel (Go ➤ Administer Workforce ➤ Administer Workforce U.S. ➤ Use ➤ Personal Data ➤ Name/Address). A new row is inserted to represent the new effective date.

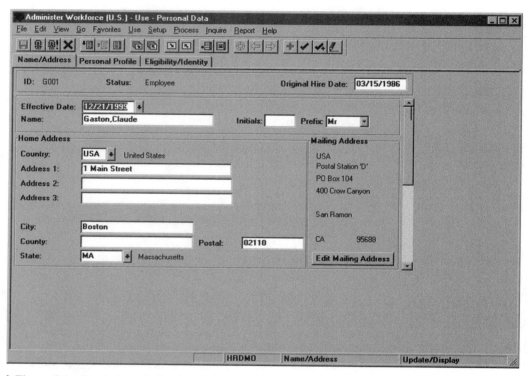

▶ **Figure 6-1**   Panel view of effective-dated personal data.

The new row appears as shown in Table 6-6.

▶ **Table 6-6**   Looking at the personal data update field

The query	`SELECT PD.EMPLID,`
	`       PD.EFFDT,`
	`       PD.NAME,`
	`       PD.UPDATE_PERS_DATA`
	`FROM PS_PERS_DATA_EFFDT PD`
	`WHERE EMPLID = 'BOZO'`

Returns the data set	EMPLID	EFFDT	NAME	UPDATE_PERS_DATA
	------	-----------	----------------	----------------
	BOZO	21-DEC-1998	Smith,Bozo	Y
	BOZO	15-JUL-1998	Clown,Bozo	N
	BOZO	15-MAR-1986	Clown,Bozo	N

The field UPDATE_PERS_DATA is flagged with a 'Y' to indicate that this row contains new information that needs to be in sync with the row on the PS_PERSONAL_DATA table. The update personal data field is a yes/no flag that indicates whether the PS_PERSONAL_DATA table needs to be updated with information from this row in PS_PERS_DATA_EFFDT. The flag is *yes* if the update needs to be performed, or *no* if the update does not need to be performed.

Every day, usually just after midnight, the batch process PERSDATA executes in the Application Engine. (This process can be set to automatically run using the Process Scheduler, or can be run manually in Go ➤ Administer Workforce ➤ Administer Workforce U.S. ➤ Process ➤ Update Personal Data.) The PERSDATA routine takes all of the rows where UPDATE_PERS_DATA is 'Y' and updates the PS_PERSONAL_DATA table with the new information.

How an update occurs depends on the situation. For different effective dates and update flags, the process of updating personal data functions differently:

The effective date is less than the current date but *after* the most recent 'N' record. The PS_PERSONAL_DATA table is updated with this row and the UPDATE_PERS_DATA flag is set to 'N.'

The effective date is less than the current date and *before* the most recent 'N' record. By default, users cannot enter an effective date previous to the most recent effective date. If the user is in Correction mode, changes do not affect the UPDATE_PERS_DATA field. This field is always marked 'N.' If a change is made, however, to the most recent row, these changes are made to PS_PERSONAL_DATA. For example, if we forgot to indicate Bozo's marital status change and used

Correction mode to fix it on the 12/21/1998 row, the change would be reflected the next day on the PS_PERSONAL_DATA table. If we made the change on the 7/15/1998 row, the change would not appear since a more current value exists. In both cases the UPDATE_PERS_DATA field will never change.

The effective date is equal to the current date. The PS_PERSON-AL_DATA table is updated with this row and the UPDATE_PERS_DATA flag is set to 'N.'

The effective date is greater than the current date. The PS_PER-SONAL_DATA table is not updated until the effective date is less than or equal to the current date. The UPDATE_PERS_DATA flag remains 'Y' until the appropriate day arrives.

There are two rows. Only one update is allowed on a single day. If the batch program is not executed daily and two rows are placed on PS_PERS_EFFDT with an UPDATE_PERS_DATA flag of 'Y,' only the most recent row is used to update PS_PERSONAL_DATA. The flag for this row is set to 'N,' but the previous row remains 'Y' forever.

Let's look at the PS_PERS_DATA_EFFDT table (Table 6-7). Remember, this is the table where only effective-dated personal data is stored.

▶ **Table 6-7**   Personal data effective dated: PS_PERS_DATA_EFFDT

Structure	Many rows per person
Keys	Employee ID
	Effective date
Alternate keys	Full name or last name only
Sub-records included	Home address
	Mailing address, used for sending out letters (COBRA, benefit summary, etc.)
	Home phone
	Name (global)
	Name (Japan only)
Panels to look at	Go ➤ Administer Workforce ➤ Administer Workforce U.S. ➤ Use ➤ Personal Data (see Go ➤ Administer Workforce ➤ Administer Workforce U.S. ➤ Process ➤ Update Personal Data for the update process)

There are two groups of fields on PS_PERS_DATA_EFFDT. Some fields store the history of fields on the PS_PERSONAL_DATA table (see Table 6-8). Other fields are unique to the PS_PERS_DATA_EFFDT table (see Table 6-9) and are explained here.

▶ **Table 6-8** PS_PERSONAL_DATA fields found on PS_PERS_DATA_EFFDT

Field	Description
EMPLID	Employee ID
ADDRESS_SBR	Home address
ADDRESS_OTH_SBR	Mailing address
MAR_STATUS	Marital Status
SMOKER	Smoker
REG_REGION	Regulatory Region
NAME	Name
NAME_INITIALS	Name Initials
NAME_PREFIX	Name Prefix
NAME_SUFFIX	Name Suffix
NAME_ROYAL_PREFIX	Name Royal Suffix
NAME_ROYAL_SUFFIX	Name Royal Prefix
NAME_TITLE	Name Title
LAST_NAME_SRCH	Last Name Search
FIRST_NAME_SRCH	First Name Search
LAST_NAME	Last Name
FIRST_NAME	First Name
MIDDLE_NAME	Middle Name
PREFERRED_NAME	Preferred name
NAME_AC	Alternate Character Name

Fields in Table 6-8 trigger a new effective-dated row in the PS_PERS_DATA_EFFDT table. For example, the smoker field indicates if the employee is a smoker, which is used to determine benefit rates. It is a yes/no value. When this value changes, a new effective-dated row is required in the PS_PERS_DATA_EFFDT table. The effective date in PS_PERS_DATA_EFFDT is the date the employee started/stopped smoking.

▶ **Table 6-9** Fields unique to PS_PERS_DATA_EFFDT

Field	Description
EFFDT	Effective date
UPDATE_PERS_DATA	Update Personal Data
REG_REGION	Regulatory Region
NAME_INITIALS	Name Initials
NAME_TITLE	Name Title
LAST_NAME	Last Name
FIRST_NAME	First Name
MIDDLE_NAME	Middle Name
PREFERRED_NAME	Preferred name

Name Differences

As you can see in Table 6-6, there are several unique fields for storing pieces of the NAME field. These fields are useful for queries, although they are not always automatically filled in.

The regulatory region on PS_PERS_DATA_EFFDT drives the rules for the employee name. Depending on the region the employee is in, the name must be formatted in a certain manner. Since the name is initially stored on PS_PERS_DATA_EFFDT, the regulatory region is stored along with it.

The name is split into first, last, and middle name fields. These fields are used by certain delivered programs, and are populated automatically by PeopleSoft when the name is entered. PeopleSoft uses the comma in the NAME field to split the name, and looks for a single space to split the first name from the middle name. Unlike the name search fields on PS_PERSONAL_DATA, these name fields are left in their original format without capitalization, and with special characters left intact.

Several other unique fields are stored on PS_PERS_DATA_EFFDT for pieces of the name, but are not populated automatically. For example, a user can enter initials in the NAME_INITIALS field, which appears on the personal data panels. The initials are not derived from the name, but are entered by the end-user. The end-user may enter the initials with or without periods, or may not enter initials at all. The initials field is not used by any delivered programs.

> The NAME_TITLE field only appears on panels for Belgium, Germany, and the Netherlands.
>
> The PREFERRED_NAME field is in the NAMEGBL_SBR sub-record but is not used by PS_PERS_DATA_EFFDT.

USING SOCIAL SECURITY NUMBERS IN PEOPLESOFT

Before version 7.5, finding the Social Security number was a breeze—it was right at the top of the PS_PERSONAL_DATA table.

With version 7.5, PeopleSoft added the capability of storing different national identification numbers and provided edits and validations for each type. So, if you are from Canada, PeopleSoft expects a Social Insurance Number and can detect if the number is invalid.

The name of the field became NATIONAL_ID, and it is 15 characters long to accommodate all countries. Easy enough, but trying to find it can be difficult. PeopleSoft created almost 15 different tables and views to keep track of the national ID.

The NID Table and Identifiers

Let's look at the table where the SSN is stored (Table 6-10). This table is simple, tracking the country and type of each national ID it stores. For Social Security numbers, the country will be USA—depending on the national ID, different edits will be used for each country.

▶ **Table 6-10** National ID: PS_PERS_NID

Structure	One row per person
Keys	Employee ID
	Country
	National ID Type
Alternate keys	None
Sub-records included	National ID Sub-record

The national ID type (NATIONAL_ID_TYPE) field is a required field that specifies what the national ID is used for. Currently PeopleSoft is delivered with two values, 'None' and 'Payroll.' The payroll process looks for national IDs with a type of 'Payroll,' so that is a good one to use. Other types of ID numbers can be stored if desired. Values are verified against both the PS_NID_TYPE_TBL and the XLATTABLE.

National IDs

National ID (NATIONAL_ID) is the field where the actual number is stored. For the U.S., this is the field where the Social Security number is stored. This field is not required, and can be (and often is) left blank. Since the SSN is required for certain government reports and files, these reports and files often audit the field to make sure that it is populated, generating error messages when it is blank. PeopleSoft does not make this field required because users are likely to enter 'dummy' numbers, which are even more difficult to weed out of the system when running government reports and files. It is better to leave the field blank and populate it later. Also, with the ability to store national IDs for different countries, and many for a single person, it is difficult to require a particular ID.

What Is an Accurate National ID?

In PeopleSoft, the SSN field is not required. A warning is issued to a user if the SSN is left blank, but the record can still be saved. There is also a warning issued for duplicate SSNs in the system, but again the record can be saved. The SSN field can quickly become an abused field, and when it comes time to generate paychecks or tax forms such as W-2s, an inaccurate SSN is not your friend. It is advisable to run a short program periodically to check for blank or duplicate SSNs.

If you want to ensure the SSN is valid, there is an elaborate edit for accurate SSNs. PeopleSoft already validates the SSN before creating the annual W-2 statement. According to this edit, a Social Security number is invalid if any one of the following is true:

1. Blank
2. Equals all zeros ('000000000')
3. Equals all ones ('111111111')
4. Equals all threes ('333333333')
5. Equals numbers 1–9 ('123456789')
6. The first three numbers are '000'
7. The first three numbers are '666'
8. The first three numbers are between 729 and 749 (inclusive)
9. The first three numbers are between 764 and 999 (inclusive)

This sequence could be placed in PeopleCode, but is it advisable to add it to a batch process, such as an SQR, to detect. Forcing a user to type in an accurate national ID is against PeopleSoft's policy of not creating fake SSN numbers. And not having an SSN for a new employee is a common situation. It is better to leave it blank and perform an audit on a period basis. This way missing or invalid SSN numbers do not cause headaches at the end of the year when W-2s are processed.

Querying the National ID

Obtaining a national ID accurately (see Table 6-11) requires a few extra steps because of the additional key, NATIONAL_ID_TYPE. This value must be hard coded into the query. Since the NATIONAL_ID_TYPE field tells PeopleSoft which *kind* of national ID you are looking for, there is no default value stored in PeopleSoft.

In SQR, PeopleSoft uses a common module, STDVAR.SQC, to set the NATIONAL_ID_TYPE to 'PR' (payroll) by default. Generally this is the value to place in a query against the PERS_NID table, since it is the only delivered value.

▶ **Table 6-11** Retrieving the national ID (SSN)

| The query | ```
SELECT  PD.EMPLID,
        PD.NAME,
        PN.NATIONAL_ID
FROM PS_PERSONAL_DATA PD,
     PS_PERS_NID PN
WHERE PD.EMPLID = 'BOZO'
  AND PN.EMPLID = PD.EMPLID
  AND PN.COUNTRY = 'USA'
  AND PN.NATIONAL_ID_TYPE = 'PR'
``` |
|---|---|
| Returns the data set | ```
EMPLID  NAME                NATIONAL_ID
------  ------------------  ------------
BOZO    Clown,Bozo          123456789
``` |

Don't Be Fooled By Imitations

The national ID appears in several different places—and sometimes it appears in its former guise as SSN. It is important to note that the only place it is accurately stored is the PS_PERS_NID table. Several other areas copy it and store it with additional information as a convenience for delivered programs.

Keep in mind that the NATIONAL_ID or SSN field on other tables is updated from the PS_PERS_NID table, sometimes by a batch process. This duplication stores the historical national ID based on the date of the record, and may not be up to date.

For example, the PS_PAY_CHECK table contains the SSN of the employee as of the paycheck end date (the last day of the pay period). Although the value is originally taken from the NATIONAL_ID field, it is stored in the SSN field on this table. If the employee's national ID changes, this historical record is not changed. The same holds true for the PS_W2_DATA table, which stores the employee's W2 tax form. The SSN field on PS_W2_DATA and PS_PAY_CHECK is updated once a batch process runs (the COBOL pay run program for PS_PAY_CHECK, and TAX910LD.SQR for PS_W2_DATA).

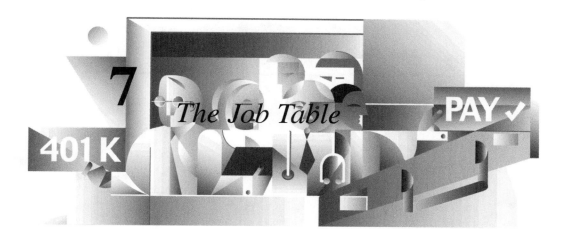

The Job Table

The PS_JOB table is the core record of the PeopleSoft HR database. This table drives every major process in PeopleSoft HRMS. In general, PS_JOB is the source of the following information:

- employee status
- compensation/Salary
- employee job/position
- employee department/location
- payroll settings
- benefits status

Job is an extremely dense and complex table. It is organized according to certain rules, and these rules are usually completely different from other legacy HR systems. PS_JOB drives many of the business process changes PeopleSoft requires of an organization.

This chapter will look at each of these categories and most of the fields that are found on the PS_JOB table. There are many important concepts surrounding the PS_JOB table, and several of them are described here. Chapters 8 through 13 discuss different issues that stem from the PS_JOB table.

Let's start with an overview of the PS_JOB table's structure, shown in Table 7-1.

▶ **Table 7-1**   Job: PS_JOB

Structure	Many rows per employee.
Keys	Employee ID
	Employee Record Number
	Effective Date
	Effective Sequence
Alternate keys	Department ID
	Job Code
	Position Number
Sub-records included	USA Job Information
	Germany Job Information
	France Job Information
Panels to look at	Go ➤ Administer Workforce ➤ Administer Workforce (U.S). ➤ Use ➤ Job Data

The employee ID field is the principal key, but it is valued from the PS_PERSONAL_DATA table. Unlike personal data, the PS_JOB table has many rows for a given employee ID. The use of the other keys on PS_JOB is critical.

IDENTIFYING JOBS ON PS_JOB

Employees may have more than one job in PeopleSoft, and this ability filters down through the table structure of PS_JOB and many other tables. In order to store several jobs per employee, the PS_JOB table has an identifier for the job, the employment record number. The employment record number field determines which job each PS_JOB table row pertains to. The field indicates the job number, from 0 to 999. Typically this field is 0 for employees with one job, and either 0 or 1 for employees with two jobs, etc.

Whether multiple jobs are allowed is determined in PeopleTools on the PSOPTIONS table. The MULTIJOBS field on this table drives the use of the employee record number. If multiple jobs is turned on, PeopleSoft will prompt for the employee record number when retrieving job data. If it is turned off, the employee record number will not be part of the prompt and will always be zero in the PS_JOB table.

It is critical to determine if your organization plans to use multiple job functionality. Often this functionality is not used, since it is rare to have a single employee in two different paid positions. It is required, though, with PeopleSoft

Pension Administration functionality. When an employee retires, a separate pension record is created on the PS_JOB table with a new employee record number.

Considering employee record number in a query requires some foresight. Should the query count a single employee as two if that employee has two jobs? If not, which job record is the appropriate one (job one or job two)? In most cases where multiple job functionality is in use, you will want to process each job record individually. For example, if you are looking for paychecks from this period, you will want to process both job records for an employee who works in two jobs. A separate check can be cut for each job, and the employee record number is contained on the paycheck record. Hard-coding the query to look for employee record number = 0 would omit some of the checks.

But if multiple job functionality is not enabled, you will want to specify employee record number = 0. Technically, all of the employee record numbers will equal zero, but just in case an additional job sneaks in, it is a good idea to specify this line in your criteria. Also, employee record number is a key, and specifying a direct value will speed up the query.

STORING HISTORY: EFFECTIVE SEQUENCE

Just as on other tables, the effective date allows the storage of historical and future information about the employee. The current row is effective starting on the effective date. This date could be in the past or future. Unlike the effective date on PS_PERS_DATA_EFFDT, the effective date on the job table relates to *every field*. Each time the value of a single field on the PS_JOB table changes, a new effective-dated row must be created.

If more than one job change occurs on a single day, the effective *sequence* indicates the order of the changes. The first job change on a given effective date will have an EFFSEQ of zero, and the second will have an EFFSEQ of one, etc. Essentially, effective sequence is the effective 'time.' For example, if Howard is hired today, and then receives a pay change on the same day, his hire record has an effective sequence of zero and his pay change has a one.

Historical rows are stored on the job table according to the combination of effective date and effective sequence. When rows are retrieved from the PS_JOB table, it is necessary to include the effective sequence with the effective date in the criteria. First, let's look at all of the PS_JOB table rows for an employee in Table 7-2.

▶ **Table 7-2** Looking at the effective date and effective sequence on PS_JOB

| The query | ```
SELECT  JO.EMPLID,
        JO.EMPL_RCD#,
        JO.EFFDT,
        JO.EFFSEQ,
        JO.ACTION
FROM PS_JOB JO
WHERE JO.EMPLID = 'BOZO'
ORDER BY JO.EFFDT, JO.EFFSEQ
``` |

Returns the data set	EMPLID	EMPL_RCD#	EFFDT	EFFSEQ	ACTION
	------	---------	-----------	------	------
	BOZO	0	15-JAN-1988	0	HIR
	BOZO	0	15-JAN-1988	1	PAY
	BOZO	0	15-MAR-1990	0	DTA
	BOZO	0	01-MAR-1991	0	PAY
	BOZO	0	01-APR-1992	0	LOA
	BOZO	1	07-MAR-1993	0	HIR
	BOZO	0	01-AUG-1994	0	RFL
	BOZO	0	01-MAR-1995	0	PAY
	BOZO	0	01-MAR-1996	0	DTA
	BOZO	0	01-MAR-1997	0	DTA
	BOZO	0	22-DEC-1998	0	PAY
	BOZO	0	22-DEC-1998	1	PAY

> *Be careful* not to mistakenly assume that the employee record number is like an effective date or effective sequence. Just because one job has employee record number = 1 and another has a record number = 0, it doesn't mean that one of them is the "correct" record and one is the "old" record. These numbers are not meant to be sequential; they simply distinguish two equal rows.

Now we will choose just the most recent row using both effective date and effective sequence in Table 7-3. This will bring back the most recent row for each unique job. The result: the most recent change to this employee's first job occurred on 12/22/1998. The most recent change to the second job occurred on 3/7/1993. Note that the most recent record for the first job has an effective sequence of '1' since it is more recent than an effective sequence of '0.'
```

▶ **Table 7-3**   Most recent row from the job table

| The query | ```
SELECT  JO.EMPLID,
        JO.EMPL_RCD#,
        JO.EFFDT,
        JO.EFFSEQ,
        JO.ACTION
FROM PS_JOB JO
WHERE JO.EFFDT =
            (SELECT MAX(JO1.EFFDT)
               FROM PS_JOB JO1
              WHERE JO1.EMPLID = JO.EMPLID
                AND JO1.EMPL_RCD# = JO.EMPL_RCD#
                AND JO1.EFFDT <= '1999-01-01')
        AND JO.EFFSEQ =
            (SELECT MAX(JO2.EFFSEQ)
               FROM PS_JOB JO2
              WHERE JO2.EMPLID = JO.EMPLID
                AND JO2.EMPL_RCD# = JO.EMPL_RCD#
                AND JO2.EFFDT = JO.EFFDT)
        AND JO.EMPLID = 'BOZO'
``` |

Returns the data set	EMPLID	EMPL_RCD#	EFFDT	EFFSEQ	ACTION
	------	---------	----------	------	------
	BOZO	0	22-DEC-1998	1	PAY
	BOZO	1	07-MAR-1993	0	HIR

Take a close look at the query in Table 7-3 that returns the maximum PS_JOB table row. It is used often. There a few things to take note of:

- Two sub-queries are necessary, and they must have different aliases (JO1 and JO2 in this case).
- All of the keys must be in each sub-query.
- While the effective date has a maximum ('1999-01-01') in order to return the most recent row, the effective sequence could be any number and has no maximum.

When Did It Happen? Tracking Actions

Many human resources databases store date and time stamps for every change that is made to the system. This makes it relatively simple to track down exact-
```

ly what happened and when. It allows programmers to select only rows that have changed and ignore the rest.

PeopleSoft is not built this way. Although many have tried, it is virtually impossible to make PeopleSoft record the date and time of every change. The effective-dated nature of PeopleSoft tables allows both retroactive and future-dated entries, which makes time stamps confusing, and in the end causes more headaches.

But, in a relentless effort to emulate existing systems, users often try to use a field that seems to provide a date stamp that indicates when someone changed the database. This field is the action date (ACTION_DT) field on the PS_JOB table.

The action date corresponds directly to any action and action reason changes on the PS_JOB table. Actions and action reasons identify changes in status, pay, or job (see the section below). While an employee's leave of absence may begin on 12/1/2001, the action date could be 4/15/1997 or 6/30/2003. The action date is the date the action *is entered, not effective.* The action date is extremely useful for detecting retroactive or future-dated transactions. By comparing the action date and the effective date, you can discover what actually happened.

Almost. All changes to the PS_JOB table are recorded with the action date, except for changes made in correction mode. Correction mode allows the user to go back in time, make a correction, and make it look like nothing was ever wrong. The action date is *not* updated to show the correction date. PeopleSoft discourages the use of correction mode, and most implementations resist using it. But it could occur, and if you are relying on action date to tell you about every single change to the PS_JOB table, correction mode will destroy the functionality of action date.

Also keep in mind that only the job table has an action date. Action dates are not stored on other tables. If you are building an interface or report according to a time stamp methodology but need data from other tables, the data selection becomes increasingly difficult and even impossible.

> An additional option for finding date and time stamps is to use PeopleSoft's audit tool, which stores a date and time stamp for all changes, even in correction mode. The required computing power, storage space, and maintenance of auditing often make this a poor solution. But if you are already using auditing then you may be able to create a type of timestamp functionality.

ACTIONS AND ACTION REASONS

There are two fields that identify exactly what happened on each job table effective date—the action and action reason. Something happens to an employee, and it is an action. The action reason explains why it happened.

The action field stores a code corresponding to an action that took place as of the effective date. When an employee is hired, this field is 'HIR'; when he is terminated, the value is 'TER.' Actions for status, compensation, and position changes are recorded in this field. Values for reasons are stored on PS_ACTN_REASON_TBL, and values for actions are verified against the translate table (see Table 7-4).

The action reason code field stores greater detail for the ACTION field. For example, a leave of absence could be for either maternity or military purposes. The ACTION_REASON field distinguishes different statuses. As a result, only the combination of the ACTION and ACTION_REASON fields provides an accurate, detailed status for an employee. Values are verified against the PS_ACTN_REASON_TBL.

Note that many types of actions appear in this field. This means that status changes, pay raises, changes in department, transfers, and promotions are all stored in one place. Picking the most recent row could return any type of action. It is necessary to consider whether you are looking for status, compensation, position, pay, or data changes.

▶ **Table 7-4** Delivered action values

Action	Description	Type
ADL	Additional Job	Status
ASC	Assignment Completion	Status
ASG	Assignment	Status
DEM	Demotion	Position
DTA	Data Change	Misc.
FSC	Family Status Change	Misc.
HIR	Hire	Status
INT	Completion of Introductory Per	Misc.
JED	Earnings Distribution Change	Compensation
JRC	Job Reclassification	Position
LOA	Leave of Absence	Status
LOF	Layoff	Status
LTD	Long Term Disability With Pay	Status
LTO	Long Term Disability	Status
PAY	Pay Rate Change	Compensation
PLA	Paid Leave of Absence	Status

▶ **Table 7-4** continued

Action	Description	Type
POS	Position Change	Position
PRB	Probation	Misc.
PRC	Completion of Probation	Misc.
PRO	Promotion	Position
REC	Recall from Suspension/Layoff	Status
REH	Rehire	Status
RET	Retirement	Status
RFD	Return From Disability	Status
RFL	Return from Leave	Status
RWP	Retirement With Pay	Status
STD	Short Term Disability With Pay	Status
STO	Short Term Disability	Status
SUS	Suspension	Status
TER	Termination	Status
TWB	Terminated With Benefits	Status
TWP	Termination With Pay	Status
XFR	Transfer	Position

As an example, let's retrieve the most recent hire or rehire row (i.e., the most recent hiring of the employee). Just like all sub-queries, additional criteria must be considered carefully (see Chapter 2 on effective dating). In the query from the previous section (Table 7-3), the criteria for the employee ID are outside of the sub-queries. In that situation, the sub-queries return the maximum row and then restrict the returned data set to the employee ID. This retrieves the most recent row for an employee ID.

If we want the most recent 'hire' or 'rehire' row (ACTION = 'HIR' or 'REH'), this criteria must be placed *inside* both of the sub-queries, as seen in Table 7-5.

▶ **Table 7-5** Most recent hire or rehire row from the job table

| The query | ```
SELECT  JO.EMPLID,
        JO.EMPL_RCD#,
        JO.EFFDT,
        JO.EFFSEQ,
        JO.ACTION
FROM PS_JOB JO
WHERE JO.EFFDT =
            (SELECT MAX(JO1.EFFDT)
               FROM PS_JOB JO1
              WHERE JO1.EMPLID = JO.EMPLID
                AND JO1.EMPL_RCD# = JO.EMPL_RCD#
                AND JO1.ACTION IN ('HIR','REH')
                AND JO1.EFFDT <= '1999-01-01')
          AND JO.EFFSEQ =
            (SELECT MAX(JO2.EFFSEQ)
               FROM PS_JOB JO2
              WHERE JO2.EMPLID = JO.EMPLID
                AND JO2.EMPL_RCD# = JO.EMPL_RCD#
                AND JO2.ACTION IN ('HIR','REH')
                AND JO2.EFFDT = JO.EFFDT)
          AND JO.EMPLID = 'BOZO'
``` |

Returns the data set	EMPLID	EMPL_RCD#	EFFDT	EFFSEQ	ACTION
	------	---------	-----------	------	------
	BOZO	0	15-JAN-1988	0	HIR
	BOZO	1	07-MAR-1993	0	HIR

What would happen if you took the criteria out of the effective sequence sub-query but left it in the effective date sub-query? The results are shown in Table 7-6.

▶ **Table 7-6** No criteria used for effective sequence

Returns the data set	EMPLID	EMPL_RCD#	EFFDT	EFFSEQ	ACTION
	------	---------	-----------	------	------
	BOZO	0	15-JAN-1988	1	PAY
	BOZO	1	07-MAR-1993	0	HIR
```

With the criteria only in one sub-query, the database engine retrieves the date for the 'HIR' record, but then retrieves the maximum effective sequence number—ignoring the ACTION for the row. Hence you get a 'PAY' action back instead of a 'HIR' action.

The different action and action reason combinations are covered in greater detail in the following three chapters:

Chapter 8:   Status-Related Actions (hire, term, leave of absence)

Chapter 9:   Compensation-Related Actions (pay change)

Chapter 10: Position-Related Actions (promotion, demotion)

Although most of the actions fall into these three categories, there are several strays. These actions should be carefully considered. For some organizations, a change in department via the 'DTA' action is considered a status or position change. In PeopleSoft, these fields have delivered meanings and functionality, but the use of these actions is up to the organization.

Most implementations also use a conversion action to form the foundation for converted employees. This action could be a custom 'CON' or 'CNV' or could be a reason for an existing action. Conversion records are often forgotten during an implementation, but once users start querying the database there is often confusion. Converted employees could look completely different from employees hired in PeopleSoft. They may not have a hire record, or even a status-related action. In these cases it is important to establish a standard initial row action or action reason, and include this code in queries against PS_JOB.

OVERLAPPING CHANGES

One of the drawbacks of the action and action reason is that many changes can occur on a single row. A PeopleSoft user is not prevented from selecting the action of 'LOA' (leave of absence) and indicating a pay change on the same row. *The action and action reason do not reveal every change. Status changes are always displayed, but other changes may be hidden.*

For example, on 8/1/1994, a user entered a row for Jennifer since she returned from a leave of absence. At the same time, Jennifer returned to a new job with a 10% pay increase. All of this information is entered in the panels at once. The resulting row (see Table 7-7) contains only the status change.

▶ **Table 7-7**   Overlapping change hidden

The query	```SELECT JO.EMPLID,```
	``` JO.EFFDT,```
	``` JO.EFFSEQ,```
	``` JO.ACTION```
	``` FROM PS_JOB JO```
	``` WHERE JO.EMPL_RCD# = 0```
	``` AND JO.EFFDT <= '1994-09-01'```
	``` AND JO.EFFDT >= '1992-01-01'```
	``` AND JO.EMPLID = 'BOZO'```

Returns the data set	EMPLID	EFFDT	EFFSEQ	ACTION
	------	-----------	------	------
	BOZO	01-APR-1992	0	LOA
	BOZO	01-AUG-1994	0	RFL

There is no record with an action of 'PAY' for the raise or an action of 'POS' for the position change. To discover that these items occur, it is necessary to look beyond the action and action reason fields to the actual fields that may have changed, as in Table 7-8.

▶ **Table 7-8**   Overlapping change revealed

The query	```SELECT JO.EMPLID,```
	``` JO.EFFDT,```
	``` JO.EFFSEQ,```
	``` JO.ACTION,```
	``` JO.CHANGE_AMT,```
	``` JO.JOBCODE```
	``` FROM PS_JOB JO```
	``` WHERE JO.EMPL_RCD# = 0```
	``` AND JO.EFFDT <= '1994-09-01'```
	``` AND JO.EFFDT >= '1992-01-01'```
	``` AND JO.EMPLID = 'BOZO'```

Returns the data set	EMPLID	EFFDT	EFFSEQ	ACTION	CHANGE_AMT	JOBCODE
	------	-----------	------	------	----------	-------
	BOZO	01-APR-1992	0	LOA	0	G060
	BOZO	01-AUG-1994	0	RFL	590.303651	G031

The fields you need to look at for each type of action are discussed in further detail in Chapters 8 through 10.

JOB TABLE FLAGS

A group of fields on the job table are simple one-character flags that identify several important characteristics of an employee.

The employee status (EMPL_STATUS) is the most prominent flag, and is required for all employees. It is used to quickly determine an employee's status. It does not contain the detail of the action and action reason, but provides overview values like active (A), terminated (T), and on leave (L). Employee status is discussed in Chapter 8.

The regular/temporary field (REG_TEMP) indicates if the employee is regular or temporary. This field is used by several processes, including benefits eligibility determination. Values are verified against the translate table, and are delivered as 'R' for regular and 'T' for temporary.

The full/part time field (FULL_PART_TIME) indicates if the employee is full time or part time. This field, like REG_TEMP, drives benefits eligibility and other processing. Values are verified against the translate table, and are delivered as 'F' for full time and 'P' for part time.

LINKING EMPLOYEES TO COMMON DATA

Most of the fields on the PS_JOB table are links to other areas of PeopleSoft (see Table 7-9). The appropriate codes for each employee will be tied to other tables with additional information. Each employee is assigned to a department, a location, and a job or position.

▶ **Table 7-9**   Links to major PeopleSoft areas

Item	Description	Table	For more info see
Department ID	Groups employees and are used for reporting	PS_DEPT_TBL	Chapter 11
Location	Specifies the building the employee works in/appears on the paycheck stub	PS_LOCATION_TBL	
Tax Location	A code that identifies locations (a building, group of buildings, or areas) where employees can be taxed	PS_TAX_LOCATION1	Chapter 18
Jobcode	Identifies a type of job that many individuals could have	PS_JOBCODE_TBL	Chapter 10
Position Number	Identifies a unique position that can be filled by one individual; most job information defaults from position data.	PS_POSITION_DATA	Chapter 10

Entry Dates

The department, jobcode, and position number are each provided along with an entry date. These dates record the date the employee entered a specific department, job, or position. It represents the effective date of the most recent change to the corresponding code.

For example, if an employee changes departments, the PS_JOB table will show a different department ID from row to row:

```
EMPLID    EFFDT       ACTION   DEPTID   DEPT_ENTRY_DT
------    ---------   ------   ------   -------------
BOZO      1/1/2001    HIR      USA023   1/1/2001
BOZO      1/15/2001   PAY      USA023   1/1/2001
BOZO      10/3/2002   DTA      USA016   10/3/2002
BOZO      1/1/2002    DTA      USA016   10/3/2002
```

The entry date changes, too. It always represents the first date of entry into the department ID shown on the same row.

This same concept can be applied to the job entry date (jobcode), position entry date (position number), salary grade entry date (grade), and step entry date (step).

HUMAN RESOURCES SETTINGS

The job table identifies settings for each module in PeopleSoft. In the HR world, the job table identifies a few key field values that specify the validation rules that apply to the employee. These fields and how they relate to validations is described in Chapter 5. Table 7-10 lists each field and its definition.

▶ **Table 7-10** HR settings found on the job table

Field	Description
Business Unit	Specifies which business unit the employee belongs to.
Department SetID	The department setID field stores the setID for the employee's department.
Jobcode SetID	The jobcode setID field stores the setID for the employee's jobcode.
Regulatory Region	The regulatory region determines the regulations that are applied to the processing of this employee. Values are stored on the PS_REG_REGION_TBL.

PAYROLL SETTINGS

In order to process a check for a person, he or she must be set up with a row on the PS_JOB table. Several fields on the PS_JOB table tell the PeopleSoft payroll process how to calculate and group a person's check.

Company and Paygroup

Two of the fields, company and paygroup, are keys to all payroll-related tables. On the job table, each employee is connected to a company code. The company field indicates the company (legal entity) the employee works for. An organization can have many companies; each employee must work for at least one company. Pay, benefits, and taxes are driven by this field.

The paygroup field determines how/when the employee gets paid. Checks are run according to paygroups. In most cases the paygroup identifies employees who are paid at different intervals or with different rules. For example, a biweekly paygroup or a monthly paygroup may exist (see Chapter 14 for more about paygroups).

Tracking Hourly Employees and FTE

The employee type field indicates if an employee is salaried, hourly, exception hourly, or not applicable. This value defaults based on the paygroup. An hourly employee is paid for hours submitted to the system. Salaried and exception hourly employees are paid according to a predetermined number of hours. If an exception hourly employee takes 2 hours off, those hours are entered as exceptions. While a salaried employee receives a set amount each pay cycle, an exception hourly employee is paid according to hours worked. The value in the employee type field also drives the payroll process since eligibility for earnings is based on employee type.

Every employee, whether salaried or hourly, has a standard hours value (STD_HOURS). The standard hours field stores the standard number of hours the employee works in a week. The number of hours defaults from the job code or the position number. If no value is specified, the defaults specified for the operator ID (the user who is modifying the job table row) or the company will be used. The hours must be between the minimum and maximum on the PS_INSTALLATION table.

The standard hours field drives the calculation of FTE (fulltime equivalent). In PeopleSoft, an FTE = standard hours on PS_JOB divided by the standard hours on the default control table used (job code, salary administration plan, operator preferences, or installation table).

Other Payroll Identifiers

Several fields further identify certain characteristics of employees for payroll processing.

The employee classification field (EMPL_CLASS) provides an additional method for grouping employees. It is also used for certain reports and variable compensation. The employee class field typically indicates if an employee is a consultant, expatriate, agency temp, intern, or trainee. Organizations often add an employee classification to maintain an existing identifier for an employee. By default, employee class is blank for other employees.

An officer code identifies employees for Nondiscrimination Testing (401k and 401m reports). This code indicates which type of officer an employee is. Variable compensation eligibility can also be driven by officer code.

> The PIN number (short for Pay Information Number) is not used by delivered PeopleSoft processes. It is for information only.
>
> The pay basis number field is used for European payroll only.

Compensation

The job table stores many compensation-related fields. These fields identify the amount of compensation an employee should receive, whether it is based on a common salary plan or individually.

Salary Plans

The salary administration plan (SAL_ADMIN_PLAN) defines how the employee's salary is calculated and increased. The salary plan defaults from PS_LOCATION_TBL or is entered for each individual. Values are stored on PS_SAL_PLAN_TBL.

The salary grade field (GRADE) determines the employee's minimum, maximum, and midpoint values for each salary range. Usually several salary grades are specified within a salary plan, but the employee can be linked to only one grade within the plan. Values are stored on PS_SAL_GRADE_TBL.

Grades are broken down further into steps. The step field identifies the employee's step level. Values are stored on PS_SAL_STEP_TBL.

Increases to a salary can be based on a plan as well—these are called salary matrix codes. The salary matrix code determines how increases to an employee's salary are made. Salary matrix codes drive salary increase functionality. Values are stored on PS_SAL_MATRIX_TBL.

General Ledger Information

The general ledger pay type field (GL_PAY_TYPE) is an optional field which can specify a cost center to charge the employee to. Other general ledger fields exist in PeopleSoft at different levels; general ledger pay type is at the lowest level, the employee level.

The account code field is used to specify particular accounts to charge an employee to. It is similar to the general ledger pay type, but can be used for other 'accounts' that need to be linked to an employee. The use of account codes is optional and varies from one organization to the other. Values are stored on the PS_ACCT_CD_TBL.

When using account codes, you can identify how pay should be split among different accounts. The earnings distribution type field is used if dollars are charged to different accounts for an employee. Earnings can be distributed among accounts by hours, by percent, or by amount (only for salaried employees). PeopleSoft does not do this distribution; a custom program would need to read the distribution type and manually distribute the dollars among different accounts.

Compensation

The critical data for payroll to calculate compensation amounts for each paycheck is found on the job table for each employee. These fields can be used together to find changes in the compensation rate and look up an employee's salary based on an annual, hourly, and monthly rate.

Two fields, compensation rate and compensation frequency, determine the employee's salary. The compensation frequency is used in conjunction with the COMPRATE field. The compensation rate is the compensation rate of the employee according to the compensation frequency. The frequency of compensation values are from the translate table (annual, biweekly, hourly, monthly, etc.). This field does not need to be (and often is not) the same as the frequency of the employee's pay check.

Whenever compensation is entered or changed, PeopleSoft calculates the annual, monthly, and hourly rates. This calculation happens in PeopleCode, so if compensation is loaded through behind-the-scenes programs, be sure to populate these three fields with the appropriate information. The split into annual, monthly, and hourly rates is detailed further in Chapter 9.

BENEFITS SETTINGS

The job table is an integral part of PeopleSoft benefits and benefits administration processing. We discuss benefits and how the job table can trigger different benefits actions in section 4, which is all about benefits. Several fields that are stored on the job table are required for benefits processing.

The principal requirement for employees in benefits administration processing is a BAS group ID (BAS_GROUP_ID). Employees are placed in different BAS group IDs in order to process them separately through benefits administration.

Benefits Status

The benefits employee status (BEN_STATUS) is a separate status that drives benefits eligibility determination. This status is determined from the ACTION and ACTION_REASON fields. Values are verified against the translate table, but are derived from the PS_ACTN_REASON_TBL, which associates an action and action reason combination to a benefits status value.

The benefits administration action field (BAS_ACTION) is the corresponding benefits action to the action and action reason. Each ACTION and ACTION_REA-SON combination is associated in the PS_ACTN_REASON_TBL with a BAS_ACTION. So a 'LOA' action and 'LTD' reason may translate to a 'TER' benefits administration action. The benefits administration action triggers a corresponding event in benefits administration. Benefits administration is covered in Chapter 24.

The COBRA action field works just like the benefits administration action. A COBRA action is specified on the PS_ACTN_REASON_TBL for each action and action reason combination. The COBRA action drives COBRA events.

Benefits Base Rate

The annual benefits base rate field (ANNL_BENEF_BASE_RT) contains a base rate used for calculating benefits. Typically this field is only used for certain employees, who have a benefit that must be based on a specific group of earnings. For example, an employee could be covered by life insurance for two times his or her annual salary. If the salary should be different from the annual rate (ANNUAL_RT) specified on PS_JOB, a new value should be entered as the annual benefits base rate. PeopleSoft benefits always uses the benefits base rate when it is populated.

Custom Fields

The eligibility configuration fields (1–9) are user-defined and drive benefits administration processing. These fields are configured to provide additional criteria to benefits administration. Each field either contains a different user-defined value, or it isn't used, depending on how benefits administration is set up.

FLSA Status

The FLSA status indicates whether the employee is exempt or nonexempt from the Fair Labor Standards Act (FLSA). This field drives benefits eligibility. The value of this field defaults from the job code for the employee. Values are verified against the translate table (Admin., Management, Non-Exempt, etc.).

Employee status is one of the common pieces of data that are extracted from PeopleSoft. Is the employee active, terminated, on leave, or retired? This question comes up often, so it is useful to look at the different ways employee status can be obtained and the pitfalls with PeopleSoft's storage method.

There are two basic levels of status in PeopleSoft. The first, embodied by the employee status flag (EMPL_STATUS), gives a high-level overview of the employee's current status. A single character represents the status.

The second is a much more detailed look at the employee's history. Using fields called actions and action reasons, PeopleSoft tracks the what and the why of each change in status. A status of on leave could have a reason of maternity, FMLA, education, health, military, or short-term disability. PeopleSoft is unique in that it considers the reason for a status separately from the status itself.

This chapter will look at the employee status, action and action reason fields, and when each should be used. It also provides the detail logic for retrieving an employee's current status-related action and action reason, which can be a tricky process.

THE EMPLOYEE STATUS FIELD

The default method of getting an employee's status is to look at the employee status field (EMPL_STATUS). This field, as delivered, provides 11 delivered options for indicating an employee's status (see Table 8-1).

▶ **Table 8-1** Employee status indicator: EMPL_STATUS

Status	Translate Value
A	Active
D	Deceased
L	Leave of Absence
P	Leave With Pay
Q	Retired With Pay
R	Retired
S	Suspended
T	Terminated
U	Terminated With Pay
V	Terminated Pension Pay Out
X	Retired-Pension Administration

The employee status field resides on every row of the PS_JOB table. If you retrieve the most recent row from the PS_JOB table, the value of EMPL_STATUS will be the employee's current status. Or, you can use the PS_EMPLOYEES table (see Chapter 4) to quickly retrieve the EMPL_STATUS value.

The employee status field is an indicator, no more. It is *not* the place where a user records a status change. Status changes are recorded with actions and action reasons. Certain actions translate to a new employee status. PeopleSoft looks at the action and determines which employee status to assign according to a set of rules.

In the previous chapter we discussed different kinds of actions, and saw that not every action is status-related. PeopleSoft, though, looks only at the status-related actions when determining the appropriate value for the employee status field. Every time a status-related action occurs, PeopleSoft changes the employee status field. If a non-status-related action occurs, such as a pay change, PeopleSoft will not change the employee status field. The old value will be copied to the new PS_JOB table row. Table 8-2 shows how the different delivered status-related actions map to the employee status field.

▶ **Table 8-2** Status action map to employee status indicator

Action/Reason Criteria	Description	Employee Status	Value
ADL	Additional Job	Active	A
ASC	Assignment Completion	Terminated	T
ASG	Assignment	Active	A
HIR	Hire	Active	A
LOA	Leave of Absence	Leave of absence	L
LOF	Layoff	Suspended	S
LTD	Long Term Disability With Pay	Leave with pay	P
LTO	Long Term Disability	Leave of absence	L
PLA	Paid Leave of Absence	Leave with pay	P
REC	Recall from Suspension/Layoff	Active	A
REH	Rehire	Active	A
RET	Retirement	Retired	R
RET and PER_TYPE on PERSONAL_DATA ='P'	Retired- Pension Administration	Retired- Pension Administration	X
RFD	Return From Disability	Active	A
RFL	Return from Leave	Active	A
RWP	Retirement With Pay	Retired with pay	Q
STD	Short Term Disability With Pay	Leave with pay	P
STO	Short Term Disability	Leave of absence	L
SUS	Suspension	Suspended	S
TER	Termination	Terminated	T
TER and reason = DEA	Termination, Death	Deceased	D
TER and PER_TYPE on PERSONAL_DATA ='P'	Terminated Pension Pay Out	Terminated Pension Pay Out	V
TWB	Terminated With Benefits	Terminated with pay	U
TWP	Termination With Pay	Terminated with pay	U

The relationships shown in Table 8-2 are stored in PeopleCode. Each action reason is connected to an employee status. Certain action/action reason combinations will translate to a certain status. To look at how it works, you can find the code on the PS_FUNCLIB_HR table, 'FieldFormula' PeopleCode for the EMPL_STATUS field.

You are asking for trouble if you change these associations. PeopleSoft looks for a select set of employee status values when processing paychecks and benefits. If you map someone on long term disability (action LTD) to an employee status of 'T' instead of 'L,' delivered processes will be affected. Long-term disability employees would be excluded from certain queries and programs, and there could be significant functional issues caused by such a change.

THE STATUS DATE

Getting the employee status is easy, but getting the status date is another issue. Since an employee can have many different rows in the PS_JOB table, and not all of them have to contain a status-related action, the most recent row is not always the right date. Table 8-3 demonstrates this phenomenon.

▶ **Table 8-3** Searching for the status date

The query	SELECT JO.EMPLID,
	            JO.EFFDT,
	            JO.EFFSEQ,
	            JO.EMPL_STATUS
	       FROM PS_JOB JO
	       WHERE JO.EMPL_RCD# = 0
	         AND JO.EMPLID = 'BOZO'

Returns the data set	JO.EMPLID	JO.EFFDT	JO.EFFSEQ	JO.EMPL_STATUS
	---------	-----------	---------	--------------
	BOZO	15-JAN-1988	0	A
	BOZO	15-JAN-1988	1	A
	BOZO	15-MAR-1990	0	A
	BOZO	01-MAR-1991	0	A
	BOZO	01-APR-1992	0	L
	BOZO	**01-AUG-1994**	**0**	**A**
	BOZO	01-MAR-1995	0	A
	BOZO	01-MAR-1996	0	A
	BOZO	01-MAR-1997	0	A
	BOZO	22-DEC-1998	0	A
	BOZO	22-DEC-1998	1	A

The most recent employee status is active, but the status date is 8/01/1994. To retrieve just a single row for the employee, showing status and status date, the query in Table 8-4 is required.

▶ **Table 8-4**   Retrieving the status date

| The query | ```
SELECT MIN(JO.EFFDT),
        JO.EMPL_STATUS
FROM PS_JOB JO
WHERE JO.EMPL_RCD# = 0
  AND JO.EFFDT >
        (SELECT MAX(JO1.EFFDT)
          FROM PS_JOB JO1
         WHERE JO1.EMPLID = JO.EMPLID
           AND JO1.EMPL_RCD# = JO.EMPL_RCD#
           AND JO1.EMPL_STATUS <>
               (SELECT JO2.EMPL_STATUS
                 FROM PS_JOB JO2
                WHERE JO2.EMPL_RCD# = 0
                  AND JO2.EMPLID = JO1.EMPLID
                  AND JO2.EFFDT =
                      (SELECT MAX(JO3.EFFDT)
                        FROM PS_JOB JO3
                       WHERE JO3.EMPL_RCD# = JO2.EMPL_RCD#
                         AND JO3.EMPLID = JO2.EMPLID)
           AND JO2.EFFSEQ =
               (SELECT MAX(JO4.EFFSEQ)
                 FROM PS_JOB JO4
                WHERE JO4.EMPL_RCD# = JO2.EMPL_RCD#
                  AND JO4.EMPLID = JO2.EMPLID
                  AND JO4.EFFDT = JO2.EFFDT)))
  AND JO.EMPLID = 'G001'
GROUP BY JO.EMPL_STATUS
``` |
| Returns the data set | ```
MIN(JO.EFFDT)    JO.EMPL_STATUS
-------------    --------------
01-AUG-1994      A
``` |

Quite a query! And it doesn't even consider effective sequence, which would add about five more sub-queries! In other words, even this large query does not accurately return the status date.

What can be done to retrieve the status date simply? The first step is to stop looking at the employee status field for status information. This is where its efficacy drops off—significantly. Instead, lets look at the action and action reason fields, and try to detect when they change. The action and action reason fields eliminate the need for such a complex query, simply because status action/action reasons combinations are not repeatable. Once you change an employee's status and reason, you cannot change it to the same status and reason tomorrow. PeopleSoft has built-in rules for which status action/action reasons can come before or after another status action/action reason. For example, you *cannot* put someone on maternity leave that is already on maternity leave. You *can* put someone on medical leave that is on maternity leave because it is a different reason.

Let's look at the action/reason combinations for Bozo (Table 8-5), and then create a simpler query using action/action reason. From the results of this query, we can see the row we desire, '01-AUG-1994.' We can also see that every status-related action is distinct from the previous and the next. Non-status-related actions, though, can be repeated (you can receive two successive department corrections, one in March 1996 and another in March 1997).

▶ **Table 8-5** Action and action reason for status

The query	```SELECT JO.EMPLID,```
	`        JO.EFFDT,`
	`        JO.EFFSEQ,`
	`        JO.ACTION,`
	`        JO.ACTION_REASON`
	`FROM PS_JOB JO`
	`WHERE JO.EMPLID = 'BOZO'`
	`  AND JO.EMPL_RCD# = 0`
	`ORDER BY JO.EFFDT, JO.EFFSEQ`

Returns the data set	JO.EMPLID	JO.EFFDT	JO.EFFSEQ	JO.ACTION	JO.ACTION_REASON
	BOZO	15-JAN-1988	0	HIR	TMP
	BOZO	15-JAN-1988	1	PAY	MER
	BOZO	15-MAR-1990	0	DTA	STC
	BOZO	01-MAR-1991	0	PAY	MER
	BOZO	01-APR-1992	0	LOA	FML
	BOZO	01-AUG-1994	0	RFL	
	BOZO	01-MAR-1995	0	PAY	MER
	BOZO	01-MAR-1996	0	DTA	CDP
	BOZO	01-MAR-1997	0	DTA	CDP
	BOZO	22-DEC-1998	0	PAY	OTH
	BOZO	22-DEC-1998	1	PAY	MER

The fact that an action/action reason combination will never occur twice in succession greatly simplifies the query. There is a small price to pay. In return, we must deal with the presence of non-status-related actions in the PS_JOB table. These actions must be *excluded* from the query (we could also *include* only status-related actions, but there are many of them). Table 8-6 shows the result.

▶ **Table 8-6** Selecting only status related actions

| The query | ```
SELECT JO.EFFDT,
       JO.EMPL_STATUS,
       JO.EFFSEQ,
       JO.ACTION,
       JO.EMPL_STATUS
FROM PS_JOB JO
WHERE JO.EMPL_RCD# = 0
  AND JO.EFFDT =
       (SELECT MAX(JO1.EFFDT)
           FROM PS_JOB JO1
         WHERE JO1.EMPLID = JO.EMPLID
           AND JO1.EMPL_RCD# = JO.EMPL_RCD#
           AND JO1.EFFDT <= '01-JAN-1999'
           AND JO1.ACTION NOT IN ('DEM', 'DTA', 'FSC',
                                  'INT', 'JED', 'JRC',
                                  'PAY', 'POS', 'PRB',
                                  'PRC', 'PRO', 'XFR'))
  AND JO.EFFSEQ =
       (SELECT MAX(JO2.EFFSEQ)
           FROM PS_JOB JO2
         WHERE JO2.EMPLID = JO.EMPLID
           AND JO2.EMPL_RCD# = JO.EMPL_RCD#
           AND JO2.EFFDT = JO.EFFDT
           AND JO2.ACTION NOT IN ('DEM', 'DTA', 'FSC',
                                  'INT', 'JED', 'JRC',
                                  'PAY', 'POS', 'PRB',
                                  'PRC', 'PRO', 'XFR'))
       AND JO.EMPLID = 'BOZO'
``` |
|---|---|

	JO.EMPLID	JO.EFFDT	JO.EFFSEQ	JO.ACTION	JO.EMPL_STATUS
Returns the data set	---------	-----------	---------	---------	--------------
	BOZO	01-AUG-1994	0	RFL	A

Success! You can see the status related actions we needed to exclude. The process is cumbersome, but it is the only way to retrieve an accurate status entry date for an employee.

> Don't forget to consider any conversion records your organization might be using. Often when an employee has no recent history, a conversion record is created in PS_JOB so that the employee has a status-related row. This row is usually considered status-related and should be included in any queries.
```

Finding the Date of the First Action

Retrieving the status date for an action and action reason combination is fairly simple. But what if the employee goes on leave, then changes from one leave to the other? If you are looking for the date of the initial leave, the query in Table 8-6 won't work. In order to find out the initial date, a query must first pick the most recent row to get the current status, then get the most recent different status before it, and *then* get the next row, the first row of the current status. This is definitely a pain.

If you knew what status you were looking for, things would be much smoother. Often this is the case. Perhaps you want to retrieve the termination date for an employee, or the date the employee went on leave. Armed with the status you seek, it is much easier to retrieve a status date. Let's look at a new set of job records for BOZO in Table 8-7 and how to retrieve the first leave date in Table 8-8.

▶ **Table 8-7**   View of job table records for BOZO

| The query | ```
SELECT JO.EFFDT,
       JO.ACTION,
       JO.ACTION_REASON,
       JO.EMPL_STATUS
FROM PS_JOB JO
WHERE JO.EMPLID = 'BOZO'
  AND JO.EMPL_RCD# = 0
ORDER BY JO.EFFDT, JO.EFFSEQ
``` |

Returns the data set	JO.EFFDT	JO.ACTION	JO.ACTION_REASON	JO.EMPL_STATUS
	----------	---------	----------------	--------------
	11-OCT-1998	HIR	HAF	A
	25-OCT-1998	LOA	MAT	L
	15-NOV-1998	LOA	MED	L
```

▶ **Table 8-8** Retrieving the first occurrence of a status action

| The query | ```
SELECT JO.EFFDT,
       JO.ACTION,
       JO.ACTION_REASON,
       JO.EMPL_STATUS
FROM PS_JOB JO
WHERE JO.EMPLID = 'BOZO'
  AND JO.EMPL_RCD# = 0
  AND JO.EFFDT  =
            (SELECT MIN(JO1.EFFDT)
               FROM PS_JOB JO1
              WHERE JO1.EMPLID = JO.EMPLID
                AND JO1.EMPL_RCD# = JO.EMPL_RCD#
                AND JO1.EMPL_STATUS IN ('L','P')
                AND JO1.EFFDT >=
            (SELECT MAX(JO2.EFFDT)
               FROM PS_JOB JO2
              WHERE JO2.EMPLID  = 'BOZO'
                AND JO2.EMPL_RCD# = 0
                AND JO2.EMPL_STATUS NOT IN ('L','P')))
``` |

Returns the data set	JO.EFFDT	JO.ACTION	JO.ACTION_REASON	JO.EMPL_STATUS
	-----------	---------	----------------	--------------
	25-OCT-1998	LOA	MAT	L

The query in Table 8-8 selects the first 'on leave' row after the most recent row where the employee was not on leave. This retrieves the accurate entry date for the employee's leave status.

THE LONG-TERM DISABILITY ISSUE

There is one situation where you will find yourself using the techniques described in this chapter time and time again—selecting long-term disability employees. The issue provides a good vehicle for understanding the PS_JOB table and the action/action reason fields.

First, a functional look at the issue. Employees who are on long-term disability are out of the office for an extended period of time. These employees continue to be employed by the company. Although the employee can return, often he or she will not. From the employee's point of view, his or her employment continues but his or her pay comes from a long-term disability insurance plan. Yet for the company, the employee needs to be removed from budgets, head counts,
```

and reports. In many human resources systems the employee is marked terminated to facilitate this process.

PeopleSoft considers long-term disability employees as on leave, not terminated. This is because the employee is technically not terminated. PeopleSoft also considers the employee on leave in order to facilitate the processing should the employee return. Different actions must take place for an employee who is returning from leave versus a rehire.

What does this mean in technical terms? HR professionals need to think proactively about the long-term disability population, including or excluding them where appropriate. If these employees were terminated in a former system, then either a functional change needs to occur or these employees need to be identified and excluded from queries and programs.

Here is the standard (almost universal) criteria for selecting employees:

```
WHERE EMPL_STATUS IN ('A','P','L)
```

(where the employee current status is active, on paid leave, or on leave). Since only the most current employee status is on the PS_EMPLOYEES table, this is typically the table that is used for status queries. Note, however, that these criteria include long-term disability employees (under the 'L'). In order to exclude them, several obstacles must be overcome:

The PS_EMPLOYEES table cannot be used. The employee status field does not distinguish employees on long-term disability, so the action/action reason combination is the only indicator we can use. Yet the PS_EMPLOYEES table contains the most recent action/action reason, not the most recent *status-related* action/action reason. Since the action could be DTA, we never know if the employee is active, terminated, on leave, or on long-term disability.

Action/action reason must be limited to status-related combinations only. By excluding actions that are not status-related, we can get the status of the employee. If this action is 'LTD' or 'LTO,' the employee is on long-term disability.

Always remember the other criteria. If you need all employees in a specific department, remember that if you exclude non-status-related actions, you are no longer picking the most recent row from the PS_JOB table. Only the department ID on the most recent row is the accurate department ID. We look at this situation in the section below about using two job table rows.

The queries in the following sections are useful for gaining a better understanding of some of the job table issues. Although the job table is organized simply, to retrieve the necessary data can require patience.

Using Two Job Table Rows

The last factor for long-term disability employees, remembering other criteria, brings us to the climax of the chapter. We know how to retrieve status and status date, but what if we add additional criteria, say, a department ID?

For example, what if you are looking for a list of active or on-leave employees in department '10400,' excluding long-term disability employees? First let's look at the raw data in the PS_JOB table in Table 8-9.

▶ **Table 8-9**   Contents of the job table

The query	`SELECT JO.EMPLID,`
	`       JO.EFFDT,`
	`       JO.ACTION,`
	`       JO.ACTION_REASON,`
	`       JO.EMPL_STATUS,`
	`       JO.DEPTID`
	`FROM PS_JOB JO`
	`WHERE JO.EMPL_RCD# = 0`
	`ORDER BY JO.EMPLID, JO.EFFDT, JO.EFFSEQ`

Returns the
data set

EMPLID	EFFDT	ACTION	ACTION_REASON	EMPL_STATUS	DEPTID
6601	**15-JUN-1996**	**HIR**		**A**	**10400**
6602	15-JUN-1996	HIR		A	20700
6602	01-JAN-1997	DTA		A	20700
7707	**15-JUN-1996**	**HIR**		**A**	**21700**
7707	**11-JUL-1996**	**PRO**		**A**	**21700**
7707	**01-MAR-1997**	**PAY**	**MER**	**A**	**21700**
7707	**01-MAR-1998**	**PAY**	**MER**	**A**	**10400**
8105	23-JUN-1982	HIR		A	10500
8105	23-JUN-1983	PAY	MER	A	10400
8105	31-JAN-1984	TER		T	10400
BOZO	11-OCT-1998	HIR	HAF	A	10100
BOZO	25-OCT-1998	LTO		L	10100
BOZO	15-NOV-1998	DTA		L	10400
BOZO	01-DEC-1998	PAY		L	10400

In Table 8-10 we pick everyone in department 10400 who has a status of A, P, or L as of the current date. We cannot tell what status these employees are, so we need to pick only the most recent, status-related row. First let's execute the query *without* limiting our result to department 10400.

▶ **Table 8-10** Employees in department 10400 who are A, P, L

| The query | ```
SELECT  JO.EMPLID,
        JO.EFFDT,
        JO.ACTION,
        JO.ACTION_REASON,
        JO.EMPL_STATUS,
        JO.DEPTID
FROM PS_JOB JO
WHERE JO.EMPL_RCD# = 0
  AND JO.EFFDT = (SELECT MAX(JO1.EFFDT)
                    FROM PS_JOB JO1
                   WHERE JO1.EMPLID = JO.EMPLID
                     AND JO1.EMPL_RCD# = JO.EMPL_RCD#
                     AND JO1.EFFDT   <= '01-JAN-1999')
  AND JO.EFFSEQ = (SELECT MAX(JO2.EFFSEQ)
                     FROM PS_JOB JO2
                    WHERE JO2.EMPLID = JO.EMPLID
                      AND JO2.EMPL_RCD# = JO.EMPL_RCD#
                      AND JO2.EFFDT   = JO.EFFDT)
  AND JO.DEPTID = '10400'
  AND JO.EMPL_STATUS IN ('A','P','L')
ORDER BY JO.EMPLID
``` |
| --- | --- |

Returns the data set	EMPLID	EFFDT	ACTION	ACTION_REASON	EMPL_STATUS	DEPTID
	------	-----------	------	-------------	-----------	------
	6601	15-JUN-1996	HIR		A	10400
	7707	01-MAR-1998	PAY	MER	A	10400
	BOZO	01-DEC-1998	PAY		L	10400
```

▶ **Table 8-11** Employees who are A, P, L, all departments

| The query | ```
SELECT JO.EMPLID,
       JO.EFFDT,
       JO.ACTION,
       JO.ACTION_REASON,
       JO.EMPL_STATUS,
       JO.DEPTID
FROM PS_JOB JO
WHERE JO.EMPL_RCD# = 0
  AND JO.EFFDT =
      (SELECT MAX(JO1.EFFDT)
         FROM PS_JOB JO1
        WHERE JO1.EMPLID = JO.EMPLID
          AND JO1.EMPL_RCD# = JO.EMPL_RCD#
          AND JO1.EFFDT   <= '01-JAN-1999')
          AND JO1.ACTION NOT IN ('DEM', 'DTA', 'FSC',
                                 'INT', 'JED', 'JRC',
                                 'PAY', 'POS', 'PRB',
                                 'PRC', 'PRO', 'XFR'))
  AND JO.EFFSEQ =
      (SELECT MAX(JO2.EFFSEQ)
         FROM PS_JOB JO2
        WHERE JO2.EMPLID = JO.EMPLID
          AND JO2.EMPL_RCD# = JO.EMPL_RCD#
          AND JO2.EFFDT   = JO.EFFDT
          AND JO2.ACTION NOT IN ('DEM', 'DTA', 'FSC',
                                 'INT', 'JED', 'JRC',
                                 'PAY', 'POS', 'PRB',
                                 'PRC', 'PRO', 'XFR'))
  AND JO.EMPL_STATUS IN ('A','P','L')
ORDER BY JO.EMPLID
``` |

Returns the data set	EMPLID	EFFDT	ACTION	ACTION_REASON	EMPL_STATUS	DEPTID
	6601	15-JUN-1996	HIR		A	10400
	6602	15-JUN-1996	HIR		A	20700
	7707	15-JUN-1996	HIR		A	21700
	BOZO	25-OCT-1998	LTO		L	10100

We can now identify employee BOZO as a long-term disability employee. Note, however, that only one employee seems to be in department 10400. What happened to all of the others? The issue now comes to light. Once we limited ourselves to status-related actions, we only retrieve the department associated with that action. Any department changes that occurred after that date are ignored.
```

To accurately retrieve data for this query, there is a trick. All we need is to join the most current record with the most recent status-related record. We can use the PS_EMPLOYEES table to retrieve the group of employees in department 10400, and link that to those employees who match the status criteria, as in Table 8-12.

▶ **Table 8-12**   Employees who are A, P, L, all departments

| The query | ```
SELECT JO.EMPLID,
       JO.EFFDT,
       JO.ACTION,
       JO.ACTION_REASON,
       JO.EMPL_STATUS,
       JO.DEPTID
FROM PS_JOB JO,
     PS_EMPLOYEES EM
WHERE EM.EMPL_RCD# = 0
  AND EM.DEPTID = '10400'
  AND JO.EMPLID = EM.EMPLID
  AND JO.EMPL_RCD# = EM.EMPL_RCD#
  AND JO.EFFDT =
        (SELECT MAX(JO1.EFFDT)
           FROM PS_JOB JO1
          WHERE JO1.EMPLID = JO.EMPLID
            AND JO1.EMPL_RCD# = JO.EMPL_RCD#
            AND JO1.EFFDT    <= '01-JAN-1999'
            AND JO1.ACTION NOT IN ('DEM', 'DTA', 'FSC',
                                   'INT', 'JED', 'JRC',
                                   'PAY', 'POS', 'PRB',
                                   'PRC', 'PRO', 'XFR'))
  AND JO.EFFSEQ =
        (SELECT MAX(JO2.EFFSEQ)
           FROM PS_JOB JO2
          WHERE JO2.EMPLID = JO.EMPLID
            AND JO2.EMPL_RCD# = JO.EMPL_RCD#
            AND JO2.EFFDT   = JO.EFFDT
            AND JO2.ACTION NOT IN ('DEM', 'DTA', 'FSC',
                                   'INT', 'JED', 'JRC',
                                   'PAY', 'POS', 'PRB',
                                   'PRC', 'PRO', 'XFR'))
  AND JO.EMPL_STATUS IN ('A','P','L')
  AND JO.ACTION NOT IN ('LTO','LTD')
ORDER BY EM.EMPLID
``` |
|---|---|

Returns the data set	EMPLID	EFFDT	ACTION	ACTION_REASON	EMPL_STATUS	DEPTID
	------	-----------	------	-------------	-----------	------
	6601	15-JUN-1996	HIR		A	10400
	6602	15-JUN-1996	HIR		A	10400
```

Finally we retrieve the data we are searching for. This final query demonstrates several points we have covered in this chapter. It selects only status-related information from the job table. It looks at the most recent status row for each employee. And it considers the most recent row, status or non-status related, to look up other information.

SIMPLIFYING JOB TABLE DATA WITH A MODIFICATION

If this process becomes too cumbersome, there are some simple fixes that can cure the problem. An indicator field for long-term disability status can be created relatively simply and populated with PeopleCode every time an employee action or action reason is changed.

Or, the PS_EMPLOYEES table can be modified to add a status-related action, status-related action reason, and effective date. This would provide three fields which could be used beyond the scope of long-term disability employees. Any status-related action or status date could be retrieved quickly. And modifying the PS_EMPLOYEES table to add three extra fields involves no PeopleCode or major revisions (it would be wise to create a new, distinct PS_EMPLOYEES table to modify, keeping it entirely separate from the delivered table). The revisions would involve a version of the query above, but would prevent users from tying up the system with this complex logic during the day. The complex query could be executed once each night, making the system easier to use and increasing performance.

If status-related fields are added to the PS_EMPLOYEES table, the above query would look quite different. Table 8-13 demonstrates the difference.

▶ **Table 8-13** Using a modified PS_EMPLOYEES table

The query	```SELECT EM.EMPLID,
	        EM.STATUS_DATE,
	        EM.STATUS_ACTION
	        EM.STATUS_REASON,
	        EM.DEPTID
	FROM PS_EMPLOYEES EM
	WHERE EM.EMPL_RCD# = 0
	  AND EM.DEPTID = '10400'
	  AND EM.EMPL_STATUS IN ('A','P','L')
	  AND EM.STATUS_ACTION NOT IN ('LTO','LTD')
	ORDER BY EM.EMPLID```

Returns the data set	EMPLID	STATUS_DATE	STATUS_ACTION	STATUS_REASON	DEPTID
	------	----------	-------------	-------------	------
	6601	15-JUN-1996	HIR	A	10400
	6602	15-JUN-1996	HIR	A	10400

With a small modification to the PS_EMPLOYEES table, the basic query to retrieve the status and status date of each employee is simplified. The modification has little impact to the system, and could facilitate training for end-users if they are trying to find status date information.

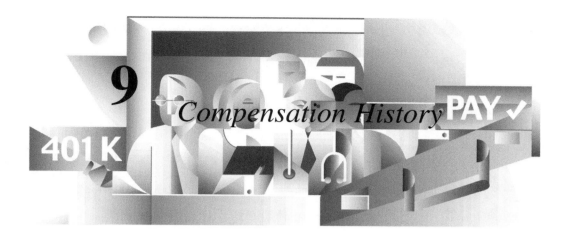

9 Compensation History

Searching for dollars often generates some initial confusion. Money is stored in so many places in PeopleSoft. Employee level information is found on the job table, PS_JOB. Salary planning data, such as the company-wide definitions of levels and steps, is found on the salary administration tables, which begin with 'PS_SAL_.'

Table 9-1 outlines where some common pieces of salary information are located. Compensation data is stored both under salary administration, which is under Go ➤ Compensate Employees, and on the job table, which is under Go ➤ Administrate Workforce (U.S.).

▶ **Table 9-1** Looking for money in all the right places

Looking for	Look in
Employee salary*	PS_JOB table
Changes to salary*	PS_JOB table
Salary history*	PS_JOB table
Pay frequency	Paygroup table, PS_PAYGROUP_TBL
Salary ranges	PS_JOB and Salary Administration tables (PS_SAL...)
Actual earnings	Payroll tables, such as PS_PAY_CHECK
Bonuses	Payroll tables, such as PS_PAY_EARN and PS_PAY_OTH_EARN
Salaried or Hourly	PS_JOB table

* Note that while the salary is stored on PS_JOB, the actual money paid to an employee can only be found on payroll tables.

This chapter discusses the compensation-related fields on the job table and gives a brief overview of the salary administration tables.

DETERMINING THE RATE

PeopleSoft stores the employee's compensation rate in several different forms. These fields can be confusing, since they all seem to have similar numbers. Although each organization tracks salaries differently, the definitions of these fields remain the same:

Compensation rate, frequency.   The compensation fields on the PS_JOB table are interrelated. They do not represent the employee's actual pay frequency or pay amount. The compensation frequency defaults to a value based on how PeopleSoft is set up. The PS_INSTALLATION table and the PS_JOBCODE_TBL (Chapter 10) contain the default values for compensation frequency. Once an employee is set up and the frequency is defaulted, the user enters a compensation rate to correspond with the frequency. Table 9-2 demonstrates how the compensation rate and frequency fields work together to produce the final rate amounts.

▶ **Table 9-2**   Compensation rate and frequency for $100,000 annual rate (ANNUAL_RT = 100000.00)

Frequency COMP_FREQUENCY	Factor used	Compensation rate COMPRATE	Annual rate ANNUAL_RT
Annual (A)	1	100,000	100,000
Biweekly (B)	26	3,846.15	100,000
Hourly (H)	2080	48.08	100,000
Monthly (M)	12	8,333.33	100,000
Semimonthly (S)	24	4,166.67	100,000
Weekly (W)	52	1,923.08	100,000

Annual, monthly, hourly rate.   PeopleSoft takes the compensation rate and multiplies it by the compensation frequency factor to arrive at the actual rates for the employee. Three rates are calculated by the system, and are not user-entered: annual rate, monthly rate, and hourly rate. The monthly rate is the annual rate divided by 12. The hourly rate is the annual rate divided by 2080. The factors in Table 9-2 are always used to calculate the compensation fields.

Change amount, percent.   These fields indicate changes to the employee salary. The amount, or percent, relates to the change in compensation rate, not the annual rate. For example, if a salary increases from $104,000 to $116,000, and the compensation frequency is weekly, the change amount will be $1000, not $12,000.

Annual benefits base rate.   This is a separate field from the annual rate, and is optional. If this field is used, it indicates the annual rate used by benefit processes for calculations. For example, a life insurance policy could cover an employee for two times his or her salary. The salary amount is taken from the annual benefits base rate. If the rate is blank, the regular annual rate is used.

DETECTING CHANGES IN PAY

Changes in compensation are stored on the job table. There are two ways a user can enter a change in salary:

Go ➤ Administer Workforce ➤ Administer Workforce (U.S.) ➤ Use ➤ Job Data

Go ➤ Administer Workforce ➤ Administer Workforce (U.S.) ➤ Use ➤ Pay Rate Change

In an ideal situation, every time an employee receives a pay increase, the user goes to the Pay Rate Change panel. This panel adds a separate row to the PS_JOB table with an action of 'PAY.' But, since users can also enter a compensation change along with any action/action-reason code on the Job Data panel, there may not be a separate row. As shown in Chapter 7 (see Overlapping Changes), changes in pay can be recorded under other action codes. For example, an employee switches into a new jobcode and receives a new salary. The action is 'data change,' but the compensation rate at the end of the job record changes due to a concurrent pay increase.

Detecting a pay change simply requires a look at the CHANGE_AMT or CHANGE_PCT fields on the job table. If there is a value, the pay was changed on the effective date of the row. Keep in mind that the change amount or percent reflects the *compensation rate* change, not the annual rate change, or salary.

> There is a field on the PS_EMPLOYMENT table called *last increase date*. We discuss this field in Chapter 12. It stores the most recent compensation rate change for certain action and action reason combinations.

An additional challenge is determining the reason for a pay change when there isn't a 'PAY' action with an action reason. When actions overlap, the reason code is not directly relevant, but it may provide enough information. For instance, an employee is promoted for outstanding performance ('PRO' and

'OPR'). The pay rate for the new job is different from the existing job, and a concurrent pay change is made to the employee's job record. Although there is no 'PAY' record, the change amount field indicates the pay change, and the action/action reason provides somewhat of an explanation. Unfortunately, this is the closest we can get to the reason for the pay change. A query for determining changes to pay is shown in Table 9-3.

▶ **Table 9-3** Compensation history for an employee

| The query | ```
SELECT
JO.EFFDT,
JO.ACTION,
JO.ACTION_REASON,
JO.ANNUAL_RT
FROM PS_JOB JO
WHERE JO.CHANGE_AMT <> 0
    AND JO.EMPLID    =    'BOZO'
ORDER BY JO.EFFDT
``` |

Returns the data set	JO.EFFDT	JO.ACTION	JO.ACTION_REASON	JO.ANNUAL_RT
	-----------	---------	----------------	------------
	01-MAR-1987	PAY	MER	21496.8
	15-MAR-1990	PAY	MER	23474.506
	01-MAR-1991	PRO	OPR	27230.426
	01-MAY-1991	PAY	ATB	29136.556
	01-APR-1992	PAY	PRO	34963.868
	01-JUN-1992	PAY	ADJ	38110.616
	01-MAR-1993	PAY	MER	41445.295
	01-MAR-1994	PRO	OPR	49734.354
	01-AUG-1994	PAY	ADJ	57194.507
	01-MAR-1995	PAY	MER	61770.067
	01-MAR-1996	PAY	MER	65476.271
	01-MAR-1997	PAY	MER	68088.774
	01-MAR-1998	PAY	MER	70812.438
	22-DEC-1998	PAY	OTH	70836.438
	23-DEC-1998	PAY		77920.082
	02-JAN-1999	DTA		79120.082
```

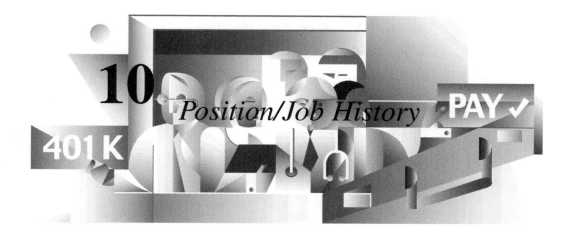

10

Position/Job History

A position in PeopleSoft can mean several things. In this chapter, we will discuss job history, which is tracked by *jobcode*, and position history, which is tracked by *position number*. The two are not mutually exclusive, but work together to track an employee's progression through the different jobs within an enterprise.

THE JOBCODE TABLE

A jobcode in PeopleSoft refers to a particular kind of job in the organization. It rarely refers to the job of a single person. Jobcodes apply default job information to employees with similar job descriptions. Choosing a jobcode for each employee is mandatory.

Several different important pieces of information reside on the jobcode table, PS_JOBCODE_TBL. By tying an employee to the jobcode table using the JOB-CODE field on the PS_JOB table, several additional fields describing an employee's job can be obtained. Table 10-1 explores the structure and the major fields on the jobcode table.

▶ **Table 10-1**   Jobcode: PS_JOBCODE_TBL

Structure	Many rows per jobcode
Keys	SetID
	Jobcode
	Effective Date
Alternate keys	Description
Sub-records included	USA Jobcode Information
	Canada Jobcode Information
	Germany Jobcode Information
	France Jobcode Information
	United Kingdom Jobcode Information
Panels to look at	Go ➤ Define Business Rules ➤ Manage Human Resources (U.S.) ➤ Setup ➤ Job Code Table

The jobcode table is a control table, but it is also used to configure defaults for the job table (PS_JOB). When an employee is hired and a jobcode selected, several field values are taken from the jobcode table and copied to the employee level (the job table). The values of these fields can be overridden at the employee level, since only the defaults are set on the jobcode table. The fields in Table 10-2 are common to both the jobcode table and the job table. Look through Chapter 7 for more information about these fields.

▶ **Table 10-2**   Default values found on PS_JOBCODE_TBL for PS_JOB

Field	Description
SAL_ADMIN_PLAN	Salary administration plan (defaults if plans are not associated with locations)
GRADE	Salary grade (always defaults from jobcode)
STEP	Salary step (always defaults from jobcode)
CURRENCY_CD	Currency code
STD_HOURS	Standard hours
COMP_FREQUENCY	Compensation frequency
REG_TEMP	Regular/temporary employee
DIRECTLY_TIPPED	Tipped

The fields that are unique to the jobcode table are described in the following subsections. These fields represent items that do not need to be stored at the employee level. All employees with the same jobcode will have the same values for these fields.

Major Fields on the JobCode Table

Job Title

The description for a jobcode is an important field. Since it is the description of the job, it is the title of the job. In effect, this field is the employee title, the one also found on the employee's business card. The title/description field is necessary for many delivered reports and functions.

The short and long descriptions are the cousins of the description field, but are not required. These fields are useful for obtaining the really long title of the employee or the much-abbreviated form.

Identifying Managers

The manager level field identifies whether the employee is considered a manager. This field is required. A standard set of management roles is listed. As a rule, employees who are not managers are number '9'—'Non-Manager.' The manager level field is not used in any delivered reports, but is helpful for quickly distinguishing a manager from a non-manager. The department table ties to managers via a manager ID number (the employee ID). If you are using the manager level and manager ID, be sure your converted data accurately uses employee IDs that have a manager level other than '9' for the manager ID field. Chapter 11 has more information on the manager ID field.

Unions

The union code (UNION_CD) stores the union the jobcode belongs to. This code is used for labor relation functionality in PeopleSoft. Historical information about union membership can be found in the PS_JOB_LABOR table. Fields are verified against the PS_UNION_TBL.

Job Families

The job family is a higher-level job classification. If several jobcodes are similar, they can be grouped together in a job family. Job families are also used for grouping competencies (employee abilities).

Workers' Compensation Code

The workers' compensation code links the jobcode to a workers' compensation plan. The workers' compensation code is an informational field, and is not used in any delivered processes.

FLSA Status

The FLSA status field (FLSA_STATUS) indicates if a jobcode is exempt from the provisions of the Fair Labor Standards Act (FLSA). This status becomes the default for all employees in the jobcode.

EEO-1, 4, 5, 6 Job Category, EEO Job Group

The classifications for the jobcode under Equal Employment Opportunity (EEO) are located in these fields. These values are used for EEO reporting and are required. The EEO job group is an optional field for grouping jobcodes into broader EEO categories. These values are not automatically populated. They are used only on EEO reports to classify employees.

Standard Occupational Classification

The standard occupational classification field (US_SOC_CD) identifies the U.S. standard occupational classification (SOC) code for Alaskan employees. If a jobcode could be used by an employee in Alaska, this code is required. The SOC code is used in unemployment insurance reporting for Alaska and is verified against PS_US_SOC_TBL.

Jobcode History

Jobcode history is stored on the job table (PS_JOB) just as other changes are stored. An action and action reason code identify when a jobcode change occurs. Typically this code is a promotion or demotion ('PRO' or 'DEM'). But, just as with compensation changes, jobcode changes can be buried in a status or other change. An employee can change jobs without a separate row on the job table.

Of course, the jobcode changes. This is the first identifier of a change. The second value to look for is the job entry date field (JOB_ENTRY_DT). When this field has a new date, the employee has a new jobcode. Table 10-3 demonstrates how to accurately determine an employee's jobcode history using a SQL query.

▶ **Table 10-3** Detecting jobcode history

The query	SELECT DISTINCT(JO.JOBCODE), JO.JOB_ENTRY_DT FROM PS_JOB JO WHERE JO.EMPLID = 'BOZO' GROUP BY JO.JOBCODE, JO.JOB_ENTRY_DT ORDER BY JO.JOB_ENTRY_DT;

```
The query          SELECT
                   DISTINCT(JO.JOBCODE),
                   JO.JOB_ENTRY_DT

                   FROM PS_JOB JO
                   WHERE JO.EMPLID = 'BOZO'
                   GROUP BY
                   JO.JOBCODE,
                   JO.JOB_ENTRY_DT
                   ORDER BY JO.JOB_ENTRY_DT;
```

```
Returns the        JO.JOBCODE    JO.JOB_ENTRY_DT
data set           ----------    ---------------
                   G850          15-MAR-1986
                   G250          15-JAN-1988
                   G061          01-MAR-1991
                   G033          01-APR-1992
                   G060          01-MAR-1994
                   2002          01-JUL-1994
                   G031          23-DEC-1998
                   G033          02-JAN-1999
```

This query uses a 'group by' statement to group similar jobcode and job entry dates together, so only one jobcode and date are returned for each combination.

POSITION MANAGEMENT

Jobcodes and positions are two different things. A position number identifies a position in the company, not a job or a person. An employee fills the position. Employees move in and out of different positions. A location, department, even mail stop and phone number can be allocated to a position.

In general, each position has one employee. A jobcode, however, has many employees. Jobcodes are a broader classification.

Jobcodes are required. The use of positions is optional. If positions are used, they are used in addition to jobcodes. If your organization is continually creating and removing positions, you should probably turn off position management. But if your organization is unchanging, positions may help with staffing, budgeting, and succession planning.

PeopleSoft also provides for partial position management. Certain departments or locations can be managed according to position, while others only by jobcode. Partial position management is required for pension management. Retired employees who receive a pension through PeopleSoft cannot be associated with a position.

Position Tables and the Job Table

Employee positions, if used, are identified on the PS_JOB table in the POSITION_NBR field. The number in this field ties to the PS_POSITION_DATA table, which stores the control values for the position.

Certain values on the jobcode table are copied to the job table as defaults. In position management, the same thing occurs, except that many more employee-level fields are defaulted by the system. Table 10-4 explains the difference.

▶ **Table 10-4** Jobcode values versus position number values

Change	Result
Enter a new standard hours value on the **jobcode table** for a certain jobcode.	No current records are changed. If a new employee is hired, the new standard hours value will appear as the default if the jobcode is selected.
Enter a new department ID for a certain position on the **position data table**.	The employee currently in the position will receive a new automatic row in the job table with an action of position change ('POS'). The row will have the same effective date as the change to the position.

Any changes to a position are copied to the employee level. This process is automatic, but requires some care by the user. It is important to make the changes to the position data table first, so that these changes are copied to the employee level. Then changes at the employee level can be made.

The automatic rows on the job table created by position management are identified by a 'Y' value in the POSITION_CHANGE_RECORD field on PS_JOB. Position changes do not have to be automatic, however. Like all changes to the job table, position changes can overlap with other actions. The sure-fire way to identify a position change is to look at the position number and the position entry date (Table 10-5). When they change, a position change occurred for an employee.

▶ **Table 10-5** Detecting position history

| The query | ```
SELECT
DISTINCT(JO.POSITION_NBR),
JO.POSITION_ENTRY_DT

FROM PS_JOB JO
WHERE JO.EMPLID = 'BOZO'
GROUP BY
JO.POSITION_NBR,
JO.POSITION_ENTRY_DT
ORDER BY JO.POSITION_ENTRY_DT;
``` |
| --- | --- |

Returns the data set	JO.POSITION_NBR	JO.POSITION_ENTRY_DT
	---------------	--------------------
	00000019	15-MAR-1986
	00000027	15-JAN-1988
	00000008	01-MAR-1991
	00000007	01-APR-1992
	00000004	01-MAR-1994
	00000006	23-DEC-1998
	00000007	02-JAN-1999

Using a 'group by,' all of the distinct position numbers and their associated entry date are retrieved, excluding all of the other information in the job table that does not relate to positions.
```

11 *Corporate Hierarchy*

T he department field has several meanings in PeopleSoft. Departments group employees, determine PeopleSoft security, and through the department tree provide the corporate hierarchy of reports-to relationships.

The definition of a department is deliberately vague. Consider a company of 25,000 employees. Each employee has a supervisor who reports to another who reports to another, up to the Chief Executive Officer. To set up and maintain all of these relationships on an employee level would be an extraordinary task. Each employee would have his or her own reports-to field. If a group of 500 employees shifts in the hierarchy, how long would it take to reconfigure everyone? PeopleSoft resolves this issue with the department ID and the department tree.

UNDERSTANDING THE USE OF DEPARTMENTS

Departments often represent a change to the way business is organized in many companies. Often employees are organized at different levels, and these levels each have their own name. An employee could have a department, but also a business unit, area, section, division, subsidiary, etc. As long as there are names for groups of people, companies have further and further divided employees according to functional needs.

Typically these multiple groups of people relate to one another hierarchically. A subsidiary is higher or lower (groups greater or fewer people) than a division in the hierarchy. PeopleSoft is organized the same way, with one key difference— all groups of employees are called departments. There are no hierarchical naming conventions, because they hinder flexibility.

A department can be anywhere in the structure of the company. The CEO is in a department, and so is someone in the mailroom. They are in different departments, but they are both in departments.

The secret to the success of this method is the department tree. With a graphical interface, departments can move around the tree. Reports-to relationships follow automatically. And since everything on the department tree is called a department, the change is seamless. No need to issue everyone new ID tags, no need to give the employees a new business unit code. Extreme changes in the structure of the organization can happen with ease. Just click on a department and drag it to the new location. Figure 11-1 shows the department tree in graphic form.

Keep the technical advantages in mind as you map your company to the department tree. Combining all of the different groups in an organization into departments is a challenge. People are used to the old names, and telling users that both a subsidiary and a division are now departments can be extremely confusing.

Although this is how PeopleSoft wants the process to work, it is not a requirement. There are several alternatives to implementing the ideal department struc-

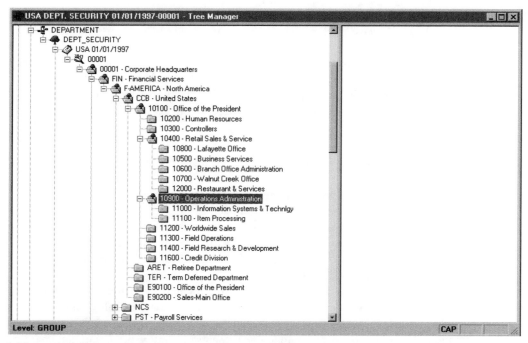

▶ **Figure 11-1** Example PeopleSoft department tree, as seen in the Tree Manager

ture, each with positives and negatives (see Table 11-1). Each company has a unique structure. Sometimes the structure aligns with PeopleSoft, and sometimes the PeopleSoft methodology is completely foreign. Creativity can go a long way, but ultimately PeopleSoft is designed to have everyone in hierarchical departments. Weighing the costs and benefits of the implementation effort and future benefits is an essential first step.

▶ **Table 11-1** Options for mapping departments

Option	Positive	Negative
Map all employees into departments at the lowest level in the tree. Create dummy departments for higher levels of groupings.	Uses PeopleSoft's department tree flexibility and maintains the existing structure in a hierarchical manner.	Dummy departments do not provide a reports-to hierarchy. The CEO should be at the highest level, not residing in a department at the lowest level.
Map all employees at the lowest level in the tree, placing the higher-level group names into the department name.	Easy to figure out the employee's groups since they are in the department name.	Flexibility is compromised, since to move a group of employees requires a change to the names of several departments.
Map employees into departments, but create custom fields on the job table to identify other groupings for each employee.	Easy to figure out the employee's groups since they are in the department name. Departments can be reorganized easily, which is useful for security purposes.	Each time a department changes, the fields on an employee's job record must be manually changed.
Re-map all groups of employees into the PeopleSoft ideal—a hierarchical department structure.	Flexibility is maintained, and reports-to relationships easily determined. Departments can be quickly reorganized with little impact to employees.	Organizational changes might be required.

THE DEPARTMENT TABLE

The department table stores each department code along with additional attributes. It is a control table that is connected to the job table by the department ID code, DEPTID. Each department ID represents an organizational entity in the company—and also drives PeopleSoft payroll and application security. Table 11-2 looks at the department table in detail.

Be careful not to choose the 'other' department table. The real department table is PS_DEPT_TBL. The decoy is PS_DEPARTMENT_TBL, which is used for Payroll Interface processing. They look almost identical, but the PS_DEPT_TBL has essential items that PS_DEPARTMENT_TBL lacks, like manager ID and location. Plus the PS_DEPARTMENT_TBL is not used by the system, anywhere, to identify or update department information.

▶ **Table 11-2**   Department: PS_DEPT_TBL

Structure	Many rows per department ID
Keys	SetID
	Department ID
	Effective Date
Alternate keys	Description
	Company
	SetID Location
	Location Code
Sub-records included	USA Department Information
	Canada Department Information
	Germany Department Information
	France Department Information
Panels to look at	Go ➤ Define Business Rules ➤ Manage Human Resources (U.S.) ➤ Setup ➤ Department Table

Basic Department Settings

Several fields are specified on the department table so that when an employee is placed in a department, they are defaulted into a company and location.

The company field links a department ID to a particular company code. Company codes are verified against PS_COMPANY_TBL. If a department is associated with a company, employees in the department are automatically placed into that company. If the company field is left blank on the department table, employees who are in the department can belong to different companies, specified on their PS_JOB table record.

A location for the department can be specified as well. The location field specifies the location the department is based in. The value specified here appears as the default for employees placed into the department. Individual employees do not have to reside in the default location. The location can be changed on the PS_JOB table for each employee. A location may refer to a building, group of buildings, city, or state depending on how locations are defined.

The setID location field specifies the setID value for the location that the department resides in. This setID may be different from the department setID. For instance, a department could be in the global setID, but could reside in a location that is part of the USA setID. Use the setID location field to link the department to the appropriate location code on PS_LOCATION_TBL.

A tax location code can also be specified at the department level. The tax location code field stores a unique code specifying where the employee resides for tax purposes. A tax location is not the same as a location. Several locations, for example, may be taxed out of a single tax location code. Values are verified against the PS_TAX_LOCATION1 table.

Manager ID

The manager ID field (MANAGER_ID) identifies the employee ID of the employee who manages the department. This employee may or may not reside in the actual department. Since this is unknown, you cannot tie managers together to move through the department tree. For example, you could get the manager ID, then get the manager's department, and then get that department's manager ID, and so on. But if managers reside in their own departments, which commonly occurs, you won't get very far. Table 11-3 shows a typical query that retrieves the department and manager name for an employee.

▶ **Table 11-3** Manager name

| The query | ```
SELECT
JO.EMPLID,
PD.NAME,
DT.DESCRSHORT,
DT.MANAGER_ID,
PD1.NAME
FROM PS_JOB JO,
     PS_PERSONAL_DATA PD,
     PS_DEPT_TBL DT,
     PS_PERSONAL_DATA PD1
WHERE JO.EMPLID = 'BOZO'
  AND JO.EMPL_RCD# = 0
  AND PD.EMPLID = JO.EMPLID
  AND DT.DEPTID = JO.DEPTID
  AND DT.SETID = JO.SETID_DEPT
  AND PD1.EMPLID = DT.MANAGER_ID
  AND JO.EFFDT =
``` |
```

▶ **Table 11-3** continued

```
              (SELECT MAX(JO1.EFFDT)
                 FROM PS_JOB JO1
                WHERE JO1.EMPLID = JO.EMPLID
                  AND JO1.EMPL_RCD# = JO.EMPL_RCD#
                  AND JO1.EFFDT <= [current date])
          AND JO.EFFSEQ =
              (SELECT MAX(JO2.EFFSEQ)
                 FROM PS_JOB JO2
                WHERE JO2.EMPLID = JO.EMPLID
                  AND JO2.EMPL_RCD# = JO.EMPL_RCD#
                  AND JO2.EFFDT = JO.EFFDT)
          AND DT.EFFDT =
              (SELECT MAX(DT1.EFFDT)
                 FROM PS_DEPT_TBL DT1
                WHERE DT1.DEPTID = DT.DEPTID
                  AND DT1.SETID = DT.SETID
                  AND DT1.EFFDT <= JO.EFFDT)
```

Returns the data set	JO.EMPLID	PD.NAME	DT.DESCRSHORT
	---------	---------------	-------------
	BOZO	Clown, Bozo The	HR
	DT.MANAGER_ID	PD1.NAME	
	------------	--------------------------	
	9001	Ringling,Simon	

A second field on the department table identifies managers. The manager position field works like the manager ID field. If position management or partial position management is turned on, the manager position field can be used. This field identifies a position number as the manger of the department. If an employee is assigned to this position, the position number can be linked to the employee ID. When the manager changes for a department, no manual intervention is necessary since the position remains the same but is now tied to a new individual.

If you specify a manager ID, a manager position cannot be used.

> When using PeopleSoft Query to perform a manager selection, you may run into an issue with the delivered security tables. This issue arises when performing the double lookup seen in table 11-3. More on this issue can be found in chapter 25.

General Ledger Account Number

The general ledger account number (GL#_EXPENSE) can store a general account number for charging the expenses of a department (employee salaries, taxes, etc.). The value of this field is placed on the earnings table when paychecks are calculated, and associates the account number to the earning according to department ID. The field is informational only, and is commonly used to store the account number for GL interfaces to the finance area of an organization.

THE DEPARTMENT TREE

PeopleSoft takes all of the departments (the groups of people) in your organization and organizes them in a tree, with 'branches' and 'leaves.' The placement of a department in the tree determines the hierarchical position of the department in the organization.

The tree breaks down into *levels*. Each department reports to a higher level until the top of the tree is reached. In Figure 11-2, the six departments make up three different levels. A tree can have any number of levels, but it is best to keep the number low to improve performance.

The Tree Manager program delivered with PeopleSoft (Go ➤ PeopleTools ➤ Tree Manager) is used to make changes to the department structure in an organization. Each department on the tree is called a *node*. Nodes can be dragged from branch to branch, with no restrictions. You can grab a department or an entire branch (a department with several departments under it). Double clicking on a node allows you to change the attributes of a department.

Behind the Scenes

Keeping the department tree flexible requires some complex logic behind the scenes. Each time a department is moved in the department tree, the PSTREENODE table is reconfigured. Each node of the tree is stored on this table and receives a range of node numbers depending on its position in the tree. Since the position can change, even very drastically, the node numbers are continually reassigned. A glimpse of the PSTREENODE table behind Figure 11-2 is shown in Table 11-4.

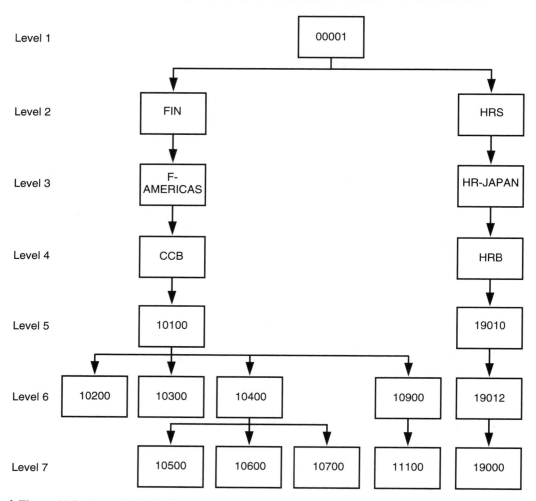

▶ **Figure 11-2** Example department tree structure

▶ **Table 11-4** Tree table: PSTREENODE

The query	SELECT

```
SELECT
PT.TREE_NODE_NUM,
PT.TREE_NODE,
PT.TREE_NODE_NUM_END,
PT.PARENT_NODE_NUM
FROM PSTREENODE PT
WHERE PT.TREE_NAME = 'DEPT_SECURITY'
  AND PT.TREE_NODE LIKE '10%'
  AND PT.SETID = 'USA'
```

Returns the data set

TREE_NODE_NUM	TREE_NODE	TREE_NODE_NUM_END	PARENT_NODE_NUM
39770031	10100	39770371	39770000
39770062	10200	39770092	39770031
39770093	10300	39770123	39770031
39770124	10400	39770278	39770031
39770186	10500	39770216	39770124
39770217	10600	39770247	39770124
39770248	10700	39770278	39770124
39770279	10900	39770371	39770031

Note how the parent node numbers tie back to the tree node numbers in the left-hand column. This is how the hierarchy is stored. By jumping from one parent node to another we can move from one level of the tree to the other. If a node is moved to a different level, the start and end node numbers for that node change as well as the parent node number.

Unfortunately it is much more difficult to navigate in the other direction. Often a report or program needs to select everyone under a specific department that is high up on the tree. All of the departments under that department, and so on down the tree, must be included. Performing this iterative query requires significant processing time. Let's look at the typical tree queries and the methods we can use to execute them.

Queries That Use the Tree

There are two basic queries that use the department tree. Each is simply the reverse of the other:

1. Finding an employee's supervising department (bottom up).
Often we need to see which high-level department an employee

falls under. Since high-level departments are not directly linked to an employee ID, we need to see where the employee's department falls in the department tree. We need to return a single value that is "above" the employee.

2. **Grouping employees according to a supervising department (top down).** The high-level departments that group other departments represent real entities in an organization. Head counts, budgets, general ledger data, or benefits may be processed according to a high-level department. Employees are not directly linked to high-level departments. The department tree is necessary to produce a list of employees that are in a high-level department, that is, many employee IDs that are "below" the high-level department.

PeopleSoft Query Method

PeopleSoft's method for performing these queries uses the delivered Query tool (discussed in Chapter 25). This method uses the PSTREENODE table along with the PSTREESELECT10 table to quickly navigate the tree. The process is complex. It is demonstrated here to fully explain the delivered process before we discuss alternative methods.

The PeopleSoft Query tool constructs elaborate SQL behind a command called *in tree*. This command, used in the criteria section of Query, selects everything under a node of the tree. For example, if we were to select all of the employees in department 10100 and in each department below 10100 on the tree, this is the SQL statement Query would create:

```
SELECT A.EMPLID
  FROM PS_JOB A
  WHERE A.EFFDT =
    (SELECT MAX(EFFDT) FROM PS_JOB
      WHERE A.EMPLID = EMPLID
        AND A.EMPL_RCD# = EMPL_RCD#
        AND EFFDT <= CURRENT DATE)
  AND A.EFFSEQ =
    (SELECT MAX(EFFSEQ) FROM PS_JOB
      WHERE A.EMPLID = EMPLID
        AND A.EMPL_RCD# = EMPL_RCD#
        AND A.EFFDT = EFFDT)
  AND EXISTS
    (SELECT 'X' FROM PSTREESELECT10 A3
      WHERE A3.SELECTOR_NUM=109
        AND A.DEPTID=A3.RANGE_FROM_10
        AND A3.TREE_NODE_NUM BETWEEN 39770031
                                AND 39770371)
```

The part in bold is what PeopleSoft Query constructed based on the department node of 10100. The process Query went through is:

1. Look up the department node on the PSTREENODE table, and retrieve the TREE_NODE_NUM and TREE_NODE_NUM_END where TREE_NODE equals the department ID, '10100.' In this case they are 39770031 and 39770371.

2. Look up the selector number on the PSTREESELNUM table for the tree being used. The selector number is 109.

3. Add the EXISTS clause to the query. The PSTREESELECT10 table contains each department ID in the RANGE_FROM_10 field. If the employee's department can be found in this table, where the selector number is for the appropriate tree (109) and the node number is within the range of department 10100, the employee is selected.

You can see why PeopleSoft hides this procedure behind a simple 'in tree' statement in Query. It is a difficult process, and one that is challenging to those users who are not using Query. Other reporting tools, both graphics-oriented and programming-oriented like SQR, do not have an 'in tree' function. To navigate the tree, you must perform this complex process—or look into the alternative we discuss next.

Tree Navigation Alternative

So the PeopleSoft Query method is a bit complex. It may or may not be practical depending on the environment you are in and the information you are looking for. In SQR, a common module could perform this function. But even a common module forces users to understand the process. It becomes a dependency for other programs.

One easier-to-stomach alternative is a user-friendly department tree table. Every night, or each time a department change is made, a batch program populates a custom table with the department tree information. Each department is listed in this custom table along with the different tree levels the department belongs to. The process flattens out the tree, creating duplicated information but a much quicker solution to tree navigation.

The custom table takes the tree we are using in Figure 11-1 and converts it into a grid of rows and fields, as shown in Table 11-5.

▶ **Table 11-5** Custom department tree table for reporting

Department	Level 1	Level 2	Level 3	Level 4	Level 5	Level 6	Level 7
00001	00001						
FIN	00001	FIN					
F-AMERICAS	00001	FIN	F-AMERICAS				
CCB	00001	FIN	F-AMERICAS	CCB			
10100	00001	FIN	F-AMERICAS	CCB	10100		
10200	00001	FIN	F-AMERICAS	CCB	10100	10200	
10300	00001	FIN	F-AMERICAS	CCB	10100	10300	
10400	00001	FIN	F-AMERICAS	CCB	10100	10400	
10500	00001	FIN	F-AMERICAS	CCB	10100	10400	10500
10600	00001	FIN	F-AMERICAS	CCB	10100	10400	10600
10700	00001	FIN	F-AMERICAS	CCB	10100	10400	10700
10900	00001	FIN	F-AMERICAS	CCB	10100	10900	
11100	00001	FIN	F-AMERICAS	CCB	10100	10900	11100
19000	00001	HRS	HR-JAPAN	HRB	19010	19012	19000

Each department is listed, and depending on the number of levels in the tree, it is associated with the levels above it. If the level is not above the current node, that level field is left blank. This table makes it much easier to see how departments relate to one another right away.

Navigating a custom department tree table

The query in Table 11-6 demonstrates the bottom-up approach using a custom department tree table. We are looking for the level 2 department for all employees, no matter what their level.

▶ **Table 11-6** Bottom up using custom department tree table

| The query | ```
SELECT
JO.EMPLID,
JO.DEPTID,
TR.DEPT_LEVEL_2
FROM PS_CUSTOM_TREE_TBL TR,
     PS_JOB JO
WHERE JO.EMPL_RCD# = 0
  AND TR.DEPTID = JO.DEPTID
  AND TR.SETID = JO.SETID_DEPT
  AND JO.EFFDT =
      (SELECT MAX(JO1.EFFDT)
         FROM PS_JOB JO1
        WHERE JO1.EMPLID = JO.EMPLID
          AND JO1.EMPL_RCD# = JO.EMPL_RCD#
          AND JO1.EFFDT <= [current date])
  AND JO.EFFSEQ =
      (SELECT MAX(JO2.EFFSEQ)
         FROM PS_JOB JO2
        WHERE JO2.EMPLID = JO.EMPLID
          AND JO2.EMPL_RCD# = JO.EMPL_RCD#
          AND JO2.EFFDT = JO.EFFDT)
  AND TR.EFFDT =
      (SELECT MAX(TR1.EFFDT)
         FROM PS_DEPT_TBL TR1
        WHERE TR1.DEPTID = TR.DEPTID
          AND TR1.SETID = TR.SETID
          AND TR1.EFFTR <= JO.EFFDT)
``` |
|---|---|

Returns the data set	EMPLID	DEPTID	DEPT_LEVEL_2
	------	--------	------------
	BOZO	19010	HRS
	9002	10100	FIN
	9003	19012	HRS
	9004	HR-JAPAN	HRS
	9005	00001	

Each employee in Table 11-6 is linked to a higher department level (level 2) in the tree. Employee 9005 does not have a level 2 department because she is at a higher level, level 1.

The query in Table 11-7 demonstrates the top-town approach. We are retrieving a list of the employees under a department at level 2.
```

▶ **Table 11-7** Top down using custom department tree table

| The query | ```
SELECT
JO.EMPLID,
JO.DEPTID
FROM PS_CUSTOM_TREE_TBL TR,
     PS_JOB JO
WHERE JO.EMPL_RCD# = 0
  AND TR.DEPTID = JO.DEPTID
  AND TR.SETID = JO.SETID_DEPT
  AND JO.EFFDT =
        (SELECT MAX(JO1.EFFDT)
           FROM PS_JOB JO1
          WHERE JO1.EMPLID = JO.EMPLID
            AND JO1.EMPL_RCD# = JO.EMPL_RCD#
            AND JO1.EFFDT <= [current date])
  AND JO.EFFSEQ =
        (SELECT MAX(JO2.EFFSEQ)
           FROM PS_JOB JO2
          WHERE JO2.EMPLID = JO.EMPLID
            AND JO2.EMPL_RCD# = JO.EMPL_RCD#
            AND JO2.EFFDT = JO.EFFDT)
  AND TR.EFFDT =
        (SELECT MAX(TR1.EFFDT)
           FROM PS_DEPT_TBL TR1
          WHERE TR1.DEPTID = TR.DEPTID
            AND TR1.SETID = TR.SETID
            AND TR1.EFFTR <= JO.EFFDT)
  AND (TR.DEPT_LEVEL_1 = '10100'
    OR TR.DEPT_LEVEL_2 = '10100'
    OR TR.DEPT_LEVEL_3 = '10100'
    OR TR.DEPT_LEVEL_4 = '10100'
    OR TR.DEPT_LEVEL_5 = '10100'
    OR TR.DEPT_LEVEL_6 = '10100')
``` |
| Returns the data set | ```
EMPLID   DEPTID
------   ------
0325     10100
6234     10400
1328     10400
1150     10900
``` |

The group of 'OR' statements at the end goes level by level through the custom tree table. If the specified high-level department ID is stored in level 1, 2, 3, 4, 5, or 6 (all of the levels of this custom tree—you may have more) for a department, then the department is valid. This method only works if the custom tree is constructed properly, with each department ID found only in the appropriate level slot. The query in Table 11-7 checks each slot because department 10100 could move to a different level.

STORING DEPARTMENT TREE HISTORY

The history for a department is easy to browse—it is stored on the department table, PS_DEPT_TBL. The department tree, though, is also an important part of a corporate hierarchy. Where is the history of the department tree stored, and how is it used?

PeopleSoft's tree manager provides an effective date field for each tree. Every time a change is made to a tree, including a department tree, the user has the option of creating a new effective-dated row. By tying a job history record to the department tree using the same effective date, an accurate picture of the organization on a given date can be constructed.

> Remember to use the same maximum effective date for the department tree and the job record in order to get an accurate point-in-time picture.

This is the best way to store tree history, but it isn't the most efficient way of changing the tree. In a large organization, departments move around and change attributes often. Saving an entirely new tree for every change creates a huge department tree table and poses a performance threat. As a result, users often effective date a tree only when major changes are made and just update the tree for minor changes.

Once a field is updated in the tree without a new effective date, there is no way to determine the previous state of the tree. These relationships are often critical for tracing the reports-to relationship of different departments at a specific historical point in time. Without knowledge of the tree structure at that time, such an analysis cannot be performed.

It is therefore important to consider how often a copy of the tree should be saved. One could determine that a new tree be created weekly, or monthly. Although the organization cannot be seen in between historic trees, at least a before-and-after image that span a short time can be found. This is a data warehousing issue—how often should the tree be captured and stored?

It depends on the importance of department tree history to your organization. Perhaps daily history is essential but does not need to be easily accessible. Each day a copy of the tree could be archived to a flat file. Maybe the tree could be archived monthly, or annually. Regardless of the solution you choose, make sure you consider department tree history during implementation. It is often a legal requirement to be able to trace where an individual is in the organization at a point in time. PeopleSoft's tree manager makes it too easy to lose this critical information.

12 *Employment Information*

Most static information about an employee's tenure with an organization is stored on the employment table, PS_EMPLOYMENT. This information rarely changes, and if it does, the old values are not stored. This chapter will describe each field in detail, especially the various employment dates.

THE EMPLOYMENT TABLE

Let's look at the structure of the employment table in Table 12-1.

▶ **Table 12-1** Employment: PS_EMPLOYMENT

Structure	One row per employee ID and record number
Keys	Employee ID
	Employee Record Number
Alternate keys	Business Title
Sub-records included	Phone
	Address
	France Employment Information
Panels to look at	Go ➤ Administer Workforce ➤ Administer Workforce (U.S.) ➤ Use ➤ Current Job ➤ Employment Data

The employee ID and employment record number fields form the unique keys for the employment table. The employment record number indicates the job the employment record pertains to. Each is a separate entity. For example, if an employee terminates from one job, the termination date will appear only for that job, not the others. The employment table must store separate rows for each job, and these employment record numbers tie back to the PS_JOB table.

MULTIPLE SETS OF EMPLOYMENT DATA

Although no history is stored on the PS_EMPLOYMENT table, often multiple records for a single employee can be found. These records have a separate employment record number which ties to PS_JOB. But additional fields on the table also provide detailed information that sometimes explains the difference between two records.

Multiple Benefits Selections

An additional record number is located on PS_EMPLOYMENT. The benefit record number (BENEFIT_RCD#) is not a key, but the values correspond to the employment record. The default is zero, but an employee can have additional benefit programs for additional jobs. An employee can have three jobs (employment record numbers 0 to 3) and two benefit programs. Two of the jobs could be under one benefit program and one under the other program. PeopleSoft requires that a benefit record number match the associated employment record numbers—but not vice versa. The case of three jobs and two programs is shown in Table 12-2.

> The employment table is the only place where employment record numbers and benefit record numbers are linked together.

▶ **Table 12-2** Employment table with multiple jobs/benefit programs

Employee ID	Employment Record Number	Benefit Record Number
BOZO	0	0
BOZO	1	0
BOZO	2	2

In this case, job 0 has a benefit record number of 0. Job one is also in this benefit program. In other words, both job 0 and job 1 share the same benefits options, elections, and rates. Job 2 has a separate set of benefits, and is identified by a corresponding benefit record number of 2.

Employees on Global Assignments

Employees who are on global assignments can have both a row for home information (base) and one for host information (abroad). The home/host classification field (HOME_HOST_CLASS) indicates if the row contains employment information regarding the home location of the employee or the host location. Host information includes benefits participation. The Home/Host Classification field is not a key, so different employment records are required—one for home and one for host. The home/host classification field is verified against the translate table, using values 'M' for home and 'S' for host. The default value is 'M.'

DATES OF EMPLOYMENT

The employment table is known as the table for dates—hire, term, service, etc. These dates are meant to be permanent.

Hire/Rehire Date

The hire date stores the effective date of the employee's hire record. Once the hire date is initially set, it does not change. There is one exception—if the date of the hire record is changed in correction mode, the hire date will change to match it. The hire date field is only populated if a hire record exists for the employment record number on the job table. If the employee has a second job without a hire record, no hire date will appear for that record number on the employment table. The hire date cannot be edited online.

> The original hire date, found on PS_PERSONAL_DATA, can be edited online and is sometimes different from the hire date.

The company seniority date is automatically set to the effective date of the job table hire record, just like the hire date field. Although the hire date cannot be edited online, the seniority date can be changed. The date can change according to whatever seniority rules you wish to apply and is not used for length of service calculations in benefits.

The rehire date is often used in conjunction with the hire date. It stores the effective date of the employee's rehire record. If the employee is not a rehire, the rehire date field is blank. In order to get the most recent hire date, both rehire date and hire date must be queried. If rehire date is blank, the hire date should be used.

Length of Service

The service date field stores the equivalent of the service time for an employee. When this date is subtracted from the current date, the service years/months/days is the result. The service date starts out as the hire date, but must be manually changed to reflect a leave of absence, termination, or suspension as necessary. The service date has no additional functionality over the company seniority date (explained above), but it is the date that benefit plans refer to. Minimum and maximum ranges and cutoffs are set by service for certain benefit plans, and these plans look at the service date. The database audit prior to payroll runs checks to make sure the service date exists and is within the range 01/01/1900 through the current date.

An associated field, the professional experience date, is optional. PeopleSoft suggests that you use it to store the date the employee began gaining experience in the field he or she is currently in. This date must be manually entered online. The field is used only by the batch SQR report OHS001FR (Health and Safety France Report).

Expected Return from Leave of Absence

The expected return date stores the date the employee is expected to return from a leave of absence. This field is manually entered when the employee goes on leave. It is used on the Employees on Leave of Absence report, SQR PER005, which also identifies those employees without an expected return date. The expected return date does not automatically process the return from leave. It is for information only.

Using Termination Date and Last Day Worked

The termination date field stores the date the employee terminated, but it has several caveats. It is automatically set to the day before the termination record effective date entered on the job table. For example, if George has a job table record showing a termination on 1/15, the termination date will be 1/14. This field is recorded when the action is entered, and is blanked out when the employee is rehired. When a future rehire action is placed on the job table, the termination date is blanked out at the time of data entry, not at the future date. If a subsequent termination occurs, the termination date is updated with the new date.

The last-worked date stores the last day the employee is to be paid for. This field is used for terminations and employees on a leave of absence. For a terminated employee this date is equal to the termination date. It is blanked out when an employee returns from leave or is rehired. Like the termination date, a future-dated return will remove the date last worked from the employment record. If the employee is on a leave of absence when he is terminated, the date last worked will still be the leave of absence last date worked, not the termination date. Also, if a subsequent termination occurs, the date last worked will remain the initial date the employee last worked.

Pay Increases

The last increase date stores the date of the most recent pay increase. PeopleSoft uses the compensation rate field on the job table to determine a pay increase. Only the following action/action reasons will change the last increase date:

- PRO and any action reason (promotion)
- PAY and MER (merit)
- PAY and PRO (promotion)
- PAY and SPG (special increase)
- PAY and no action reason

All other changes to the compensation rate (i.e., a change when an employee terminates or is returned from a leave of absence) are not reflected in the last increase date. Since these changes are possible, the date of last increase is not always accurately valued.

Probation Date

The probation date indicates the start date of a probation period for an employee. Probations are used in conjunction with employee contracts, which are stored under Go ➤ Administer Workforce ➤ Administer Workforce (U.S.) ➤ Use ➤ Contract Data. If a period of probation is scheduled using this panel group, the probation date is copied to the PROBATION_DT field on the employment table. If multiple probation dates exist for one or more contracts, the earliest probation date is placed on the employment table.

POSITION MANAGEMENT FIELDS

The following fields on the employment table are only used when position management is enabled. They help track employee-level information about positions.

Business Title

The business title field stores the employee's official business title. This title defaults from the position title if position management is used; otherwise it is blank unless manually entered. The business title can be different from the title of the employee's job (on the job code table). The business title is used on several delivered reports.

Reports-To Position Number

The reports-to position number is only used if position management is at least partially enabled (see Chapter 10). It is automatically set to the default position that the employee's position reports to. It can be entered manually online to override the default. The delivered SQR POS006 will produce a warning message if the reports-to field is blank or creates a circular reference. The position number is verified against the PS_POSITION_DATA table.

Supervisor ID

The supervisor ID field is only used if partial position management is enabled. It is used as an alternative to the reports-to position number; if the reports-to is blank, the supervisor ID can be used. Supervisor ID is never used for full position management since full position management requires a reports-to position. The supervisor ID is the employee ID of the employee's supervisor. The supervisor ID is verified against the PS_PERSONAL_DATA table. A warning is issued if the supervisor ID is the same as the employee ID.

Phone Subrecord

The phone sub-record on the employment table stores the work phone for the employee, as established by position management. Phone information from the position data table automatically updates the work phone if position management is used. The PS_EMPLOYEES table stores the contents of this field under the name WORK_PHONE to differentiate it from the phone field on other tables.

PAYROLL SETTINGS

Many basic settings for payroll are located on the employment table. While the job table stores the compensation rate information, company and paygroup, the employment table deals with the details of deductions and check distribution.

Deductions and Deduction Subsets

The employment table stores the settings for which deductions an employee is allowed to receive. The deductions taken field provides a flag indicating how these rules are specified: by the deduction table (D), by a subset of the deduction table that is identified with a subset ID (S), or no deductions should be taken at all (N). Information is entered on the Go ➤ Compensate Employees ➤ Maintain Payroll Data U.S. ➤ Use ➤ Payroll Data 2 panel.

The deduction subset ID field works in conjunction with the deductions taken field. If a subset of the deduction table is chosen for the deductions taken field, the subset ID field is required. A deduction subset contains only certain deductions, and specifying the ID of this subset limits the deductions taken from the employee's paycheck to just the subset. The deduction subsets are stored on PS_DED_SUBSET_TBL.

Paycheck Distribution

The distribution mail option field (PAYCHECK_DIST_OPTN) indicates whether an employee's paycheck is distributed using company mail or the postal service. The field is set for each employee on the Payroll Data 1 panel. This and other settings tell the payroll process which address to use for the employee's paycheck.

If the paycheck is distributed using the postal service, the paycheck address option field will store the address type for the paycheck address. The default value is specified on PS_PAYGROUP_TBL but can be manually changed on the Payroll Data 1 panel for each employee. The paycheck can go to the employee's home address specified on the personal data table (H), to the mailing address specified on personal data (M), or to a check address (C) specified on Payroll Data 1. When the default on PS_PAYGROUP_TBL is overridden, the value on PS_PAYGROUP_TBL is set to (E), specifying that the address option is selected at the employee level on the Payroll Data panel. In such cases, the address fields on PS_EMPLOYMENT are populated with the appropriate paycheck address.

If the paycheck is distributed internally, several fields can be populated. The location option field stores the employee location for the sorting of paychecks. Locations are defined on PS_LOCATION_TBL. Like the paycheck address option, the paycheck location default is on PS_PAYGROUP_TBL. On the

Payroll Data panels the paycheck can be associated with the location of the employee's home department (H), job department (J), or with a different location. The home department is the location linked to the employee's department. The job department is the location on the employee's job record.

Other locations can be specified on the Payroll Data panel and are stored in the SETID and LOCATION fields. This is only necessary if the employee's paycheck location is different from his or her department location and job location.

In addition, a paycheck can be sent to a particular internal mailbox. The mail drop ID field stores the internal mail location for the employee's mail. The mail drop ID is defaulted from the position if position management is used. It is also specified on the PS_PAYGROUP_TBL for each paygroup. The payroll process can use the mail drop as a sorting option.

Paycheck Name

The paycheck name field allows you to specify a name other than that specified on PS_PERSONAL_DATA for the employee's paycheck. The paycheck creation process uses this field if it is not blank.

Payroll System

The payroll system field stores which payroll system the employee is paid under. The payroll system could be NA (North American), European, or Other. The payroll system determines the payroll data, rules, and calculations necessary for processing each employee's paycheck. The flag is set on the Go ➤ Administer Workforce ➤ Administer Workforce (U.S.) ➤ Use ➤ Job Data ➤ Payroll panel.

BENEFITS ADMINISTRATION FLAG

One field on the employment table is benefits-related. The benefit system flag (BENEFIT_SYSTEM) indicates whether benefits administration or the base benefits process handles the employee's benefits. This information is set on the Go ➤ Administer Workforce ➤ Administer Workforce (U.S.) ➤ Use ➤ Job Data ➤ Benefits Program panel. See Chapter 21 for more information on benefits processing options.

13 *Background Information*

$\mathbf{A}$ll background information in PeopleSoft is stored as accomplishments. An accomplishment specifies a distinct achievement, such as learning a language, completing a degree, or obtaining a license.

COMPETENCIES VS. ACCOMPLISHMENTS

PeopleSoft uses accomplishments to track employee progress using position management, but position management is not a prerequisite for using accomplishments functionality. The system can be set up to associate certain accomplishments with a particular position. You can then make sure that all managers have MBAs or that all auditors are licensed. PeopleSoft provides extensive functionality for organizing employees according to skills and achievements.

Succession planning, matching employees with skills, and gap detection are all handled by PeopleSoft's manage competencies process. Both competencies and accomplishments are associated with positions in PeopleSoft. A competency is a skill, something that is at a lower level than an accomplishment. You may have a computer science degree, but can you program in PeopleCode? Skills are finite requirements that can be linked to positions.

We will discuss accomplishments in this chapter, which most organizations use to track employee backgrounds. It should be noted, though, that PeopleSoft provides extensive functionality and reference material on using accomplishments in conjunction with competencies to track employee/position fits.

159

ACCOMPLISHMENTS

Accomplishments let you track the achievements of your employees. All accomplishment information is stored in two basic tables: PS_ACCOMP_TBL stores the control values, and PS_ACCOMPLISHMENTS stores the accomplishments of the entire employee population.

Although only two tables track accomplishments, they contain widely varied kinds of information. Table 13-1 describes the different accomplishment categories.

▶ **Table 13-1**   What is an accomplishment?

Accomplishment Category	Description
TST	Test Results
DEG	Degrees
HON	Honors and Awards
MEM	Memberships
LNG	Languages
LIC	Licenses and Certifications
NVQ	NVW (United Kingdom only)

Accomplishment Values

Let's look at the PS_ACCOMP_TBL to see how it is structured. Note that there are only three sub-records in Table 13-2 but seven accomplishment categories in Table 13-1. Sub-records are included for information beyond the code and a description. Awards, tests, memberships, and languages only have a description in the PS_ACCOMP_TBL.

▶ **Table 13-2**   Accomplishments: PS_ACCOMP_TBL

Structure	Many rows per accomplishment category; no effective dates
Keys	Accomplishment
Alternate keys	Description
Sub-records included	License/Certification Information
	Degree Information
	National Vocational Qualifications UK Information
Panels to look at	Go ➤ Develop Workforce ➤ Administer Training (U.S.) ➤ Setup ➤ Degree Table/ License and Certification Table/ Membership Table/ Test Table

Identifying an Accomplishment

The accomplishment field is the unique identifier of an accomplishment. Since accomplishments can be degrees, awards, tests, languages, etc., the accomplishment field values vary widely. Some examples include: 3003 (Driving Test), AR (Arabic), BA (Bachelor of Arts), VYA (Volunteer of the Year Award). PeopleSoft is delivered with over 200 values. The PS_ACCOMP_TBL is the control table for these values. Note that the different categories of accomplishments are not distinguishable in the accomplishment code (no embedded fields); the ACCOMP_CATEGORY field provides this function.

An accomplishment category distinguishes different types of accomplishments. About seven different categories are stored on the PS_ACCOMP_TBL table (see Table 13-1).

Licenses and Certifications

The renewal required, renewal period, and renewal length fields store information about licenses and certification renewal. If the accomplishment is a license or certification (category = 'LIC'), these fields may be used. These fields are informational only and are not used by the PeopleSoft system.

Degrees

The years of education and education level fields form the DEGREE_SBR subrecord, which tracks information on accomplishments in the 'DEG' category. Years of education is the number of years required to obtain the degree. Education level specifies the degree level: trade school, university, or university advanced. Country specifies where the degree is earned. Additional information may be entered for degrees earned in Germany. All degree fields are for information only.

NVQ Accomplishments

The NVQ sub-record stores National Vocational Qualifications for employee accomplishments in the United Kingdom.

Employee Accomplishments

While PS_ACCOMP_TBL stores the control values for each accomplishment, the PS_ACCOMPLISHMENTS table contains the actual accomplishments for each person in the organization. Detailed information about each person's accomplishments can be stored. Since this information differs from the control values (which by their nature are the same for each employee with the same accomplishment), different sub-records are used. Carefully note the difference in names to detect a control sub-record versus an employee-level sub-record. Let's look at the personal accomplishments table (Table 13-3).

▶ **Table 13-3** Personal Accomplishments: PS_ACCOMPLISHMENTS

Structure	Many rows per person
Keys	Employee ID
	Accomplishment
	Organization
	Description
	Date Issued
	Major Code
Alternate keys	None
Sub-records included	Test
	License/Certification
	Language
	Language France
	Membership
	Education
	Education France
	Education Germany
	Honors and Awards
	Honors and Awards France
Panels to look at	Go ➤ Develop Workforce ➤ Administer Training (U.S.) ➤ Use ➤ Education/Language/Licenses and Certifications/Memberships/Test Results

Both employees and non-employees are found on the accomplishments table. The accomplishment field identifies the accomplishment. A single employee can have several accomplishments, and can even have the same accomplishment twice (two degrees, two awards, etc.).

The organization field (ORG) is used as a key, but only for memberships. It is an additional key for distinguishing accomplishments since an individual may belong to several organizations with the same accomplishment code.

The date issued is used for each accomplishment to track the date the accomplishment is obtained. It is also a key in case the exact same accomplishment is acquired twice.

Identifying the Employee's Major

The major code field (MAJOR_CODE) is used for degree accomplishments. It is a key in order to allow the same accomplishment on the same day, in different majors. For example, someone could earn a bachelor's degree in Business and one in Architecture on the same day. The major code distinguishes the two accomplishments, which share the same category and issued date. Major codes are stored on PS_MAJOR_TBL.

Several other fields track information about degree accomplishments. The major is copied from the PS_MAJOR_TBL but can be overridden on PS_ACCOMPLISH-MENTS. If the major doesn't exist in the PS_MAJOR_TBL, the user can just enter a description in the major field. Date acquired provides an additional date, since date issued is also found in this table. Although PeopleSoft does not specify how each date field should be used, it is a good idea to keep them consistent.

The school code and school field work just like the major. If a school code exists, the description is copied from PS_SCHOOL_TBL. If not, the user can type in a description. The state and country track where the degree was earned; they are labeled 'other' because the state and country for licenses is also contained on this table ('other' is for degrees, without other is for licenses).

Tracking Licenses and Expirations

The LIC_CERT_SBR sub-record stores information about licenses and certifications. The license number and issued-by fields store text about the license. The state and country provide information on where the accomplishment was issued (a license to practice law in NJ, in England, etc.). The expiration date stores a date that you can use to track when licenses will expire. The license verified and renewal-in-progress fields are yes/no values. These values can be used to periodically determine when licenses and certifications will expire. A delivered SQR, PER034, provides a listing of accomplishments and contains the expiration date for licenses and certifications.

Linking Accomplishments By Category

Here is a perfect example of a minor relational database headache. When you want information about a person's educational background, you cannot just go to the PS_ACCOMPLISHMENTS table. Although the background is stored there, it is lumped together with the six other accomplishment categories. Nearly always, you must link to the PS_ACCOMP_TBL control table to determine the category. Table 13-4 shows how it's done. Simply linking the accomplishment back to the control table allows us to get the category and then restrict the rows returned.

▶ **Table 13-4** Retrieving only one accomplishment category

The query	```SELECT AC.ACCOMPLISHMENT, AC.SCHOOL, AT.EDUCATION_LVL FROM PS_ACCOMPLISHMENTS AC, PS_ACCOMP_TBL AT WHERE AC.EMPLID = 'BOZO' AND AT.ACCOMPLISHMENT = AC.ACCOMPLISHMENT AND AT.ACCOMP_CATEGORY = 'DEG'```

```
The query        SELECT
                 AC.ACCOMPLISHMENT,
                 AC.SCHOOL,
                 AT.EDUCATION_LVL

                 FROM PS_ACCOMPLISHMENTS AC,
                     PS_ACCOMP_TBL AT
                 WHERE AC.EMPLID = 'BOZO'
                   AND AT.ACCOMPLISHMENT = AC.ACCOMPLISHMENT
                   AND AT.ACCOMP_CATEGORY = 'DEG'
```

```
Returns the      ACCOMPLISHMENT    SCHOOL            EDUCATION_LVL
data set         --------------    ----------------  -------------
                 BA                Miami University  U
                 MBA               Georgetown        A
```

Payroll

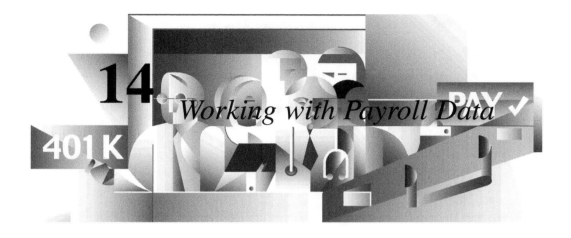

14 Working with Payroll Data

Everything on an employee's paycheck must be crystal clear and consistent. It is a challenge for any large or small corporation, but an important one.

This chapter introduces the payroll process, a series of programs delivered with PeopleSoft. These programs generate paychecks using settings for salary, deductions, taxes, special earnings, and garnishments.

A pay calendar specifies when checks should be written, and keeps track of them once they are created. We'll look at the pay calendar table to get a better understanding of how the data is organized, and later, how PeopleSoft calculates each check and stores the results.

PAYROLL TABLES

There are numerous tables associated with the payroll process. Tables are named according to the stage in the payroll run. For example, to find the tax an employee is supposed to pay next period, you need to look at:

- PS_JOB for the employee's tax location.
- PS_TAX_DISTRIB to determine the employee's home state and locality.
- PS_STATE_TAX_DATA for the employee's state elections.
- PS_FED_TAX_DATA for the employee's federal elections.
- PS_LOCAL_TAX_DATA for the employee's local elections.

- PS_STATE_TAX_TBL for state and federal tax rates.
- PS_LOCAL_TAX_TBL for local tax rates.

But if you are searching for post-payroll data, you should look for a "PS_PAY" table: PS_PAY_TAX has all of the resulting tax amounts for the employee. The tables that contain post-payroll data are always prefixed with PAY in PeopleSoft. There are over 100 PAY tables—the common ones are listed in Table 14-1. These tables comprise a good 90% of the payroll tables you'll ever need.

▶ **Table 14-1**   Major payroll tables

Table	Stores
PS_PAY_CALENDAR	The core of the group: a list of pay period dates. This table is a control table (i.e., does not contain employee data).
PS_PAY_CHECK	Finished checks with gross and net
PS_PAY_EARNINGS	Regular and overtime earnings and hours
PS_PAY_OTH_EARNS	Special earnings and hours (auto allowance, bonus, etc.)
PS_PAY_DEDUCTION	Deductions taken
PS_PAY_TAX	Federal, state, and local taxes taken
PS_PAY_GARNISH	Garnishments against paycheck taken
PS_PAY_DISTRIBUTN	Where the check went (mail or direct deposit)

Figure 14-1 shows the relationships between the various tables used in the payroll process.

LOOKING AT A SPECIFIC PAYROLL RUN

The pay calendar table in PeopleSoft stores each payroll period for all of the companies and paygroups you establish. It is set up before you begin running payrolls, with all of the dates for the future payroll periods. It doesn't have to be set in stone; calendars can be added, changed, and removed.

A COBOL process, PSPCLBLD (Go ➤ Compensate Employees ➤ Manage Payroll Process U.S. ➤ Process ➤ Pay Calendar Creation), can fill the pay calendar table with entries automatically, based on parameters you provide.

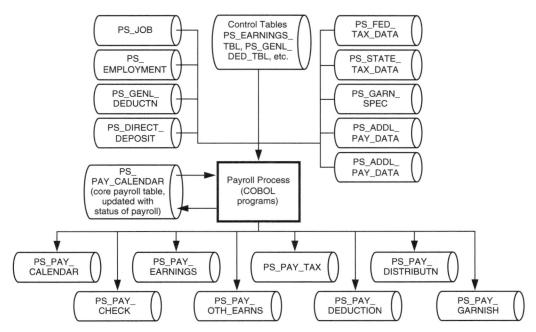

▶ **Figure 14-1** This diagram is a high-level overview of the major payroll process inputs and outputs (many minor tables are omitted).

For batch processing, it helps if you define your calendar ahead of time and stick to it. Most programs, including delivered programs, need to know which pay calendar you wish to use. Even the payroll programs require this information—they will run checks for any time period you like. If the calendar is permanent, these programs (and you) can easily tell what runs next. Timing the processing of earnings and deductions in time for each payroll is much simpler when you've nailed down a schedule for the next three years.

Let's look at the fields in the pay calendar table to get a better understanding of how calendars are stored and used by the payroll process (Table 14-2).

▶ **Table 14-2** Pay calendar: PS_PAY_CALENDAR

Structure	Many rows per pay date
Keys	Company
	Paygroup
	Pay end date
Alternate keys	Run ID
Sub-records included	None
Panels to look at	Go ➤ Define Business Rules ➤ Define Payroll Process ➤ Setup 2 ➤ Pay Calendar Table

Using the Paycheck Table with Payroll Queries

All information on the PAY tables ties back to a specific check for a specific calendar. The key structure that forms this bond is the same on every PAY table. Hence, a check can be traced through and identified in each table according to the same keys.

There is one key, the employee ID, that is only found on two tables: PS_PAY_CHECK and PS_PAY_EARNINGS. This means that we cannot go straight to the PS_PAY_DEDUCTION table and bring up an employee's deductions. We first look at PS_PAY_CHECK, find the employee's checks, and then tie to the other payroll tables. PS_PAY_CHECK is the starting point for every payroll query. Without it, you have no idea whose information you're looking at. The example in Table 14-3 demonstrates why a simple query on PS_PAY_DEDUCTION brings back inaccurate results unless the paycheck table is used.

▶ **Table 14-3** Retrieving deductions (inaccurately) without an employee ID

The query	```SELECT
PD.DED_CD,
PD.DED_CUR,
PD.PAGE#,
PD.LINE#
FROM PS_PAY_DEDUCTION PD,
PS_JOB JO
WHERE PD.COMPANY = JO.COMPANY
AND PD.PAYGROUP = JO.PAYGROUP
AND PD.PAY_END_DT = '15-OCT-1999'
AND PD.OFF_CYCLE = 'N'```

▶ **Table 14-3** continued

Returns the data set	DED_CD	DED_CUR	PAGE#	LINE#
	------	----------	-----	-----
	A01	60.75	1	3
	A02	14.32	2	2
	A01	20.01	1	1
	B23	3.07	1	1
	B23	16.42	3	1
	A01	18.91	2	1

Without the EMPLID field, we get back lots of indistinct deductions, with just a line number and page number. Even though we specified a specific payroll, company, and paygroup, we need the PS_PAY_CHECK table to translate the line and page number into an employee, as in Table 14-4.

▶ **Table 14-4** Retrieving deductions (the right way) with an employee ID

The query	
| | ```
SELECT
PD.DED_CD,
PD.DED_CUR,
PD.PAGE#,
PD.LINE#
FROM PS_PAY_DEDUCTION PD,
      PS_JOB JO,
      PS_PAY_CHECK PC
WHERE PC.COMPANY      = JO.COMPANY
  AND PC.PAYGROUP     = JO.PAYGROUP
  AND PC.PAY_END_DT   = '15-OCT-1998'
  AND PC.OFF_CYCLE    = 'N'
  AND PC.EMPLID       = 'BOZO'
  AND PD.COMPANY      = PC.COMPANY
  AND PD.PAYGROUP     = PC.PAYGROUP
  AND PD.PAY_END_DT   = PC.PAY_END_DT
  AND PD.OFF_CYCLE    = PC.OFF_CYCLE
  AND PD.PAGE# =  PC.PAGE#
  AND PD.LINE# =  PC.LINE#
  AND PD.SEPCHK       = PC.SEPCHK
``` |

Returns the data set	DED_CD	DED_CUR	PAGE#	LINE#
	------	----------	-----	-----
	B23	3.07	1	1
```

The result shows the page number and line number of the check that employee 'BOZO' received for this particular payroll. Note in particular how we linked the paycheck table to the pay deduction table by every key (7 total). Also, since we do not know the page number, line number, or separate check value, we cannot specify these items. This is okay—if there are numerous lines, we will simply get back numerous checks for the employee.

Payroll Keys

In order to keep track of the thousands and thousands of checks PeopleSoft will generate over time, up to five join keys are necessary. Understanding these keys is essential to understanding PeopleSoft payroll from both a functional and technical perspective. The keys are based on the setup of the payroll process. They also provide the link between data in different areas.

> Always make sure that you are using every key when joining two PAY tables. If you miss one key, you will probably get multiple rows back and the bug will be difficult to detect.

Let's look at the keys in greater detail. The first four keys identify the payroll run that generated the check. Each key identifies an aspect of the payroll. To retrieve checks for a given payroll, you can use the PS_PAY_CALENDAR table to select a payroll and then use these four keys to link to other payroll tables that contain the data you need.

Company

The company field associates a company code with a payroll run. This field is found on numerous tables, but at the employee level it is on the PS_JOB table. Since in PeopleSoft an employee can work for two different companies and receive two different checks (using the employment record number described in Chapter 7), company must be a key. If you are implementing for several different companies, each company must have a separate payroll, and hence a separate pay calendar. They don't have to be different or occur at different times—but they must be set up as separate entries. Each company has its own tax identification number and could have different settings which affect payroll. The company field is verified against PS_COMPANY_TBL.

Paygroup

A paygroup is a value given to a group of employees, providing a separate set of parameters for payroll runs for each group. Paygroups usually split groups of employees by country, by the bank that cuts the check, by pay frequency, by check/direct deposit advice stock differences, by work schedule, or by earnings program. Of course it depends on your implementation, but typically two or three paygroups are created—one for biweekly payrolls and one for weekly or monthly payrolls. The payroll process creates checks according to paygroup; each paygroup is processed separately in sequence. You can establish the employee level paygroup on the PS_JOB table. An employee can only be in one paygroup per job; if the employee has two job records, he or she can conceivably receive two checks cut in different payroll runs.

The paygroup table determines the pay frequency. This one field, PAY_FREQUENCY, determines how an employee's pay is calculated. You will find that you are looking for it quite often. Since paygroups are often defined according to pay frequency, you may be able to just look at the code ('BW' for instance) and tell what the frequency is (biweekly). The code is arbitrary, however. To accurately figure out the pay frequency, you need to look at the paygroup table.

While we're on the topic of paygroups, it is important to point out that many other settings appear on the paygroup table. We won't go into each setting, but you should know that pay maximums, retroactive pay settings, and check sorting parameters are recorded by paygroup. Also, many of the field values on the 'results' tables (PAY tables) are copied directly from the paygroup table. As we look at each PAY table we will take a detailed look at these fields.

Pay Period End Date

The pay period end date field (PAY_END_DT) is the last date of the payroll period. Each check written for an employee has a different pay end date unless it is an off-cycle run (see the off-cycle calendar field). The payroll calculation program uses the pay end date to determine which earnings and deductions to take, to prorate earnings, and to determine holidays and work schedules. Although there are other dates associated with pay calendars, you're nearly always safe if you identify a payroll period by the pay end date. It represents a real date, whereas the check date could be any arbitrary date, and the pay begin date could be the same for two different pay end dates.

Off-Cycle Calendar?

The off-cycle field (PAY_OFF_CYCLE_CAL) tells you whether a payroll run was executed on the normal automatic cycle (e.g., every two weeks), or for a special run. It identifies an *off-cycle calendar.* This is a calendar that strays from the normal payroll calendar. Off-cycle runs usually include a bunch of checks that either didn't make it into an automatic cycle, are intended to correct mistakes made in the automatic cycle, or just need to be written immediately. Off-cycle runs are at the discretion of the user.

An off-cycle calendar entry must have its own pay end date. Note that an off-cycle *check* does not need to appear on an off-cycle *calendar*. A single check that is calculated and confirmed online (using Online Check) will be marked as an off-cycle check, but it does not run on a calendar.

> Off-cycle calendar is one of those fields where you have to stop and think. If it is yes, what does that mean? A yes indicates off-cycle, and a no indicates on-cycle (normal).
>
> The pay off-cycle calendar field links to other payroll tables using the Off-cycle field (OFF_CYCLE). The name is different, but the function is the same. A yes is off-cycle, a no is on-cycle (normal). It is safe to link these two fields: OFF_CYCLE = PAY_OFF_CYCLE_CAL.

Also, consider the processes that need to occur for an off-cycle run. Will the bank need an EFT (Electronic Fund Transfer) file, will the pay check program be used, and will you send data to FLS (Federal Liaison Services)? An off-cycle run, even though it happens irregularly, could trigger many other processes.

The Current Payroll

One of the most basic questions involving payroll is, "What is the most recent payroll run?" To retrieve the most recent pay run, pick the most recent pay end date with a confirmation flag of yes. Now that we've looked at the keys for the PS_PAY_CALENDAR table, let's look in Table 14-5 to see how the recent pay run is retrieved.

▶ **Table 14-5** The most recent confirmed pay run

| The query | ```
SELECT
PC.COMPANY,
PC.PAYGROUP,
PC.PAY_END_DT,
PC.RUN_ID
FROM PS_PAY_CALENDAR PC
WHERE PC.PAY_END_DT =
        (SELECT MAX(PC1.PAY_END_DT)
           FROM PS_PAY_CALENDAR PC1
          WHERE PC1.COMPANY = PC.COMPANY
            AND PC1.PAYGROUP = PC.PAYGROUP
            AND PC1.PAY_END_DT <= '2000-06-01'
``` |
```

▶ **Table 14-5** continued

```
                           AND PC1.PAY_CONFIRM_RUN = 'Y')
           ORDER BY PC.COMPANY, PC.PAYGROUP
```

Returns the data set	COMPANY	PAYGROUP	PAY_END_DT	RUN_ID
	-------	--------	-----------	------
	DKB	BW1	11-MAY-2000	52K
	DKB	MO1	30-NOV-1996	M11
	CBB	MO2	31-JAN-1995	J95
	HRB	BW	23-MAY-2000	B5K
	HRB	SBW	28-FEB-2000	S2K

The returned data set gives us the most recent pay end date for each company and paygroup combination. In the table above, the organization has three companies. Companies DKB and HRB have two paygroups. The most recently confirmed checks correspond to the pay end date for each company and paygroup combination. So company DKB/paygroup MO1 hasn't been paid since late 1996. Employees in company CBB haven't been paid since 1995.

Pay Run ID

Run ID is the key that isn't a key. It's easy to get confused about the function of a run ID. Technical users know that if run ID isn't a key, it won't uniquely define a pay calendar entry. But functional users see run ID in all of the payroll panels and see a setup table called PS_PAY_RUN_TBL.

Another point of confusion: a pay run ID is not a user run ID. Often a panel asks for a "run control ID" when you open it. It is just asking for you to identify which parameter set you want to use. For example, I use a parameter set called 'ATB.' Every time I run something from PeopleSoft, I type in ATB, and PeopleSoft brings back the parameters I used last time. Maybe I ran a report for 3/28/2010. The next time I go to run that report, I type in ATB and up comes 3/28/2010.

When a process asks for "Run control ID:" before opening the panel, it is asking for ATB. If you don't have your own run ID, make sure you choose "Add," and simply type in a new one.

When a process opens a panel, and on that panel asks for a "Pay Run ID:", it usually has a drop down box. In this case it is a *pay run* ID. It is very easy to think run ID = parameters for both types of run IDs. A *pay run* ID is defined in the PS_PAY_RUN_TBL and identifies a particular pay calendar. It has nothing to do with your run ID.

Although pay run ID is not a key, it is an essential element of the payroll process. The pay run ID is used to group several payroll runs (pay calendar entries) into a single run. For example, your organization has six companies, and each company has two paygroups. When you set up your pay calendar table for the 1/15/2000 pay end date, you must create twelve rows, one for each paygroup within each company. Going through all of the payroll calculation and confirmation steps twelve times seems like overkill. So you create a pay run ID, call it A01, and link these calendars to it. Voila, you can run the whole group at once.

In fact, you *must* use pay run IDs. When PeopleSoft creates paysheets, it asks for a pay run ID, and nothing else. In other words, you cannot create paysheets for a single calendar entry unless you assign a unique pay run ID to every calendar entry. One way or another, you'll have to use pay run IDs.

One of the principal functions of the pay run ID is to keep track of dollars that go with a particular payroll. If you execute a payroll run and then realize that 100 employees need a $5 adjustment, you can launch an off-cycle run and attach it to the confirmed pay run ID. You cannot make an off-cycle calendar with the same pay end date as the on-cycle run, but you can give it the same pay run ID. The off-cycle run is then 'linked' with the on-cycle run. Type in the pay run ID, and checks from both runs are returned. The ripple effect is enormous, since all delivered payroll reports ask for a pay run ID. When you tie off-cycle calendars to on-cycle run IDs, the data never gets lost. Pay run IDs are provided to make payroll easier—use them.

Payroll Dates

When we were looking at pay end date above, we noted that this is the only unique date you should use to identify a payroll calendar. There are numerous other dates associated with the calendar, and they have their purposes, too. Let's look at the different dates you need to establish for each calendar.

Pay Period Begin Date

The pay period begin date is the first date of the pay period. It goes hand in hand with the pay end date, but is not a key. The pay begin date should be the day after the pay end date of the previous pay end date, but does not need to be. Pay begin dates often indicate that two pay calendar entries are for different paygroups. A biweekly paygroup will have a pay begin date that is more recent than a monthly paygroup at the end of the month.

Paycheck Issue Date

The paycheck issue date (CHECK_DT) is the date that is printed on the check. It is typically a number of days before the pay end date, since pay checks must be cut, confirmed, mailed, and in your hands near the pay end date at most companies. So the payroll process is run early, and the check date used is often the date the check lands in your mailbox. Since the check date can be anything, do not use it to select checks. It does not delineate different payroll periods— two periods could have the same check date. On the other hand, the check date is useful for figuring out balances. If you are looking at a balance table, the period (1–12) is determined according to the check date, not the pay end date. See the end of this chapter for more on balances.

Weeks in This Period

The number of weeks in a pay period is based on the number of Wednesdays that fall in the period. PeopleSoft doesn't calculate it, so be careful when you do! The period weeks field (PERIOD_WEEKS) is only used in certain states for tax reporting.

Pay Period

The pay period is the number of the pay period, consecutively, in the current month. So if your pay end date is 10/07/2001, this is probably the first pay period of the month (PAY_PERIOD = 1). If it is 10/23/2001, maybe it is the third pay period, depending on your pay frequency. Like the period weeks field, PeopleSoft doesn't calculate this field; it is entered online. The pay period is used by payroll calculation to determine which deductions and additional pays are associated with the pay calendar. If a deduction is to be taken the second period each month, PeopleSoft links it using the PAY_PERIOD field.

Pay Periods Per Year

The pay periods per year field identifies how many periods occur during the year. This is stored for every single calendar and is used for proration. If a calendar is monthly or semi-monthly, it is automatically set to 12 or 24, respectively. But if it is weekly or biweekly, there could be 26, 27, 52, or 53 periods. You must set up your pay calendar appropriately depending on the actual payroll dates that will fall in the current year. The payroll system prorates pay by annualizing an amount by the standard 12, 24, 26, or 52. Then it divides that amount by the number of pay periods per year.

Date Closed

The pay period close date can be set for the pay calendar, but it defaults to the pay end date. The Time and Labor module looks at this date to determine if the hours reported are part of the current pay period. If the Time and Labor module is not installed, the field will not appear on the pay calendar definition panel.

On-Cycle Pay End Date

The on-cycle pay end date field is used for FLSA (Fair Labor Standards Act) processing. Its name is confusing, since the field can only be used for off-cycle calendars. The field determines when the pay period ends for FLSA calculation of overtime, for those paygroups (or companies) where FLSA tracking is turned on. In other words, what should the on-cycle end date be for this off-cycle calendar? When the calendar is entirely off-cycle, this field allows you to change the FLSA tracking end date to a custom value.

Multiple Jobs

The single check for multiple jobs (SINGLE_CHECK) field indicates if employees in this payroll run received a single check for two different jobs (two job records). In order to get one check for two jobs, the two jobs must share the same benefits (same benefit number). The single check option can be set at the paygroup level; the SINGLE_CHECK field only indicates if the payroll run contains single checks.

Taking Deductions

The deductions taken (DED_TAKEN) field indicates how deductions are taken for the pay calendar: the deduction table governs (D), no deductions are taken (N), or the deduction table subset governs (S). A deduction table subset only includes certain deductions that you want to take with this payroll run. For example, if you run bonus checks, you probably want to create a deduction subset that doesn't include deductions like health plan and dental plan. When PeopleSoft cuts the bonus checks, it only takes the deductions you've specified, not all of the usual deductions. The subset ID is placed in the DED_SUBSET_ID field to link to the appropriate subset. For more on deductions, see Chapter 17.

GENERAL LEDGER

Payroll runs are linked to general ledger systems. Each time a payroll runs, the data usually needs to be sent to a processing system in the financial area, called General Ledger (GL), that charts each paycheck on a financial ledger. PeopleSoft HRMS isn't meant to be an accounting system and knows that paycheck data needs to be sent to GL. You'll find that GL fields are sprinkled throughout PeopleSoft, allowing you to link earnings, deductions, and taxes to GL account numbers.

On the pay calendar table there are several fields to use for GL processing. The GL interface run field (GL_INTERFACE_RUN) tells you if the delivered General Ledger interface was executed. If you're not using the delivered interface, this field will probably be no, but you can set up your program to use it. Once the flag is set to yes, you can't make any adjustments to the payroll—so think about it first.

The pay calendar also provides a way to prorate your payroll dollars to fit a GL accounting cycle. Ledgers are often closed for a month on an off-beat date, like March 25, as the last day of the month. This makes it difficult to decide which paychecks fall in which GL period. To compensate, the accrual percent field (ACCRUAL_PCT) on the pay calendar table lets you enter a rate to apply to make payroll periods jive with the GL calendar. If your pay end date is 3/23/2001, and GL wants dollars as of 3/25/2001, the percentage can add two prorated days of pay. You enter this percentage only in the 3/23 pay calendar.

Then, in your next calendar, 4/05/2001, you leave the percentage blank and turn on the reverse accruals field (REVERSE_FLAG) to deduct those two days. The reverse accruals field tells a pay calendar to reverse the proration it took in the previous pay period.

THE PAYROLL PROCESS

The payroll process can be a stressful part of implementation—after all, if PeopleSoft can't cut a check, what good is it? Implementing PeopleSoft payroll can come down to one rule: If you can't get payroll to run, the whole thing is a failure.

PeopleSoft caught on quickly, and in each new version it provides better tools to debug your payroll process. Payroll error messages are carefully evaluated and have detailed descriptions in the user documentation. And the process has just three simple steps. We will look at each step individually, paying particular attention to the state of the payroll data at the end of each step. The three steps are:

1. Paysheet creation (open up the payroll)
2. Payroll calculation (calculate the checks)
3. Payroll confirm (close the payroll)

1. Paysheets

A paysheet is PeopleSoft's terminology for "the place we put the checks." In truth, it is a couple of tables: PS_PAY_LINE/PS_PAY_PAGE and PS_PAY_CHECK. But if you think of a green ledger book, and think of each paycheck occupying a line in the book, the terminology is easier to grasp. A page contains lines and each line represents a check.

The first step in the payroll process is to create paysheets. When PeopleSoft creates paysheets, it does a thorough job. Pages and lines are created, and PeopleSoft also calculates gross earnings amounts for each employee, figures out holidays, proration, and more. The to-do list includes:

- Set up earnings records, which allows you to make adjustments and apply overrides to the employee's earnings, one-time deductions/taxes/garnishments, and hours.
- Establish holidays during the pay period and calculate hours and earnings for them.
- Figure out prorations for employees who have job changes mid-period.

Basically, paysheet creation gets things moving by doing the initial calculations for earnings. PeopleSoft takes the employee's salary or hourly rate, figures out how many hours he or she worked, figures out earnings, and makes any necessary adjustments due to one-time events or job changes. These rows are created on the PS_PAY_EARNINGS and PS_PAY_OTH_EARNS tables during paysheet creation. Depending on the circumstances, several rows for a single employee might be created. Sometimes earnings are split between two departments, the employee has a mid-period pay rate change, the employee has two jobs, or the employee works in two locations. All of these factors are considered during paysheet creation.

The process does *not* create a paycheck record on PS_PAY_CHECK. The regular deductions, taxes, and garnishments are all missing. PeopleSoft has created paylines, which are stored in the PS_PAY_LINE table with a copy of certain job table fields. This payline is fed into the payroll calculation process (the next step) to produce the actual paychecks.

Running the paysheet creation process separately from payroll calculation has one advantage—you can make adjustments. If you just let PeopleSoft figure out all of the earnings, you will have some issues. What about someone who just terminated, or someone who worked extra overtime recently? These adjustments can be made to the paysheets anytime before the payroll calculation, using online panels.

Because adjustments are continually being made after the paysheet creation, PeopleSoft automatically looks at the job table for any changes to department, location, salary, etc. when performing the next step, pay calculation. Each payline can be set up to accept these changes or to reject these changes. If you enter a one-time change directly to a paysheet, however, the payline will be set to reject subsequent changes to JOB information.

OK to Pay

One of the fields on each payline is the OK-to-pay field. The payroll process uses the OK-to-pay field to skip certain checks. Often OK-to-pay is set to no for hourly employees since their hours must be manually entered into the system. And if a process fails, like payroll calculation, you can set the offending paylines to have an OK to pay of no.

If OK-to-pay is no, the last step of the payroll process will remove any earnings calculations associated with the payline. The payroll confirmation performs this cleanup effort. The checks for these employees will need to be regenerated with new paysheets.

Payroll Calculation Audit

Before running the payroll calculation you can execute a delivered SQR program, PAY035, to report on possible errors. This program reviews the basic integrity of the data—do items link correctly, and are valid codes used throughout? The program can be run from the menu Go ➤ Compensate Employees ➤ Manage Payroll Process ➤ Report 2 ➤ Precalc Audit. Table 14-6 lists the items this SQR checks.

▶ **Table 14-6** Precalculation audit SQR

Error message
Pay page missing pay calendar entry.
Pay tax override missing pay earnings.
Canadian tax override missing pay earnings.
Pay garnishment override missing pay earnings.
Invalid North American pay rate code in pay earnings.
Invalid North American overtime rate code in pay earnings.
Invalid North American other pay rate code in pay earnings.
Payline missing pay page.
Pay earning missing payline.

▶ **Table 14-6** continued

Pay earnings employee ID does not match payline employee ID.

State tax data missing unemployment/disability insurance jurisdiction selection.

Earning has missing/invalid state tax data.

Earning has missing/invalid company local tax data.

Pay other earning line missing pay earning line.

Pay one time missing pay earning line.

---

2. Payroll Calculation

The pay calculation is the core of the whole payroll process. PeopleSoft takes the earnings, figures out the taxes, deductions, and garnishments that should/can be taken and comes up with the net check amount.

There are a couple of options for payroll calculation. You can run the payroll calculation in a preliminary mode (see the payroll flags section later on) to get out all of the bugs. You can also tell the payroll calculation program to recalculate all check amounts or to use the amounts as they are, applying employee-level changes. This feature updates the earnings calculations performed during the paysheet creation. PeopleSoft automatically detects changes to employee-level tables that could affect pay and applies these changes during the calculation process. If you changed a non-employee-level table (like department or location), you need to select the option to re-calculate, since many employees could be affected.

Payroll calculation is principally concerned with taxes. The pay calculation program figures out taxable earnings, determines before-and after-tax deductions and combines these amounts to arrive at a net pay figure.

Once you have worked through any errors in the payroll calculation, you can turn off the preliminary calculation run option and run the final calculation. This sets a flag on the pay calendar table that tells pay confirmation that everything is okay. If you try to run pay confirmation with the preliminary calculation flag on, you will receive an error message.

3. Payroll Confirmation

Now the checks are ready to be cut. Some additional processing occurs:

- Balance tables are updated (see the section on accumulators, later in this chapter).
- Deduction arrears and leave accruals are updated.
- Check numbers/advice numbers are assigned.

The amounts for the current check are applied to the appropriate period in the balance tables. This period is based on the check date. Note that amounts can only be added to the balance tables in order of date. So if you've confirmed your February checks and then go to confirm your January checks, the January amounts won't make it into the balance tables. Nor will your payroll confirm successfully. To prevent this from happening, *always confirm payroll runs in order of check date.*

Error Resolution

When running a large payroll for the first time, relax. Things will come up that you didn't expect. Work through each roadblock and record the steps you take so you can move quickly the next time. Usually there is an error somewhere in the setup information for an employee, whether it is benefits calculations, additional pay restrictions, deduction errors, or tax issues.

To find the errors, look under Go ➤ Compensate Employees ➤ Manage Payroll Process U.S. ➤ Inquire ➤ Payroll Error Messages. Each message is listed in detail. Where possible, an employee ID and record number is provided for reference.

Sometimes there is no error at all—just a big crash. In these cases, take a careful look at the volumes of data you are processing. The COBOL programs use arrays, which are restricted in size. An array is a place for storing a table of information in memory—like a spreadsheet—accessed using cell-like references (such as 'A2'). If PeopleSoft places all of the benefit plans in an array and you have 600,000 plans, you could hit the upper limit and crash. The solution involves opening up the COBOL program and setting the maximum to a higher number. Be sure to communicate with your PeopleSoft account manager when making these changes.

The Continue with Errors Feature

The continue-with-errors field (CONFIRM_ERRORS) tells PeopleSoft if it should keep going when it encounters an error during the payroll calculation process. Only certain error messages are considered "continue" messages. You can define which errors PeopleSoft should ignore on the Go ➤ Define Business Rules ➤ Define Payroll Process ➤ Setup 2 ➤ Pay Message Table panel. When PeopleSoft encounters one of these errors, it skips the check and goes on to the next one. If the error is not defined as one that can be continued, it creates an error message and could halt the payroll process.

When checks do error out, the error pay end date (ERR_PAY_END_DT) identifies the date errant checks should be re-processed on. So if a check has an error, and it is a "continue" error, the record will be skipped. That check will then be automatically linked to the payroll for the pay end date stored here. You must fix the error before the next payroll run.

Identifying Payroll Process Achievements

To see where you are in the process, look at the pay calendar table. Several flags indicate where each calendar is—the flags can also be viewed at Go ➤ Define Business Rules ➤ Define Payroll Process ➤ Setup 2 ➤ Pay Calendar Table. This is a strange place to go when you just need to know if the paysheets were created successfully, but it gives you a good overall picture of the process.

At the bottom of the panel you'll see several grayed-out flags. These flags indicate what has run and what still needs to be done. Let's look at each individual flag.

Paysheets Run

The paysheets run field (PAY_SHEETS_RUN) tells you if the paysheets have been created. If the PSPPYBLD COBOL program has executed successfully, and paysheets exist for the pay calendar, this field is set to yes. Paysheet creation opens the sheets and creates earnings for each employee that is to be paid. Once paysheets are created, users can create checks through the payroll process or online, and can place these checks on the paysheets. Typically paysheets remain uncreated until the payroll process begins. Paysheet creation is the first step—it "opens" the payroll period.

Payroll Preliminary Calculation Run

The payroll preliminary calculation run field (PAY_PRECALC_RUN) is set to yes if a preliminary calculation was run. Preliminary calculations are performed to correct errors before the final calculation. Both a preliminary calculation and a final calculation perform exactly the same functions, but the payroll confirm won't confirm you unless you've run the final calculation. If a preliminary calculation was run, checks, deductions, and taxes will exist.

A preliminary calculation is not always executed. In these cases the flag will remain off. Always use this flag in conjunction with the payroll calculation run flag, which could be set to yes if no preliminary run occurred.

Payroll Calculation Run

The payroll calculation run field (PAY_CALC_RUN) stores a yes value when the final payroll calculation is successfully executed. It essentially means that PeopleSoft took the employee's earnings (calculated during paysheet creation), deductions, taxes, and garnishments, and created records in the database for each. Prior to this step, you can't look up these items for the pay period. The PS_PAY_CHECK table is also populated by the payroll calculation. Checks are complete at this point, but no check numbers are assigned.

Payroll Confirmation Started

The payroll confirmation started field (PAY_CONFIRM_START) tells you that the confirmation has begun but is not yet complete. Errors are probably being corrected. The pay confirm process sets this flag to yes as soon as it starts.

Payroll Confirmation Run

The payroll confirmation run field is *the* indicator (PAY_CONFIRM_RUN). It tells you when you can finally breathe easily again. When it is set to yes, all of the paychecks are done and have check numbers. All of the balances (earnings, tax, etc.) are updated. A confirmed payroll cannot be edited without running the payroll unconfirm process.

Paychecks Run

This field has a very simple-sounding name, and as it so happens, no function at all. PeopleSoft does not use this field, and it is usually just defaulted to no.

Off-Cycle Calculations Outstanding

If off-cycle calculations are outstanding for the pay calendar, this flag (PAY_OFF_CYCLE) is set to yes. Remember, only on-cycle checks are calculated when the payroll calculation process executes. An off-cycle check, by definition, is calculated and confirmed outside of the payroll process. If off-cycle checks reside on the pay pages for the current on-cycle calendar, and they are not calculated, this flag will be set to yes.

Off-Cycle Closed

When no additional off-cycle checks can be created for a payroll run, the off-cycle closed flag (PAY_OFF_CYCLE_CLS) is set to yes. Once the payroll is confirmed, and this flag is set, no further off-cycle checks can be created for that payroll run.

BATCH PROCESSING PAYROLL DATA

One of the huge challenges of running payroll interfaces and reports is figuring out how to select data. PeopleSoft is flexible enough to allow you to cut checks on-cycle, off-cycle, for the same or different run IDs, and for any pay end date. Determining which records should go to the general ledger system or appear on a deduction report can be tricky.

PeopleSoft's delivered processes are a useful guide. The payroll process asks for different parameters at different times. Table 14-7 lists each process and the parameters requested.

▶ **Table 14-7**   A guideline: PeopleSoft payroll process parameters

Process	Parameters
Paysheet Creation	Pay run ID
Pay Calculation	Full pay run options (see table 14-8): pay run ID or particular calendar
Pay Confirmation	Full pay run options (see table 14-8): pay run ID or particular calendar
Check Print	Full pay run options (see table 14-8): pay run ID or particular calendar
Direct Deposit File	Pay run ID or a company/paygroup/pay end date combination. Cannot run only on-cycle or only off-cycle calendars for a run ID, and cannot run for only a specific set of paysheet pages.

Three of these processes use a common module for determining parameters. It lets you select according to run ID or according to a particular on- or off-cycle pay calendar. These parameters are listed in Table 14-8.

▶ **Table 14-8**   PeopleSoft's delivered payroll parameter set

Field	Function
Pay run ID	Enter a run ID.
On/Off Cycle	Choose On (O), Off (F), or Both (B) on-and off-cycle calendars.
Process All Calendars?	There is more than one pay calendar for the run ID—process them all or just one?
Company, Paygroup, Pay End Date	If you choose just one calendar, type in the company, paygroup, and pay end date of the calendar.
Off-Cycle Page Range	If you choose off-cycle processing, you can enter a page-from and a page-through. If you don't enter anything, PeopleSoft will use 1 through 9999.

These parameters handle most of the possibilities, but automating these parameters is challenging. How do you know which run ID to use this period without looking it up? Doesn't the PeopleSoft database contain this information?

There are two possibilities for resolving this issue. If you predefine every run ID and never define them on-the-fly, you can simply store a list of run IDs. Each pay period, you can run with the next one. That is the easy way, but often payroll departments need to define run IDs during production. Perhaps an off-cycle calendar needs its own paysheets, or maybe an off-cycle calendar needs to be processed before the on-cycle paysheets are opened. In these situations, batch payroll interfaces and reports need to consider which records to send according to the dates on the pay calendar table.

Associating Batch Requirements with Payroll Dates

Technically you should be able to choose a date, let's say the pay end date, and run for all dollars between that date and the previous pay end date.

That works fine for most applications. Certain programs, though, like a direct deposit file, need to send the money right away even if it is off-cycle. They cannot wait until the next on-cycle pay run. These programs need to be executed separately. And, when the on-cycle does run, you must make sure you do not include the dollars you have already sent.

Programs that execute off-cycle should run for every unique pay end date. If an off-cycle run occurs, it will have a new pay end date. Run for that pay end date. Then, when the on-cycle comes around, run for the on-cycle pay end date. And so on. Since pay end dates must be unique for each calendar, you won't have to worry about sending something twice.

For normal programs that do not execute right away, you *must* pick up any off-cycle calendars with your regular on-cycle run. In this case, you can use the on-cycle calendar as your time frame (if all paygroups share pay end dates) and select everything in between:

1. Look at the pay calendar; retrieve the pay begin and end dates of the most recently confirmed on-cycle payroll.

2. Select all calendars, on or off-cycle, that have pay end dates which fall between the begin and end dates selected in step 1.

This method ensures that all calendars are retrieved, even if off-cycle calendars were added during production. It is only necessary if you are adding run IDs on-the-fly during production for special off-cycle runs. If you can keep your run ID definitions permanent, your interfaces and reports can simply ask for a run ID. The run ID can be looked up on the pay calendar table, and all related pay calendars can be retrieved.

ACCUMULATORS AND BUCKETS

Often you need a cumulative amount, such as the employee's pay year to date, or the amount deducted for health insurance in a given month. You don't care how many paychecks the employee received and how much each one was for. You just want to know the total by year, quarter, or month.

PeopleSoft's balance tables provide this information. The payroll confirmation process makes sure that these tables are absolutely accurate. They reflect confirmed paychecks. Table 14-9 provides descriptions of the major balance tables.

▶ **Table 14-9**   Major payroll balance tables

Table	Stores
PS_EARNINGS_BAL	Regular and overtime earnings and hours, special earnings and hours (auto allowance, bonus, etc.)
PS_DEDUCTION_BAL	Deductions taken
PS_GARN_BALANCE	Garnishments against paycheck taken
PS_TAX_BALANCE	Federal, state, and local taxes taken

Although the balance tables provide a great convenience—all of the numbers in one place—they can be tricky to navigate. Let's look at the different keys we need to provide to get data returned:

Employee ID.   Easy to obtain—look at PS_JOB.

Company.   Use the company from the employee's PS_JOB record.

Balance ID.   The balance ID lets you create different types of balances. PeopleSoft is delivered with the calendar year balance (i.e., a balance amount for every month). This balance ID is 'CY' and is usually the one to use. If your organization uses a custom calendar to track balances, you may want to use that ID. Essentially the balance ID determines what a period means (see Balance Period below).

Balance Year.   This is the year for the balance, in numeric form.

Balance Quarter.   This is the quarter for the balance. If you want the balance for a particular quarter, use this field. If you want it for a particular period (i.e., month), there is no need to provide the quarter field.

Balance Period.   A period is a portion of a year. If your balance ID divides the year into 20, then the period would be 1 through 20. The common balance ID of 'CY' divides the year into 12 months, or 12 periods.

Special balance.   The special balance field identifies custom-designed buckets of earnings. An accumulator can be set up to combine earnings into a single earnings code. If you have a performance bonus and an attendance bonus, you can set them both up to accumulate into a unique earnings code called 'BON.' If the earnings balance is for 'BON.' the special balance field will be 'Y.' Two other rows will also exist for the employee—one for each bonus earning code, but their special balance fields will be set to 'N.'

Earnings code.   The earnings code tells you which earning the balance is for. You can look up the name on PS_EARNINGS_TBL. Each balance table has its own code (deduction, garnishment, tax).

Table 14-10 shows what is returned when we do a select on the earnings balance table when the current date is 06/07/2000.

▶ **Table 14-10**   Earnings balances

The query	`SELECT`
	`EB.ERNCD,`
	`EB.SPCL_BALANCE,`
	`EB.GRS_YTD,`
	`EB.GRS_QTD,`
	`EB.GRS_MTD`
	`FROM PS_EARNINGS_BAL EB`
	`WHERE EB.EMPLID          = 'BOZO'`
	`   AND EB.COMPANY        = 'CBB'`
	`   AND EB.BALANCE_ID     = 'CY'`
	`   AND EB.BALANCE_YEAR   = 2000`
	`   AND EB.BALANCE_PERIOD =`
	`(SELECT MAX(EB1.BALANCE_PERIOD)`
	`   FROM PS_EARNINGS_BAL EB1`
	`  WHERE EB1.EMPLID        = EB.EMPLID`
	`    AND EB1.COMPANY       = EB.COMPANY`
	`    AND EB1.BALANCE_ID    = EB.BALANCE_ID`
	`    AND EB1.BALANCE_YEAR  = EB.BALANCE_YEAR`
	`    AND EB1.BALANCE_PERIOD <= 6)`

Returns the data set	ERNCD	SPCL_BALANCE	GRS_YTD	GRS_QTD	GRS_MTD
	PER	N	2075	900	300
	FLX	N	420	180	60
	REG	N	39726.03	17430.76	5901.04
	401	Y	39726.03	17430.76	5901.04

We get a lot of data back. What does it mean? It looks like this employee had three earnings this year: performance bonus, flexible spending, and regular. The 401 is an accumulator of earnings that apply to a 401(k) plan. It contains duplicated dollars from previous 401(k) earnings. The employee earned $5,901.04 this period, $17,430.76 this quarter so far, and $39,726.03 this year so far. If you look at the FLX earning, you can readily see that the earning is about $60 per month, and seven months have passed (=$420). The seventh month is the third month of the second quarter of the year (=$180).

To figure out the total year-to-date earnings for the employee, you can use a modified version of the query above, as shown in table 14-11.

Deduction, tax, and garnishment balances are stored in the same fashion. We discuss each of these items in a separate chapter. Apply the keys detailed in these chapters, and the balances are simple to retrieve.

▶ **Table 14-11** The total earnings year to date

The query	``` SELECT SUM(EB.GRS_YTD) FROM PS_EARNINGS_BAL EB WHERE EB.EMPLID = 'BOZO' AND EB.COMPANY = 'CBB' AND EB.BALANCE_ID = 'CY' AND EB.SPCL_BALANCE = 'N' AND EB.BALANCE_YEAR = 2000 AND EB.BALANCE_PERIOD = (SELECT MAX(EB1.BALANCE_PERIOD) FROM PS_EARNINGS_BAL EB1 WHERE EB1.EMPLID = EB.EMPLID AND EB1.COMPANY = EB.COMPANY AND EB1.BALANCE_ID = EB.BALANCE_ID AND EB1.BALANCE_YEAR = EB.BALANCE_YEAR) ```
Returns the data set	``` SUM(GRS_YTD) ----------- 42221.03 ```

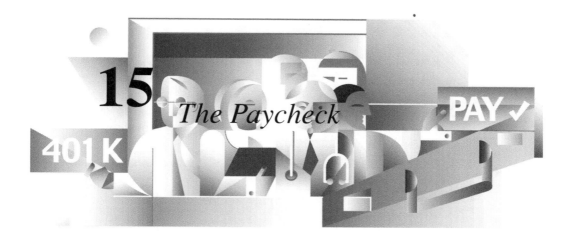

15
The Paycheck

The paycheck table is the one place in PeopleSoft payroll where you must inevitably look. Although only a few fields are unique to each paycheck, like net pay and total gross pay, the paycheck links each pay line on a paysheet to an employee ID. In Chapter 14 we discussed the major payroll keys and demonstrated how to link to the paycheck table. Here we will look at the other fields on the paycheck table and at some alternative ways users might cut a check.

> Note that although everything is called a paycheck, this includes pay advices/ direct deposit statements. An advice is simply a paycheck that doesn't get printed; it is sent on an interface file. Up until that point, it is considered a paycheck and is stored on the paycheck table like any other check.

HOW DO CHECKS GET CREATED?

Sometimes the way checks get created in PeopleSoft can be confusing. There are so many different kinds—online checks, on- and off-cycle checks, final checks, reversals and reprints. How do they all relate?

The process is actually quite simple. Start by considering the normal payroll process. Let's say our pay frequency is biweekly. Every two weeks, we run the payroll process. We follow a routine, in an order roughly like this:

1. Hire employees, establishing their salary and tax location and benefits elections.

2. Enter any additional pay settings (repeating earnings other than regular earnings). Enter general deduction settings (repeating basic deductions).

3. At the end of the pay period, perform necessary batch processing. This could require feeding hours into the system for earnings, and/or dollar amounts for deductions.

4. Run benefits administration (see section 4) to create benefits deductions settings.

5. Execute the on-cycle payroll process (described in Chapter 14).

All other PeopleSoft check-writing functions are outside of this normal routine. Each time a special check is written there are two options. You can either place the check on an on-cycle payroll (i.e., write it, but let it be paid later), or make an off-cycle payroll/off-cycle page and print it now. The features you choose, of course, depend on the timing of what you need to do.

THE PAYCHECK TABLE

First let's explore the paycheck table in detail (Table 15-1).

▶ **Table 15-1** Paycheck: PS_PAY_CHECK

Structure	Several rows per pay end date, per employee ID. Typically one row per employee ID and pay end date.
Keys	Company
	paygroup
	Pay end date
	Off cycle
	Page #
	Line #
	Separate Check #
Alternate keys	Check #
	Employee ID
	Name
Sub-records included	Address sub-record
Panels to look at	Go ➤ Compensate Employees ➤ Manage Payroll Process ➤ Inquire ➤ Paycheck Data

The Rest of the Payroll Keys

Now that we're looking at actual checks, there are several additional keys to be aware of. These keys tie a paycheck to a pay line on a pay page and uses this page/line combination link to earnings, deductions, taxes and garnishments.

The page number (PAGE#) represents the "page" the check is stored on, using the paysheet metaphor. Paychecks are stored on "paysheets," similar to how a manual payroll system works. A group of checks is stored on each page. The number of paylines (one line per employee) that falls on each sheet can be specified on the company table. The page number is verified against the PS_PAY_PAGE table.

The payline number (LINE#) represents a single employee on a paysheet. Paylines are created during the paysheet creation process. One line is set up per employee, unless more are required. An employee could have transferred to a new company or paygroup, and PeopleSoft knows that two checks will be needed (i.e., two paylines). If the employee changed locations or jobs mid-period, a new pay earnings line is created, but not necessarily a new check (the separate check flag must be activated). The payline number is verified against the PS_PAY_LINE table.

Together, the page, line number, and separate check number indicate where the paycheck is on the 'ledger' of checks for this payroll run.

When there is an additional check for an employee, a separate check number further identifies the specific items on it. When scheduling an additional pay, you can specify that the additional earnings be placed on a separate check. In the separate check field, you can enter a sequence number from 1 through 9. This number is used as a key to identify a separate paycheck. Typically the separate check number is set to zero for every check. When a separate check does occur, the sequence numbering begins with one. These checks appear on the same page and line number as the base check and are only distinguished by the separate check number.

Alternate Keys for Finding a Check

Employee ID

The paycheck table, as the core of the process, stores information about the employee. An employee ID is associated with each paycheck. This field is required, and you can use it to look up checks. With a pay end date and an employee ID, you can easily query for all checks the employee received. Remember, though, that the presence of a record on the paycheck table does not guarantee that the check actually made it through confirmation and into the employee's hands.

If an employee is working in more than one job, and receives a different paycheck for each job, the employee record number will identify which job the paycheck is linked to. Employee record number is not required, since most employees work at only one job, in which case the field will be zero.

Name

Another way to look up paychecks is by name. The name field is placed on the check from the PS_PERSONAL_DATA table. It represents the name of the employee as of the day the check was cut. This is different from the personal data name today.

There is another name on the check—the paycheck name (PAYCHECK_NAME). This field can be set separately from the employee name on the employment table (see Chapter 11).

Check number

If you have the actual check in your hand and can obtain a check number, this is the best way to get information. The check number is assigned after payroll confirmation and is exactly what is printed on the check, just like the check number in a checkbook. Note, however, that check number is not a key, nor is it required.

PeopleSoft automatically populates this field according to the last check number used for the particular form ID (if you are using different paycheck stocks). If stock A is used, the next check number might be 10, but for stock B the next check number could be 200. You must define a form ID on PS_PAY_FORM_TBL for each type of stock you plan to use. Then you can specify which forms are used on the paygroup table. PeopleSoft populates the form ID when you create paysheets according to the form ID on the paygroup table, and gets the check number according to the last-used number on PS_PAY_FORM_TBL.

The check number can be reset, so the same number can be used twice in PeopleSoft—and often is. You may have a form ID for checks, and one for advices. In this case, it is likely that you'll encounter two checks with the same check number—one will be a check, the other will be an advice. In other words, don't rely on a check number to identify a check in PeopleSoft. Use the full set of keys.

Social Security Number

The Social Security number for the employee is placed on the paycheck table mostly for the convenience of other programs. Direct deposits to the bank must include the Social Security number, and the paycheck statement includes the SSN. Although you can use it like an employee ID, remember that it is not a unique, nor a required field (see Chapter 6 on personal data).

Delivering Paychecks

One might think that the payroll process ends with payroll confirmation, but the process does not end until the check lands in the employee's hands. Sorting and delivering paychecks, especially for a large company, is a major concern. PeopleSoft accommodates employers who send checks home through the mail as well as companies that rely on internal distribution.

You can choose how employees receive their paychecks on the employment table. When payroll runs, it copies this value and the appropriate address. The two are written to the paycheck table. The address, then, is printed on the check itself. Table 15-2 provides a description of the available options. The default value is 'H' (mail to home).

▶ **Table 15-2**   Paycheck address options

Value	Delivery Method	Address to Use	Description
1	Internal	Home Address	Place home address on check.
2	Internal	Mailing Address	Place mailing address on check.
3	Internal	Custom Address	Place custom address on check.
C	Mail	Custom Address	Place custom address on check and mail to this address.
E	N/A	N/A	This option is not used on the PS_PAY_CHECK table.
H	Mail	Home Address	Place home address on check and mail to this address.
M	Mail	Mailing Address	Place mailing address on check and mail to this address.

When the address is copied to the paycheck table, it is stored in the address sub-record. This address could come from PS_PERSONAL_DATA (home and mailing) or PS_EMPLOYMENT (custom).

If the check is distributed internally, the location field can be used. On the payroll data panels, under Maintain Payroll Data U.S., you can specify which location code is used for paycheck sorting for each employee. The location field on the paycheck table identifies which location was used for the particular paycheck.

Sorting

Regardless of the distribution method, PeopleSoft needs to know the sort order for the checks. Two fields, the distribution keys (PAYCHECK_DIST_KEY1, 2), are used to sort paychecks. PeopleSoft populates these fields with a sequence of values separated by forward slashes (/). You can define these values on the Go ➤ Define Business Rules ➤ Define Payroll Process ➤ Setup 2 ➤ Paygroup Table 6 panel. Checks can be sorted according to department, name, employee ID, FLSA status, location, mail drop, shift, employee type, or supervisor ID. PeopleSoft then takes the actual values of the two 90-character fields and combines them into one long field to use for sorting. You'll notice that the key 2 field doesn't quite start with anything; that's because it is only a continuation of the key 1 field.

Paycheck Accounting

Paychecks must be linked to a department in the organization. This allows financial areas to determine the expenses of each department individually and can assist with computing profitability of the company.

This link also helps when an employee works in two different departments, splitting his time. The department ID field on the paycheck clarifies such situations, where hours and dollars are split. If an employee works in department 002, the paycheck will reflect department 002. If time is split between two departments (usually when an employee switches departments mid-period), the department ID will identify which paycheck amounts go to which department.

With the advent of version 7.5, PeopleSoft added the capability of linking checks to a business unit. Time and money are not split according to business unit—if they are, it will appear to be a department change. Business unit is simply a way to sort payroll data, and several delivered reports sort checks by it.

How Much Did I Get?

The payroll calculation process is complex. A few fields post some of the results to the paycheck for quick reference. For example, the employee type is on each paycheck, since the calculation depends on whether an employee is hourly or salaried. Employees can change their type often (especially if they are temporary), so this field is essential to know for each check. Employee type is discussed further in Chapter 7.

The total fields on the check table provide actual amounts rather than calculation parameters. When combined, these amounts give a quick overview of what happened during payroll calculation. They provide the sum total of the major pieces of the paycheck: earnings, other earnings, taxes, and deductions. Earnings and other earnings are combined to form the total gross. The total taxes field includes all employee taxes (employer taxes, usually identified by an 'ER' in the description, are not included). The total deductions field includes all before-and after-tax deductions, excluding deductions set up as taxable and nontaxable benefits. When you add all these figures together, you get the net pay. The detailed calculation of gross earnings less deductions and less taxes to determine net pay is what a payroll person refers to as the "gross to net."

Table 15-3 demonstrates how all the pieces fit together for a sample paycheck, and Figure 15-1 shows what an actual PeopleSoft-generated check looks like.

▶ **Table 15-3** Sample paycheck total calculations

Table	Class	Description	Amount	Used in calculation
PS_PAY_EARNINGS		Regular earnings	3333.69	3333.69
PS_PAY_OTH_EARNS		Holiday	161.31	161.31
		Car Allowance	250	250
		Flex Credits	60	60
PS_PAY_CHECK		**Total Gross**		**$3805.00**
PS_PAY_DEDUCTION	A (after tax)	Parking	50	50
	A	U.S. Savings Bond	50	50
	A	United Way	5	5
	B (before tax)	Medical Plan	74	74
	B	Dental Plan	15	15
	A	Vision Plan 8 8		
	B	Life Insurance Plan	3.57	3.57
	A	Supplemental Life Deduction	21.84	21.84
	B	401(k) Deduction	166.68	166.68
	P (non-taxable pretax benefit)	401(k) Deduction	83.34	
	B	Health Care FSA Deduction	50	50
	B	Dependent Care FSA	50	50
PS_PAY_CHECK		**Total Deductions**		**$494.09**
PS_PAY_TAX	D	Federal OASDI/Disability EE	235.91	235.91
	E	Federal OASDI/Disability ER	235.91	
	F	Federal FICA Hospital Ins. EE	55.18	55.18
	H	Federal Withholding	405.61	405.61
	Q	Federal FICA Hospital Ins. ER	55.18	
	U	Federal Unemployment ER	25.56	
	D	California OASDI/Disability EE	38.05	38.05
	H	California Withholding	85.12	85.12
	U	California Unemployment ER	111.82	
PS_PAY_CHECK		**Total Taxes**		**$819.87**
PS_PAY_CHECK		**Net Pay** ($3805 less 494.09 less 819.87)		**$2491.04**

Test Company   Pay Group: MO1-Monthly Payroll   Business Unit: USADM
Main Street   Pay Begin Date: 12/15/1999   Check #:   0100114
Cupertino, CA 95014   Pay End Date: 01/01/2000   Check Date: 01/03/2000

Bozo T. Clown	Employee ID: BOZO		TAX DATA:	Federal	CA State
1 Main Street	Department: 10201		Marital Status:	Married	Married (one income)
Cupertino, CA 95014	Location: Corporate Headquarters		Allowances:	1	1
	Job Title: Chief Executive Officer		Addl. Pct.:		
SSN: 999-99-9999	Pay Rate: $6,593.35 Monthly		Addl. Amt.:		

HOURS AND EARNINGS

| | | Current | | YTD | | **TAXES** | | |
Description	Rate	Hours	Earnings	Hours	Earnings	Description	Current	YTD
Regular			6,289.04	192.00	12,578.08	Fed Withholdng	531.52	1,399.04
Holiday (Statutory)	38.038558	8.00	304.31	16.00	608.62	Fed MED/EE	101.28	202.56
Car Allowance			300.00		600.00	Fed OASDI/EE	433.05	866.10
Flex Credits			60.00		120.00	CA Withholdng	124.10	337.47
						CA OASDI/EE	34.77	69.53
Total:		8.00	6,953.35	208.00	13,906.70	Total:	1,224.72	2,874.70

| **BEFORE-TAX DEDUCTIONS** | | | **AFTER-TAX DEDUCTIONS** | | | **EMPLOYER PAID BENEFITS** | | |
Description	Current	YTD	Description	Current	YTD	Description	Current	YTD
Medical Plan	309.00	618.00	Garnishment - Tax Levy	345.00	345.00	Life Insurance Plan	22.91	45.82
Dental Plan	18.75	37.50	Parking	75.00	150.00	Life Insurance Plan*	31.32	62.64
Life Insurance Plan	22.91	45.82						
Short-Term Disability Plan	14.00	28.00						
Health Care FSA Deduction	400.00	600.00						
Dependent Care FSA	2,000.00	3,000.00						
Total:	2,764.66	4,329.32	Total:	420.00	495.00	* Taxable		

	TOTAL GROSS	**FED TAXABLE GROSS**	**TOTAL TAXES**	**TOTAL DEDUCTIONS**	**NET PAY**
Current:	6,953.35	4,220.01	1,224.72	3,184.66	2,543.97
YTD:	13,906.70	9,640.02	2,874.70	4,824.32	6,207.68

PTO HOURS	YTD		**NET PAY DISTRIBUTION**	
Start Balance:	80.0		Check #0100114	2,543.97
+ Earned:	80.0			
+ Bought:			Total:	2,543.97
- Taken:				
- Sold:				
+ Adjustments:				
End Balance:	160.0			

MESSAGE: This is a test message.

Test Company   90-1021/1221   FEDERAL AMERICA BANK   Check No.
Main Street   12 Elm Street   100114
Building 6   Cupertino, CA 95014
Cupertino CA 95014

Date: 01/03/2000   Pay Amount: $2,543.97 *****

Pay   ****TWO THOUSAND FIVE HUNDRED FORTY-THREE AND 97/100 DOLLARS****

To The
Order Of

     Bozo T. Clown
     1 Main Street
     Cupertino, CA 95014

     Location: Corporate Headquarters

                                  signature font

C0100114C A122100218A C

▶ **Figure 15-1**   Actual PeopleSoft-generated paycheck.

Rather than go through each of the pay tables, selectively eliminating certain deductions and taxes, you can just grab the total number from the paycheck table—which does it all for you.

DIFFERENT KINDS OF PAYCHECKS

In Chapter 14 we saw that a payroll can go through several different stages and has flags for each stage. The same applies to each individual paycheck. As a paycheck goes through the stages, the paycheck status field (PAYCHECK_STATUS) changes. A pay calendar may be confirmed, but sometimes a check does not make it through, and is still set to "Calculated," not confirmed. The possible values are described in Table 15-4.

▶ **Table 15-4** Paycheck status

Value	Description
A	Adjusted; this check reflects an adjustment to the paycheck, which was made using the reversal process.
C	Calculated; the check is calculated, but not confirmed.
F	Confirmed; the check is confirmed and complete.
R	Reversed; the check is no longer valid; it has been reversed.

PeopleSoft also provides a paycheck cashed flag which tells you if a check has already been cashed. Since PeopleSoft isn't a bank and has no way of knowing this, usually this field is just set to no. This field must be manually populated to reflect when a check is cashed. It does not have any functionality in PeopleSoft.

Once you know the status, there are some additional fields that are of interest. Since a check can be many things—a correction, reversal, reprint, or final check, it is a good idea to look at these fields.

The paycheck option field tells you additional specific information about the entire check—is it an advice, is it a reversal? Table 15-5 explains the values.

▶ **Table 15-5** Paycheck option

Value	Description
&	Check and Advice; the employee receives part of the paycheck as a physical check and part is direct deposited.
A	Advice; the check is direct deposited.
C	Check; a physical check is cut.
M	Manual Check; a manual check was cut (i.e., someone took out a checkbook, wrote the employee name and amount, tore it off, and later entered it into PeopleSoft).
R	Check Reversal; the paycheck is a reversal. Usually it has a negative amount.

Adjustments

The paycheck adjust field identifies a paycheck that is an adjustment. If a check is off by, say, $10, then you can process a paycheck adjustment. PeopleSoft will reverse the incorrect check and also create an off-cycle check with the pay data that appeared on the original check. The adjustment payline should be updated with what needs to be different. PeopleSoft can then calculate and cut the new, adjusted check, like any other check. Because the adjustment process was used, the paycheck adjust field will be set to yes for the adjustment check. To process an adjustment, go to Go ➤ Compensate Employees ➤ Manage Payroll Process U.S. ➤ Process ➤ Paycheck Reversal/Adjustment.

Reprints

If a paycheck must be reprinted, a new check is issued as a replacement, and this check has a paycheck reprint flag set to yes. The old paycheck is moved to the dead paycheck table. Paychecks are often reprinted due to printer errors and jamming (lost checks are usually stopped and reissued). To generate a reprint, go to Go ➤ Compensate Employees ➤ Manage Payroll Process U.S. ➤ Process ➤ Paycheck Reprint. You will need to specify the starting and ending check number to reissue more than one check.

Online Check

Using the online check feature (Go ➤ Compensate Employees ➤ Manage Payroll Process U.S. ➤ Use ➤ Online Check) you can write checks instantly. For example, maybe mid-period Andy needs a huge lump-sum payment. You can apply any one-time deductions, taxes, or garnishments right in the panel and calculate the check and choose how it will be paid. The check can be part of an off-cycle payroll run, an off-cycle page, or part of an on-cycle run.

Manual Check

A manual check is similar to an online check, except you do all of the work. When you write a check using a checkbook instead of using PeopleSoft, you must record the earnings, deductions, taxes, etc. in PeopleSoft. To do this, you work directly with the paysheet itself. A manual check requires the creation of a paysheet (typically an off-cycle sheet), the manual entry of data onto that sheet, and the usual payroll process of calculation and confirmation. The paysheet is marked for manual check entry so PeopleSoft is aware that most of the check data will be provided.

Final Checks

A final check is the last check the employee will receive from the employer. You generate final checks when an employee terminates and you still owe him or her salary. To create such a check, go to Go ➤ Compensate Employees ➤ Manage

Payroll Process U.S. ➤ Use ➤ Final Check Request. The final check can be linked to the next payroll run or generated online immediately.

To identify a check as a final check, look at the paysheet source field on the paycheck table. The paysheet source identifies how the paycheck was created. The paysheet could be from a regularly scheduled payroll(R), an on-line paysheet (O), an on-line final check (L), a batch of on-line final checks (K), or from an FLSA paysheet.

16 *Earnings*

Earnings are the first piece of the pay-check in PeopleSoft. They are the part everyone likes—the positive dollars you get before deductions, taxes, and garnishments are taken out. They are also the first product of the payroll process. Without running payroll, your earnings are zero. PeopleSoft takes care of converting each employee's job information (salary, pay frequency, standard hours) into dollars during the payroll process using the rules you specify.

DEFINING EARNINGS

Earn Codes

All earnings are stored according to an *earn code*. This is a code of up to three characters that identifies an earning. PeopleSoft delivers many useful codes, but each implementation requires new earn codes. Because most companies want to avoid an unnecessary learning curve for their online data processors, they will create earnings codes from scratch that have similar values to their legacy system codes. It's a good idea to use a logical three-character code, since the descriptions for the codes are hidden away on a control table, often requiring an extra lookup. Codes like REG (regular pay) and AUT (auto allowance) make immediate sense. Table 16-1 contains a list of the delivered earn codes.

▶ **Table 16-1** Delivered earnings codes

Code	Table	Code	Table
ADJ	Adjustments	OTP	Overtime
ADV	Advance	OTS	Straight Overtime
AUT	Automobile Allowance	PDP	Per Diem Pay
AWD	Award—Non Cash	PRM	Premium Pay at .5
BEP	Beeper Pay	PW	Piecework
BNS	Bonus	REG	Regular
CAL	Car Allowance	REL	Relocation Reimbursement
CBN	Bonus	RLC	Relocation—Taxable
CLA	Cost of Living Adjustment	RLN	Relocation—NonTaxable
CMP	Comp Time	RTC	Reimbursement—Tuition Costs
COM	Commission	RTD	Retro/Deduction Refund
DBL	Double Time	RTE	Retro Pay/Earnings
DCR	Dental Credits	RTN	Retro—Negative Offset
DRW	Accumulative Draw	RTO	Retroactive Pay—Overtime
EXP	Expense Reimbursement	RTP	Retro Pay—Premium/Extra
EXT	Extra pay above regular	RTR	Retroactive Earnings—TRG
FER	Float Pay—Emergency Room	S60	Short Term Disability at 60%
FLT	Float Pay	SCK	Sick Pay
FLX	Flex Credits	SCO	Sick Payoff
FMA	Family Med. Leave Adjustment	SEV	Severance Pay
FML	Family Medical Leave	SHF	Shift 2 Differential
FOR	Float Pay—Operating Room	SOI	Stock—Ordinary Income
FRH	Foreign Housing—Rent	SPB	Special Bonus
FRU	Foreign Housing—Utilities	STD	Short Term Disability
GSD	Goods & Services Differential	STP	Stock-Tax Payment
HBN	Holiday Bonus	TOP	Top-up Earnings
HCR	Health Credit	TPA	Tips Allocation
HNS	Holiday (Non-Statutory)	TPC	Tips Credit
HOL	Holiday (Statutory)	TPJ	Tips Adjustment
HRS	Hours Only—No Pay	TPR	Tips Reported
ILH	Interim Living—Host	UIC	Unemployment Insurance

▶ **Table 16-1** continued

Code	Table	Code	Table
JUR	Jury Pay	UNI	Uniform Reimbursement
LCR	Life Insurance Credits	UNP	Unpaid Leave
LTD	Long Term Disability	VAC	Vacation
LVP	Legislated Vacation Pay	VAD	Vacation Advance
MIL	Mileage Reimbursement	VAM	Visits Pay A.M.
NCA	Non Cash Award	VAO	Vacation Payoff
NOE	No Earnings	VBY	Vacation Buy
NTP	Night Pay	VPM	Visits Pay P.M.
OCL	On Call Earnings	VSL	Vacation Sell
OCP	On-Call Pay	WCB	Workers' Compensation
ORP	Orientation Pay	WEP	Weekend Pay

As you can see, there are many codes, and they are broad in scope. Your implementation probably won't use all of these codes, and PS_EARNINGS_TBL will look quite different.

Defining an Earning: The Earnings Table

The earnings table stores the basic rules for an earn code in PeopleSoft. You can define an earn code by going to Go ➤ Define Business Rules ➤ Define Payroll Process ➤ Setup 1 ➤ Earnings Table. There are four panels containing numerous rules for the code. All of these rules are stored on PS_EARNINGS_TBL.

Payments

Payment Type.   When an earning is entered, you have the option of typing in the hours worked or the total amount earned. The payment type field (PAYMENT_TYPE) tells PeopleSoft which entry method is allowed for the earning. You can enter:

- amount only (A)
- hours only (H)
- only both (B)
- either (E)
- a flat amount defined for the earnings (F).

The flat amount PeopleSoft uses is stored in EARN_FLAT_AMT. If you choose unit/override rate (U), you can specify a particular hourly rate for this earning only. The override rate is stored in PERUNIT_OVR_RT.

Effect on FLSA.   The earning can be added to the accumulators that track FLSA (Fair Labor Standards Act) amounts. If the earning should be included, you can specify to include amounts (A), hours (H), or both (B). The default is none (N).

The FLSA category field (FLSA_CATEGORY) tells PeopleSoft whether the earning is to be applied to regular earnings (R) or overtime earnings (O) accumulators, or excluded from FLSA calculation (X). The regular_pay_included field (REG_PAY_INCLUDED) is used in conjunction with an FLSA category of overtime. This field tells PeopleSoft if your overtime multiplication factor contains regular pay. You might calculate overtime by multiplying regular pay by 1.5—does this include the regular pay, or is the result just overtime pay?

Retro Pay Processing.   Retroactive pay is entered after the pay period it was earned in. If an employee didn't get paid last period, you would enter a retroactive earning amount and cut a new check. PeopleSoft provides a process which identifies a payroll-related job action whose effective date is after the last processed pay period and does most of the retroactive pay automatically. To perform this process PeopleSoft needs to know which earnings can be paid retroactively. Eligible earnings have an eligibility value of yes (ELIG_FOR_RETROPAY).

Sometimes special earnings are used to pay retroactive earnings. Perhaps the employee missed some REG earnings. To pay them retroactively, you might use a special earning code. In this case, the USED_TO_PAY_RETRO field is set to yes.

Payback Deduction Code.   Certain earnings need to be returned, such as an advance. You can link a deduction code to the earnings code so PeopleSoft can automatically try to recover the funds. Place the deduction code in the DEDCD_PAYBACK field.

Allowable Earnings

Employees are eligible for different earnings according to the earnings programs they are enrolled in. An earning program is a group of valid earn codes for a paygroup. For example, the earnings program 'AAA' includes regular, overtime, and a performance bonus. But it does not include an auto allowance, tips, or commissions. You link all employees in a paygroup with one earnings program on the paygroup table. Earnings programs form the basic earning rules—which earn codes can be used by which employees.

One additional criterion for an employee to receive a particular earning is the employee type. Certain earnings are set for hourly employees (H) and others for salaried employees (S). If both groups can use the earning, the allowable employee type field (ALLOW_EMPLTYPE) is set to (A).

United States Taxes

Tax Method. The earnings table provides numerous check-box fields to appropriately set up taxes for each earning. The tax method field (TAX_METHOD) determines how taxes are taken for the earning (see Table 16-2).

▶ **Table 16-2** Tax methods

Code	Method	Description
A	Annualized	The tax is calculated based on the annualized amount of the earning, and then divided by the number of pay periods associated with the employee.
B	Bonus	Canadian tax method.
C	Cumulative	Uses the year-to-date withholding and the number of periods specified on the paysheet definition to determine what to withhold.
G	Aggregate	Combine additional pay with regular pay, and withhold the annualized amount from the total.
L	Lump Sum	Canadian tax method.
M	Commission	Canadian tax method.
P	Specified on Paysheet	Uses the method specified on the paysheet definition.
S	Supplemental	Uses the federal and state supplemental tax rates defined on the tax tables (e.g., 28% for federal) for additional pay.

Subject to FWT, FICA, FUT, Withhold FWT. The subject to… fields (SUBJECT_FWT, _FICA, _FUT) define whether the earning is subject to federal taxes. Most earnings are, but certain earnings (e.g., expense reimbursements) may not be subject to one or more of the taxes.

The taxable gross component ID (TAX_GRS_COMPNT) is used in the calculation of state and local taxes. If certain states do not follow the federal guidelines for taxable gross amounts, a taxable gross definition can be established to set the appropriate gross amounts. If you provide the ID for the definition on the earnings table, that definition will apply when state and local taxes are calculated.

Earnings Allocation

Add to Gross Pay.   If the earning amount should be added to an employee's gross pay, the add- to-gross field (ADD_GROSS) should be checked. This field is used for cases where the earning does not represent actual dollars, and the amount should not be added to gross pay. An employee could use an apartment or a car, but not actually receive funds. The earnings need to be taxed, but should not be included in the gross pay calculation.

Maintain Earnings Balances.   The PS_EARNINGS_BAL table is updated with all amounts for an earning code if the maintain balances (MAINTAIN_BALANCES) check box is set to yes. All earnings should be recorded on the balance table. If you record earnings amounts but leave them off the balance table, that table will not accurately represent the total earnings for an employee. Some delivered programs use this table to get balance information— it is best to keep it accurate and send every earning code to the balance table.

Eligible for Shift Differential.   When an employee is working on a shift, PeopleSoft looks at the earnings that are eligible for shift differentials and applies the appropriate factor (defined on the job table). The shift differential field tells PeopleSoft which earnings those are.

Hours Only.   The use of this field depends on how you are recording hours. If the hours only field is set to yes, PeopleSoft will take the hours or earnings for the earn code and subtract them from the employee's regular earnings. For some earn codes, such as vacation leave, this feature can save data entry time.

Subject to Garnishments.   This strangely named field (ADD_DE) tells PeopleSoft if an earning should be used or added in the calculation of disposable earnings for garnishments. All garnishable earnings for an employee are then used as the basis for calculating the amount of garnishment payments. Some earnings may not be subject to garnishments (e.g., expense reimbursements), and PeopleSoft will retain them during the payroll calculation process. A 'yes' value indicates that the earning should be used in the disposable earnings calculation.

Budgets/ General Ledger Account Number.   If you use earning codes to track general ledger expenses, you can associate a general ledger account number (GL#_EXPENSE) with each earn code. The budget effect field is for information only (it has no effect).

Calculating the Earning Amount

Earnings Calculation Sequence. When PeopleSoft calculates a paycheck, it figures out each earning in a certain order. Earnings with a lower sequence number are figured out first. The sequence is only relevant when one earning depends on the amount of the other. In this case, order the earnings in the sequence of calculation. PeopleSoft suggests setting the sequence for regular earnings to '001' to ensure that it is calculated first. Then subsequent earnings can use this amount in their calculation.

The system calculates earnings for hourly employees according to the following formula:

```
Earnings = [(Pay Rate or Unit/Override Rate
    + Shift Rate + Rate Adjustment Factor)
    * (Hours + Hours Adjustment Factor)
    * Multiplication Factor]
    + Earnings Adjustment Factor
```

Earnings for salaried employees are calculated as follows:

```
Earnings = Earnings amount
    * Multiplication Factor
```

Factors. PeopleSoft will apply a custom factor to the calculation of an earning amount (see Table 16-3). For both hourly and salaried employees, a flat multiplication factor can be applied. This factor is stored in FACTOR_MULT. Often this factor is used for overtime (1x, 2x, 3x, etc.) earnings.

▶ **Table 16-3** Earning calculation using factors

Item	Calculation
Rate	Pay rate + shift rate + rate adjustment factor
Hours	Hours + hours adjustment factor
Multiplication Factor	Applied to (rate × hours)
Earnings Adjustment	Added to above (rate × hours × multiplication factor)

For hourly employees, there are several additional options. A rate adjustment factor (FACTOR_RATE_ADJ) can be applied to the rate of the earning. PeopleSoft takes the pay rate or unit/override rate, adds the shift rate, and adds the rate adjustment factor to arrive at the final rate.

Hours can be adjusted with the hours adjustment factor in a similar fashion. PeopleSoft adds this factor (FACTOR_HRS_ADJ) to the actual number of hours.

There is also an earnings adjustment factor (FACTOR_ERN_ADJ). You can use this factor to specify a flat amount that is added to an earning. If you are specifying a flat earning, such as a bonus to all employees, make sure you set the multiplication factor to zero in order to prevent hour/rate calculation. Then PeopleSoft will just use the earnings adjustment.

Maximums.   PeopleSoft will calculate earnings amounts up to a set maximum, if specified on the earnings table. The maximum yearly amount (EARN_YTD_MAX) will prevent earnings after the year to date balance for the earning has reached the maximum specified.

The hourly rate maximum (HRLY_RT_MAXIMUM) is not used by the payroll process and is for information only.

Earnings Based on Type.   An earning can be based on another earning code or an accumulator code, specified in the based-on fields (BASED_ON_ERNCD and BASED_ON_ACC_ERNCD). With this feature, the earning amount will be based on the other earning amount—it could be a percentage or a rate applied to the hours of the other earning.

The value of the based-on amount or hours field (AMT_OR_HOURS) determines how the earning is calculated. If amount is selected (E), the multiplication factor is applied to the other earning amount. To take 10% of regular earnings, you would specify a based-on earning code of REG and a multiplication factor of .10. If hours is selected (H), just the hours for the other earning code are used to calculate a new earning.

Special Calculations.   If you modify the payroll calculation programs (in COBOL) to perform a special routing for an earning, you can specify this in the special calculation routine field (SPEC_CALC_RTN). This is for information only, or it can be used by your routine to determine which earnings should be processed. Modifying the COBOL is a serious undertaking. Since the code is hidden from the general user, this field is an alert that something might be going on behind the scenes.

Employee Tips

Tip Categories.   If your employees receive tips, certain earning codes can be established for tips. The tip category tells PeopleSoft how tips are processed (see Table 16-4).

▶ **Table 16-4** Tips

Code	Method	Description
A	Allocation	Tips are calculated by PeopleSoft using the Tip Allocation Process.
C	Credit	Earning represents system-calculated tip credits.
N	Not tips	The earning does not represent tips (default).
R	Reported	Earning represents tips reported by the employees.
S	Other system	Earning is used to meet minimum wage requirements. Used when the salary + tips is less than minimum wage.
T	Tippable	The earning can be used for the Tip Allocation Process.

> The earnings category on the earnings table is unrelated to the tips category. Earnings category is not currently used in PeopleSoft.

RETRIEVING EARNINGS FOR AN EMPLOYEE

There are two earnings tables, PS_PAY_EARNINGS and PS_PAY_OTH_EARNS. Between these two tables you can find all of the earnings for a given employee in any calculated pay period. Regular and overtime earnings are stored in their own fields on the PS_PAY_EARNINGS table.

Each employee will receive a regular earning amount (usually identified by the code 'REG'). Other earnings, such as allowances, bonuses, or vacation pay are stored separately from the regular earnings, on PS_PAY_OTH_EARNS.

> This division of earnings is not always consistent. PeopleSoft will let a user store regular earnings, for example, on the PS_PAY_OTH_EARNS table. It is possible to store any and all earnings on PS_PAY_OTH_EARNS. Although it is possible to place 'REG' on PS_PAY_OTH_EARNS, most companies do not. Check first—if not—then just concentrate on PS_PAY_EARNINGS for regular earnings.

Retrieving earnings for a given employee is simple. Join the tables on the payroll keys, and know which fields contain the actual amounts. Tables 16-5 and 16-6 demonstrates the two typical queries.

▶ **Table 16-5** Retrieving earnings for an employee: earnings

| The query | ```
SELECT
PE.PAGE#,
PE.LINE#,
PE.ADDL#,
PE.PAY_END_DT,
PE.REG_EARNS,
PE.REG_HRLY_EARNS
FROM PS_PAY_EARNINGS PE
WHERE PE.COMPANY     = 'HRB'
   AND PE.PAYGROUP    = 'BW'
   AND PE.OFF_CYCLE   = 'N'
   AND PE.EMPLID      = 'BOZO'
``` |
|---|---|

Returns the data set	PAGE#	LINE#	ADDL#	PAY_END_DT	REG_EARNS	REG_HRLY_EARNS
August	1	1	0	31-AUG-1999	3245	0
	1	1	1	31-AUG-1999	0	0
September	1	1	0	30-SEP-1999	3095.23	0
	1	1	1	30-SEP-1999	0	0
October	1	1	0	31-OCT-1999	3245	0
	1	1	1	31-OCT-1999	0	0
November	1	1	0	30-NOV-1999	2945.46	0
	1	1	1	30-NOV-1999	0	0

▶ **Table 16-6** Retrieving earnings for an employee: other earnings

| The query | ```
SELECT
PO.PAY_END_DT,
PO.ADDL#,
PO.ERNCD,
PO.OTH_EARNS
FROM PS_PAY_OTH_EARNS PO
WHERE PO.COMPANY = 'HRB'
   AND PO.PAYGROUP = 'BW'
   AND PO.OFF_CYCLE = 'N'
   AND PO.PAGE# = 1
   AND PO.LINE# = 1
``` |
|---|---|

▶ **Table 16-6**   continued

Returns the data set	PAY_END_DT	ADDL#	ERNCD	OTH_EARNS
August	31-AUG-1999	0	AUT	15
	31-AUG-1999	1	CAL	250
September	30-SEP-1999	0	HOL	149.77
	30-SEP-1999	1	CAL	250
October	31-OCT-1999	0	CAL	250
November	30-NOV-1999	0	HOL	299.54
	30-NOV-1999	1	CAL	250

According to the returned data, the employee received regular earnings of $3245 in August, as well as two additional earnings: AUT and CAL. The total earnings for this pay end date would be $3245 + $15 + $250 = $3510. In October, the employee received regular earnings, but only one additional earning of $250. If we combined these two queries into a single query, an outer join would be required. Otherwise we would have dropped the October regular earnings, since there are two earning rows and only one other earning row. This is a join that leaves many users mystified. To prevent confusion, look at earnings in two *separate* queries to make sure you're seeing all of the earnings.

The Pay Earnings Table

All detailed information about pay earnings is stored on the basic tables mentioned above: PS_PAY_EARNINGS (Table 16-7) and PS_PAY_OTH_EARNS. These tables store the *results* of the payroll earnings process. Let's explore the fields on these two tables in greater detail to understand what is recorded where.

▶ **Table 16-7**   Pay earnings: PS_PAY_EARNINGS

Structure	Several rows per pay end date, per employee ID. Typically one row per employee ID and pay end date.
Keys	Company
	paygroup
	Pay end date
	Off cycle
	Page #

▶ **Table 16-7** continued

	Line #
	Additional Pay Line #
Alternate keys	None
Sub-records included	None
Panels to look at	Go ➤ Compensate Employees ➤ Maintain Payroll Data U.S. ➤ Inquire ➤ Paycheck Data ➤ Paycheck Earnings

The Keys/ Additional Pays

The earnings table shares the common payroll key structure explained in Chapters 14 and 15. Each earning is stored according to company, paygroup, pay end date, off-cycle/on-cycle, page number, and line number. Pay earnings are also stored with an employee ID, employment record number, and benefit record number for easy lookup. (Pay other earnings, however, do not have an employee ID.)

Additional Payline # Key.   An additional payline number field (ADDL#) is provided to keep track of additional earnings lines. The additional number is used to distinguish one earnings record from another. For instance, an employee may have an earnings record for one week and a separate earnings record for another. Or the employee has an additional pay. Or an employee has one line charging some earnings to one department, and another line charging earnings to another department. The additional number field breaks earnings down further.

> The additional number is an important key for linking pay earnings and pay other earnings. Each other earning is tied to a specific pay earning additional number.

Additional Pays.   An additional pay is anything that is in addition to an employee's regular pay. Additional pays occur for multiple pay periods and at a regular interval—every pay period, every month, year, etc. A car allowance, an annual bonus, or a regular-paid advance are set up as additional pays (Go ➤ Compensate Employees ➤ Maintain Payroll Data U.S. ➤ Use ➤ Additional Pay).

When setting up an additional pay, you can specify a reason. The reason is not used by PeopleSoft—it is informational only.

Be sure to look at the disable-direct-deposit field when looking for additional pay records. This field indicates when the direct deposit is turned off for the additional pay amount—for a special bonus check, for instance.

Earnings Begin and End Dates. Earnings are stored with a begin and end date for each line. These fields do not necessarily correspond to the pay end date, since earnings can occur over any subset of time within a pay period. For example, if Fred works in one department for two days, and then in another for eight days, he will have two earnings records. The begin and end dates will all connect to span a single two-week pay period. In addition, the pay end date should equal the last earning end date in the sequence.

Status of the Earning

To track the status of an earning through the payroll process you can look at the payline calculation status field. This field provides greater detail than the paycheck table status fields since it relates to each pay earning line. Descriptions of each status are listed in Table 16-8.

▶ **Table 16-8** Pay line status

Code	Status	Description
C	Calculated	The record is calculated.
E	Calculation Error	The record is not calculated due to a payroll error. The payroll calculation process will not end until no records have errors (ignoring records marked not OK to pay).
F	Confirmed	The record is confirmed.
I	Initial Load	A pay earnings record was created, but no earning amount was calculated. When a record's OK to pay field is not marked, records are created but not calculated. When pay confirm runs, these records (I status) are deleted.
P	Pay in Progress	While payroll calculation runs, it sets this status to 'in progress.' Typically a record with a 'P' status didn't make it through the calculation process due to an error.
U	Updated by Operator	A manual update online was made since the original calculation.

OK to Pay. The OK-to-Pay field determines whether the data in a payline will be processed for payment. The default for this flag on the payline is derived from the paygroup table and impacts all employees within the paygroup. In addition, on the additional pay table, earnings must be set up to process as OK to pay, or a user must manually 'OK' each earning every payroll period. This 'OK' is translated to the pay earnings table. If the field is set to 'N,' this record will be bypassed by the calculation process.

Job Pay/Override Hourly Rate.   The payroll process takes time to get through. When paysheets are created (the first step), earnings are calculated according to the salary on the job table. If the information on the job table changes after this step, PeopleSoft can check before confirming the paycheck. If the job pay field on the earning is set to yes, PeopleSoft will check for changes, and make any necessary adjustments (see Table 16-9).

The job pay field is used in conjunction with the override hourly rate field. When the override is set to yes, the override rate on the paysheet will be used in lieu of the rate on the job table for the employee.

▶ **Table 16-9**   Rate changes during payroll calculation

Job Pay	Override Hourly Rate	Rate Changes Applied?	Rate Used	Hours, etc. Changes Applied?
On	Off	Yes	Updated Job	Yes
Off	Off	No	Original Job	No
On	On	No	Paysheet override	Yes
Off	On	No	Paysheet override	No

Combining Checks.   The single check feature combines separate earnings into a single check for employees that have more than one job. The single check field identifies how the pay line is used. Typically records have an 'N' for not applicable. But if a single check is issued, the field will be 'C' for check only. When a check is issued only on the paysheet, and not actually processed through to the confirm level, the field will be 'P' for paysheet only. When querying the pay earnings table, it is a good idea to restrict your retrieval to SINGLE_CHECK_USE IN ('C', 'N') so you retrieve only real, confirmed earnings.

Earning Amounts

One of the most confusing parts of the earnings table is figuring out where the dollars are kept and why. Each of the "amount" fields is explained in Table 16-10.

▶ **Table 16-10**   Earning amount fields

Field	Contains	Description
REG_PAY_HRS	Entered hours	The hours supplied to PeopleSoft.
REG_PAY	Entered pay	The pay supplied to PeopleSoft.
REG_HRS	Hours (hourly)	Hours used to calculate earning amount.

▶ **Table 16-10** continued

Field	Contains	Description
REG_EARN_HRS	Hours (salaried)	Hours derived from earning amount (using standard hours on job table).
REG_EARNS	Earning (salaried)	Earnings derived from compensation information on job table.
REG_HRLY_EARNS	Earning (hourly)	Earnings derived from REG_HRS and rate on job table.
OT_HRS	Overtime hours	Overtime hours worked.
OT_HRLY_EARNS	Overtime earnings	Overtime earnings derived from OT_HRS.

Regular, Overtime Hours Earnings Type.   The regular hours earning type field (ERNCD_REG_HRS) is not an amount—it's the code that is used for regular earnings. PeopleSoft allows you to specify different earning codes for regular and overtime earnings based on paygroup. One paygroup could receive regular earnings as REG, while another might receive AAA earnings as regular pay. Similarly, the overtime hours earning type field could be OT for one paygroup, and OT2 for another, since that paygroup receives 2× overtime. When you look at the earnings in the pay earnings table, you can identify the appropriate earning code for each amount.

Unlike the pay other earnings table, regular and overtime earnings are stored in their own fields on the pay earnings table. Although one amount might be OT and another OT2, the amounts are located in the same field—overtime earnings.

Regular Hours Input/Regular Salaried Earnings.   The pay amount fields (REG_PAY_HRS, REG_PAY) represent items that are entered into PeopleSoft. When entering hours or earnings, a user enters amounts into the pay process. It is input either by a custom batch process, manually, or by the time and labor module. The hours and earnings these fields represent are not the final hours and earnings used on the paycheck.

Regular Hours/Regular Earnings Hours.   The hours for a pay earning can be obtained by adding these two fields (REG_HRS, REG_EARN_HRS) together. Employees who are paid with an amount (i.e., salaried employees) will have hours calculated and stored in the regular earnings hours field. PeopleSoft calculates this value from the salaried earnings and divides it by the standard hours field on the job table. Employees who are hourly will have their hours stored in the regular hours field. If you always add these two fields together, you'll be assured of getting back the total hours an employee worked.

Regular Earnings/Regular Hourly Earnings.   The actual dollar amount of the earning is stored in these two fields (REG_EARNS, REG_HRLY_EARNS). Again, if you add them together, you will obtain the total amount earned. These fields follow a similar formula to the hours: Regular earnings are for earnings calculated using standard hours (salaried employees), and regular hourly earnings are for earnings calculated using reported hours (hourly employees).

Overtime Hours/ Overtime Hourly Earnings.   Overtime hours (OT_HRS) can apply to any type of employee. In all cases, PeopleSoft needs to know how many hours were worked. This hours amount is moved directly into the overtime hours field. PeopleSoft also calculates the earnings due to the employee based on these hours (OT_HRLY_EARNS). This earnings amount is stored in the overtime hourly earnings field.

Tax Amounts

Most of the tax information about an earning defaults from the earnings table. Certain additional fields, however, can be set at the detail level, earning by earning.

The state and locality, for instance, are applied for each earning depending on the earning location. PeopleSoft uses the state and locality fields to associate earnings with the appropriate tax rates. If Joe works in New York and Massachusetts, a certain percentage of his earnings might be in different places. The PeopleSoft payroll process calculates Joe's income tax according to the rates for the different locations. Joe's state and locality, as established on the job table tax location and corresponding tax distribution table, are copied to the earning line.

There are also two options for calculating taxes at the earning level. First, by specifying a tax period, PeopleSoft can tax an earning according to the time span it covered, rather than in one lump sum. If the earning should be taxed as if it were paid over four biweekly pay periods, then the pay frequency would be biweekly and the tax periods set to four. The payroll calculation process will take the taxes for the earning according to these settings.

Second, an earning can accept or reject the additional taxes that are defined on the tax data panels. If the additional taxes field is set to yes (default), the additional taxes are taken. When set to no, the payroll calculation process ignores the additional taxes.

Rates Used

For a useful overview on the rates used, refer to the paycheck data panels. All of the rates for a pay earning are shown in Go ➤ Compensate Employees ➤ Maintain Payroll Data U.S. ➤ Inquire ➤ Paycheck Data ➤ Paycheck Earnings.

The rate used for an earning can be the hourly rate (R) or the FLSA rate (F). The hourly rate field is used in conjunction with the regular hours field to arrive at the regular hourly earnings. For salaried employees the rate is taken from the job table.

If the FLSA rate applies, it is also stored on the pay earnings table. Earnings with an eligibility for FLSA will typically have this rate. The rate is the product of the settings on the earning table for the earn code.

If a shift applies to an earning, it is indicated in the shift field. The shift and the appropriate rate are stored for each earning.

Gross-Up. A gross-up is when the earnings of a payment is increased to cover the amount of taxes an employee must pay which results in the net pay being the full amount of the award. If Andy receives a $5000 bonus for his recruiting efforts, the company might want to prevent the tax hit he would take on the extra income. Increasing the value of the bonus to the point where the grossed-up earnings value less the taxes on the value equals the $5000 original value means Andy will not incur a tax hit in the payout. When an earning is grossed-up, this check box is set to yes.

Comp Rate Used for Regular. Once pay earnings are calculated, the compensation rates that were used are stored in these two fields. One rate is for regular earnings and the other is for overtime earnings. When regular hours is equal to zero, PeopleSoft hides the rate on the pay-check panel—the same is true for overtime hours. These rates, therefore, represent the rates applied to hours supplied to PeopleSoft, not derived by PeopleSoft.

Accounting/Sources

Earnings can be distributed among different accounts (ACCT_CD), general ledger pay types (GL_PAY_TYPE—see Chapter 7), departments (DEPTID), job codes (JOBCODE), or position numbers (POSITION_NBR). Every earning must be linked to a department ID, but the other fields are often linked to an earning as well. When an employee switches jobs, for example, it is useful to show one earning for the first job and another for the second job when the switch happens mid-period. The presence of these fields on the earnings table allows these allocations.

Business Unit. The Business Unit field is on the pay earnings table to indicate which business unit the department resides in.

Time & Labor Source Flag. When time and labor data is automatically entered into the pay earnings table, the time and labor source is set to T to indicate the source of the amounts. The field can also be set to user-updated/created record (U). This field is read by the payroll process to determine whether to run time and labor functions against the pay earnings. For records not manually entered or sent through time and labor, the default for this field is blank.

Other Earnings

Other earnings are stored in a logical format: earn code and amount. The other hours and other pay fields (OTH_HRS, OTH_PAY) receive input during the payroll process. They are used to calculate the other earnings amount (OTH_EARNS). These hours and earnings are associated with the value in the earnings code (ERNCD) field (see Table 16-11).

▶ **Table 16-11**　Pay other earnings: PS_PAY_OTH_EARNS

Structure	Several rows per pay end date per employee check.
Keys	Company
	paygroup
	Pay end date
	Off cycle
	Page #
	Line #
	Additional pay line #
	Earnings code
Alternate keys	None
Sub-records included	None
Panels to look at	Go ➤ Compensate Employees ➤ Maintain Payroll Data U.S. ➤ Inquire ➤ Paycheck Data ➤ Paycheck Earnings

Additional Pay Sequence Number.　This field is unrelated to the additional number (ADDL#) on the pay earnings table. An additional pay sequence number relates only to additional pays, which are usually stored on the other earnings table.

The sequence number is used to store additional pay instructions on the PS_ADDL_PAY_DATA table. Instruction one could be sequence number one, two is sequence two, and so on. The sequence number is provided on the other earnings table to tie the earning back to each additional pay instruction.

The other earnings table is used principally to record additional pay, but PeopleSoft-delivered processes also use it to store all incoming earnings. The time and labor module, for example, will feed regular earnings to the other earnings table. These earnings will not have an additional sequence number.

Other Sources. In addition to the two basic earnings tables, there is a standard control table and a useful balance table for earnings. Table 16-12 describes the different earnings tables.

▶ **Table 16-12** Earnings tables

Table	Description
PS_EARNINGS_TBL	The earnings table stores the control values for every earnings code. The table contains a description, precedence (which earnings to calculate first), and other calculation rules for each earnings code.
PS_PAY_EARNINGS	Stores the calculated earnings for an employee for each pay period. Contains regular and overtime earnings.
PS_PAY_OTH_EARNS	Stores the calculated other earnings for an employee for each pay period. See Table 16-1 for earnings codes stored on this table.
PS_EARNINGS_BAL	Consolidates the pay earnings and pay other earnings tables into balances, stored by earnings code for each employee (see Chapter 14 for information on balance tables). Contains all earnings, even 'REG,' and balances stored monthly, quarterly, and annually.

When deciding between the earnings balance table and the pay earnings/pay other earnings tables, consider the time slice you are looking for. The earnings balance table cannot get more detailed than a monthly balance. If you need to report on earnings every pay period, you most likely need to look at the pay earnings tables. But if you are reporting monthly, the balance table is much simpler to access. Most of the keys involved are easy to obtain, whereas the pay earnings table must be combined with the pay other earnings table.

FEEDING PEOPLESOFT

For a large implementation, there are thousands of special earnings each pay period. While PeopleSoft can handle the calculation of regular earnings for salaried employees with ease, the rest must be augmented with additional data. For hourly employees, PeopleSoft needs to know how many hours they worked this period. If bonuses need to go out to a group of employees, PeopleSoft needs to know how much and to whom. Outside systems can feed this data using interface files. The files are loaded into the PeopleSoft tables every pay period before pay calculation begins.

The program that loads these tables can be extremely complex, and timing is key. The process usually looks like this:

1. Run paysheet creation. PeopleSoft calculates the regular earnings (and special earnings it knows about) automatically.
2. Run the earnings interface.
3. If a check exists for the employee, use the page and line number of the existing check.
4. If a separate or new check is required, create a new page and/or line number for the employee.
5. Validate the fields on the file to make sure they conform to the established rules for earnings. There could be a maximum, or the earn code could be invalid for the employee.
6. Determine the appropriate additional taxes for the earning based on the PS_TAX_DISTRIB table.
7. When the earnings are successfully loaded, calculate payroll.

This process is not easy. The earnings interface, especially for large implementations with many earn codes, is complex. For guidance, look to the PeopleSoft delivered interface, PAYUPDT.SQR (pay update). It performs the basics but has some limitations:

- It does not perform off-cycle runs—earnings can only coincide with on-cycle pay runs.
- It assigns all earnings to PS_PAY_OTH_EARNS, rather than placing regular and overtime earnings on PS_PAY_EARNINGS.
- The correct pay end date must be on the input file—there is no routine to get the pay end date from PS_PAY_CALENDAR.
- Although certain actions should depend on settings in the control table for earnings (such as Add Gross?), the delivered program defaults these fields to hard coded values.
- There is no verification procedure or report that comes out of the delivered program.

While not a comprehensive earnings interface, the PeopleSoft-delivered program demonstrates the logic and SQL statements necessary to perform a feed into PeopleSoft payroll.

Deductions are items subtracted from payroll earnings. Often these items belong to a third party, such as a health care provider, 401K plan administrator, or charity. PeopleSoft handles all of the aspects of taking a deduction. It prioritizes the different items, takes each one from the employee's earnings, and stops when instructed—usually when earnings are fully depleted. Using arrears balances, PeopleSoft can continue to deduct the remaining amount over future payroll periods. When correctly set up, deductions require little user intervention.

GETTING TO KNOW DEDUCTIONS

Deductions cover a wide range of vendor types. Some are simple amounts taken each pay period for a retirement account, and others are deductions for participation in a medical plan. PeopleSoft connects certain deductions with benefits plans and handles enrollment through benefits administration. Depending on the information you're seeking, you may need to look through benefits as well as payroll tables.

Deduction Code and Class

Similar to an earning, a deduction is identified by a code of three to six characters, the deduction code (DEDCD). Delivered codes in the demonstration database a customer receives from PeopleSoft are listed in Table 17-1.

▶ **Table 17-1** Delivered deduction codes (see Table 21-1 in Chapter 21 for plan type descriptions)

Plan type	Code	Description	Plan type	Code	Description
00	ADVPBK	Advance Payback	15	NQMED	Non Qualified Medical
00	ADVTVL	Travel Advance	16	NQDNTL	Non Qualified Dental
00	BUY1	Buyback Pension Srvc—Repay 1	17	NQVSN	Non Qualified Vision
00	BUY2	Buyback Pension Srvc—Repay 2	20	LIFE	Life Insurance Plan
00	BUY3	Buyback Pension Srvc—Repay 3	20	LIFEA	Life After-tax Deduction
00	CAFE	Cafeteria Charges	20	NYLIFE	New York Life Life Ins
00	CHILD	Child Care Center-On Site	21	LIFSUP	Suplemental Life Deduction
00	CREDUN	Credit Union	21	NYLIFE	New York Life Supplementl Life
00	CSB	Canada Savings Bonds	22	AD/D	AD/D Deduction
00	CSBRSP	Canada RRSP Bonds	22	ADD	Accidental Death & Dismmbrmnt
00	DRAW	Accumulative Draw	25	LIFDEP	Dependent Life
00	EXPTAX	Assignment Country Tax	25	NYLIFE	New York Life Dependent Life
00	GARNSH	Garnishment	30	STD	Short-Term Disability Plan
00	GSINCM	Goods'n Serv Spendable Income	31	INSDIS	Long-Term Disability
00	HEALTH	Health Club Dues	31	LTD	Long-Term Disability Plan
00	HYPOTX	Hypothetical Tax	31	LTDA	Long-Term Disability After Tax
00	LOAN	Loan Payback	40	401A	401(a) Deduction
00	NETPAY	Net Pay Adjustment	40	401K	401(k) Deduction
00	PAYADJ	Payback Adjustment	40	WELLS	Wells Fargo 401k Plan
00	PHARM	Pharmacy Charges	41	PROFIT	Canadian Savings Contributions
00	PRKING	Parking	4A	ESPP	Employee Stock Purchase Ded
00	PURCH1	Purchase of Service 1	50	SICK1	Sick Pay Benefit Deduction
00	RDCRSS	Canadian Red Cross	51	VACATN	Vacation Pay Deduction
00	RESP	Regstrd Education Savings Plan	53	FMLA	Family Medical Leave Act
00	STOCK	Stock Purchase	60	CCB	Health Care—FSA
00	UNION	Union Dues	60	FSAHC	Health Care FSA
00	UNIONC	Union Dues—Canada	60	HEALTH	Health Care FSA Deduction
00	USBOND	U.S. Savings Bond Deduction	61	CCB	Dependent Care—FSA
00	UWAY	United Way	61	DEPFSA	Dependent Care FSA
00	VACADV	Vacation Advance Payback	61	FSADC	Dependent Care FSA
01	CRED	General Flex Credit	65	HCCAN	Health Care CAN Spending Acct

▶ **Table 17-1** continued

Plan type	Code	Description	Plan type	Code	Description
10	BASMED	Basic Medical	66	RCCAN	Retirement Counseling CANADA
10	MEDIC	Medical Plan	70	CCB	Public Employees Retirement
10	MEDICA	Medical After-Tax Deduction	80	PRUD	Standard Pension
11	DENTAL	Dental Plan	81	PRUD	Supplementary Pension
11	DNTLA	Dental After-Tax Deduction	82	CONT	Consolidated Pension Contribtn
11	INSDEN	Dental Insurance	90	VACBS	Vacation Buy Deductn (AftTx)
12	MMAJOR	Major Medical Deduction	90	VBUY	Vacation Buy—BfrTx
13	MMAJOR	Major Medical	91	VACSL	Vacation Sell Deductn (AftTx)
14	VISION	Vision Plan	91	VSELL	Vacation Sell—BfrTx

As you can see, most of the deductions relate directly to a benefit. Many of the deductions include an embedded code for the deduction class. These codes are used to quickly identify a deduction as a certain class, but the class field is always recorded as well.

What is a deduction class? The class specifies whether a deduction is taken before taxes or calculated after tax. For example, you may be enrolled in a pre-tax 401(k) plan which will deduct money from your total earnings before taxes are calculated so that your earnings to be taxed are reduced. The before-tax removal of funds is the advantage of a 401(k)—essentially you avoid being taxed on these funds. Certain deductions can be taken before tax. Others, like a parking allowance, might be taken after tax—from the employee's net pay.

The tax class is also used to identify nontaxable, nontaxable pre-tax, and taxable benefits. Health benefits are often nontaxable, and a 401(k) is usually a nontaxable pre-tax benefit. Employer contributions to an employee benefit are taxable. Table 17-2 shows all of the possible deduction classes.

▶ **Table 17-2** Deduction class

Code	Description
A	After-tax deduction
B	Before-tax deduction
L	Deduction that affects Quebec income tax
N	Nontaxable benefit deduction
P	Nontaxable pre-tax benefit deduction
T	Taxable benefit deduction

Some deductions can be classified as separate classes. In fact, an entire table is devoted to deduction classes. The PS_DEDUCTION_CLASS table associates a deduction code with a deduction class. Hence a life deduction could be associated with three different classes. There could be an after-tax life deduction, a nontaxable benefit life deduction, and a taxable benefit life deduction. Depending on the rules established for the deduction, all three could be used on a single paycheck.

Suppose, for example, that Todd and his employer share the cost of a life insurance plan. For the employer, it is a nontaxable benefit. But for Todd, it is an after-tax deduction. And if the employer goes over a certain level of coverage, the federal government collects tax on the benefit. So in a single paycheck, PeopleSoft could use the LIFE deduction three times, with different deduction classes.

Defining a Deduction: The Deduction Table

Deductions are relatively simple to create. You define a code, give it a priority, and set up how it should be taxed. Look at the panels under Go ➤ Define Business Rules ➤ Define Payroll Process ➤ Setup 1 ➤ Deduction Table for a guide to the elements of a deduction code.

Unlike earnings, deduction information is not all stored on one table. Basic information, like the description, priority, and maximum arrears, is stored on PS_DEDUCTION_TBL. Tax information is stored separately, since a single deduction can have several tax options. These options are stored on PS_DEDUCTION_CLASS.

For information on the key structure of these tables, refer to Chapter 3 on control tables. To link the two tables, simply join on plan type and deduction code, choosing the maximum effective date from each.

Plan Type

The plan type key is actually a benefits designation. Different benefit plans are categorized into plan types. For example, you could have 500 possible medical plans. They're all under plan type '10.' All 401(k) plans are under plan type '40'. PeopleSoft delivers a fairly comprehensive list of plan types. Tables 4-5 and 4-6 in Chapter 4 list the code structure for plan types. General deductions are stored in plan type '00.'

Using plan type as a key means that PeopleSoft permits a single deduction code to be used for two different plan types. You can set up a life plan deduction called LIFE and a medical deduction called LIFE. It wouldn't be a good idea to do this unless the two deductions are somehow related. Users can be easily confused by two deduction codes that are the same. In addition, the employee's paycheck/advice detail would be confusing to the employee since they are delivered to show only the deduction code and not the plan type.

Priority

The deduction priority (DED_PRIORITY) establishes the order in which deductions are taken. Since an employee's earnings could be too little for the assigned deductions, it is important to decide which deductions *must* be taken out, and which could be deducted later.

The chart in Table 17-3 describes how PeopleSoft takes deductions. In the sample, Eric makes $4000 in a pay period, claims no withholding allowances, receives taxable benefits of $1000, and has deductions for $400 before tax and $600 after tax.

▶ **Table 17-3** How PeopleSoft calculates net pay

Step	Description	Sample (Eric's paycheck)
1	Calculate earnings.	$4000
2	Subtract before-tax deductions from the earnings to determine how much of the earning is taxable.	$4000 less $400 = $3600
3	Add taxable benefits to the earnings to be taxed to determine the "taxable gross," which is the amount against which the taxes will be computed.	$3600 plus $1000 = $4600
4	Determine taxes.	Taxes come to $1012 (22% for sake of example)
5	Subtract taxes from taxable gross.	$4600 less $1012 = $3588
6	Subtract after-tax deductions from result.	$3588 less $600 = $2988

When PeopleSoft reaches step six, and there isn't enough money to take deductions, it starts over from step one. For example, if Eric's calculated net was $500, and after-tax deductions were $600, PeopleSoft could not take the deductions. At this point PeopleSoft recalculates the net pay and applies the priorities you have established.

This priority overrides the before-and after-tax assignments. A garnishment, for example, could be set up with a very high priority. PeopleSoft takes the garnishment before taking any before-tax deductions.

Deductions with the same priority are taken together. They are also avoided together if there is not enough money. PeopleSoft recommends that each deduction receive a unique priority to prevent this situation. If you have several deductions of one type, and an employee will only receive one of them, using the same priority is not a concern.

Another important note about deduction priorities—they work in conjunction with the tax priorities set up on the company table (DED_PRIORITY_FED and DED_PRIORITY_STATE). You must set up higher priorities for these fields and make sure all deductions have lower priorities in order to take taxes first and deductions next. If these priorities are set up incorrectly the process described in Table 17-3 will not work.

Arrears—Flat and Factor

Arrears occur when PeopleSoft cannot take a deduction. The amount goes into arrears, and PeopleSoft will try to take it when the next paycheck is cut. The maximums allow you to impose limits on what PeopleSoft will try to collect.

The rule is established with the maximum payback code. The payback can be set to a flat maximum (Y), no maximum (N), or a maximum of a factor times the regular deduction amount (F). For example, let's say that Barbara receives a deduction of $1500 for her limousine service. If a flat maximum of $2000 is set, that maximum is stored in MAX_ARREARS_PAYBK. When she is in arrears over $2000, PeopleSoft will keep trying to collect only $2000. If no maximum is set, Barbara won't be so lucky—the charges will keep mounting and PeopleSoft will continue to collect the full amount. The third option, using a factor, could be set up to collect only 50% of the arrears. The factor of .5 is stored in the MAX_ARREARS_FACTOR field. Then PeopleSoft will only collect a maximum of 50% of $1500, or $750. Of course, the factor could be greater than one, which wouldn't be very nice to Barbara. This, in effect, would be charging interest for the balance due.

Processing

PeopleSoft has added functionality for processing bond deductions and garnishment deductions. By checking one of these boxes, PeopleSoft will associate the deduction code either with U.S. bond processing functions or garnishment processing.

Negative Amounts

The easiest thing to forget about deductions is that a negative deduction can occur. Suppose the recipient of your medical deduction realizes they've instructed PeopleSoft to take $10 too much for your medical coverage. The vendor could process a deduction for negative $200 to cover the last 20 pay periods. PeopleSoft will store this deduction and will take it just like any other deduction—except that the result will be an addition to net pay (in essence, an earning).

Usually this does not occur. PeopleSoft is typically the culprit, not the vendor. When a check is reversed, or a correction made, negative deductions are often created. It is important to check with your vendor whether they can receive negative amounts. These amounts will definitely appear on the PS_PAY_DEDUCTION table.

ENROLLING EMPLOYEES IN DEDUCTIONS

With large populations of employees enrolling in several different deductions, it makes sense to interface the enrollments, terminations, and amounts into PeopleSoft. This is a complicated process, since each vendor is sending different information, there are many files, and thorough error-checking and validation must be performed. The process typically occurs with the following steps:

1. PeopleSoft sends a file to the vendor of employee name and SSN.
2. The vendor records enrollments in the deductions. This depends on the vendor and the implementation. If you are recording enrollments in a deduction in PeopleSoft, the process only involves steps #4 and #5. For example, a medical plan deduction is set up in PeopleSoft, and benefits administration enrolls employees. No input is necessary, but the medical plan needs to know who is participating (and receives the file described in step #5).
3. Before the payroll, the vendor sends a file to PeopleSoft with SSN, deduction start date, deduction code, and deduction amount. The file might also have termination records, instructing PeopleSoft to stop taking a deduction.
4. PeopleSoft payroll runs.
5. PeopleSoft sends a file to the vendor with SSN and the deduction amount taken.
6. The process continues at step #2.

Essentially, you'll need to create an interface to set up or modify deductions and a set of interfaces that pass information back on deductions taken. If you are constructing these interfaces or using the delivered PeopleSoft deduction interface, be sure to distribute the file layout to your vendors and stress the importance of following it closely. Receiving all of the files in the same format will make things easier.

Also carefully consider how deductions will be fed into the system. Should the vendor send a social security number or an employee ID? Remember, PeopleSoft can store duplicate social security numbers—or none at all. Will the vendor need to send the actual deduction code? When will the vendor send the file? Does the vendor send a new deduction record every pay period, or only a list of the new enrollments and terminations? What should occur if a deduction is already established, or set up for a future effective date? Do the deductions need to be processed right away but loaded to the PeopleSoft tables at a later date? These questions determine how the inbound deduction process will function, and which tables will be used to accept the files.

The General Deduction Tables

The general deduction tables establish the calculations for deductions and which basic deductions are taken for an employee. There are two tables. The PS_GENL_DED_TBL is a control table for deduction codes (see Chapter 3 for key structure). It stores the default calculation for a deduction code. The PS_GENL_DEDUCTION table stores which *non-benefit* deductions an employee is set up to receive (see Table 17-4). Both tables only store information for general deductions, that is, deductions that are not set up in the benefits module. The employee level data on PS_GENL_DEDUCTION always overrides the default level information for a deduction.

▶ **Table 17-4**   General deductions: PS_GENL_DEDUCTION

Structure	Several rows per employee ID, one for each deduction code/ effective date.
Keys	Employee ID
	Employee Record Number
	Deduction Code
	Effective Date
Alternate keys	None
Sub-records included	None
Panels to look at	Go ➤ Compensate Employees ➤ Maintain Payroll Data U.S. ➤ Use ➤ General Deduction Data

Deductions are calculated according to the values in three principal fields: deduction calculation, additional amount, and rate percentage. Table 17-5 describes each calculation option and which fields will be populated when it is used. The additional amount field is an additional amount that applies to each pay period.

▶ **Table 17-5** Deduction calculation

Code	Description	Values stored in
A	Flat Amount	DED_ADDL_AMT
B	Percentage	DED_RATE_PCT
C	Calculated by salary system—an outside system calculates the deduction.	
D	Default to Deduction Table (PS_GENL_DED_TBL)—used only on PS_GENL_DEDUCTION.	
E	Percent of special earnings, i.e. an accumulator. A 401K accumulator of specific earnings can be used. Cannot be set at employee level.	DED_RATE_PCT, ERNCD_SPCL
F	Percent of employee's Federal gross amount	DED_RATE_PCT
G	Percent of employee's total gross amount	DED_RATE_PCT
H	Rate × total hours for the pay period	DED_RATE_PCT
N	Percent of net pay, the amount when the deduction is taken (net pay used would reflect previous deductions and will not reflect subsequent deductions)	DED_RATE_PCT
P	Rate × special hours, i.e. hours linked to an accumulator. Cannot be set at the employee level.	DED_RATE_PCT, ERNCD_SPCL
S	Special deduction calculation—a custom calculation is used, which requires modification to PeopleSoft delivered code.	
W	Rate × hours worked, using the earnings that have the FLSA hours worked field set to yes.	DED_RATE_PCT

Deduction Dates

The effective date tells PeopleSoft when to start taking the deduction. As long as the effective date is less than or equal to the pay end date, the deduction will be started in that period. So if the effective date is March 15 and the pay end date is March 15, the deduction will be taken.

The deduction end date tells PeopleSoft when to stop taking the deduction. If the end date is less than or equal to the pay end date, the deduction will not be taken in that period. The deduction will not be pro-rated based on the date; it is either taken or not taken. If a deduction should end on the last day of a pay period, set the deduction end date to the day after the pay period ends so that the deduction is active for the entire pay period. For example, a pay period that ends March 28 should have a deduction end date of March 29. PeopleSoft only takes a deduction if the end date is greater than the pay end date for the payroll run.

Goals

A goal amount is the maximum PeopleSoft should take for the employee. If a United Way contribution is $200, the goal amount can be $200 and PeopleSoft will take a deduction until that amount is reached (for example, if a percentage of earnings is the deduction calculation method). The goal balance field stores the current balance and is updated each time the deduction is taken. The goal balance holds the amount that has been taken already.

The maximum yearly amount found on PS_DEDUCTION_TBL overrides the goal amount. Once the yearly amount is reached, PeopleSoft stops trying to fulfill the goal amount.

Updates

To keep track of all of the changes to the deductions for an employee, the last action and date fields record who changed what when. The last action could be recorded as system (C), the hire process (D), an online user (O), or a web user (W). The date of last update records the date the table was last changed. This provides a timestamp and is not related to the effective date.

Verifying Eligibility

Benefits Program Participation

Benefit deductions aren't as easy to decipher as general deductions. They are set up with elaborate rate structures that depend on the employee's age, level of coverage, time with the company, etc. Section 4 goes into these rate systems in greater detail. If you are looking for the amount PeopleSoft tries to take from a paycheck for a benefit plan, it can be found on the BAS_PARTIC_COST table. The method for retrieving this information is also found in section 4.

It is important to look at benefit tables, however, when setting up any deduction for an employee. In the benefits tables, an employee is linked to a benefit program. This program contains all of the plans they can sign up for, as well as the eligible deduction codes.

For example, Christen is in the BAS benefit program (base benefits). This program includes numerous different possible plans she could join. The plans are stored according to the plan type. For a medical plan type, there may be 50 different plans.

But the program is not limited to benefits deductions. General deductions are part of the program too, stored under plan type '00' (general deductions). The available deductions Christen can enroll in are listed here. The query in Table 17-6 shows how to retrieve a list so you can verify that an employee can receive a particular deduction. Each deduction code is stored with a different option ID, so this field is excluded from the WHERE clause.

▶ **Table 17-6**   Checking the benefit program for permissible deductions

| The query | ```
SELECT
BD.DEDCD
FROM PS_BEN_PROG_PARTIC BP,
     PS_BEN_DEFN_OPTN BD
WHERE BP.EMPLID    = 'C0001'
  AND BD.BENEFIT_PROGRAM = BP.BENEFIT_PROGRAM
  AND BD.PLAN_TYPE   = '00'
  AND BP.EFFDT = (SELECT MAX(BP1.EFFDT)
                       FROM PS_BEN_PROG_PARTIC BP1
                      WHERE BP1.EMPLID = BP.EMPLID
                        AND BP1.EFFDT <= [as of date])
  AND BD.EFFDT = (SELECT MAX(BD1.EFFDT)
                       FROM PS_BEN_DEFN_OPTN BD1
                      WHERE BD1.BENEFIT_PROGRAM =
                                  BD.BENEFIT_PROGRAM
                        AND BD1.PLAN_TYPE = BD.PLAN_TYPE
                        AND BD1.DEDCD   = BD.DEDCD
                        AND BD1.EFFDT <= [as of date])
``` |
| Returns the data set | ```
DEDCD
-------
CHILD
HEALTH
PRKING
GARNSH
USBOND
UWAY
LOAN
CREDUN
UNION
CAFÉ
PHARM
ADVTVL
``` |

Checking for Deduction Stop at Termination

On the PS_DEDUCTION_CLASS table, a deduction can be set up to stop at termination. If an employee receives a check after termination, the deduction is not processed for that check. The field is STOP_DED_TERM.

When feeding deduction information into PeopleSoft, you should look at the job table to retrieve status and the deduction class table to determine if the deduction is valid when an employee terminates. If a stop-at-term deduction is sent for a terminated employee, it should be rejected.

RETRIEVING DEDUCTIONS

The Pay Deduction Table

When payroll runs, deductions taken are recorded to the PS_PAY_DEDUCTION table (see Table 17-7). In addition to the regular payroll keys, plan type and benefit plan for each deduction, there are several additional amounts that are useful to know.

▶ **Table 17-7** Pay deductions: PS_PAY_DEDUCTION

Structure	Several rows per employee ID, one for each deduction code for each check.
Keys	Company
	Paygroup
	Pay End Date
	Off Cycle
	Page Number
	Line Number
	Separate Check
	Plan Type
	Benefit Plan
	Deduction Code
	Deduction Class
	Deduction Sales Tax Type
Alternate keys	None
Sub-records included	None
Panels to look at	Go ➤ Compensate Employees ➤ Maintain Payroll Data U.S. ➤ Inquire ➤ Paycheck Data ➤ Paycheck Deductions

Deduction Amounts

When a deduction is calculated, the amount actually taken is stored in the current deduction field (DED_CUR). If an arrears payback or deduction refund affects this amount, it is stored in the refund or payback field for reference (DED_CUR_PAYBK, DED_CUR_REFUND).

Deductions Not Taken

When a deduction amount is not taken, PeopleSoft stores the amount not taken in the deduction-not-taken field. A reason is stored to help decipher what happened (see Table 17-8).

▶ **Table 17-8** Reasons deductions are not taken

Code	Description
A	Annual limit reached
B	Annual limit rollover from previous check
D	Benefit plan limit reached
E	Benefit plan limit rollover from previous check
H	Highly compensated employee limit reached
I	Highly compensated employee limit rollover from previous check
K	415 (U.S. pension) limit reached
L	415 (U.S. pension) limit rollover from previous check
M	Deduction maximum reached
N	Insufficient net pay to take deduction
R	Deduction maximum exceeded by rollover from previous check
S	Benefits base limit reached
T	Benefits base limit rollover from previous check
Z	Multiple reasons

Benefits Base Salary

For life benefit plans, such as a life insurance plan, the calculated base (CALCU-LATED_BASE) is the salary amount used to determine coverage. An employee receives coverage based on their salary—one times their salary, two times, etc. The calculated base is the employee's salary PeopleSoft considers for benefit coverage as of when the deduction was taken.

The Query

The query in Table 17-9 demonstrates the common method for retrieving deductions PeopleSoft calculated and took from an employee's paycheck.

▶ **Table 17-9**   Finding deductions taken for a payroll period

| The query | ```
SELECT
PC.EMPLID,
PC.SSN,
DE.PAY_END_DT,
DE.DEDCD,
DE.DED_CUR
FROM PS_PAY_DEDUCTION DE,
     PS_PAY_CHECK PC
WHERE PC.PAY_END_DT        = '28-FEB-2000'
  AND PC.OFF_CYCLE         = 'N'
  AND PC.PAYCHECK_STATUS   = 'F'
  AND DE.DEDCD             = 'UWAY'
  AND PC.COMPANY           = DE.COMPANY
  AND PC.PAYGROUP          = DE.PAYGROUP
  AND PC.PAY_END_DT        = DE.PAY_END_DT
  AND PC.OFF_CYCLE         = DE.OFF_CYCLE
  AND PC.PAGE#             = DE.PAGE#
  AND PC.LINE#             = DE.LINE#
  AND PC.SEPCHK            = DE.SEPCHK
``` |

Returns the data set	EMPLID	SSN	PAY_END_DT	DEDCD	DED_CUR
	8553	934556778	28-FEB-2000	UWAY	10
	G001	047663321	28-FEB-2000	UWAY	15
	E001	632648090	28-FEB-2000	UWAY	5

Note how we link the paycheck table to the pay deduction table to identify the employee with the deduction. Deductions are only stored according to the payroll check keys and do not have an associated employee ID or SSN. Linking to the paycheck table provides this link.
```

18 Taxes

Taxes are a low-maintenance item in PeopleSoft. Rates and rules are delivered and updated regularly by PeopleSoft. Codes to identify local jurisdictions and states are also provided. Based on the rules you set up on the data tables for each employee, PeopleSoft payroll will calculate the appropriate taxes, deduct them from the paycheck, and store them on the PS_PAY_TAX table.

There are several tables for storing tax rules and settings. Table 18-1 describes each table. Note the two types of set-up tables: *control* tables, which contain the rules for a given taxing authority (federal, state or local), and *data* tables, which contain employee tax specifications.

▶ **Table 18-1**   Tax tables

Type	Table	Description
Federal	FED_TAX_DATA	Employee-level federal tax elections
State	STATE_TAX_DATA	Employee-level state tax elections
Local	LOCAL_TAX_DATA	Employee-level local tax elections
State/Federal	STATE_TAX_TBL	Control table for federal and state taxes, stores federal and state tax rules
State/Federal	ST_OTH_TAX_TBL	Control table for other special state taxes.
Local	LOCAL_TAX_TBL	Control table for local taxes, stores local tax rules
State/Local	TAX_DISTRIB	Stores the percentage tax to take for each employee's work location (state and local jurisdiction). Most employees have one work location and 100% distribution.

▶ **Table 18-1**   continued

Type	Table	Description
All	PAY_TAX	Contains the tax amounts taken from each of the employee's paychecks.
All	TAX_BALANCE	Stores summary yearly, quarterly, and monthly balances of tax amounts taken from employee paychecks

TAX LOCATIONS

State and Locality

PeopleSoft provides lists of states and local jurisdictions. The state code is six characters, and is verified against the PS_STATE_NAMES_TBL, which also contains the full state name and U.S. numeric code. Local jurisdictions are given a locality code. Localities are ten characters and are defined on PS_LOCAL_TAX_TBL. They often have embedded codes—see the section on Pennsylvania localities for more information.

The Other States

Federal and local information is sometimes stored on state tax tables when their rule structures are similar. PeopleSoft created special codes to identify these pseudo-states. Whenever you see a state called '$U,'this is not a state—it is a code that means Federal. A '$E' indicates an earned income credit (EIC payment). A 'Z1' is the New York City local tax, and a 'Z2' is the Yonkers local tax. PeopleSoft continues to define new Z codes based on the taxing rules of certain localities. If the locality uses taxes similar to a state, a Z code is established.

Be sure to look out for these codes when accessing the state names table or state tax table. If you are only reporting on states, you'll want to exclude these codes.

Tax Location Code

States and localities can be grouped into unique location codes, such as 'Corporate Headquarters.' A tax location is a distinct location you will process payroll and tax data for. It could contain more than one state, or just more than one locality tax (for instance, earned income tax and occupational privilege local taxes in Pennsylvania).

A tax location code is usually just a three character code. Employees are linked to a tax location on the job table (detail) and on the department table (default). PeopleSoft uses this tax location as a default value to determine which taxes to take for an employee. If the installation table (PS_INSTALLATION) is set up to support the automatic setup of taxes for employees, the distribution of taxes is then stored on PS_TAX_DISTRIB for each state and locality found within the tax location code. The data populated into the PS_TAX_DISTRIB can be overridden for employees who have work taxes that differ from the default tax location setup.

DEFINING A TAX

The tax control tables store the definition of a tax. The formula for computing withholding tax, local tax rates, minimum and maximum taxes, and other basic information about a tax are stored according to the state or locality. Let's look at the structure of the local tax table (PS_LOCAL_TAX_TBL) to get an idea of how tax rules are stored.

Tax Class

If you are looking at the local tax table or state other tax table, you need to identify which tax you desire by choosing a tax class. The tax class specifies what the tax is—withholding, unemployment, employee or employer, etc. It is used as a key on the pay tax table, tax balance table, and other state tax table. The tax class is not used as a key on the local tax table, since each type of tax on the local tax table has its own locality code.

> Note that the state tax table, PS_STATE_TAX_TBL, also does not have a tax class field. That's because it only defines base withholding taxes.

Table 18-2 explains each tax class and identifies it as employer or employee. If you are looking only for employee taxes or employer taxes, be sure to specify the appropriate tax class. Often these are reported on separately, since employer taxes do not appear on an employee paycheck. *Employee* taxes are deducted from the total gross earnings and paid to the government. *Employer* taxes come straight from the employer's pocket and are unrelated to the taxes an employee pays (we'll call them company taxes to make things easier to understand).

▶ **Table 18-2** Tax class

Code	Company/ Employee	Description
C	Employee	Earned Income Credit
H	Employee	Withholding
K	Employee	Excise
M	Employee	New Jersey WFDP (Workforce Development Partnership Fund)
N	Employee	New Jersey HCSF (Health Care Subsidy Fund)
S	Employee	Unemployment—Special
P	Employee	Occupational Privilege Tax
R	Company	Local
B	Both	Local—Employer and Employee
D	Employee	OASDI/Disability (Social Security)
E	Company	OASDI/Disability (Social Security)
G	Employee	OASDI—tips (Social Security)
J	Company	OASDI—tips (Social Security)
V	Employee	Unemployment
U	Company	Unemployment
W	Employee	Voluntary Disability Plan
X	Company	Voluntary Disability Plan
F	Employee	FICA Medical Hospital Insurance
Q	Company	FICA Medical Hospital Insurance
T	Employee	FICA Medical Hospital Insurance—tips
Z	Company	FICA Medical Hospital Insurance—tips

Keep in mind that these classifications are used in conjunction with state and locality codes to uniquely identify a tax. Even though you could create it, you won't find anyone in Arkansas with a tax class of M or N (New Jersey taxes).

Local Taxes

Maintenance

PeopleSoft maintains the local tax table and provides updates to it when required (see Table 18-3). You can still modify the local tax table, but as soon as you do, PeopleSoft flags the new locality as "customer responsibility" (the

MAINT_RESPONSBLTY field). When updates to the table are made, localities with customer responsibility are left alone.

Local Jurisdiction

A locality code does not represent a city or town. Yes, locality codes follow the boundaries of cities and towns, but they often represent even smaller subsets or crossovers between towns. An employee could receive a local tax for the town she lives in (municipal tax), plus a local tax for the school district she belongs to. Or she may receive one local tax that combines a school district and a municipal tax. The local jurisdiction field tells you which is which. A value of 'D' means school district, 'M' means municipality, and 'C' stands for combination. The values 'S' (state), 'T' (county), and 'O' (other) are not currently used.

▶ **Table 18-3** Local tax table: PS_LOCAL_TAX_TBL

Structure	Several rows per state and locality depending on effective date
Keys	State
	Locality
	Effective Date
Alternate keys	Locality name
	County
Sub-records included	None
Panels to look at	Go ➤ Define Business Rules ➤ Define Payroll Taxes ➤ Setup ➤ Local Tax Table

Tax Type/ Rates

The basic rule for the calculation of the local tax is based on the tax type. This defines whether the tax is a rate, a set amount, based on state taxes or is on a state tax table (graduated tax table). When a local tax is similar to state rules, the tax is stored on the PS_STATE_TAX_TBL, given a state code that begins with 'Z,' and the local tax type is set to 'T' for graduated tax table. In these cases the 'Z' code is stored in GRADUATED_TBL_CD on the local tax table in order to link to the state tax table record.

For a tax type involving a rate, the rates are stored for residents and non-residents (RESIDENT_TAX_RT, NONRESIDENT_TAX_RT).

Handling Pennsylvania

Localities in Pennsylvania have special codes with embedded meanings. Table 18-4 explains each of the codes and what they stand for.

▶ **Table 18-4** PA locality codes

Code	Example	Meaning
Starts with I	I010033S	Income tax
Starts with O	O010033C	Occupational privilege tax
Ends with I	46592I	An old code PeopleSoft will be deleting
Ends with O	46592O	An old code PeopleSoft will be deleting
Ends with C	I300455C	Combination municipality and school district
Ends with M	I300455M	Municipality
Ends with S	I300455S	School district
Ends with number after letter	I320275C1	Subset, indicates that the school district applies to more than one municipality

Note that two of the possibilities, ending with an I or an O, are scheduled for deletion. PeopleSoft left these codes in to facilitate the conversion to the new codes. They are all inactivated, but PeopleSoft provides an SQR to re-activate them. In future releases PeopleSoft will delete these codes entirely.

In addition to these codes, the local tax table provides several fields specific to Pennsylvania.

Other Localities. The other locality field (OTH_LOCALITY) is used to define a corresponding locality, such as a school district code for a municipal locality. The name and abbreviation are also stored here. Deductions are calculated according to the value in these three fields. Table 17-5 in Chapter 17 describes each calculation option and which fields will be populated when it is used. The additional amount field is an additional amount that applies to each pay period.

Partial Indicator. When a single school district is related to several municipalities, the partial indicator is turned on (PARTIAL_IND). According to Table 18-4, any codes ending in a letter followed by a number will have this indicator turned on, since the number represents a subset number for each municipality.

State and Federal Taxes

The state tax table (Table 18-5) is different from all of the other tax tables because it only stores withholding taxes (a single tax class, 'H'). It also has a very misleading name, since it stores not only state but federal and local taxes as well. Any withholding tax that requires special rules is stored on the state tax table.

▶ **Table 18-5** State tax table: PS_STATE_TAX_TBL

Structure	Several rows per state depending on effective date
Keys	State
	Effective Date
Alternate keys	None
Sub-records included	None
Panels to look at	Go ➤ Define Payroll Taxes ➤ Setup ➤ Federal/State Tax Table

Tax Type/ Rates

State taxes can be calculated using numerous methods, and PeopleSoft is set up to handle every state-specific rule. For this reason we won't go heavily into the definition of taxes. But it's useful to know where things are and how they connect.

On the state tax table, the calculation type is the basic calculation PeopleSoft payroll will perform. A tax rate can be a flat percentage of federal tax, a percentage of taxable gross, or on a graduated scale. Graduated taxes (i.e., taxes that depend on the marital status or financial income of the employee) or other factors are identified on a separate table, the PS_STATE_TAXRT_TBL. This table contains the state, a low gross earnings, low tax, tax rate, and a tax status. The tax status identifies the type of calculation—there are over 30 different types. Some sample types are Single (S), Married (M), Non-resident (O), New Jersey Rate Table C (C), and Head of Household-Special (Y). As you can see, they are very specific.

Two fields on the state tax table identify methods for calculating tax on supplemental earnings (like a bonus payment). The concurrent method field (Paid with regular wages) is for income that is taxed using the annualized method. The separate method field (Separate payment) is for earnings paid separately from regular wages. Depending on the method chosen for each of these fields, extra income will be taxed differently. Again, these fields are set by PeopleSoft according to the laws of each state.

EMPLOYEE TAX ELECTIONS

Several data tables store information about individual employee taxes. Each employee has one record on the federal tax data table, one record for every state the employee is taxed in on the state tax data table, and one record for every locality on the local tax data table. These three tables have similar fields. We'll look at the federal tax data table, since it contains all of the types of fields in one place (Table 18-6).

▶ **Table 18-6** Federal tax data: PS_FED_TAX_DATA

Structure	One row per employee (several if different effective dates)
Keys	Employee ID
	Company
	Effective Date
Alternate keys	None
Sub-records included	None
Panels to look at	Go ➤ Compensate Employees ➤ Maintain Payroll Data U.S. ➤ Use ➤ Employee Tax Data ➤ Federal Tax Data

Special Withholding/ Allowances

The following fields specify federal withholding and allowances rules for a particular employee:

Special Federal Withholding Tax (FWT) Status. To stop PeopleSoft from calculating the standard federal tax for an employee, you can specify the employee as exempt (E) or specify an additional amount and/or percent (G) to take the place of the federal tax (see these two fields below).

FWT Marital Status. A marital status, married (M) or single (S) is stored for each employee so PeopleSoft can decide which taxes are applicable.

FWT Allowances. The number of allowances (i.e., for dependents) the employee takes is stored here. PeopleSoft will let an employee take any number of allowances. The delivered SQR report Tax106 identifies employees with more than ten allowances.

FWT Additional Amount, Additional Percent. An employee can specify an additional amount or percentage to be taxed. This additional amount is taken on top of the PeopleSoft-calculated federal amount, unless the special status field is set to 'G' (see above).

Lock-in. If the IRS sends a letter specifying the maximum number of allowances an employee may have, this is called a lock-in letter. You can check the lock-in received box to indicate the receipt of such a letter and then type in the limit in the lock-in limit field. PeopleSoft will then restrict the number of federal allowances for this and all future-dated records.

FICA and EIC

FICA Status. The FICA (Federal Insurance Contributions Act) status defaults from the company table but may be overridden here. If the employee is exempt from paying taxes on company-provided benefit payments, this field will be set to 'E' for exempt. The field can also be set to 'M' for Medicare only, but is usually specified as 'N' for Subject to FICA.

Exempt from FUT. If the employee is exempt from federal unemployment tax (FUT), this box is checked. The FUT exempt field also defaults from the company table. Since FUT is an employer-paid tax, the employee will not see this tax.

EIC Status. Earned income credits (EIC) can be paid to employees each pay period. A setting of 'M' for a married couple filing for EIC, or 'S' for a single individual filing for EIC will tell PeopleSoft to pay EICs. As mentioned above, the rates for EICs are stored in the state tax table under the state code $E.

W-2 Settings

When PeopleSoft produces a W-2 statement, it needs to know some basic information about the employee. These flags are stored on the federal tax data table since they are related to federal tax filing. Table 18-7 explains each flag.

▶ **Table 18-7** W-2 flags stored on PS_FED_TAX_DATA

Flag	Definition
Statutory employee	The employee works for the employer but is not an employee under common law.
Deceased	Employee is deceased.

▶ **Table 18-7** continued

Flag	Definition
Pension plan	The employee participated at some point during the year in a pension plan.
Legal representative	Name on the W-2 is a legal representative for the employee.
Deferred compensation	Employee deferred income into a 401(k) or 403(b) retirement plan.

State Settings

State tax data is similar to federal tax data, so we will only look at some of the unique fields for state data. In addition to the fields explained below, there are several fields you can find on the table and panel that are specific to just one state. The ANNL_EXEMPTION_AMT is only for Mississippi, SWT_ADDL_ALLOWANCES and WAGE_PLAN_CD only for California, and PERCENT_OF_FWT only for Arizona.

Resident. One of the key differences between federal tax data and state tax data is that an employee can be linked to more than one state. A resident check box (RESIDENT) identifies which state the employee resides in. The work state is determined by the employee's tax location on the job table.

Non-residency Statement Filed. An employee must inform you if he or she lives and works in different states. In several states, they need to file a notice. This field can be used to record when the employee has filed notice.

Unemployment Jurisdiction. Employees who work in several different states must specify which state takes out unemployment and disability taxes. PeopleSoft sets this flag to yes depending on how many states an employee is taxed in. If the employee is taxed in one state, that state is set to yes. If two, the nonresident state is set to yes. If more than two, PeopleSoft will tell you to specify a state manually.

SDI Status, Exempt from SUT. The SDI status identifies whether an employee is subject to state disability insurance taxes (Y), a voluntary disability plan (V), not applicable (N) or exempt (E). The SUT exempt field is yes when an employee is exempt from state unemployment tax. Both fields default from the company table.

Local Settings

The local tax data table has even fewer fields than the state tax data table. The table stores the number of allowances, additional amount and percentage, special tax status, and marital status just like the federal and state tax data tables. It has a resident indicator just like the state tax data table, except that employees can reside in several localities (remember, localities can indicate a school district and municipality, not just a town).

When more than one locality is applied to an employee work location, PeopleSoft stores the other locality code in the other work locality (LOCALITY_LINK) field.

RETRIEVING TAXES

The query in Table 18-8 demonstrates the common method for retrieving taxes calculated by PeopleSoft and taken from an employee's paycheck.

▶ **Table 18-8** Finding taxes taken for a payroll period (withholding only shown)

The query	
| ```
SELECT
PC.EMPLID,
PC.SSN,
PT.STATE,
PT.LOCALITY,
PT.TAX_CUR
FROM PS_PAY_TAX PT,
     PS_PAY_CHECK PC
WHERE PC.PAY_END_DT        = '28-FEB-2000'
  AND PC.OFF_CYCLE         = 'N'
  AND PC.PAYCHECK_STATUS   = 'F'
  AND PT.TAX_CLASS         = 'H'
  AND PC.COMPANY           = PT.COMPANY
  AND PC.PAYGROUP          = PT.PAYGROUP
  AND PC.PAY_END_DT        = PT.PAY_END_DT
  AND PC.OFF_CYCLE         = PT.OFF_CYCLE
  AND PC.PAGE#             = PT.PAGE#
  AND PC.LINE#             = PT.LINE#
  AND PC.SEPCHK            = PT.SEPCHK
``` | |
```

▶ **Table 18-8**   continued

	EMPLID	SSN	STATE	LOCALITY	RESIDENT	TAX_CUR
Returns the data set	------	---------	-----	--------	--------	-------
	BOZO	632648090	$U			1117.07
	BOZO	632648090	PA		Y	183.02
	BOZO	632648090	PA	60000I	Y	313.09
	C001	490667266	$U			320.66
	C001	490667266	CA			116.13
	C001	490667266	OH		Y	97.52

Employee BOZO has a federal income withholding tax of $1,117.07 this period. He is a resident of Pennsylvania, locality 60000I. His state withholding tax is $183.02 and local tax is $313.09. Employee C001 resides in Ohio and works in California.

The Pay Tax Table

When payroll runs, taxes taken are recorded to the PS_PAY_TAX table. In addition to the regular payroll keys, state and locality for each tax, there are several additional amount fields for each tax.

▶ **Table 18-9**   Pay tax: PS_PAY_TAX

Structure	Several rows per employee ID, for federal ($U), state, and/or local tax for each check.
Keys	Company
	Paygroup
	Pay End Date
	Off Cycle
	Page Number
	Line Number
	Separate Check
	State
	Locality
	Tax Class
Alternate keys	None
Sub-records included	None
Panels to look at	Go ➤ Maintain Payroll Data U.S. ➤ Inquire ➤ Paycheck Data ➤ Paycheck Taxes

Tax Amounts

The current tax field is the actual tax that was taken, and the taxable gross is the amount that was taxed. These will appear for every tax class. The current no-limit-gross field, though, identifies the taxable gross as if there were no limits. Certain tax classes have limits imposed, which reduce the taxable gross. Although the no-limit-gross is not used to calculate taxes, PeopleSoft does use it to report quarterly tax wages.

When a tax amount is not taken, PeopleSoft stores the amount not taken in the tax-not-taken field.

19
Garnishments

Garnishments are always the forgotten piece of the payroll process. There's earnings, deductions, taxes—but what is a garnishment? Part of this ignorance is due to the fact that garnishments, in PeopleSoft, are really a deduction—an elaborate deduction.

A garnishment occurs when an employee owes money to an external party. Dan could owe child support to the state of Illinois, or be past due on his credit card payments. Usually a garnishment means that Dan is *really* past due. Garnishments are a serious step, since they 'garnish,' or directly take, an employee's wages. The employee has no say, since typically a garnishment is a court order.

SETTING UP GARNISHMENTS

PeopleSoft stores garnishments separately from other deductions. In fact, there is only one delivered deduction code for garnishments, GARNSH. The code simply enables a garnishment in the payroll process. Setting up a garnishment is completely different from setting up a deduction.

First, let's look at all of the different tables for garnishments and how they come together. Table 19-1 lists each table and function.

▶ **Table 19-1** Garnishment tables

Table	Description
GARN_BALANCE	Stores balances of garnishments taken for an employee.
GARN_DE_DED	Defines which deductions can be taken from earnings before garnishments apply.
GARN_DE_DEFN	Disposable earnings definitions for garnishments.
GARN_DE_EARN	Lists earning codes that can be garnished.
GARN_EMPL_DED	Defines permissible deductions at the employee level.
GARN_PAYEE_TBL	Stores address information for garnishing party.
GARN_RULE	Links an employee garnishment to a garnishment law.
GARN_RULE_TBL	Defines U.S. government garnishment laws.
GARN_SCHED	Defines when garnishments should be taken for an employee.
GARN_SPEC	Employee-level garnishment order detail.
PAY_GARNISH	Stores the garnishment results of the pay process.

As you can see, garnishments are not a simple thing to set up. Luckily many of these tables are already delivered in PeopleSoft, and most of them are control settings which should almost never change. However, the PS_GARN_DE_DEFN table must be updated with customer-specific deduction codes to properly identify the disposable earnings definition. We're going to look specifically at setting up a garnishment for an employee—the PS_GARN_SPEC table.

Employee Garnishment Specifications

The garnishment specification panels (Table 19-2) allow you either to enter a new garnishment or to track an existing order. They store most of the relevant information in one place.

▶ **Table 19-2** Garnishment Specification: PS_GARN_SPEC

Structure	Several rows per employee ID, one for each garnishment.
Keys	Employee ID
	Company
	Garnish ID
Alternate keys	None
Sub-records included	Address Sub-record
Panels to look at	Go ➤ Compensate Employees ➤ Maintain Payroll Data U.S. ➤ Use ➤ Garnishment Spec Data

Identifying a garnishment

Garnishments are stored using a garnish ID number. This number must uniquely identify the garnishment. Since garnish IDs are not set up on a control table, the number need not be unique from employee to employee. For example, one employee could have a garnishment from the IRS with a garnish ID of 01. Another employee could use the 01 ID to represent a family court order. As long as a single employee with numerous garnishments uses unique garnish IDs, everything is fine.

The garnish ID is not an arbitrary number, though. It is used throughout the downstream panels and tables to identify the garnishment for an employee. You'll find it on PS_PAY_GARNISH and PS_GARN_BALANCE.

Many garnishments are set up on the fly—you look up the employee and type in the garnishment information. Certain garnishments, especially from the government, are stored in the rule table. These garnishments can be selected on the Garnishment Spec Data 6 panel. The link is stored on the PS_GARN_RULE table. Choosing a garnishment rule fills in some of the data, but you still need to manually type in some of the information at the employee level.

A garnishment type also provides an identification of a garnishment. PeopleSoft provides these types for your records; they are not used in payroll processing. Table 19-3 lists the different types and their definitions.

▶ **Table 19-3** Garnishment types

Code	Description
A	Wage assignment; a standard garnishment
B	Chapter 13 bankruptcy
C	Child support
D	Dependent support
L	Tax levy; owes taxes
S	Spousal support
W	Writ of garnishment; a standard 'failure to pay' garnishment

Child, dependent, and spousal support garnishments are used in conjunction with the support type field (GARN_SUPPORT_TYPE), which identifies the support as current or arrears.

General information about the garnishment, such as the court name, IDs associated with the order, and general remarks can be entered as well to identify the garnishment.

Payees

The payee information (i.e. the people who are taking the wages) is stored at the employee level with the garnishment information. Common payees are stored on the PS_GARN_PAYEE_TBL—it is just their name and address. When setting up a garnishment, you can choose from this table or type in a new payee name and address. This is the address that the garnishment is sent to. If you choose a name, the payee information is automatically copied into the employee-level fields on PS_GARN_SPEC.

There is also an AP Vendor ID field, which can be used if you plan to use an accounts payable system to process garnishment payments (discussed later in this chapter). Contact information is also stored here, but is for your information only.

Status

Garnishments, you'll find, are a manual process. When the status of a garnishment changes, it is your responsibility to modify the status field at the employee level. There are five different codes that identify the status of a garnishment order, listed in Table 19-4. PeopleSoft will take the garnishment only if the status is 'A' or 'R.'

▶ **Table 19-4** Garnishment status

Code	Description
R	Request received—the first status, but rarely used (garnishments are often approved or rejected before they're typed in).
A	Request approved—you are informing the court that you will comply.
J	Request rejected (employee could be terminated, or there are no wages)
S	Request suspended—the garnishment continues but PeopleSoft temporarily stops taking it from the employee's paycheck.
C	Deduction completed, the garnishment is paid.

Deduction Rules

Numerous fields affect how the garnishment is taken from a paycheck, including the priority, limits, calculation routine, and amount.

Garnish Priority.   A garnishment priority is not the same as a deduction priority, although they work in a similar fashion. A lower priority number means that the deduction will be taken before a higher number. If you enter the same priority number for two deductions, PeopleSoft takes the lower Garnish ID first. Keep in mind that the priority is only in relation to the employee you are working with. Priorities do not carry over from one employee to another. Priority is not used when you are prorating garnishments.

Company/ Payee Fees. These two 'include' checkboxes indicate how garnishment fees should be taken. A fee for handling the garnishment may be taken by the payee (the people garnishing), or the company. To make sure that you get the fee, it can be automatically removed from the disposable earnings for an employee. This way, when PeopleSoft goes to take the garnishment, the disposable earnings already reflect the removal of the fee. The include in disposable earnings fields turn this function on.

Limit Amount, Limit Balance, Monthly Limit. Limitations exist for how long a garnishment can be taken, or on how many garnishments are allowed can be entered. PeopleSoft will keep track of the balance deducted in the limit balance field, until the limit amount is reached. A monthly limit is also sometimes imposed. Keep in mind that PeopleSoft considers paychecks as part of a given month when the paycheck date falls within the month, not the pay end date.

Stop Dates. PeopleSoft needs to know when to stop taking the deduction. It will accept a date, but some garnishment laws impose a restriction of days that a garnishment can be taken. For example, a garnishment might need to be taken for no more than 30 days. Without knowing when your next check will occur, you could not enter a stop date. But if you set the auto calculation stop flag to yes and enter in a number of days, PeopleSoft will figure out the date and handle the stop automatically.

Payment Mode and Schedule. The garnishment deduction schedule allows a particular schedule for deducting garnishments. Perhaps an employee should only receive the deduction every third payroll period. The PS_GARN_SCHED table and Garnishment Spec Data 5 panel allow the construction of a custom schedule. If such a schedule is used, the deduction schedule field is set to 'S.' Otherwise, by default the schedule is 'A' for all payrolls.

The payment mode looks like an important processing field, but it serves no function. You can use it for information or to feed another system. The payment mode identifies whether the payee should receive a check when the collection is complete ('C'), every time an amount is deducted ('D'), or every month ('M').

Calculation Routine, Percent and Amount. There are two simple ways PeopleSoft can take a garnishment. It can take the maximum possible ('M'). Or it can apply a percentage and/or a flat amount to the employee's disposable earnings ('P'). When a flat amount is taken, enter the frequency (daily, monthly, or weekly) so PeopleSoft can figure out how much should be taken for the employee based on his or her particular pay frequency.

RETRIEVING GARNISHMENTS

The query in Table 19-5 demonstrates the common method for retrieving garnishments calculated by PeopleSoft and taken from an employee's paycheck.

▶ **Table 19-5**   Finding garnishments taken for a payroll period

The query	`SELECT`				
	`PC.EMPLID,`				
	`PC.SSN,`				
	`PG.GARNID,`				
	`PG.DEDUCT_AMT,`				
	`PG.DEDUCT_GARN_AMT,`				
	`FROM PS_PAY_GARNISH PG,`				
	`     PS_PAY_CHECK PC`				
	`WHERE PC.PAY_END_DT`		`= '28-FEB-2000'`		
	`  AND PC.OFF_CYCLE`		`= 'N'`		
	`  AND PC.PAYCHECK_STATUS`		`= 'F'`		
	`  AND PC.COMPANY`		`= PG.COMPANY`		
	`  AND PC.PAYGROUP`		`= PG.PAYGROUP`		
	`  AND PC.PAY_END_DT`		`= PG.PAY_END_DT`		
	`  AND PC.OFF_CYCLE`		`= PG.OFF_CYCLE`		
	`  AND PC.PAGE#`		`= PG.PAGE#`		
	`  AND PC.LINE#`		`= PG.LINE#`		
	`  AND PC.SEPCHK`		`= PG.SEPCHK`		

Returns the data set	EMPLID	SSN	GARNID	DEDUCT_AMT	DEDUCT_GARN_AMT
	------	---------	------	----------	---------------
	BOZO	632648090	03	1750.89	1741.55
	BOZO	632648090	04	345.00	345.00

BOZO had two garnishments taken from his paycheck—one for $1741.55 and another for $345. Since a fee applies to garnish ID 3, the actual hit to Bozo is $1750.89.

The Pay Garnish Table

When payroll runs, garnishments taken are recorded to the PS_PAY_GARNISH table. Some of the information comes directly from the PS_GARN_SPEC table, where garnishments are set up. Other fields are results of the payroll process—let's look at the fields you'll commonly use to determine what happened in Table 19-6.

▶ **Table 19-6** Pay garnish: PS_PAY_GARNISH

Structure	Several rows per employee ID, one for each garnishment taken
Keys	Company
	Paygroup
	Pay End Date
	Off Cycle
	Page Number
	Line Number
	Separate Check
	Plan Type
	Benefit Plan
	Deduction Code
	Deduction Class
	Garnish Priority
	Garnish ID
Alternate keys	None
Sub-records included	None
Panels to look at	Go ➤ Compensate Employees ➤ Maintain Payroll Data U.S. ➤ Inquire ➤ Paycheck Data ➤ Paycheck Garnishments

The Strange Keys

The pay garnish table has many keys. Most of them, however, don't provide important functions. Payroll keys (the first 7) are standard. Then the structure is similar to the pay deduction table, with a plan type, benefit plan, deduction code and deduction class.

In most situations, the plan type is '00' for general deduction, the benefit plan is blank, the deduction code is 'GARNSH' and the deduction class is 'A' (after-tax). That clears up some of the confusion. Then garnishments are listed according to priority and ID number.

Of course, the presence of this key structure means that garnishments can be set up with other deduction codes for benefit plans, different plan types, or different deduction classes. But these situations are unlikely.

The Resulting Garnishment Amounts

The deduction amount, garnish amount, company fee and payee fee fields identify what was deducted and how much of that was a garnishment and how much was a fee. The formula is simple:

```
Deduction amount - Company fee - Payee fee = Garnish amount.
```

The deduction amount is taken from the paycheck, but the garnish amount is what you need to pay the garnishing party (plus the payee fee).

AN ACCOUNTS PAYABLE INTERFACE

PeopleSoft stores a great deal of information about garnishments, but what does it actually do with it? The answer is not much. The different control tables manage most of the rules governing how garnishments are taken out, and some fields at the employee level affect payroll. Most of the other fields simply store data about the garnishment.

That is because PeopleSoft does not write garnishment checks. These checks don't go to employees—they go to the garnishing party. If Georgia is garnishing 100 employees for spousal support, Georgia wants one check covering all of these garnishments and a report showing who contributed what. PeopleSoft just won't do it without some funny business (setting up fake employees, for instance).

Many choose to write a custom SQR to generate a file that can be used by an accounts payable (AP) system. An AP system typically writes checks for vendors in a company. It can easily cut a check to a garnishing party. When you send information to the AP system, you'll find that many of the "information only" fields in PeopleSoft are suddenly useful, like address or AP vendor ID number. At the tail end of this process, think about how you can provide a report of garnishment payments along with the check that your AP system creates.

20

Year-End Processing: The W-2

Each year, after the year is over (i.e, January), certain reports need to be produced. We'll concentrate on the W-2, the government form that details how much an employee earned and paid in taxes. A W-2 must be produced for each employee by the end of January so it can be used in individual tax returns. PeopleSoft's W-2 process is designed to make this process simple, and more importantly, accurate.

Many things can go wrong with producing W-2s. An employee could find an error, and a new W-2 will need to be produced. Errors in individual payrolls, which you've ignored so far, pop up again. Few people look forward to producing W-2s. At least in PeopleSoft most of the processing is handled automatically.

THE W-2 DESIGN

PeopleSoft's W-2 process has many programs to run which update tables and produce audit reports. The steps are detailed in Table 20-1. As an overview, there are really just a few basic steps. You load the W-2 tables, you audit the data, fix it, print the W-2s, and create the file for the government.

▶ **Table 20-1**　Steps for producing W-2s

Step	Description
Prepare	Make sure the data in the following tables is in tip-top shape: PS_COMPANY_TBL PS_TAXFORM_TBL PS_TAXFORM_FORM PS_TAXFORM_PRT PS_W2_COMPANY
Set Federal Tax Data	Run Tax504 to set the federal tax data flags for the employee. This program looks to see if the employee participated in a pension plan, had a before-tax deduction (i.e., deferred compensation), or passed away (deceased flag).
Run Tax900	Lists possible errors, such as employee negative tax balances or invalid Social Security numbers. Review the report, correct the errors, and run again until no errors exist.
Run Tax910LD	Takes personal, payroll, and tax data and loads it to the PeopleSoft W-2 tables.
Run Tax910ER	Identifies additional errors.
Run W-2 reports	Tax910AU lists detail data of individual W-2s. This is an audit report that will report errors. Tax916ST State W-2 Tax Totals Report. Tax916LC Local W-2 Tax Totals Report. Review these reports and correct errors until no errors exist.
Re-run Tax910LD and Tax910ER	Final W-2 records are now loaded.
Final run of W-2 reports	Run the W-2 reports for a final reference.
Run Tax910PR	Prints copies of the W-2 for employees.
Run Tax910FD	Creates the tape for the federal government.

The first major step is to prepare for the W-2 process. This involves setting up W-2 company information and establishing parameters for how W-2s will print.

W-2 Parameters

Boxes

Using several panels, you can define exactly how PeopleSoft calculates a W-2. These panels are under Go ➤ Compensate Employees ➤ Manage Annual Tax Reporting U.S. ➤ Setup ➤ Tax Form Definition. Here is where each box is defined, named, and associated with a tax, taxable gross, or deduction. Using these panels, several balances can be combined together into a single box.

Printing

Under Tax Form Print Parameters you can specify how PeopleSoft prints a W-2. This is useful for adapting PeopleSoft to your company's specific W-2 form. PeopleSoft will create W-2 forms in several styles or can accept pre-printed forms. Each individual item that appears on the W-2 can be adjusted using the print parameters. The line number, column number, and edit mask can all be specified. These parameters are read by the W-2 print program, TAX910PR, making it one of the most flexible delivered SQRs. In an effort to keep customer modifications to a minimum, the print parameters allow customization without changing the actual SQR program. This is especially important for an SQR that changes nearly every year due to W-2 changes. Since PeopleSoft will keep revising Tax910PR, it makes little sense to modify it.

Reporting

The tax reporting parameters panels and table store data about the tape created for the government. These fields are provided to comply with federal government standards. Company information, such as address and federal EIN number(s) is provided on the company panel and table.

Auditing Data Using Delivered Reports

The delivered reports provide an excellent audit of payroll data. Table 20-2 lists the different error checks each report provides. You'll find that PeopleSoft is quite comprehensive when it comes to tax reporting.

▶ **Table 20-2**   W-2 Audit Errors

Validation	Program
Medicare or Medicare tips tax amount is greater than limit	Tax900
Medicare or Medicare tips tax and tax balance not equal	Tax900
Medicare or Medicare tips tax withheld is greater than limit	Tax900
No federal tax data record	Tax900
OASDI or OASDI tips taxable > OASDI limit	Tax900
OASDI or OASDI tips tax withheld > OASDI tax withheld limit	Tax900
OASDI or OASDI tips tax and tax balance not equal	Tax900
Negative gross taxable	Tax900
Federal Withholding Tax (FWT) balance for Puerto Rico employee	Tax900

▶ **Table 20-2** continued

Validation	Program
Puerto Rico tax expected, another state found	Tax900
Puerto Rico tax balance in a non-Puerto Rico company	Tax900
FWT balance for Guam employee	Tax900
Earned Income Credit (EIC) for Puerto Rico employee	Tax900
Earned Income Credit (EIC) advance payment exceeds limit	Tax900
Negative tax Tax900 Tips Medicare Gross < Tips OASDI gross	Tax900
Medicare gross < OASDI gross Tax900 Missing or invalid EIN	Tax900
Imputed income is negative	Tax900
EIC advance exceeds maximum EIC amount	Tax900
Social Security taxable is negative	Tax900
Social Security HI taxable is negative	Tax900
Social Security tax is negative	Tax900
Incomplete employee address	Tax910er
Social Security HI tax is negative	Tax900
City taxable is negative	Tax900
City tax is negative	Tax900
State taxable is negative	Tax900
State tax is negative	Tax900
Federal/state taxable equal to imputed income	Impcalc
Employee has fringe but not federal taxable	Tax910er
Employee has no taxable W-2 earnings	Tax910ld
Earned Income Credit (EIC) should be < 0	Tax900
Missing SSN or SSN is invalid (see validation in Chapter 6)	Tax900
Box 11 > box 1	Tax910er
Box 12 > box 1	Tax910er
Box 13C < 0	Tax910er
Box 13D, E, F, G, or H > 0 but deferred compensation not marked	Tax910er
401(k) amount is negative	Tax900

Most of the error checking in Tax910er is a duplicate of the checks made in Tax900, just to ensure that nothing sneaks through.

Limitations and Multiple W-2s

The PeopleSoft W-2 has limits, but most of them are handled on separate W-2 forms. States and localities do not limit the W-2s—PeopleSoft will keep creating new W-2 records for however many states and localities the employee is taxed in. Similarly, only three entries can appear in box 13. If there are more, PeopleSoft will generate new W-2 records.

Employees working in two different companies will also receive two W-2 records. If the companies share a Federal EIN, however, their W-2 data will eventually be combined on the printout and file.

USING W-2 TABLES

The W-2 tables store payroll balances for employee W-2s separately from the regular payroll balances. This ensures that the balances are frozen and cannot be changed as time passes. Of course, you can run the Tax910ld SQR to reload the tables, and then they'll change. But the theory is that after W-2s are produced, this data will stay the same forever. Additionally, PeopleSoft will warn you if you try to reload a previous year.

Table 20-3 demonstrates a simple query looking at employee W-2 information after it is loaded to the tables.

▶ **Table 20-3** W-2 Data: PS_W2_AMOUNTS

| The query | ```
SELECT
WD.SSN,
WA.EMPLID,
WA.BOX,
WA.STATE,
WA.LOCALITY,
WA.W2_AMOUNT
FROM PS_W2_AMOUNTS WA,
      PS_W2_DATA WD,
      PS_W2_EE WE
WHERE WE.PROCESS_FLAG      = 'C'
   AND WE.CALENDAR_YEAR    = 1999
   AND WE.TAXFORM_ID       = 'W'
   AND WE.EMPLID           = 'BOZO'
   AND WD.COMPANY          = WE.COMPANY
   AND WD.EMPLID           = WE.EMPLID
   AND WD.CALENDAR_YEAR    = WE.CALENDAR_YEAR
   AND WD.TAXFORM_ID       = WE.TAXFORM_ID
   AND WA.COMPANY          = WD.COMPANY
``` |
| --- | --- |
```

▶ **Table 20-3** continued

```
              AND  WA.EMPLID            = WD.EMPLID
              AND  WA.CALENDAR_YEAR     = WD.CALENDAR_YEAR
              AND  WA.TAXFORM_ID        = WD.TAXFORM_ID
              AND  WA.SEQUENCE_NUMBER   = WD.SEQUENCE_NUMBER
```

Returns the data set	SSN	EMPLID	BOX	STATE	LOCALITY	W2_AMOUNT
	632648090	E001	01	$U		78469.36
	632648090	E001	02	$U		13629.42
	632648090	E001	03	$U		654.00
	632648090	E001	04	$U		4054.80
	632648090	E001	05	$U		78469.36
	632648090	E001	06	$U		1137.81
	632648090	E001	14G	PA		0
	632648090	E001	17	PA		78469.36
	632648090	E001	18	PA		2197.15
	632648090	E001	20	PA	60000I	78469.36
	632648090	E001	21	PA	60000I	3778.34

A little explanation is necessary. Here we are looking at three tables. The base table, PS_W2_EE, lists each employee along with a process flag for the W-2. A 'C' process flag means complete. The taxform ID of 'W' selects only W-2 data. The next table, PS_W2_DATA, stores employee-specific data, such as the name, SSN, address, and different W-2 flags. Note the addition of a new key, sequence number. This number keeps track of multiple W-2s for the same employee. Finally, we link to the PS_W2_AMOUNTS table to get the actual boxes and their amounts.

Benefits

21
Navigating Benefits

$\mathbf{T}$his chapter will break down the different benefits areas and explain how they interrelate. We'll go through an extensive overview of PeopleSoft benefits functions and the changes that occur in the database behind the scenes. First, we will consider the various modules and how they connect to human resources and payroll functions. Next, we will explore the table structures and how to navigate them. What are the keys you need to know, and where is the data stored? Then, in the following chapters in this section, we will look at how each benefits function works in detail.

AN INTRODUCTION TO BENEFITS

A company provides benefits to employees as part of their employment. A benefit is sometimes paid for by the employee through a deduction, partly by the employee and partly by the employer, or entirely by the employer. It could be provided to every employee or to employees who match certain criteria. For some benefits, employees can choose which benefit they wish to receive out of a pool of possible options.

To track benefits, PeopleSoft considers all of the steps in the process—determining eligibility, recording employee elections, and performing the appropriate deductions and billing. The benefit modules are fully integrated, with many ties back to both human resources and payroll tables.

This section deals with the general benefits table setup and looks at health and life insurance plan types. There are several other plan types and other PeopleSoft functions that are not discussed here. Table 21-1 lists some sample benefits plan types that are delivered with PeopleSoft. We will concentrate on the 1x and 2x plans (health and life plans).

▶ **Table 21-1** Benefit plan codes

Plan Type	Description
10	Medical
11	Dental
12	Major Medical
14	Vision
15	Nonqualified Medical
20	Basic Group Life Insurance
21	Supplemental Group Life Insurance
30	Short-Term Disability
40	401(k)
61	Flexible Spending Account, Dependent Care
90	Vacation Buy Plan

There are also several functions that PeopleSoft offers which are not covered in this section. The following modules are *not* covered:

- Cash billing
- FMLA administration
- Leave balances/vacation balances
- COBRA (continuation of benefits)

Benefits is an incredibly extensive area of PeopleSoft, occupying a great deal of PeopleSoft's overall functionality. Many of these functions are specific to certain plans that your organization may or may not be implementing. For this reason, we will concentrate on the core benefits offerings:

- PeopleSoft benefits terminology
- Base benefits control table setup
- Benefits administration setup (events, rules) and processing
- Health plan data
- Life plan data

- Dependents and beneficiaries, and their enrollment
- Benefits rate structures

These basic benefits functions are complex and require our full attention over the next four chapters. We will look at how values are stored and how commonly used benefits information can be accurately retrieved from the PeopleSoft database.

Understanding Benefits Administration

In PeopleSoft, benefits can be maintained in two ways. You can manually determine everything once you've determined whether a participant fulfills your benefits criteria, or you can let PeopleSoft do it. When you manually tell PeopleSoft to stop or start a person's benefits, you are working in *base benefits*. If you run the event maintenance process, where PeopleSoft ultimately decides if the employee's benefits should begin or end, you are working in *benefits administration*. They are not mutually exclusive. Benefits administration sits on top of base benefits, performing some of the manual labor involved in determining eligibility and coverage begin and end dates for you.

If your company needs a system that automatically determines eligibility and processes an enrollment, you should use benefits administration. Benefits administration does not automate all enrollment activity. Manual intervention must occur to enroll a participant.

If your company is smaller and these transactions can occur manually, you should avoid the potential headaches of the event maintenance process and type things into the appropriate panels on your own.

Either way, base benefits is *always* the main source of benefits data. A benefits administration table never stores the final enrollment records for an employee. Since benefits administration only administers the process of enrollment, it does not store the official enrollment record. This is still found on the base tables—benefits administration simply changes the base tables when necessary.

For example, Greg is getting married. This is considered a life event, and allows him to change his benefits enrollments. In the benefits administration setup, a change in marital status ('FSC,' or family status change) is associated with an FSC benefits event. During the benefits administration process, the change in marital status triggers a benefits event, alerting PeopleSoft to the potential for a benefits change. PeopleSoft determines which plans Greg is eligible for. Greg receives this list at home, and calls in his selection to the benefits department. Using benefits administration, a PeopleSoft user goes to Go ➤ Compensate Employees ➤ Administer Automated Benefits ➤ Use ➤ Data Entry (By Participant). Here the user can see which plans Greg is eligible for, and enroll him in the new health plan he chooses.

When the benefits administration process runs again (often each night), it sees that Greg has switched plans. It writes a new, more recent effective-dated row with his new plan information. It also determines how much should be deducted from Greg's paycheck for the new plan. The administration programs look up the appropriate rate and set up a standard amount to be charged each pay cycle. They also double-check Greg's eligibility for the plan he has chosen, as well as the eligibility of his dependents who may be enrolled.

As the last step, the benefits administration process updates the table that stores health plan enrollment. This table, PS_HEALTH_BENEFIT, stores information about the current plan Greg is enrolled in. Although his election went through numerous other tables during the process, it is not a confirmed election until it is found in this base benefit table.

Event Maintenance vs. Open Enrollment

When we talk about benefits administration, we are referring to a set of programs that executes to determine eligibility and process elections. There are two major sets of programs that can be used to perform benefits administration. Event maintenance (EM) often occurs nightly to pick up employee changes.

The other major process is annual enrollment, called open enrollment (OE) in PeopleSoft. Open enrollment is when employees have the ability to change their plans or coverage level each year. Although running event maintenance is similar to performing an open enrollment, PeopleSoft will process open enrollment elections using separate program processing schedules to establish the new benefits. In open enrollment, employees are eligible to change their benefits without a valid life event.

Both event maintenance and open enrollment are considered benefits administration processes. When we refer to the "benefits administration process" we are referring to either possibility—event maintenance or open enrollment.

BASIC BENEFITS TERMINOLOGY AND SETUP

The core elements of PeopleSoft benefits are shown in Figure 21-1.

These terms are easy to confuse because they sound very similar. They are used throughout the PeopleSoft benefits areas. We will look at how benefit programs are defined, and how plan type, benefit plan, and coverage code combinations are assigned to these programs. The assignment of these values is a setup task, involving control tables and the definition of many values. It is useful to understand how these control tables are set up and administered, since they are the only way to link an employee election back to common benefits information.

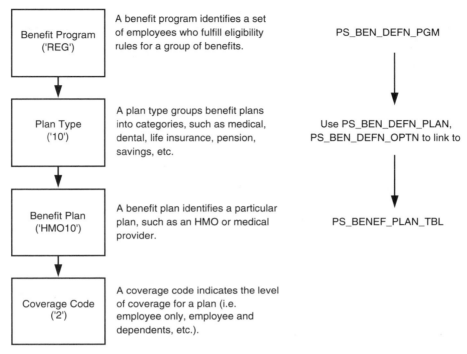

Benefit Program ('REG')	A benefit program identifies a set of employees who fulfill eligibility rules for a group of benefits.	PS_BEN_DEFN_PGM
Plan Type ('10')	A plan type groups benefit plans into categories, such as medical, dental, life insurance, pension, savings, etc.	Use PS_BEN_DEFN_PLAN, PS_BEN_DEFN_OPTN to link to
Benefit Plan ('HMO10')	A benefit plan identifies a particular plan, such as an HMO or medical provider.	PS_BENEF_PLAN_TBL
Coverage Code ('2')	A coverage code indicates the level of coverage for a plan (i.e. employee only, employee and dependents, etc.).	

▶ **Figure 21-1**   Basic organization of PeopleSoft benefits.

The fields shown in Figure 21-1 are the core keys to the PeopleSoft benefits tables. Let's look at each key and how it is defined to see how the basic control values for PeopleSoft benefits are established and stored. This will introduce the major areas of PeopleSoft base benefits.

Benefit Plans and Plan Type

The benefit plan table, PS_BENEF_PLAN_TBL, is the control table for benefit plans. A benefit plan is a code that represents a medical plan, HMO plan, dental plan, life insurance plan, etc. Each benefit plan code identifies a unique plan, although this plan code should be used in conjunction with a plan type.

A plan type is a simple two-digit code used to group benefit plans. Table 21-2 presents some sample delivered benefit plan values, their plan type, and their translation.

▶ **Table 21-2** Benefit plan codes

Benefit Plan	Plan Type	Description
BASMED	10	Basic Medical
HMO1	10	HMO Medical Plan
COMP	11	Basic Dental
MAJMED	12	Major Medical Plan
VILO	14	Vision–Low
NQMED	15	Nonqualified Medical
BLIFE	20	Basic Group Life Insurance
SL2X	21	Supplemental Group Life Insurance (2x salary)
STD	30	Short-Term Disability
FIDLTY	40	Fidelity 401(k)
DCFSA	61	Flexible Spending Account, Dependent Care
VBUY	90	Vacation Buy Plan

The benefit plan is a detailed field describing the actual plan the employee is enrolled in. If your company offers 35 possible HMO plans, each may require a separate benefit plan code to identify it.

Benefits Programs

A benefit program is the highest order in benefits—it contains a set of benefit plans. One benefit program could permit an employee to enroll in an HMO or a medical plan, as well as a life insurance plan. Another program could allow the same HMO and life insurance plan, but not the medical plan. Benefit plans and their options can be grouped in any combination to form benefit programs. So yet another program could include an HMO and life insurance plan but only allow HMO coverage for the employee (spouse and dependents prohibited).

Benefit programs are used to group the set of benefit offerings provided to a specific group of employees. Eligibility rules you set up allow PeopleSoft to determine which specific benefit program and benefit options an employee should receive. Programs also are an essential element of the event maintenance and open enrollment processes, since they provide information on benefits options.

You must create benefit programs from scratch, based on your organization's benefit plan offerings. They can be created for any combination of benefit plans and plan options.

Defining a Benefit Program

The first item on the base benefits panels is the benefit program participation. Although the table behind Go ➤ Compensate Employees ➤ Administer Base Benefits ➤ Use ➤ Benefit Program Participation, PS_BEN_PROG_PARTIC, only has one field, benefit program, it is one of the most important fields in base benefits. This is where an employee ID is linked with a benefit program. The link is made when event maintenance runs and determines through eligibility rules which program is correct. Initially, an employee will receive a default program based upon their paygroup.

There are several fields you can define for a benefit program. These fields are stored on the PS_BEN_DEFN_PGM table and can be set on the Go ➤ Define Business Rules ➤ Define Automated Benefits ➤ Setup ➤ Benefit/Deduction Program Table panels.

Effective Date

Benefit programs, like most benefit control values, are effective-dated. Since they are at such a high level and link both benefit plans and benefit rules, the effective dates must all tie together. This means that a benefit plan that is part of a benefit program must be effective-dated on or after the effective date of that benefit program. The same holds true for the rules, which must be dated on or before their corresponding benefit *plan* effective date. PeopleSoft cannot do this three-way check (from rule, to plan, to program), so it is possible to set up programs and plans with mismatched effective dates. It is up to you to make sure these dates correspond.

Program Type

Benefit programs can be two different types: automated (A) or manual (M). PeopleSoft sets this field according to the installation table (PS_INSTALLA-TION), where you can turn the benefits administration module on or off. If the module is off, all programs you create will be manual. The only way to change this field online is to change the installation table.

Dependent Age Limits

The limits for dependent ages can be defaulted in the benefit program definition. Many companies impose a restriction on how old a child can be in order to be claimed as a dependent. For example, often after age 21 a child cannot be claimed as a dependent unless he or she is a student, in which case the age limit is 25. Both a dependent limit and a student limit can be stored. You can also choose whether disabled dependents should be excluded from this restriction, and whether married dependents are automatically ineligible.

Retrieving Benefit Program Information

Often it is useful to list benefit programs or obtain a description for an employee's program. The query in Table 21-3 demonstrates how to find a list of benefit programs and their type.

▶ **Table 21-3** Listing benefit programs

| The query | ```SELECT
BP.BENEFIT_PROGRAM,
BP.DESCR,
BP.PROGRAM_TYPE

FROM PS_BEN_DEFN_PGM BP
WHERE BP.EFFDT =
        (SELECT MAX(BP1.EFFDT)
          FROM PS_BEN_DEFN_PGM BP1
        WHERE BP1.BENEFIT_PROGRAM = BP.BENEFIT_PROGRAM
            AND BP1.EFFDT <= '2000-01-01')
ORDER BY BP.PROGRAM_TYPE;``` |
|---|---|
| Returns the data set | BENEFIT_PROGRAM   DESCR   PROGRAM_TYPE |
| | ---------------   ----------------------   ------------ |
| | REG   Full-time regular   A |
| | LOA   Leave of absence   M |
| | LTD   Long-term disability   A |
| | RET   Retiree   A |

The values in Table 21-3 are not defined by PeopleSoft—they are provided as sample benefit programs. Each implementation requires a different set of benefit program configurations depending on the possible benefit plans, eligibility rules, and employee status selections.

Defining Plan and Plan Type Settings for a Program

The second panel of the benefit program definition is complex. This panel represents two setup tables: the plan type settings, stored on PS_BEN_DEFN_PLAN, and the actual plans linked with the program, found on PS_BEN_DEFN_OPTN.

First let's look at PS_BEN_DEFN_PLAN. This is where default settings are stored for each plan type. Most importantly, this is where benefits administration rules are associated with a plan type within a program and hence tied back to an employee. As an example, we will use plan type '10' (medical).

Event Rules ID

This ID field is used only for benefits administration. The event rules ID links a plan type within a benefit program to a group of event rules defined for the benefits administration process. All of the employees under benefit program ABC will use the event rules defined for their program. Then within their program a different set of event rules can be specified for each plan type (medical, life, disability, savings, etc.). We discuss event rules in greater detail later in the chapter.

Minimum and Maximum Annual Contribution

These fields are also benefits administration fields. They are used only for FSA plans within plan types 60 and 61. Unlike the fields we saw in the initial benefit program definition, these fields are not related to the FSA functionality. Even if you are processing FSA claims outside of PeopleSoft, the minimum and maximum annual contributions need to be tracked. They prevent PeopleSoft from accepting an annual pledge during data entry that is less than or greater than the specified limits.

Waive Coverage

The waive coverage field tells PeopleSoft whether employees can waive their coverage of plans in this plan type. This field is used by benefits administration. If you are only using base benefits, the waive option is set at the plan level, so it should be defaulted to 'no' at the program/plan type level. When using benefits administration, the waive coverage setting can apply to the plan type. It can be set to not allowed (N), allowed with proof (P), not applicable (X), or always allowed (Y).

COBRA and HIPAA

If the plan type is covered under COBRA, the COBRA plan check box should be 'yes.' COBRA (Consolidated Omnibus Budget Reconciliation Act) requires employers to allow qualified employees to continue their benefits coverage after termination. Only certain plan types are covered under COBRA. A medical plan, for example, would be a valid COBRA option, while a pension plan may not be.

The HIPAA plan field refers to another legal requirement, the Health Insurance Portability and Accountability Act. PeopleSoft produces a HIPAA report, which a terminated employee can take to a subsequent employer. If the plan type is eligible for the HIPAA report, the check box should be 'yes.'

Linking Plans with a Program Using Options

Connecting benefit plans with a high-level program can be confusing because PeopleSoft specifies each plan as an option. On the second panel of the benefit program definition, the appropriate plans are stored. The link between the program and the plans occurs on the PS_BEN_DEFN_OPTN table. This table contains the benefit program code and the benefit plan code—but there is also an option code sandwiched between them.

Imagine you're setting up a new benefit program. You navigate to Go ➤ Define Base Benefits ➤ Setup ➤ Benefit/Deduction Program Table. You complete the first panel and move on to the second. Here you set up a plan type (i.e., '10' for medical). Then there is a large empty grid at the bottom, where you must link benefit plans according to options. Click 'insert row,' and choose a benefit plan. The benefit plan row appears in the grid, with the option ID of '01.' Insert another, and that is '02.' and so on.

The option ID is a key that stores the link between programs and plan options. A plan option includes both a plan and a coverage level. The option ID is unique only within a benefit program. If an employee, Dan, is choosing a medical plan (plan type '10'), he could have fifteen different options to choose from, each with an option ID, one through fifteen. These options could be made up of five distinct plans, each with three possible coverage levels.

Specifying Benefit Plan Settings

When you link a plan to a program, there are several settings to establish. They are listed in the grid on the panel along with the benefit plan code. Each of these fields is stored on the PS_BEN_DEFN_OPTN table:

> **Option ID.** This field is the key that PeopleSoft provides when you link a plan to a program (explained above, under Linking Plans...).

> **Option Type.** The option type field identifies special options, such as general deductions, credits, and waivers. Table 21-4 lists each option type and what it represents.

▶ **Table 21-4** Option types

Type	Ben. Admin.?	Description
P	Only Ben. Admin.	Only specified for the benefit program row (type '01'), which is used for defaults. Does not pertain to other plan types. See the Special Plan Type Rows section in this chapter.
D	Base Benefits/Ben Admin.	For the general deduction row (plan type '00'). Does not pertain to other plan types. See the Special Plan Type Rows section in this chapter.

▶ **Table 21-4** continued

Type	Ben. Admin.?	Description
G	Only Ben. Admin.	Provides an option for receiving a general credit in lieu of choosing a benefit plan. Only one option in a plan type can be a credit.
O	Base Benefits/Ben Admin.	This is the standard option type. It means that the option is indeed an option.
W	Only Ben. Admin.	Provides an option for waiving the plan type. Follows the waive setting for the plan type.

Option Sequence. This field specifies the order in which options should appear in PeopleSoft and on letters and reports. Your option ID fields could be in a different order that you wish to provide on printed output.

Option Code. This field is the code that users will type into the data entry panels to specify an option.

Option Level. This is used for plans where coverage is at a certain level, such as 1 or 2 times salary. Benefits administration looks at the value of this field when an employee changes plans. For example, if an event rule does not allow a change from level 1 to 2, benefits administration rejects the change. PeopleSoft also uses level to determine the lowest option, which is automatically chosen as the default if specified in an event rule.

Coverage Code. Certain plan types require a coverage code. The combination of a plan and a coverage code will constitute an option. An employee can elect, for instance, HMO23 with employee coverage, HMO23 with family coverage, etc. The Coverage Codes section in this chapter explains these codes in greater detail.

Default Option Checkbox ('Def' on the panel). If the option is the default (i.e., if the employee does not make a choice), this check box is set to 'yes.' The event rules designation as well as this checkbox would signify which default option should be chosen. There can only be one default per plan type. When setting an option as the default, you should choose an option that does not require proof. Also, plan types starting with 4, 6, and 9 (savings, FSA, vacation) can only default to a waive option.

Deduction Code. This field links the benefit plan within the option to a deduction code. The combination, not just the benefit plan, is linked to a deduction code.

Geographic Location, Eligibility ID. These two fields are used to link eligibility rules to a particular option. This determines who is eligible for a particular plan option. See the Eligibility Rules heading in this chapter for more information.

Cross Plan Values. When enrollment in one plan is contingent on enrollment in another, the two plans are linked with 'cross-plan' values. You can link a plan type (XPType) and benefit plan code (XPlan) to an option to have benefits administration cross-check eligibility. For life plans, a percentage limit can be specified (XLimPct). First the system cross-checks eligibility; then it compares the coverage amounts using the percentage you specify. For medical plans, you can specify that only the dependents enrolled in one plan can enroll in the other when you set the cross-dependent checkbox (XDep) to yes for an option.

Special Plan Type Rows

You may notice some unfamiliar plan type values in the benefits program definition. The most common is the plan type '00,' which is for general deductions. On plan type '00,' the option rows do not have benefit plans but instead list deduction codes. This is where the eligible general deductions are listed for a group of employees associated with this benefit program. The options for plan type '00' do not have many of the fields filled in because they are not relevant.

The other unique plan type is '01.' This is called a program row, since it is actually the default row for the entire benefit program. If a plan type is not defined for this program, PeopleSoft will default to the settings on the '01' row.

Retrieving Common Benefit Plan Characteristics

For an overview of the benefit plans an employee can choose from, the plans the employee actually chose, and the costs involved, you can use the BAS tables. Some of this information is not located on the individual plan type tables (health and life tables) that we will go into in subsequent chapters.

The result of the query in Table 21-5 is a list of the employee's most recently elected benefit plans. The schedule ID 'EM' stands for event maintenance.

▶ **Table 21-5** Finding plan elections

| The query | ```
SELECT
BP.PLAN_TYPE,
BP.OPTION_CD,
BO.BENEFIT_PLAN
FROM PS_BAS_PARTIC_PLAN BP,
     PS_BAS_PARTIC_OPTN BO
WHERE BP.EMPLID          = 'BOZO'
  AND BP.SCHED_ID        = 'EM'
  AND BO.SCHED_ID        = BP.SCHED_ID
  AND BO.EMPLID          = BP.EMPLID
  AND BO.BENEFIT_RCD#    = BP.BENEFIT_RCD#
  AND BO.EVENT_ID        = BP.EVENT_ID
  AND BO.PLAN_TYPE       = BP.PLAN_TYPE
  AND BO.OPTION_CD       = BP.OPTION_CD
  AND BP.EVENT_DT        =
       (SELECT MAX(BP1.EVENT_DT)
          FROM PS_BAS_PARTIC_PLAN BP1
         WHERE BP1.SCHED_ID      = BP.SCHED_ID
           AND BP1.EMPLID        = BP.EMPLID
           AND BP1.BENEFIT_RCD#  = BP.BENEFIT_RCD#
           AND BP1.PLAN_TYPE     = BP.PLAN_TYPE)
``` |

Returns the data set	PLAN_TYPE	OPTION_CD	BENEFIT_PLAN
	---------	---------	------------
	01		
	10	14	MDBC
	11	14	DDDD
	14	16	VILO
	20	13	LIF2X
	40	11	FIDLTY
	60	11	HC
	61	11	DC

In this query we are joining the plan table, which stores the election that was manually entered, to the option table, which contains the benefit plan names. In a twist of terminology, the plan table only contains the option code, not the benefit plan. The PS_BAS_PARTIC_OPTN table links an option code to a benefit plan code.
```

Don't be confused by the option ID and option code fields. The option ID is an automatic key field that identifies an option. It is used to link together the PS_BAS_PARTIC_COST table and the PS_BAS_PARTIC_OPTN table. You will also find an option code on PS_BAS_PARTIC_OPTN—this code represents an option for a particular plan type. The option code resets for each plan type. A medical plan type, for example, could have options 1–4, and so could a life plan type. When the option code and plan type are used together they can identify a benefit plan on PS_BAS_PARTIC_PLAN.

Note that the first plan type returned is '01.' As mentioned above, this is the default row for the employee.

Benefit Program Costs

The third panel in the benefit program definition series provides cost information connections. The various methods for calculating the cost of a plan to an employee are stored on four different rate tables:

- age graded—based on the employee's age (today or at a certain point in time)
- flat amount
- salary percentage—based on employee's salary
- years of service

A different rate table can be associated with each benefit option. For example, medical plans could be calculated according to age, while life plans are calculated according to salary. The key of the settings from the rate tables is stored in the Rate Table ID field; this ID could contain a value that matches the ID on any of the four tables. The cost ID is different—it is an automatic key PeopleSoft assigns each time you make a link between a benefit program and a rate table.

Chapter 24 is dedicated to the different rates PeopleSoft uses to calculate benefits.

BENEFITS CONTROL TABLES

As you might suspect, there is a system of organization behind the benefits functional processes. Table 21-6 is a convenient guide to the terminology of benefits table names.

▶ **Table 21-6** Benefits table names

Naming convention	Function of tables using this prefix	Sample Table
BAS	Benefits administration tables (eligibility, options, participation)	BAS_PARTIC_OPTN
BEN_BI	Benefits cash billing	BEN_BI_DETAIL
BEN_DEFN	Control tables	BEN_DEFN_COST
BEN_PER/BEN_PLAN	Snapshot of employee benefits (see chapter 4)	BEN_PLAN_DATA
BEN_PROG	Benefit program definitions and employee participation	BEN_PROG_PARTIC
HEALTH	Health plan elections, employee & dependent	HEALTH_BENEFIT
PARTIC	Stands for the output of a benefits process, such as CBR_PARTIC for the COBRA process and BAS_PARTIC for benefits administration	BAS_PARTIC_PLAN
LIFE	Life plan elections, employee & beneficiary	LIFE_ADD_BEN
DEP/DEPENDENT	Dependents and beneficiary information	DEPENDENT_BENEF
DISABILITY	Disability plan elections	DISABILITY_BEN
SAVINGS	Savings plan elections	SAVINGS_PLAN
LEAVE	Leave plan elections	LEAVE_PLAN
FSA	Flexible Spending Account elections	FSA_BENEFIT
VACATION	Vacation plan elections	VACATION_BEN
AGE/ SALARY/	Rates for benefit plans, based on age, salary,	AGE_RATE_TBL,
FLAT/ SVC	flat amount, years of service	SALARY_RATE_TBL, FLAT_RATE_TBL, SVC,_RATE_TBL
CALC	Benefits calculation rules	CALC_RULES_TBL

The benefits administration tables are separated from other benefits areas by the BAS prefix. Each different benefit plan type has its own prefix, such as HEALTH and LIFE. This makes it easy to know what kinds of data you are retrieving.

Table 21-7 below provides a short overview of the different control tables you will encounter in this section. As we look at the control table settings for base benefits and benefits administration, use this table to avoid getting lost in all of the different areas and their connections.

▶ **Table 21-7** Benefits control tables described in this chapter

Table	Function name
Base Benefits	
PS_PROVIDR_TBL	Provider table (address for the HMO, etc.)
PS_PROV_POLICY_TBL	Policy table (plan policy numbers)
PS_LIFE_ADD_TBL	Life/Accidental Death plan details
PS_DISBLTY_PLN_TBL	Disability plan details
PS_SAVINGS_PLN_TBL	Savings plan details
LEAVE_PLAN_TBL	Leave accrual plan details
PS_FMLA_PLAN_TBL	Family Medical Leave Act plan details
PS_FSA_BENEF_TBL	Employer contributions to FSA plan detail
Benefits administration	
PS_BAS_GROUP_TBL	Definition of group IDs, which group employees for processing
PS_BAS_ELIG	Contains rules for determining whether an employee is eligible for a plan
PS_BAS_PASSIVE_EVT	Passive event definitions, for events that occur based on age or years of service
PS_BAS_EVENT_RULES	Definition of benefits events, i.e. when an employee event should trigger a benefits action
PS_BAS_EVENT_CLASS	Identifies events that can occur based on actions or other triggers, such as new hire 'HIR' and family status change 'FSC'
PS_BAS_SCHED	Schedule for processing groups of employees through event maintenance or open enrollment

Base Benefits Control Tables

The core tables you will look at most often are base benefit tables. They store the actual enrollment in benefit plans and are used to determine coverage levels, dependent information, and FSA account balances. Let's look at the commonly used control tables for base benefits to get a good foundation before exploring the benefits administration enrollment tables.

Providers

The provider table, PS_PROVIDR_TBL, stores information about the plan provider, like the HMO company or the insurance agency, and its address.

Providers are stored according to four types: general provider (GEN), industrial insurance board (IIB), implementation partner (IMP), and National Health Service (NHS), but general provider is the standard setting for most plans.

> A provider ID must be identified. If you do not wish to store provider data in the system, you can define one ID and reuse it.

An adjunct table, the provider policy table PS_PROV_POLICY_TBL, stores information about the particular policy with an insurer, including the policy number and start and end dates. This information is optional too, and does not affect any delivered functions. PeopleSoft knows when an employee's coverage starts and stops but does not pay attention to the expiration date of a plan for the entire company.

Coverage Codes

Coverage codes are used for plan types 1x (health, medical, dental, vision, etc.). They indicate what level of coverage, or how much coverage, an employee has. This is a separate control table with a full set of panels, since PeopleSoft allows you to set up additional coverage codes from the delivered. A coverage code includes several parameters. Minimum and maximum number of dependents allowed can be established (for no limit, type in 99). Spouse coverage (SPOUSE_COVERAGE) can be set to allowed (A), not allowed (N), or required (R). The nonqualified dependent coverage (DOMESTIC_COVERAGE) can be set to required or not allowed. A nonqualified dependent refers to federal tax regulations that define who is and who is not a dependent, such as a domestic partner. Since benefit plans may vary in their adoption of these regulations, this field can record whether the coverage includes these individuals.

Table 21-8 explains the delivered values. These values are often altered to suit each implementation; sometimes just the description is altered to better explain the coverage level.

▶ **Table 21-8** Delivered coverage codes

Code	Description
1	Employee only
2	Employee and spouse
3	Employee and dependents (no spouse)
4	Family
5	Nonqualified adult (no spouse, nonqualified required)

▶ **Table 21-8**   continued

Code	Description
6	Nonqualified children (no spouse, nonqualified required)
7	Nonqualified adult and children (no spouse, nonqualified required)

Life Plan Coverage

Most benefit plans have one or two fields that must be defined in addition to the information specified on the benefit plan table (PS_BENEF_PLAN_TBL).

> Health plans are the exception—information about plan type '10' (health) is limited to the coverage codes you associate with each plan on the benefit program definition.

Life plans, unlike other plans, store a coverage amount (i.e., how much the plan covers you for) on the PS_LIFE_ADD_TBL. If you have a million-dollar life insurance policy, the coverage amount can be determined from a flat amount or a percentage. Usually the employee benefits base salary is used for percentage amounts. The coverage can also be a special calculation routine, the sum of dependent coverage, or stored at the employee level ('Specified on Employee Record'). Just as in payroll, the special calculation routine only indicates that you have modified the delivered COBOL programs to calculate a special coverage.

> Don't be confused by different uses of the word coverage. A coverage code is universal among benefit plans—it identifies the *level* of coverage. The coverage amount, on the other hand, is a *dollar amount* of coverage, usually associated with a life plan. Coverage groups, explained in Chapter 22, relate to this second definition, not the coverage code.

Disability, Savings, Leave Accrual Plans

The detail for these plans can get quite involved. Since the likelihood is that you will need to look at these panels once and then leave them be, we will look at each of them only at a high level.

Disability Plans. You can store detail parameters for disability panels on the PS_DISBLTY_PLN_TBL.

This table stores a maximum monthly benefit amount (should the employee go out on disability) and a salary replacement percentage amount, which is limited by the monthly amount. If the percentage of salary is greater than the monthly maximum, the employee will receive the maximum only.

Savings Plans. The savings plan definition panels (and PS_SAVINGS_PLN_TBL) allow you to set up employee savings plans with many flexible options. A 401(k) plan, for example, can be set up with matching employer contributions, years of service restrictions, and rollovers to other plans when maximums are reached. The settings here work in conjunction with accumulators you may have established in payroll to track 401(k) earnings.

> Savings plans settings such as these should only be used if you are using PeopleSoft to manage your savings plans. A 401(k), for example, could be a deduction in payroll, with the eligibility handled by an outside system.

Leave Accrual Plans. The leave plan table (PS_LEAVE_PLAN_TBL) contains parameters for leave of absence accrual plans. The accrual is set up based on a number of hours reached. If you reach x number of hours, you accrue a factor of each hour. There are also fields for storing bonus levels and maximum yearly amounts.

FMLA Plans. Family Medical Leave Act plans provide continued benefit coverage and job restoration for employees who must take a leave for family medical reasons. The detail panels (and PS_FMLA_PLAN_TBL) store parameters for how the permitted twelve-week leave is taken. Since only twelve weeks may be taken in a given year, you can choose when the year starts and ends for tracking this balance. You can also change the annual entitlement to a number of weeks other than 12, set minimum service requirements, and link to a special FMLA hours accumulator.

FSA Plans. Flexible Spending Accounts allow employees to use pre-tax funds to pay for miscellaneous health care and dependent care expenses. The frequency of contribution and calculation rules for the employer and employee contribution is defined on the FSA detail setup panels and PS_FSA_BENEF_TBL table.

PeopleSoft can track employee FSA claims using an FSA run ID that is linked to a benefit program. If PeopleSoft processes FSA claims, the FSA run ID determines which employees should be included.

Benefits Administration Control Tables

Most of the rules for benefits administration are stored in control tables prefixed with BAS. These rules are defined under the menu Go ➤ Define Business Rules ➤ Define Automated Benefits ➤ Setup. Remember that benefits administration is the automated determination of eligibility and processing of enrollment based on manually entered elections. In order to process benefits using benefits administration, you must set up the eligibility rules, events and event classes, and other miscellaneous control tables.

BAS Groups

Employees are linked to benefits administration groups with an ID field, BAS_GROUP_ID. Group IDs are defined on the group ID panels at Go ➤ Define Business Rules ➤ Define Automated Benefits ➤ Setup ➤ Group ID Table. A group ID links an employee to a benefits administration group. The group ID value is stored on the job table PS_JOB as well as the group table, PS_BAS_GROUP_TBL.

Groups are used to process only certain employees through open enrollment or periodic event maintenance. Rather than process all of the employees at once, groups allow you to split up the employee population however you like. An employee can be assigned to any group ID.

Eligibility Rules

The eligibility rule settings are used by benefits administration to determine an employee's benefit program and if an employee is allowed to select a particular plan option. The eligibility rule ID is specified in the definition of a benefit program. PeopleSoft lets you configure the eligibility using numerous fields. These rules are set on Go ➤ Define Business Rules ➤ Define Automated Benefits ➤ Setup ➤ Eligibility Rules Table, and stored on tables prefixed with PS_BAS_ELIG. For each field, any number of possible values can be specified as eligible or ineligible. If one benefits status is eligible, you can just list that value. Or, if ten are ineligible, you can list the ten values and set the flag to ineligible. The rules you set can be based on the following fields:

1. Have a minimum or maximum standard hours
2. Be within a minimum or maximum age (can set an as of date)
3. Worked for a minimum or maximum number of months (can set an as of date)
4. Have a particular value for the following fields:
   a) Benefits Status

b) Employee Class

c) Employee Type

d) Full/Part Time

e) FLSA Status

f) Officer Code

g) Regular/Temporary

h) Regulatory Region

i) Salary Administration Plan

j) Grade

k) Work Location (by state)

l) Work Location (by location code)

m) Union Code

n) Company/Paygroup (combination)

o) Custom Eligibility Configuration Fields 1–9 (found on PS_JOB)

If this list is not sufficient, there is also an override panel where an employee ID and benefit record number can be specified. This will override the rules for certain employees.

Events

In benefits administration, an event indicates that something happened to an employee that may allow a benefit change to occur. There are three types of events:

- Triggered Events
- Manual Events
- Passive Events

Triggered events are caused by a change to an employee's job table data. If Albert becomes a temporary employee, the reg/temp field becomes 'T.' Once the change on the employee's job record is saved, PeopleCode triggers an event in Benefits Administration that will be processed during the next event maintenance run (most likely that evening).

Manual events are entered directly into benefits administration panels. Under the BAS Activity panels, you can manually cause an event to occur. Then, when event maintenance runs, the manual entry will trigger the appropriate event rules. The BAS Activity panels are described later in this chapter.

Passive events require nothing but the passage of time. If there is a passive event rule that says all benefits must change when an employee works at the company for over 80 years, Albert must wait until that occurs. Each time benefits administration runs, it will check to see if Albert qualifies. If so, the passive event process is included in the run.

Passive events are defined on the Go ➤ Define Business Rules ➤ Define Automated Benefits ➤ Setup ➤ Passive Event Definition panel and are stored on PS_BAS_PASSIVE_EVT. For each event you can specify the months and days required, and the date the event is based on—birth date or service date. You also must specify an event class for each passive event.

Event Classes

An event class categorizes events into several categories. To view or define event classes, navigate to Go ➤ Define Business Rules ➤ Define Automated Benefits ➤ Setup ➤ Event Class Table, or look at the PS_BAS_EVT_CLASS table.

Event classes are compared with benefits administration actions listed on the action/reason table for each action/reason combination. So if an employee terminates and the action is TER, PeopleSoft will look for an event class called TER. The event class use (EVENT_CLASS_USE) field determines how the event class works. In most cases, the event class use is set to 'S' for specific event class. The other settings are for particular cases: 'O' for open enrollment event class, 'D' for default (only one class can be a default class), and 'N' for snapshot event class. PeopleSoft delivers a set of event classes, which are listed in Table 21-9.

▶ **Table 21-9**   Delivered event classes

Event class	Use	Description
FSC	S	Family status changes (action = FSC) or manual event with no action
HIR	S	New hires (action = HIR)
MSC	D	Miscellaneous change (default)
OE	O	Open enrollment use only
SNP	N	Snapshot use only
TER	S	Terminated employees (action = TER)

Event Rules

The definition of a particular event rule is somewhat more complex than that of the high-level event class. Event rules are defined on the next panel in the

Setup menu, and are stored on PS_BAS_EVENT_RULES. They are linked to benefit program types using the event rule ID (for information about this link, see the Benefit Programs section above).

Within each rule definition, the different event classes are listed. You must specify what each rule should do when it encounters each event class. For example, if Albert has a family status change, what does the rule say should occur for the 'FSC' class? The information about a class within a rule is stored on PS_BAS_EVENT_CLASS.

Under the event classification you can establish how benefits administration should treat plan types that are linked to this rule. Should an election be required? Should PeopleSoft look at the history of an employee's eligibility for the plan when determining if a change needs to occur, or only at the current election? Or should PeopleSoft ignore a particular event?

PeopleSoft's benefit administration programs take the event, apply the rule, and then decide what to do next. If an employee had a serious enough change in status, PeopleSoft might terminate current benefits and set up a new list of options. The settings found in the event rules panels and tables are much more detailed. They provide settings for the allowable levels of coverage for life insurance plans and the default begin and end dates for plan elections. They also decide when to turn on and off cash billing.

> Cash billing is a PeopleSoft feature we will not cover. It allows you to produce bills to collect payments for benefits when an employee is no longer receiving a paycheck. The process of collecting and tracking these funds is called cash billing. In the case of event rules, cash billing would be triggered by an event, such as a termination.

PeopleSoft provides many defaults for these rules, and with luck only a select few fields will need to be changed to correspond to your company's benefit rules. Let's look at some of the fields you may need to work with.

Default Method.   The default method determines what happens when an employee does not make an election but has a status change. Depending on the change, a particular rule is kicked off and the defaults are defined on the event rule table. The different defaults are listed in Table 21-10.

▶ **Table 21-10** Default Methods

Method	Description
C	Assign current coverage else option (the option defined as the default for the plan type)
E	Assign current coverage else low option*
L	Default to lowest eligible option*
N	Assign current coverage else none (in other words, the employee loses the plan coverage if he or she is not eligible for the current coverage)
O	Default to option and coverage (the option defined as the default for the plan type)
T	Terminate coverage

* The lowest eligible option means that PeopleSoft looks at the options available, and chooses the lowest option level, and then the lowest option sequence within that level (see above for definitions of these fields).

Select Allowed.   The select allowed field defines the extent of the changes benefits administration will allow when an event occurs. The setting could be none (N), all options (A), or coverage code only (C).

Scheduling

Schedules are used to run benefits administration processes. There are schedules for open enrollment, and there are usually many schedules for event maintenance. Many schedules can be set up for different groups of employees. You could have a schedule for each open enrollment year, and a schedule for event maintenance for hourly employees.

Each schedule allows you to define a company code or a BAS group ID field to process. All employees within the company code, or who have the appropriate group ID, will be processed when the schedule is executed. The schedule ID field identifies the schedule and is often requested as a parameter for benefits administration processes.

The schedule table (PS_BAS_SCHED) also contains status flags for the open enrollment and snapshot processes. The process could be scheduled to run ('S'), or unprocessed ('U').

Geographic Location

Geographic locations are ranges of postal codes that can determine eligibility. If employees in a set of 400 postal codes are eligible for a certain HMO plan, but others aren't, you'll need to set up a geographic location, which is identified by a location table ID. The HMO plan must be linked to this ID on the benefit program definition panels in order for PeopleSoft to know that these postal codes determine eligibility.

Snapshot

The snapshot is used to set up your PeopleSoft benefits eligibility picture for the first time. Usually when PeopleSoft is implemented, the benefit elections must be brought over from another system. Unless this coincides with an open enrollment period, you will need to run the snapshot to establish the eligibility starting point in PeopleSoft.

There are two reasons for running the snapshot. First, when you go to run event maintenance for the first time, it needs to refer to previous and current benefit eligibility. If you only enter elections, the process cannot determine eligibility history. Second, the event maintenance process only looks at employees who have an event occur. For most employees, no events will occur in a given pay cycle. In order to ensure that the elections for each employee fulfill the rules you've established, you will need to run either open enrollment or snapshot, which looks at every employee by default.

A Control Table Summary: Looking at Benefits ID Fields

PeopleSoft benefits is a confusing area of the PeopleSoft database. There is a great deal of information to track and process. You no doubt will forget the differences among a schedule ID, group ID, option ID, and program ID. There are a lot of IDs in PeopleSoft benefits. As a reference, Table 21-11 lists each ID with a description.

▶ **Table 21-11** Benefit IDs

Field	Name	Description
AGE_RATE_TBL_ID	Age-Graded Rate Table ID	Groups together age rates on PS_AGE_COVG_TBL to provide information for calculating premiums (stored on PS_AGE_RATE_TBL). A benefit plan that uses an age rate will have an age rate table ID stored in the rate table ID field (RATE_TBL_ID).
BAS_GROUP_ID	BAS Group ID	Found on the PS_JOB table, this ID groups employees for benefits administration processing (see Groups in this chapter).
CALC_RULES_ID	Calculation Rules Table ID	Identifies a calculation rule, used to set up as-of dates for rate or coverage calculation. Must be linked to a plan definition when defining a benefit program. See Chapter 24.

▶ **Table 21-11** continued

Field	Name	Description
COBRA_EVENT_ID	COBRA Event ID	Although the COBRA_EVENT_ID field appears on several BAS tables, it is only relevant if you are using PeopleSoft's COBRA functionality. Under COBRA a qualified employee can continue his or her benefits after termination. PeopleSoft can print COBRA notification letters and continue benefits if necessary. The event ID is an enrollment flag. An ID of zero is the default, meaning the employee is not enrolled. Anything greater than zero means the employee is enrolled in COBRA. A 900 means the employee is enrolled, but the COBRA batch processes will ignore the employee.
COST_ID	Cost ID	When defining a benefit program, each cost type (price or credit) and rate type combination for an option receives a numerical cost ID.
DEPENDENT_BENEF	Dependent/ Beneficiary ID	A dependent/beneficiary ID is a combination ID. Since both dependents and beneficiaries are stored on the same table, a single ID is used to track them along with a dependent/beneficiary type (see Chapter 23).
DEPENDENT_ID	Dependent ID	Some information about dependents is stored separately from beneficiaries. In this case a dependent ID is used, but the values are equivalent to the DEPENDENT_BENEF ID. They are actually the same field and can be joined in queries.
ELIG_RULES_ID	Eligibility Rules ID	An eligibility rules ID groups a set of eligibility rules.
EVENT_ID	Event ID	PeopleSoft benefits administration lists each event on the BAS_PARTIC tables. The event ID uniquely identifies an event for an employee. It will begin with a '1' and will be incremented as additional events occur.
EVENT_RULES_ID	Event Rules ID	See Defining Plan Type Settings in this chapter.
FLAT_RATE_ID	Flat Rate Table ID	Uniquely identifies a flat rate on the flat rate table. Links to a benefit plan rate table ID (RATE_TBL_ID) where the rate type for the plan is flat ('2').
FMLA_PLAN_ID	FMLA Plan ID	See Defining a Benefit Program section in this chapter.

▶ **Table 21-11**   continued

Field	Name	Description
GROUP_ID	Group ID	See Groups section in this chapter.
HLTH_PROVIDER_ID	Health Provider ID	This identifies a health provider, such as a primary care physician. The ID is for information only.
OE_DEFN_ID	Open Enrollment Definition ID	Defines a unique open enrollment period. The ID usually is for a particular year, such as 'OE01.'
OPTION_ID	Option ID	Automatically generated by the system for each new option created.
PASSIVE_EVENT_ID	Passive Event ID	Used to uniquely define a passive event (not caused by an action).
PLAN_ID	Plan ID	This ID is for employee internal professional education plans—not for benefit plans. The unique identifier for a benefit plan is BENEFIT_PLAN.
PROGRAM_ID	Program ID	The program ID is used to identify payroll identification numbers (PINs). It has nothing to do with benefit programs, which use BENEFIT_PROGRAM for a key.
RATE_TBL_ID	Rate Table ID	Links a benefit plan to the rate for the plan. This ID could contain values from FLAT_RATE_ID, AGE_RATE_TBL_ID, SALARY_RATE_ID, and SVC_RATE_TBL_ID. The rate table ID is stored on PS_BEN_DEFN_COST.
SALARY_RATE_ID	Percent of Salary ID	Identifies rate options for percent of salary rates. Each option is defined by a unique salary rate ID, which ties to a benefit plan via the RATE_TBL_ID field.
SCHEDULE_ID	Schedule ID	This schedule ID can be a decoy—it actually identifies an employee work schedule, not a benefits administration schedule.
SCHED_ID	Schedule ID	Identifies the benefits administration schedule. The schedule launches the benefits administration for a particular company and the employees with a particular BAS_GROUP_ID.
SNAP_DEFN_ID	Snapshot Definition ID	Uniquely defines a snapshot run; this field is a sibling of the OE_DEFN_ID.
SVC_RATE_TBL_ID	Service Rate Table ID	Identifies rate options for rates based on length of service. Each benefit plan that is based on service rates stores a service rate table ID in the RATE_TBL_ID field.

THE BENEFITS ADMINISTRATION PROCESS

Benefits administration occurs in two high-level phases. First, you will run benefits administration to determine which employees are eligible to change their benefits (i.e. determine eligibility based on events). Next, you manually enter their elections and run benefits administration again to confirm their enrollment.

Benefits administration processes events. Although each event is linked to an individual, or participant, PeopleSoft treats each event independently. Benefits administration processes one event at a time. If an employee has more than one event (such as an address change and a family status change), PeopleSoft processes the older event first and the newer event only when the first event has been processed to completion.

Throughout the benefits administration process, a status is assigned to each event. This status is stored in BAS_PROCESS_STATUS, found on the BAS_PARTIC table. The possible values are in Table 21-12. These statuses are valid during different stages of benefits administration: the scheduling of employees to process, figuring out the employee's eligibility, determining elections that were made, and confirming these elections.

▶ **Table 21-12**   Process Status

Status	Name	Description
Program Assignment		
AE	Program eligibility assignment error	The employee JOB information needs correction or the eligibility rules need to be modified; PeopleSoft is assigning the employee to multiple benefit programs.
AN	Program eligibility assignment not found	No benefit program was found for the employee. The employee will be processed as FA (assigned none) or PR (prepared), depending on whether election information is entered for the employee.
AS	Program eligibility assigned	A benefit program was found, and the employee can move on to the next stage. If at the end of Benefits Administration an event has an 'AS' status, more than one event was found for the employee, and the one you see is the ignored one. The other event was not successfully processed, causing the event with an 'AS' status to be ignored.
Option Preparation		
FA	Finalized—no benefit program	Participant has no benefit program and no elections.

▶ **Table 21-12**   continued

Status	Name	Description
FP	Finalized—prepared none	Participant has a benefit program but is ineligible to make elections based upon the processed event.
PE	Prepare error	An error occurred; this record will be re-evaluated on the next run (correct JOB data). Could indicate possible setup tables errors such as missing pay calendar entries.
PR	Prepared	Enrollment forms may be printed; the eligible options were successfully created.
NT	Notified	The enrollment form was created and printed (occurs after PR).

Entering and Loading Elections

Status	Name	Description
ET	Entered	The elections have been manually entered.
EE	Election error	An election error occurred. Corrections should be made in the data entry panels before the next run.
FE	Finalized—enrolled	The entered election has been processed and the appropriate tables updated.

Reprocessing

Status	Name	Description
RE	Re-enter	After an election is finalized (FE), any changes cause the status to become 'RE' as the changes are re-entered.

The process status enables a level of error correction that is necessary for benefits administration. Numerous errors can occur based on the complexity of eligibility and election rules. In general, these errors can be corrected in three places. The PS_JOB table contains basic benefits data about the employee, such as the BAS group ID, and also triggers eligibility to elect. When an address or a job field changes, an event is created. Changing information on PS_JOB can thereby affect benefits administration.

The second location for potential errors is the tables where elections are entered. When an employee chooses a new benefit plan, this election must be entered in the BAS activity panels. If the election kicks out with an error, it is likely that the activity panels and tables are the source.

The third source for errors can be the setup tables. If data has not been set up correctly in the control tables, an event maintenance error could occur. Typically errors due to control table setup occur at the beginning of an implementation, when testing is performed.

BAS Activity/ Manual Entry

The panels for entering manual benefits event triggers are found under Go ➤ Compensate Employees ➤ Administer Automated Benefits ➤ Use.

The BAS Activity panel provides a list of all benefits administration events, listed by employee and date that have not yet been processed by event maintenance. It is a direct view of the entire PS_BAS_ACTIVITY table. Each event has an action source; the possible types are listed in Table 21-13.

▶ **Table 21-13** Action sources

Action	Description
ME	Manual event
OE	Open enrollment
PB	Passive event—birthday
PS	Passive event—service
SN	Snapshot
TJ	Job data change
TL	Union change
TP	Address change

Remember that this is the event source, not the election source. An event can be triggered by any of the actions listed in Table 21-13, but an election must be made manually through data entry panels.

PeopleSoft provides two data entry panels that perform the same function using two different techniques. The 'by schedule' panels allow you to enter bulk elections for a group of employees. The 'by participant' panels require an employee ID. In general, you can enter elections by schedule during open enrollment when everyone is making an election, and process by participant during event maintenance when a small group of employees are making elections.

Both data entry panels only allow entry for open events. If no event exists, or all events are finalized for an employee, PeopleSoft will not load any events.

The elections entered onto these panels reside on the PS_BAS_PARTIC_PLAN table. This table stores all of the plan options and will record the actual election in the COVERAGE_ELECT field. To determine which plans an employee has elected, search the table as in the query in Table 21-5.

On-Demand Event Maintenance

An employee can be sent through event maintenance manually, separate from all other employees, using on-demand event maintenance. Using a single panel, the following actions can be performed:

- activities/events can be viewed
- eligibility can be determined
- options established
- enrollment statements printed
- elections entered
- benefits validated and finalized
- confirmation statements printed
- elections re-processed

On-demand event maintenance allows the entire benefits administration process, or a portion of it, to occur immediately. If an employee needs an enrollment statement today, makes selections, and then needs a confirmation statement, the on-demand maintenance panel can be used. The benefits enrollment process can occur while the employee is waiting.

TRACKING PEOPLESOFT BENEFITS

Since PeopleSoft benefits administration processes most of the base benefits data, what kinds of information must be extracted and reported on from the PeopleSoft benefits tables? In the following chapters we will look closely at health tables, life insurance plan tables, dependent and beneficiary participation, and rate tables. These tables reveal the results of the benefits administration, or manual benefits process. The employee and dependent elections, coverage and rates are placed on these tables by benefits administration programs.

Benefits Interfaces

PeopleSoft benefits are often extracted and sent to external systems. Benefits providers, for example, need to know which employees are enrolled in a benefit plan. The enrollment date and coverage level are important fields, as is dependent participation information. Such vendor interfaces will use SQL like that found in Chapters 22 and 23.

Other interfaces could extract or import information from IVR (Interactive Voice Response) systems. These systems can record changes to employee benefits. An employee might change his benefit plan using an IVR during an annual open enrollment process, or the contribution to a flexible spending account can be altered using an IVR. Interfaces must send the current elections to the IVR and must receive the changes into database tables.

The table and field descriptions and SQL in this and the following chapters will provide the basis for such interfaces. These chapters describe how benefits data is stored while pointing out the challenges of selecting this data accurately.

Benefits Reports

PeopleSoft delivers numerous reports for extracting benefits data. Some reports are for analyzing and reconciling benefits data. Others, though, are sent to employees directly. Employees must receive a list of eligible benefits, a confirmation of their election, and often require letters to indicate when their benefits change. There are a delivered open enrollment letter, termination letter, and several COBRA letters.

These letters often require some modification to adapt to an organization. They often do not contain complex SQL, or they require extensive amounts of database processing. Their challenge lies in the printing process and the customization for any legal policies or forms. PeopleSoft does not provide a convenient way to alter these letters, except through programming in SQR.

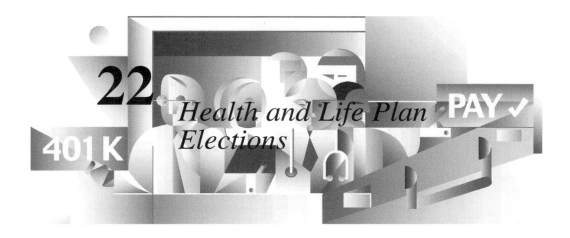

22 Health and Life Plan Elections

Most of the benefit plans in PeopleSoft fall into two categories: health and life. Health plans provide medical coverage for employees and their dependents. Life plans offer insurance for the employee, naming individuals as beneficiaries. These two plan types have extra tables that store detailed enrollment information.

These enrollment tables contain the entire enrollment history for employees and their dependents/beneficiaries. Storing this information is difficult, since the actual plan, coverage level, and enrolled dependents change from year to year. In this chapter we will look at how health and life plan information can be accurately retrieved from these tables.

HEALTH ENROLLMENTS

All enrollments for health plans are kept on the PS_HEALTH_BENEFIT table (see Table 22-1). If you are using benefits administration, this table is populated at the end of the process with the final enrollment information. The health benefit table is the place to go if you need to see the health plans that an employee is enrolled in.

▶ **Table 22-1** Health Benefits: PS_HEALTH_BENEFIT

Structure	Many rows per employee ID and plan type
Keys	Employee ID
	Employee Record Number
	Cobra Event ID

▶ **Table 22-1**   continued

	Plan Type
	Benefit Record Number
	Effective Date
Alternate keys	None
Sub-records included	None
Panels to look at	Go ➤ Compensate Employees ➤ Administer Base Benefits ➤ Use ➤ Health Benefits

The health benefit table stores only plan types that begin with '1' that is, in the 10-19 series. These plan types as delivered include medical, dental, vision/hearing, and nonqualified versions of these plans. Basic information is stored for each enrollment—coverage dates, election date, coverage level, and optional health provider information.

The panel that looks at the PS_HEALTH_BENEFIT table is usually not accessed when benefits administration is used. In benefits administration, data entry occurs on separate panels and through events, which then write rows to the health benefit table during benefits administration. When you look at the base benefits health panels (see 'Panels to look at' in Table 22-1), you are viewing the results of benefits administration programs. If, on the other hand, you are not executing benefits administration, then data entry would occur on the base benefit panels.

Elections

Rows are stored in the health benefit table according to a field called coverage elect (COVERAGE_ELECT). It is not a key, but it supplies critical information. The possible values for coverage elect are:

- elect (E)—the participant elected the plan.
- term (T)—the participant terminated coverage entirely.
- waive (W)—the participant waived coverage entirely.

Each row in the table has one of these three codes. When you look at the table and go down through each row, you can track the history using these codes, as in Table 22-2.

▶ **Table 22-2** Coverage elections

Emplid	Plan Type	Date	Coverage Elect	Coverage Code	Benefit Plan
BOZO	10	1/11/2000	E	1	MEDIC
BOZO	10	5/23/2000	E	1	HMO23
BOZO	10	10/1/2001	E	2	HMO23
BOZO	11	1/11/2000	E	2	ADENT
BOZO	11	5/23/2000	E	3	DDENT
BOZO	11	6/3/2000	W		

Notice how the coverage election, coverage code, and benefit plan work together. When an employee elects a plan for the first time or changes the coverage of a plan, a new row is created. If the employee loses eligibility in a plan or waives his or her coverage (June 3, 2000), no coverage code or benefit plan is entered. In the example in Table 22-2, BOZO elected the medical plan (MEDIC, plan type 10) on January 11, 2000. That May, he changed to an HMO plan. No termination row exists because his coverage never terminated. Then, in October of the following year, he added his spouse to the plan, changing the coverage code.

When an employee changes plans, no termination row is written to this table. An 'E' row is followed by another 'E' row. If an employee is ineligible and his or her coverage is terminated, a termination row will be written with a 'T' value. The termination of coverage in a particular plan, therefore, can be determined by both a change in plan code and by the coverage elect field.

Dates

The most difficult part of determining enrollment is understanding the different date fields. There are five date fields on the health table, all slightly different. They allow PeopleSoft to store historical information. Similar to the PS_JOB table, enrollment history presents some navigation issues. First let's look at the meaning of each date field.

Even though both elections and terminations are stored on the health benefit table, many of the fields are named "begin date" and "end date". Do not get confused—these dates are stored for each row regardless of the coverage elect value. It is common to think of the begin date as associated only with elections while the end date is associated only with terms—but this is not the case. A begin date for a 'T' row indicates when the termination begins.

Effective date

In general, the effective date is used to track history. It is the only date field that is a key, so when it is used with the employee ID and plan type it provides a unique identifier. An employee cannot have two medical enrollment entries for the same effective date.

Yet the effective date does not overtly appear on the health benefit panel. Actually, it is in disguise as the *deduction begin date*. The effective date is used to start and stop deductions. In the payroll world, the date the deduction starts is the date the employee started paying for the medical plan. It is therefore the date the plan is effective in payroll. PeopleSoft payroll uses this date to determine when to take a deduction.

The effective date/deduction begin is determined by the specifications made for deduction begin on the event rules table. For event maintenance, you can specify an event rule to use the same date, the first date of the next payroll, or the first date of the current payroll as an effective date/deduction end date. In other words, the employee either gets a few days of benefits for free, or pays for the days in the period that passed.

The effective date is also essential for linking to other tables, such as PS_HEALTH_DEPENDNT, which stores dependent enrollment according to effective date. Chapter 23 on dependents discusses this topic in detail.

> The deduction end date is no longer populated in version 7.5.

Coverage begin and end dates

The coverage begin date is equally, if not more important than the effective date. It indicates the official start (or end, if the row is a 'T' row) of coverage. The employee is covered for all claims beginning with this date.

Often the effective date (deduction begin date) will precede the coverage begin date in order to ensure that the deduction is taken before coverage starts. While payroll is interested in the deduction begin date, your health care vendors will need to know the date coverage begins and ends.

Unfortunately, providing these dates is not as simple as selecting the coverage date fields. In PeopleSoft a new row is created for every change in coverage, and the coverage begin and end dates are tied to this row. The coverage date does not indicate the enrollment date. It only provides the date for the particular coverage election. We look carefully at determining *enrollment* dates in the next section.

If you are choosing between using the coverage begin date and the effective date for the health record, consider their different meanings. The effective date (i.e. deduction begin date) is the date the employee started paying for coverage. The coverage begin date is the date coverage began. Depending on the information that is important to you, either date could be appropriate.

Elect date

The election date is a date stamp for the election. It records when the employee made the election (i.e., when the enrollment form sent in by the employee was processed). This date is often drastically different from the other dates, since employees can enter an election at any time. PeopleSoft disregards the election date and looks at an entry once the coverage begin date equals the current date. Also, election date is not a reliable date stamp, since it can be changed on the health benefits panel (unless display-only access is granted to these panels).

DETERMINING THE CURRENT ENROLLMENTS

Let's look at some examples of pulling health benefit information from PeopleSoft to get a better idea of how these dates work. First, a review of the data we are querying for the employee 'BOZO' is in Table 22-3.

▶ **Table 22-3** Health benefit data for BOZO

Emplid	Plan Type	Effective Date	Coverage Begin Date	Coverage Elect	Coverage Code	Benefit Plan
BOZO	10	1/11/2000	1/11/2000	E	1	MEDIC
BOZO	10	5/23/2000	5/23/2000	E	1	HMO23
BOZO	10	10/1/2001	10/1/2001	E	2	HMO23

Finding the most recent transaction date

The simplest query will retrieve the plan the employee is currently in and provide the most recent coverage date for his or her level of coverage. An example that retrieves the most recent coverage for a medical plan type is shown in Table 22-4.

▶ **Table 22-4** Health benefit transaction date

| The query | ```
SELECT
HB.EFFDT,
HB.PLAN_TYPE,
HB.BENEFIT_PLAN,
HB.COVRG_CD,
HB.COVERAGE_BEGIN_DT,
HB.COVERAGE_ELECT

FROM PS_HEALTH_BENEFIT HB
WHERE HB.EMPLID          = 'BOZO'
  AND HB.PLAN_TYPE       = '10'
  AND HB.COVERAGE_BEGIN_DT          =
      (SELECT MAX(HB0.COVERAGE_BEGIN_DT)
         FROM PS_HEALTH_BENEFIT HB0
        WHERE HB0.EMPLID             = HB.EMPLID
          AND HB0.EMPL_RCD# = HB.EMPL_RCD#
          AND HB0.COBRA_EVENT_ID    = HB.COBRA_EVENT_ID
          AND HB0.BENEFIT# = HB.BENEFIT#
          AND HB0.PLAN_TYPE = HB.PLAN_TYPE
          AND HB0.COVERAGE_BEGIN_DT <= [current date])
``` |

Returns the data set	EFFDT	PLAN_ TYPE	BENEFIT _PLAN	COVRG _CD	COVERAGE_ BEGIN_DT	COVERAGE _ELECT
	-----------	-----	-------	-----	-----------	--------
	01-OCT-2001	10	HMO23	2	01-OCT-2001	E

This same query could be written another way, using the effective date field instead of the coverage begin date in the sub-query. This would pull a different row, since the effective date and coverage begin date do not need to be in chronological order. For instance, a later effective date could have an earlier begin date and vice versa. If Bozo has an effective date of November 2001 (later than the row in Table 22-4) but a coverage begin date in December 2000 (before the begin date in Table 22-4), a query using effective date would pull this row instead of the one in our query. Would it be correct? That depends on what you are looking for, and how you use the system.

In most cases PeopleSoft will not contain an effective-dated row that is so disparate from the coverage begin date (i.e., the coverage begin date of one row falls before a previous coverage begin date). This will only occur when correction mode is used. Using the effective date to get the most recent row is a perfectly fine solution and, as we will see in Chapter 23, a necessary step for linking employees with their dependents. Table 22-5 demonstrates the query using
```

effective date. The same row is returned because Bozo's data was created by benefits administration and has no disparate coverage begin dates.

▶ **Table 22-5** Health benefit transaction date

The query	SELECT

```
SELECT
HB.EFFDT,
HB.PLAN_TYPE,
HB.BENEFIT_PLAN,
HB.COVRG_CD,
HB.COVERAGE_BEGIN_DT,
HB.COVERAGE_ELECT

FROM PS_HEALTH_BENEFIT HB
WHERE HB.EMPLID        = 'BOZO'
  AND HB.PLAN_TYPE     = '10'
  AND HB.EFFDT =
      (SELECT MAX(HB0.EFFDT)
        FROM PS_HEALTH_BENEFIT HB0
       WHERE HB0.EMPLID           = HB.EMPLID
         AND HB0.EMPL_RCD# = HB.EMPL_RCD#
         AND HB0.COBRA_EVENT_ID   = HB.COBRA_EVENT_ID
         AND HB0.BENEFIT#  = HB.BENEFIT#
         AND HB0.PLAN_TYPE = HB.PLAN_TYPE
         AND HB0.COVERAGE_BEGIN_DT <= [current date])
```

Returns the data set	EFFDT	PLAN_ TYPE	BENEFIT _PLAN	COVRG _CD	COVERAGE_ BEGIN_DT	COVERAGE _ELECT
	01-OCT-2001	10	HMO23	2	01-OCT-2001	E

The coverage begin date in the two previous examples represents what we will call a 'transaction' date. This is the date of the most recent transaction, i.e., change in coverage or plan. To a health provider, this date is useful for tracking the coverage level. It does not provide, however, an enrollment date.

Finding the enrollment date

An enrollment date is the date the employee first entered the benefit plan. This date is stored on the health benefit table, but is difficult to obtain. In Table 22-3 there are two enrollment dates. One is for HMO23 and one is for MEDIC. To retrieve the most recent enrollment date, you must select the first date in the most recent group of election rows. In other words, we want to look at the most recent benefit plan (HMO23) and then find the first date the employee was in that plan (5/23/2000).

There are two options for obtaining the enrollment date:

1. Get the date from PS_BENEFITS_DATA. This table is explained in Chapter 4 and Appendix A, and we will look at how it works below. The field is called ENROLLMENT_DT, and the BEN100 SQR program creates it. To select the date from the benefits data table, your query will be dependent on BEN100 executing success-fully to populate the enrollment date field.

2. Select the date from PS_HEALTH_BENEFIT by stepping back through the table for each employee.

Of course, simply selecting the value from PS_BENEFITS_DATA is the eas-iest way to get the enrollment date. Let's look at both methods.

BEN100 Method

The BEN100 program uses SQR to obtain the correct date. Here is the code that PeopleSoft uses:

```
move &HBeffdt to $enrollment_dt
begin-select
H3.EMPLID,H3.BENEFIT_PLAN,H3.EFFDT,H3.PLAN_TYPE
  if (&H3.benefit_plan != $benefit_plan)
    EXIT-SELECT
  else
    move &H3.effdt to $enrollment_dt
  end-if
from PS_HEALTH_BENEFIT H3
where H3.EMPLID             = $current_emplid
  and H3.COBRA_EVENT_ID     = #cobra_event_id
  and H3.EMPL_RCD#          = #current_empl_rcd
  and H3.PLAN_TYPE          = $plan_type
  and H3.EFFDT             <= &HBeffdt
order by H3.EFFDT DESC
end-select
```

Without going into detail about how SQR operates, this select statement retrieves all of the rows for an employee within a plan type and places them in descending order. For each row returned, it evaluates the benefit plan and, if the plan changes, exits out of the select statement. When it exits, the first date of the last series is contained in the $enrollment_dt field.

This method is very efficient but will not work using a query tool that cannot include an IF/THEN statement (i.e., additional logic). The BEN100 SQR program populates the PS_BENEFITS_DATA table with this date *because* it is nearly impossible to perform logic like this using a query tool. The ENROLLMENT_DT field can simply be selected from PS_BENEFITS_DATA once BEN100 has been executed, as in Table 22-6.

▶ **Table 22-6** Enrollment date from PS_BENEFITS_DATA

The query	SELECT

```
SELECT
BD.PLAN_TYPE,
BD.BENEFIT_PLAN,
BD.ENROLLMENT_DT

FROM PS_BENEFITS_DATA BD
WHERE BD.EMPLID = 'BOZO'
```

Returns the data set	PLAN_TYPE	BENEFIT_PLAN	ENROLLMENT_DT
	10	HMO23	23-MAY-2000
	11	DDDD	21-SEP-1996
	14	VILO	01-JAN-1997

SQL Method

The enrollment date can be obtained from the PS_HEALTH_BENEFIT table by stepping through the historical data. To retrieve only the last set of data for the plan the employee is currently in, we look at everything after the most recent termination. Table 22-7 shows all of the health benefit rows for employee BOZO.

▶ **Table 22-7** Health benefit records for BOZO

The query	SELECT

```
SELECT
HB.EMPLID,
HB.PLAN_TYPE,
HB.BENEFIT_PLAN,
HB.COVRG_CD,
HB.COVERAGE_ELECT,
HB.COVERAGE_BEGIN_DT,
HB.EFFDT

FROM PS_HEALTH_BENEFIT HB
WHERE HB.EMPLID = 'BOZO'
```

▶ **Table 22-7**   continued

	EMPLID	PLAN_ TYPE	BENEFIT _PLAN	COVRG _CD	COVERAGE _ELECT	COVERAGE _BEGIN_DT	EFFDT
Returns the data set	BOZO	10	HMO23	2	E	01-OCT-2001	01-OCT-2001
	BOZO	10	HMO23	1	E	23-MAY-2000	23-MAY-2000
	BOZO	10	MEDIC	1	E	11-JAN-2000	11-JAN-2000
	BOZO	11	DDDD	1	E	01-MAR-1998	01-APR-1998
	BOZO	11	DDDD	1	E	01-MAR-1997	01-MAR-1997
	BOZO	11	DDDD	4	E	01-JAN-1997	01-JAN-1997
	BOZO	11	DDDD	1	E	21-SEP-1996	01-SEP-1996
	BOZO	11	DDHM	3	E	01-JAN-1996	01-JAN-1996
	BOZO	11	DDDD	1	E	01-JAN-1995	01-JAN-1995
	BOZO	11			W	01-JAN-1993	01-JAN-1993
	BOZO	14			T	01-MAR-1996	01-MAR-1996
	BOZO	14	VIHI	3	E	01-JAN-1996	01-JAN-1996
	BOZO	14	VIHI	1	E	01-JAN-1995	01-JAN-1995

First, break up the data set by plan type. Then look for the most recent effective date. In the case of BOZO's dental plan, 3/1/98 is the most recent entry. For the DDDD benefit plan, the first time BOZO entered the plan is 9/21/96. Note that BOZO was in DDDD previously. The enrollment date only pertains to the most recent contiguous period of enrollment in a particular plan.

Although the logic is simple to follow, the SQL query to do it is rather lengthy. Table 22-8 demonstrates the full SQL query, retrieving both the most recent transaction date and the enrollment date.

▶ **Table 22-8**   Obtaining enrollment date using SQL

The query
```
SELECT
HB.PLAN_TYPE,
HB.BENEFIT_PLAN,
HB.COVRG_CD,
HB.COVERAGE_ELECT,
HB.COVERAGE_BEGIN_DT,
HB2.COVERAGE_BEGIN_DT

FROM  PS_HEALTH_BENEFIT  HB,
      PS_HEALTH_BENEFIT  HB2
WHERE HB2.EMPLID          = 'BOZO'
  AND HB2.BENEFIT_PLAN    = HB.BENEFIT_PLAN
  AND HB2.PLAN_TYPE       = HB.PLAN_TYPE
  AND HB2.EMPLID          = HB.EMPLID
```

▶ **Table 22-8** Obtaining enrollment date using SQL

```
            AND  HB.EFFDT              =
                (SELECT MAX(HB1.EFFDT)
                   FROM PS_HEALTH_BENEFIT HB1
                  WHERE HB1.EMPLID              = HB.EMPLID
                    AND HB1.EMPL_RCD# = HB.EMPL_RCD#
                    AND HB1.COBRA_EVENT_ID   = HB.COBRA_EVENT_ID
                    AND HB1.BENEFIT#  = HB.BENEFIT#
                    AND HB1.PLAN_TYPE = HB.PLAN_TYPE
                    AND HB1.EFFDT             <= [current date])
            AND HB2.EFFDT =
                (SELECT MIN(HB3.EFFDT)
                   FROM PS_HEALTH_BENEFIT HB3
                  WHERE HB3.EMPLID              = HB2.EMPLID
                    AND HB3.EMPL_RCD# = HB2.EMPL_RCD#
                    AND HB3.COBRA_EVENT_ID   = HB2.COBRA_EVENT_ID
                    AND HB3.PLAN_TYPE = HB2.PLAN_TYPE
                    AND HB3.BENEFIT_PLAN     = HB2.BENEFIT_PLAN
                    AND HB3.BENEFIT#  = HB2.BENEFIT#
                    AND ((HB3.EFFDT >
                        (SELECT MAX(HB4.EFFDT)
                           FROM PS_HEALTH_BENEFIT HB4
                          WHERE HB4.EMPLID    = HB3.EMPLID
                            AND HB4.EMPL_RCD# = HB3.EMPL_RCD#
                            AND HB4.COBRA_EVENT_ID   = HB3.COBRA_EVENT_ID
                            AND HB4.PLAN_TYPE = HB3.PLAN_TYPE
                            AND HB4.BENEFIT#  = HB3.BENEFIT#
                            AND HB4.BENEFIT_PLAN  <> HB.BENEFIT_PLAN
                            AND HB4.EFFDT             < HB.EFFDT))
                        OR (NOT EXISTS
                        (SELECT HB5.EFFDT
                           FROM PS_HEALTH_BENEFIT HB5
                          WHERE HB5.EMPLID              = HB3.EMPLID
                            AND HB5.EMPL_RCD# = HB3.EMPL_RCD#
                            AND HB5.COBRA_EVENT_ID   = HB3.COBRA_EVENT_ID
                            AND HB5.PLAN_TYPE = HB3.PLAN_TYPE
                            AND HB5.BENEFIT#  = HB3.BENEFIT#
                            AND HB5.BENEFIT_PLAN  <> HB.BENEFIT_PLAN
                            AND HB5.EFFDT             < HB.EFFDT))
```

Returns the data set	PLAN_ TYPE	BENEFIT _PLAN	COVRG _CD	COVERAGE _ELECT	COVERAGE _BEGIN_DT	COVERAGE _BEGIN_DT
	-----	-------	-----	--------	-----------	-----------
	10	HMO23	2	E	01-OCT-2001	23-MAY-2000
	11	DDDD	1	E	01-MAR-1998	21-SEP-1996
	14	VILO	2	E	01-JAN-1997	01-JAN-1997

The first coverage begin date is the transaction date, and the second date is the date coverage began in the particular plan. BOZO enrolled in the DDDD dental plan on September 21, 1996, and his last change to his coverage in this plan was on March 1, 1998. He enrolled in the health plan HMO23 on May 23, 2000, and changed his coverage on October 1, 2001.

The query in Table 22-8 follows a particular logic. It first selects the most recent row to obtain the transaction date. Then it links to the next (minimum) row after the most recent change in benefit plan. A change in the benefit plan code indicates that another plan was elected, or that coverage was terminated or waived (a blank plan code). For the dental plan type, the query first finds the most recent non-DDDD row from March 1, 1996 for BOZO. Then it retrieves the first election row after it. This is the first day the participant entered the most recently elected plan.

At the end of the query is an OR NOT EXISTS, which handles situations where the employee has never changed from one benefit plan to another. In such cases, the query will simply retrieve the first row.

Also, we have linked the health benefits table to itself. This allows us to pull the transaction date and the enrollment date at the same time. You could split this into two queries and pass the necessary date information between them (see how HB4.EFFDT and HB5.EFFDT must be less than HB.EFFDT in their respective sub-queries).

Locating a 'Termination'

The term 'termination' needs some clarification in PeopleSoft benefits. From the perspective of the provider (an HMO company, for example), a termination occurs when an employee is no longer covered in a particular plan. If Kate is covered in plan 'HMO1' and then switches to a different plan, her coverage in plan 'HMO1' terminates.

In PeopleSoft, the terminology is different. Kate simply changed benefit plans. No termination row is written to the PS_HEALTH_BENEFIT table. A new row is written with a new coverage begin date and plan code.

A termination row only occurs when an employee terminates coverage completely and has no coverage at all. Kate could have gone on a part-time schedule, and her eligibility for health benefits could be terminated. A termination row indicates this stop in coverage. A waiver occurs when Kate voluntarily decides to stop her coverage. Both 'T' and 'W' options are distinguished by a lack of a value for the benefit plan and coverage code fields.

If you are searching for participants in a certain plan, then you will probably also want to capture employees who terminated (changed or dropped coverage entirely) from that plan. To fulfill this requirement it is necessary to look at the row after the most recent plan row to get the termination date. Table 22-9 demonstrates how this is achieved in SQL.

▶ **Table 22-9** Finding the termination date for a plan

| The query | ```
SELECT
HB.PLAN_TYPE,
HB.COVERAGE_BEGIN_DT

FROM PS_HEALTH_BENEFIT HB
WHERE HB.EMPLID = 'BOZO'
  AND HB.EFFDT =
        (SELECT MIN(HB1.EFFDT)
          FROM PS_HEALTH_BENEFIT HB1
         WHERE HB1.EMPLID         = HB.EMPLID
           AND HB1.EMPL_RCD# = HB.EMPL_RCD#
           AND HB1.COBRA_EVENT_ID   = HB.COBRA_EVENT_ID
           AND HB1.PLAN_TYPE = HB.PLAN_TYPE
           AND HB1.BENEFIT_PLAN      = HB.BENEFIT_PLAN
           AND HB1.BENEFIT#  = HB.BENEFIT#
           AND ((HB1.EFFDT >
              (SELECT MAX(HB2.EFFDT)
                FROM PS_HEALTH_BENEFIT HB2
               WHERE HB2.EMPLID          = HB1.EMPLID
                 AND HB2.EMPL_RCD# = HB1.EMPL_RCD#
                 AND HB2.COBRA_EVENT_ID   = HB1.COBRA_EVENT_ID
                 AND HB2.PLAN_TYPE = HB1.PLAN_TYPE
                 AND HB2.BENEFIT#  = HB1.BENEFIT#
                 AND HB2.BENEFIT_PLAN     ='MEDIC'))));
``` |

Returns the data set	PLAN_TYPE	COVERAGE_BEGIN_DT
	---------	-----------------
	10	23-MAY-2000

This query looks for a particular plan ('MEDIC'), gets the most recent transaction date for the plan, and then looks at the next row in the table. This next row is either a new plan or a termination/waiver row with no plan code. The query reads the date from this row to return the true termination date for the 'MEDIC' plan.
```

LIFE PLANS

The underlying table structure and the storage of dates for life plans is similar to that of health plans. Refer to the previous section on health plans for a general introduction to the following topics:

- Enrollments
- Elections
- Dates
- Current enrollments/enrollment date
- Terminations/termination date

All enrollments for life insurance plans are kept on the PS_LIFE_ADD_BEN table (Table 22-10). If you are using benefits administration, this table is populated at the end of the process with the final enrollment information. The life benefit table is the place to go if you need to see which life insurance and accidental death/disability plans that an employee is enrolled in. Enrollments for beneficiaries are on PS_LIFE_ADD_BENEFC.

▶ **Table 22-10** Life Plans: PS_LIFE_ADD_BEN

Structure	Many rows per employee ID and plan type
Keys	Employee ID
	Employee Record Number
	Plan Type
	Benefit Record Number
	Effective Date
Alternate keys	None
Sub-records included	None
Panels to look at	Go ➤ Compensate Employees ➤ Administer Base Benefits ➤ Use ➤ Life and AD/D Benefits

The life/ADD benefit table only stores plan types that begin with '2' (i.e., in the 20-29 series). These plan types include life, supplemental life, accidental death, and supplemental accidental death plans for participants and dependents. Basic information is stored for each enrollment—coverage dates, election date, coverage type, and base benefits salary for calculating coverage.

Determining coverage amounts

Coverage, for a life plan, is the amount the participant can claim against the insurance plan. If Susan is covered for one million dollars, she can claim that one million dollars. PeopleSoft tracks coverage because often companies scale the amount of coverage a participant can have in a company-sponsored insurance plan. Coverage can depend on many factors.

To figure out an employee's coverage in a life plan, you should use the PS_LIFE_ADD_BEN table to find out how the coverage is calculated and stored, then select the appropriate fields. Coverage type values (LIFE_ADD_COVRG field) are shown in Table 22-11.

▶ **Table 22-11** Coverage type (LIFE_ADD_COVRG)

Value	Description
1	Flat amount only
2	Factor × salary + flat amount
3	Specified in employee record (i.e., right on PS_LIFE_ADD_BEN)
4	Special calculation routine (if you modify the benefits administration COBOL)
5	Sum of dependent coverage

If the information is not specified on the PS_LIFE_ADD_BEN table (value 3), then the amount and/or rate is stored with the definition of the plan itself on the plan setup table. This is usually the case. A look at the PS_LIFE_ADD_BEN table is shown in Table 22-12.

▶ **Table 22-12** Looking for coverage on PS_LIFE_ADD_BEN

The query
```
SELECT
LA.EMPLID,
LA.BENEFIT_PLAN,
LA.LIFE_ADD_COVRG,
LA.FLAT_AMOUNT,
LA.FACTOR_XSALARY,
LA.BENEFITS_BASE

FROM PS_LIFE_ADD_BEN LA
WHERE LA.PLAN_TYPE    = '20'
  AND LA.EFFDT =
        (SELECT MAX(LA2.EFFDT)
          FROM PS_LIFE_ADD_BEN LA2
         WHERE LA2.EMPLID    = LA.EMPLID
           AND LA2.EMPL_RCD# = LA.EMPL_RCD#
           AND LA2.PLAN_TYPE = LA.PLAN_TYPE
           AND LA2.EFFDT     < [current date])
```

▶ **Table 22-12**   continued

	EMPLID	BENEFIT _PLAN	LIFE_ADD _COVRG	FLAT_ AMOUNT	FACTOR_ XSALARY	BENEFITS _BASE
Returns the data set	RT_00000003	BLIFE	2	0	0	1
	7703	LIF1X	1	0	0	1
	7704	LIF1X	1	0	0	1
	G003	LIF1X	1	0	0	1
	8553	LIF2X	1	0	0	1
	6602	LIFBAS	3	10000	0	1
	7707	LIFBAS	1	0	0	1

You can see that neither the flat amount nor the factor is stored for those with a coverage type other than 3. Yet for all coverage types, the PS_LIFE_ADD_BEN table provides a guide to the benefits base salary to be used for calculation of coverage. A '1' as shown above indicates that PeopleSoft will use the annual rate for the employee (PS_JOB table, ANNUAL_RT field). A '2' means that the annual benefits base rate for the employee is used (PS_JOB table, ANNL_BENEF_BASE_RT field).

▶ **Table 22-13**   Looking for coverage on PS_LIFE_ADD_TBL

| The query | ```
SELECT
LT.BENEFIT_PLAN,
LT.LIFE_ADD_COVRG,
LT.FLAT_AMOUNT,
LT.FACTOR_XSALARY,
LT.COVG_GROUP_CD

FROM PS_LIFE_ADD_TBL LT
WHERE LT.PLAN_TYPE = '20'
  AND LT.EFFDT =
        (SELECT MAX(LT2.EFFDT)
           FROM PS_LIFE_ADD_BEN LT2
          WHERE LT2.BENEFIT_PLAN = LT.BENEFIT_PLAN
            AND LT2.PLAN_TYPE = LT.PLAN_TYPE
            AND LT2.EFFDT < [current date])
``` |
|---|---|

	BENEFIT _PLAN	LIFE_ADD _COVRG	FLAT_ AMOUNT	FACTOR_ XSALARY	COVG_GROUP_CD
Returns the data set	BLIFE	2	0	1	BSL
	LIF1X	2	200	1	CCB
	LIF2X	2	0	2	CCB
	LIF2XB	3	0	0	
	LIF3X	2	0	3	CCB
	LIFBAS	2	0	2	CCB
```

Table 22-13 demonstrates how to look up the missing flat amount and factor information on the appropriate life insurance plan definition table.

The BLIFE plan covers the individual for his or her entire salary. Life 1x covers for the individual's salary plus $200. Life 2x is just twice the individual's salary.

The calculation is simple. Find out the appropriate benefits base salary for coverage on PS_LIFE_ADD_BEN, then find out the flat amount and factor to apply to the salary on PS_LIFE_ADD_TBL.

Coverage Groups

Life plans can also be grouped using a coverage group code. If employees elect several life plans and a maximum coverage applies to the combination of these plans, a coverage group field combines the plans and stores a maximum amount that is cumulative. So, for example, if a coverage group combines a supplemental and a dependent life plan with a maximum of $500,000, my combined coverage in these two plans cannot exceed $500,000. The coverage is reduced to fit the maximum in descending order of plan type. So the coverage amount of a life plan of type 25 (such as Dependent Life) will be taken first, then a plan type of 24, 23, etc., until the maximum is reached. When the maximum is reached, it's possible that plan type 20 (Basic Life) will actually have no coverage at all.

23
Dependents and Beneficiaries

In addition to tracking the enrollment of employees, PeopleSoft stores information about the enrollment of dependents and beneficiaries in benefit plans. These individuals are separated from the employees. When PeopleSoft speaks of a participant in a plan, the word participant does *not* include dependents and beneficiaries. PeopleSoft provides some criteria for performing event maintenance on dependents and beneficiaries, but unlike employees (or other individuals in PS_PERSONAL_DATA), they do not interact with human resources independently of their employed family member or benefactor. All changes to dependents and beneficiaries must go through the employee participant.

In this chapter we will discuss how dependent and beneficiary personal data and enrollment information is stored, and how employees are linked to their dependents.

HOW ARE DEPENDENTS AND BENEFICIARIES STORED?

The distinction between dependents and beneficiaries is simple: a dependent is a family member covered under a benefit plan who can make claims on the plan, while a beneficiary is the designated recipient of funds on a life insurance, savings, or pension plan. PeopleSoft stores dependents and beneficiaries together because it needs the same information for both. This arrangement often blurs the differences between the two, but it is important to maintain these two types of individuals as distinct.

First let's look at the tables that contain information about dependents and beneficiaries in Table 23-1.

▶ **Table 23-1**   Dependent/beneficiary tables in PeopleSoft

Table	Description
PS_DEP_BENEF_NID	Contains the national ID (SSN) for each dependent and beneficiary.
PS_DEPENDENT_BENEF	Stores all personal data about each dependent and beneficiary.
PS_HEALTH_DEPENDNT	Tracks the history of dependent enrollment in health plans.
PS_LIFE_ADD_BENEFC	Tracks the history of beneficiary designations in life insurance plans.
PS_SAVINGS_BENEFIC	Tracks the history of beneficiary designations in savings plans.
PS_PENSION_BENEFC	Tracks the history of beneficiary designations in pension plans.

The relationships between these tables is straightforward. The PS_DEPEN-DENT_BENEF table forms the center, similar to the PS_PERSONAL_DATA table for employees. From there, dependents and beneficiaries are linked to health and life plans using separate historical tables. The link stores a dependent/beneficiary ID and a plan type, and any enrollment information.

LOCATING ALL DEPENDENTS FOR A PARTICIPANT

Information on dependents and beneficiaries is stored on panels under Go ➤ Compensate Employees ➤ Administer Base Benefits ➤ Dependent/Beneficiary ➤ Name/Address. When you type in an employee ID, the dependents and beneficiaries appear and can be added or deleted. The address, birth date, gender, marital status, student data/occupation, phone numbers, Medicare information, and SSN are stored on these panels for each individual. No history is stored for this data.

Using dependent/beneficiary type

To find all of the dependents for a participant, you can select from the PS_DEPENDENT_BENEF table by employee ID. The procedure also works for beneficiaries if you specify beneficiary as your dependent/beneficiary type. Table 23-2 demonstrates the appropriate SQL for dependents.

▶ **Table 23-2** Retrieving current dependents

| The query | ```
SELECT
DB.EMPLID,
DB.DEPENDENT_BENEF,
DB.RELATIONSHIP,
DB.BIRTHDATE

FROM PS_DEPENDENT_BENEF DB
WHERE DB.DEP_BENEF_TYPE IN ('D','O')
``` |
| --- | --- |

Returns the data set	EMPLID	DEPENDENT_BENEF	RELATIONSHIP	BIRTHDATE
	------	---------------	------------	-----------
	BOZO	02	S	03-MAY-1986
	BOZO	03	D	30-SEP-1990
	1680	02	S	06-JUN-1975
	1680	03	D	30-OCT-1978
	1328	02	S	11-JUL-1990

Here we specified a dependent/beneficiary type of 'D' for dependent and 'O' for both. Other possible values are: 'B' for beneficiary, 'C' for dependents who are only for COBRA, 'N' for someone who is none of the values (rare), and 'E,' 'Q,' and 'R' for individuals who are part of a qualified domestic relations order (QDRO) specifying that payments go to an estate, representative employee, or general representative.

> Remember to include 'O' (both) as a valid identification of either a dependent or a beneficiary.

The dependent/beneficiary ID (such as 01, 02, 03, etc.) does not follow a set rule. It could be any number for any dependent. Also remember that this table is not effective-dated. If a dependent is removed, he or she is gone forever until manually re-entered. The assignment of a dependent/beneficiary ID is therefore a random process.

Specifying relationships

Each dependent has some sort of relationship to the employee. Since several kinds of people can be stored on the PS_DEPENDENT_BENEF table and panels, there are many relationship options. Not all of the options pertain to the benefit plan. For example, a dependent is usually not an employee's roommate.
```

Although it is a valid selection, it is probably invalid for the employee's health plan. Table 23-3 lists all of the possible relationship types for reference.

▶ **Table 23-3** Relationships

Value	Description	Value	Description
A	Aunt	ND	Nonqualified Daughter
B	Brother	NE	Nephew
D	Daughter	NI	Niece
E	Employee	NS	Nonqualified Son
FA	Father	O	Other
FI	Father-in-Law	R	Other Relative
FR	Friend	RO	Roommate
GC	Grandchild	S	Son
GF	Grandfather	SI	Sister
GM	Grandmother	SP	Spouse
M	Mother	T	Estate
MI	Mother-in-Law	U	Uncle
N	Neighbor	X	Ex-spouse
NA	Nonqualified Adult		

The National ID

PeopleSoft stores the national ID (SSN or other international identification) for each dependent and beneficiary. This information is easily accessed on the dependent/beneficiary panel but is stored separately behind the scenes in the PS_DEP_BENEF_NID table. By storing this information in a separate table, PeopleSoft allows you to specify multiple national identification numbers for a single person.

The PS_DEP_BENEF_NID table is useful because it consolidates the basic ID numbers in one place. It has three fields: employee ID, dependent/beneficiary ID, and national ID. The employee ID is only for associating the dependent or beneficiary back to an employee; it does not mean that employee SSNs are stored in this table.

DETERMINING DEPENDENT COVERAGE

To identify dependents that are actually enrolled in a benefit plan, you must look at additional tables. Just because a dependent is stored on PS_DEPENDENT_BENEF does not mean that he or she has any of the employee's benefit plans. Only once an enrollment record is set up will the dependent/beneficiary affect benefits.

These enrollment areas are divided by plan type. Table 23-4 lists each place you can set up a dependent/beneficiary in a benefit plan.

▶ **Table 23-4** Dependent/beneficiary enrollments

Panel ➤ Go ➤ Compensate Employees ➤ Administer Base Benefits ➤ Use ➤)	Dependent/ Beneficiary	Table
Health Benefits	Dependent	PS_HEALTH_DEPENDNT
Life and AD/D Benefits	Beneficiary	PS_LIFE_ADD_BENEFC
Savings Plans	Beneficiary	PS_SAVINGS_BENEFIC
Savings Plans (Canada/International)	Beneficiary	PS_SAVINGS_BENEFIC
Pension Plans	Beneficiary	PS_PENSION_BENEFC

The process, and the storage method behind it, is simple. Type in an employee ID, and a list of the dependents for each plan, along with the historical dependents for each historical plan, is returned. To access this information using SQL, simply link all of the associated tables together to get a detailed listing. Table 23-5 provides a sample SQL statement for retrieving a list of dependents enrolled in health plans for a single employee.

▶ **Table 23-5** Retrieving dependents enrolled in health plans

The query
```
SELECT
DB.NAME,
DB.BIRTHDATE,
DN.NATIONAL_ID,
HB.BENEFIT_PLAN,
HB.EFFDT

FROM PS_DEPENDENT_BENEF DB,
     PS_DEP_BENEF_NID DN,
     PS_HEALTH_BENEFIT HB,
     PS_HEALTH_DEPENDNT HD
WHERE HB.EMPLID          = 'BOZO'
  AND HB.EMPL_RCD#       = 0
```

▶ **Table 23-5** continued

```
          AND  HB.PLAN_TYPE              =  '10'
          AND  HD.EMPLID                 =  HB.EMPLID
          AND  HD.EMPL_RCD#              =  HB.EMPL_RCD#
          AND  HD.COBRA_EVENT_ID         =  HB.COBRA_EVENT_ID
          AND  HD.PLAN_TYPE              =  HB.PLAN_TYPE
          AND  HD.BENEFIT#               =  HB.BENEFIT#
          AND  HD.EFFDT                  =  HB.EFFDT
          AND  DB.DEPENDENT_BENEF        =  HD.DEPENDENT_BENEF
          AND  DB.EMPLID                 =  HB.EMPLID
          AND  DN.EMPLID                 =  HB.EMPLID
          AND  DN.DEPENDENT_BENEF        =  HD.DEPENDENT_BENEF
```

Returns the
data set

```
                                       NATIONAL   BENEFIT
          NAME              BIRTHDATE   _ID        _PLAN     EFFDT
          ------------      ----------- ---------  -------   -----------
          Clown,Mary        25-DEC-1950 567785644  MATC      30-MAR-1999
          Clown,Jane        25-AUG-1990 665430081  MATC      30-MAR-1999
          Clown,Fred        16-MAR-1993 667389046  MATC      30-MAR-1999
          Clown,Mary        25-DEC-1950 567785644  MDTC      01-JAN-1997
          Clown,Jane        25-AUG-1990 665430081  MDTC      01-JAN-1997
          Clown,Fred        16-MAR-1993 667389046  MDTC      01-JAN-1997
          Clown,Jane        25-AUG-1990 665430081  MDTC      01-JAN-1996
          Clown,Fred        16-MAR-1993 667389046  MDTC      01-JAN-1996
```

This query shows the appropriate join between health benefit, health dependent, and the dependent/beneficiary tables. Note the line in bold, linking the effective date of health benefit with that of health dependent. This link represents the application of an important rule regarding dependent/beneficiary enrollment. *Since dependents and beneficiaries can only be enrolled in the plans an employee is enrolled in, they link to their 'owning' employee by effective date, not benefit plan.* In other words, dependents and beneficiaries cannot choose their own benefit plans or choose when to enroll or terminate their enrollment. They are at the mercy of the employee's enrollments and terminations.

Of course, a dependent might terminate his or her enrollment, or an employee could add a dependent and enroll that person. PeopleSoft requires the addition of a line of history in the employee record so that it can create a corresponding enroll/termination for the dependent.

For example, the employee in Table 23-5 had two dependents enrolled as of January 1, 1996 (Fred and Jane). On January 1, 1997, the employee added a dependent, Mary. Notice how a new effective date is created, and all of the dependent records copy over to the new date. The effective date appears on a single row in PS_HEALTH_BENEFIT and on multiple rows in PS_HEALTH_DEPENDNT.

When the employee changes benefit plans in March 1999, the dependent enrollment records are all affected. They copy again, even though there are no changes to the dependents enrolled. Since the employee has changed plans, the dependents must change their effective date to match the new plan.

Dependent enrollment date

One casualty of the configuration of these tables is the retrieval of concrete dates for dependent participation. Just like retrieving the employee enrollment date, the dependent enrollment date is the first record in a stack of numerous records. Furthermore, a dependent is not linked to a benefit plan, except through the employee. This makes the SQL more difficult.

First let's look quickly at the contents of a new set of data for Carol. Table 23-6 explains each row of the output for Carol.

▶ **Table 23-6**   Health benefit table for Carol

Coverage begin date	Effective date	Benefit plan	Coverage elect	Coverage code	Description
01-JAN-1993	01-JAN-1993	COMP1	E	1	Carol joins the COMP1 health plan.
01-JAN-1995	01-JAN-1995	MDBC	E	1	Carol switches to the MDBC health plan.
01-JAN-1996	01-JAN-1996	MDBC	E	3	Carol enrolls some dependents in her health plan.
01-MAR-1996	01-MAR-1996		W		Carol decides to waive all health coverage.
01-DEC-1996	01-JAN-1997	MDTC	E	4	Carol resumes her health coverage by electing MDTC and enrolls her dependents too, with coverage beginning the first day of December. She convinces the HR representative to start deductions for the new plan in 1997 (hence the later effective date).

▶ **Table 23-7**   Dependent health benefit table for Carol

Effective date	Dependent Beneficiary ID	Description
01-JAN-1996	02	Here is where Carol enrolled dependent #2 in MDBC.
01-JAN-1996	03	Here is where Carol enrolled dependent #3 in MDBC.
01-JAN-1997	01	Carol terminated coverage in March 1996. No changes were made to the dependent participation records at that time. When Carol enrolled in MDTC with an effective date of January 1997, her dependents received a new row with the new effective date. She added dependent #1. Note that since coverage for Carol actually begins December 1, 1996, coverage for the dependents will begin then too.
01-JAN-1997	02	Dependent #2 switches to the new plan.
01-JAN-1997	03	Dependent #3 switches to the new plan.

Using this information, we can piece together the enrollment and termination dates for each dependent in the MDBC plan (Carol's second selection). Table 23-8 demonstrates the query necessary to determine the enrollment date for a dependent.

The query uses the dates returned by a basic query on the employee's participation. A sample of this basic query is shown in Chapter 22, table 22-7. These dates, as you can see in Table 23-6 above, are January 1995 through March 1996. Since the dependent must follow the participant's coverage, these dates are used to limit the data returned.

▶ **Table 23-8**   Retrieving dependents' enrollment date

The query
```
SELECT
DB.NAME,
DB.RELATIONSHIP,
HB.COVERAGE_BEGIN_DT

FROM PS_HEALTH_DEPENDNT HD,
     PS_DEPENDENT_BENEF DB,
     PS_HEALTH_BENEFIT HB
WHERE HD.EMPLID            = 'CAROL'
  AND HD.PLAN_TYPE         = '10'
  AND DB.EMPLID            = HD.EMPLID
  AND DB.DEPENDENT_BENEF   = HD.DEPENDENT_BENEF
```

▶ **Table 23-8** continued

```
        AND HD.EFFDT =
            (SELECT MIN(HD1.EFFDT)
               FROM PS_HEALTH_DEPENDNT HD1
              WHERE HD1.EMPLID             = HD.EMPLID
                AND HD1.EMPL_RCD#          = HD.EMPL_RCD#
                AND HD1.COBRA_EVENT_ID     = HD.COBRA_EVENT_ID
                AND HD1.PLAN_TYPE          = HD.PLAN_TYPE
                AND HD1.BENEFIT#           = HD.BENEFIT#
                AND HD1.DEPENDENT_BENEF    = HD.DEPENDENT_BENEF
                AND HD1.EFFDT >= '01-JAN-1995'
                AND HD1.EFFDT <= '01-MAR-1996')
        AND HB.EMPLID             = HD.EMPLID
        AND HB.EMPL_RCD#          = HD.EMPL_RCD#
        AND HB.COBRA_EVENT_ID     = HD.COBRA_EVENT_ID
        AND HB.PLAN_TYPE          = HD.PLAN_TYPE
        AND HB.BENEFIT#           = HD.BENEFIT#
        AND HB.EFFDT              = HD.EFFDT
```

Returns the data set

```
NAME           RELATIONSHIP   COVERAGE_BEGIN_DT
------------   ------------   -----------------
Smith,Jane     02             01-JAN-1996
Smith,Fred     03             01-JAN-1996
```

In this example, Carol enrolled in a plan on January 1, 1995 and last made a change to the plan on March 1, 1996. When we go to select her dependents, we get Jane and Fred, but a coverage begin date in January 1996, not 1995. In other words, Carol enrolled in 1995, and then added her dependents in 1996. Accordingly, there is an effective-dated row on Carol's health benefits table.

Finding the termination date for a dependent

Although we retrieved an enrollment date for Carol's dependents, they may no longer be enrolled. We were only looking for the minimum date and ignored subsequent records.

An additional SQL must be executed to check if a dependent has been terminated from a particular plan. Here we look again between the employee's enrollment date and termination date. This time we limit the query to only one dependent (Table 23-9).

▶ **Table 23-9** Retrieving dependent's termination date

| The query | ```
SELECT
MIN(HB.COVERAGE_BEGIN_DT)

FROM PS_HEALTH_BENEFIT HB
WHERE HB.EMPLID = 'CAROL'
   AND HB.PLAN_TYPE = '10'
   AND HB.EFFDT >
         (SELECT MAX(HD2.EFFDT)
            FROM PS_HEALTH_DEPENDNT HD2
           WHERE HD2.EMPLID            = HB.EMPLID
             AND HD2.EMPL_RCD#          = HB.EMPL_RCD#
             AND HD2.COBRA_EVENT_ID     = HB.COBRA_EVENT_ID
             AND HD2.PLAN_TYPE          = HB.PLAN_TYPE
             AND HD2.BENEFIT#           = HB.BENEFIT#
             AND HD2.DEPENDENT_BENEF    = '02'
             AND HD2.EFFDT             >= '01-JAN-1995'
             AND HD2.EFFDT             <= '01-MAR-1996')
``` |
| Returns the data set | ```
COVERAGE_BEGIN_DT
-----------------
01-DEC-1996
``` |

To work through how PeopleSoft came up with this date, first look at the contents of the tables in Tables 23-6 and 23-7. Notice how the employee waived coverage in the MDBC plan with an effective date of March 1, 1996. But the date returned in our query is December 1, 1996, because we asked for the coverage begin date, not the effective date, after the most recent MDBC plan row.

The effective date field is the only way to tie the employee and benefit records together, but coverage begin date represents the date coverage changed. This is also the termination date for the employee in this plan and for the enrolled dependents.

The query we used in Table 23-9 looks for the last date it can find for a dependent between the enrollment and waive dates of the employee. It then picks the next row, that is, the minimum effective date that is greater than this last date. In this case, PeopleSoft picked up the January 1, 1996 effective date. Then, when it looked for the minimum coverage begin date with a corresponding effective date greater than January 1996, it found the March 1 effective date and picked December 1 as the minimum coverage begin date.

It is a bizarre path to a termination date, especially since we are jumping between dependent records and employee records, effective dates and coverage begin dates. The two rules guiding us through this maze, though, are simple:

- Employee and dependent enrollment records always have the same effective dates.
- Although effective dates join the records, the coverage begin date identifies when coverage starts and stops.

Benefits can be confusing to keep track of with all of the options available to employees. Once we consider the rate the employee pays for the plan, the confusion escalates. While enrollment in a plan can involve several factors, such as full/part time, current status, or age, these elements often break down further into rates that are based on service, age, or salary.

PeopleSoft stores all of the rates for your organization's benefits and automatically applies the appropriate rate during event maintenance and payroll processing. This feature allows PeopleSoft to deduct the appropriate amount, keep track of arrears (the amount PeopleSoft is unable to deduct), and even perform cash billing if the employee does not receive a check. It also means that downstream systems can receive the final rate, rather than all of the factors used to calculate it.

RATE TABLES

PeopleSoft stores rates according to four criteria: employee's age, length of service with the company, annual salary amount, or a flat rate. Each type of rate is stored on a separate table, with an ID, an effective date, pay frequency (annual, monthly, biweekly, etc.), and rate unit (rate is per hundred dollars or per thousand dollars of coverage).

Age

The age rate table is split in two—the rate ID table PS_AGE_RATE_TBL, and the coverage table PS_AGE_COVG_TBL. Age rate IDs are set up on the rate table with an effective date, frequency, and rate unit. This ties to the rate ID and effective date on the coverage table.

Look at the age coverage panel at Go → Define Business Rules → Define Base Benefits → Setup → Age-Graded Rate Table. The coverage table allows you to indicate gender, the age range (low and high), and the rates for smokers and nonsmokers (total rate and employer portion). The panel calculates the employee portion using those rates.

Service

The service rates are stored in the same manner. There is a rate ID table, PS_SVC_RATE_TBL, and a coverage table with the rules, PS_SVC_COVG_TBL. A quick look at the Service Rate Table panel under Setup shows how rates are specified for a length of service. A number of months of service required for the rate, the total rate, and the employer portion are stored together. PeopleSoft looks at the employee's service date on the PS_EMPLOYMENT panel to determine the appropriate rate.

Salary

Determining rates according to salary is simple. PeopleSoft applies a percentage to the employee's salary to determine the rate. Hence, there is only one panel, PS_SALARY_RATE_TBL, which stores an ID, an effective date, and a percentage (PCT_OF_SALARY). If the percentage is 5%, PeopleSoft applies this to the salary of the employee to derive a rate for the plan.

Flat Rate

The flat rate table applies the same rate to every employee in the same benefit plan option. It does not use a scale based on age, service, etc. The total rate is a dollar amount, and the rate per unit can be set to 'None,' etc. In other words, if the total rate is $15, then the plan costs $15. An employer portion can also be specified.

The provider amount field defaults to the total amount, but is not used by the system. It is informational only and can be manually overridden in the panel to reflect an administrative cost.

Service Steps

Savings plans use a separate table to track service. A 401(k), plan, for example, often has an employer portion that is scaled according to service. The service step table, which you can see in Setup ➤ Service Step Table, allows you to specify the months of service required and the deduction classification (before or after tax) of the employer contribution. It also will provide a cap at a percentage of the employee's gross salary and a percentage of employer contribution.

Multiple deductions can be set up for a single length of service. Someone who works at the company for three years could have a 25% match from the company, up to 3% of her salary, provided after tax, and also a 75% match up to 10% of her salary before tax. A separate group of tables is needed to store this rate setup. The tables involved are PS_SVC_STEP_COVG, PS_SVC_STEP_PCT, and PS_SVC_STEP_TBL.

CALCULATION RULES

A benefit program contains lists of possible benefit plan options and associates these plans with the appropriate rate table. The results are stored on the PS_BEN_DEFN_COST table. In addition to a rate table ID (which could be an age, service, salary, or flat rate ID), there is a calculation rule ID.

Calculation rules supply additional criteria to PeopleSoft for calculating the employee's rate of coverage. The PS_CALC_RULES_TBL is extensive, with numerous options:

- Choose the date to use for determining premium calculation, coverage calculation, age as-of, and service as-of. The date could be the current pay end date or a particular date from this year or last year.

- Age as-of can be specified for the employee, dependent, or spouse. Different calculation rules are required to use more than one.

- Rounding rules specify how PeopleSoft should round dollar amounts, such as coverage.

- Deductions can be limited to a percentage of gross pay.

- Coverage minimums and maximums can be specified.

- A default can be set for using benefits base rate or annual rate for calculation of coverage.

The calculation rules are an important consideration if you are trying to determine the rate an employee pays or the coverage an employee has for a benefit plan. With calculation rules, the process is not as simple as going to the appropriate rate table and pulling the rate. Limits, rounding, and as-of dates could all be manipulated by calculation rules during benefits administration, which will affect the final rate.

LOOKING UP A RATE

To find the actual rate being charged for a benefit plan, it is necessary to look at the output of benefits administration. The calculation rules have already been applied and the appropriate rate selected.

> The output of benefits administration differs from the deduction information from the paycheck. A pay deduction could be the same as the final rate for a benefit plan, but many times a deduction is too large to be taken. In this case, PeopleSoft might take part of the deduction or none at all—this is the amount the employee pays, not the amount the employee is billed.
>
> A panel group under base benefits provides a summary of benefits deductions, not rates. This group is under Go ➤ Compensate Employees ➤ Administer Base Benefits ➤ Inquire ➤ Benefits Deduction Summary. The dollars shown here are results of the payroll calculation process, not the benefits administration process.

Finding the appropriate rate requires the connection of several benefits administration output tables, similar to the requirements we saw in Chapter 21, specifically in Table 21-5. In that query we used the PS_BAS_PARTIC tables to determine what an employee elected.

A more elaborate query can also provide cost information. The amount charged to an employee's paycheck (not necessarily taken) for a particular plan can only be found on PS_BAS_PARTIC_COST. A query linking all of the BAS tables is shown in Table 24-1.

▶ **Table 24-1** Benefit cost information for an employee

The query

```
SELECT
BP.PLAN_TYPE,
BO.BENEFIT_PLAN,
BO.CALCULATED_BASE,
BC.DEDUCT_AMT

FROM PS_BAS_PARTIC_PLAN BP,
     PS_BAS_PARTIC_OPTN BO,
     PS_BAS_PARTIC_COST BC
WHERE BP.EMPLID            = 'BOZO'
  AND BP.SCHED_ID          = 'EM'
  AND BP.COVERAGE_ELECT    = 'E'
  AND BO.SCHED_ID          = BP.SCHED_ID
  AND BO.EMPLID            = BP.EMPLID
```

▶ **Table 24-1** continued

```
        AND  BO.BENEFIT_RCD#        =  BP.BENEFIT_RCD#
        AND  BO.EVENT_ID            =  BP.EVENT_ID
        AND  BO.PLAN_TYPE           =  BP.PLAN_TYPE
        AND  BO.OPTION_CD           =  BP.OPTION_CD
        AND  BC.SCHED_ID            =  BP.SCHED_ID
        AND  BC.EMPLID              =  BP.EMPLID
        AND  BC.BENEFIT_RCD#        =  BP.BENEFIT_RCD#
        AND  BC.EVENT_ID            =  BP.EVENT_ID
        AND  BC.PLAN_TYPE           =  BP.PLAN_TYPE
        AND  BC.OPTION_ID           =  BO.OPTION_ID
        AND  BP.EVENT_DT            =
            (SELECT  MAX(BP1.EVENT_DT)
                FROM  PS_BAS_PARTIC_PLAN  BP1
               WHERE  BP1.SCHED_ID         =  BP.SCHED_ID
                 AND  BP1.EMPLID           =  BP.EMPLID
                 AND  BP1.BENEFIT_RCD#     =  BP.BENEFIT_RCD#
                 AND  BP1.PLAN_TYPE        =  BP.PLAN_TYPE)
```

	PLAN_TYPE	BENEFIT_PLAN	CALCULATED_BASE	DEDUCT_AMT
Returns the data set	---------	------------	---------------	----------
	01	0		60.00
	10	MDBC	0	309.00
	11	DDDD	0	50.00
	14	VILO	0	12.00
	20	LIF2X	142000	12.07
	40	FIDLTY	0	0

This query looks at the plan table, where it determines which plans the employee elected (coverage elect = 'E'). It links these plans with the option table, which in turn links to the cost table. The dollar amount (DEDUCT_AMT or ANNUAL_AMT) on the cost table is the most recent final calculated rate.

To see how these tables connect online, look at the Go ➤ Compensate Employees ➤ Administer Automated Benefits ➤ Inquire ➤ Employee Event Summary. Follow these steps:

1. **Participant panel**—View the general program information about the employee. PeopleSoft uses this information to link all of the PS_BAS_PARTIC tables.

2. **Plan type panel**—Choose a plan type, such as '10' for medical. The election should be yes, and you can find the option code for the benefit plan the employee chose.

3. **Option and cost panel**—All of the options are listed here, so scroll down to the option number you found on the plan type panel. Remember, it is an option code, not an option sequence that you are looking for. Now you can find a cost ID for this option code and see the annual and deduction amounts.

It seems like all of the information about options, elections, enrollments and rates is all centralized in this one place. Note, however, that this is only the output of automated benefits (i.e., benefits administration). It contains the appropriate dollars being charged and tells you which plans the employee elected. For play-by-play election, coverage, and covered dependents information, you still need to look at the corresponding base benefit tables such as PS_HEALTH_BENEFIT. The PS_BAS_PARTIC tables and inquiry panels provide a quick overview but do not include the detail and may exclude any manual changes to the employee's benefit plan status.

Part 5

Query and SQR Tools

25

PeopleSoft Query

Several vendors have partnered with PeopleSoft to provide reporting tools that enhance PeopleSoft. The list of these tools, part of the standard set of PeopleTools provided with each PeopleSoft suite, has grown over the years to accommodate many new companies and capabilities. In each case, PeopleSoft provides some level of support for the tool but is clearly looking to focus its interests on the online portion of the PeopleSoft experience. PeopleSoft, in fact, is a major provider of tools from other companies.

We will look exclusively at the basic delivered reporting tools that users are likely to come into contact with: PeopleSoft Query (a home-grown tool) and SQR (a programming language for database reporting). This chapter focuses exclusively on Query, and Chapter 26 examines SQR in detail.

New reporting tools are created all the time, and recently some extremely robust ad-hoc tools have appeared on the market. PeopleSoft Query is not necessarily the best tool or the simplest tool. But it is the one provided by PeopleSoft, and hence the easiest to set up, distribute to users, and tinker with. It is a great tool to learn on.

Probably the most common question users have about the different delivered reporting tools is "Which do I use, and when?" Table 25-1 provides a quick guide to choosing the appropriate reporting tool, and some basic limitations of each.

▶ **Table 25-1** Delivered reporting tools

Tool	Best if used for	Advantages	Limitations
PeopleSoft Query	Ad-hoc/simple reports and data extracts	• Easy to use • Creates complex SQL statements behind the scenes, including searches of trees • Uses PeopleSoft row-level security • Can output to Microsoft Excel, Crystal Reports	• Performance (see appendix B on fast security to improve) • Cannot update the database; cannot INSERT data • As a query becomes more complex (more tables, special joins), the Query 'front end' starts to make things more difficult than they have to be. Query can do almost anything SQL can by itself, but often it requires more effort to use the front end than to just type in a SQL statement. • Certain advanced SQL functions are not supported
SQR	Complex batch reports and data extracts, batch system needs that require programming logic (loops, IF/THEN logic)	• Uses a simple language that facilitates report creation • Can handle complex PeopleSoft data selection • Cross-platform support • Programs can be scheduled outside of the PeopleSoft Process Scheduler.	• Requires a certain level of programming experience • Must establish a development environment • Cannot produce data in mainframe packed format without help from a utility • No row-level security
COBOL	Nightly batch jobs that require a minimal amount of processing time	• Offers enhanced performance • Not a new language—training possibly not required	• Few delivered programs are in COBOL, whereas hundreds of SQR common modules are delivered.

▶ **Table 25-1** continued

Tool	Best if used for	Advantages	Limitations
		• Can handle complex PeopleSoft data selection	• Does not offer a simple language or ease of reporting
		• Programs can be scheduled outside of the PeopleSoft Process Scheduler.	• No row-level security

Each of these three tools has distinct advantages and disadvantages. The decision should always hinge on exactly what you are trying to accomplish and with what resources. In general, implementations follow PeopleSoft's lead. SQR is the major player, and COBOL is only used for highly complex logic-ridden programs. Query is used as an ad-hoc tool. You could just as easily use COBOL for your ad-hoc needs and schedule all of your Query constructions to run every night—both languages are flexible enough. The best advice when faced with these questions is to consider all of the tools for each program, rather than restricting the choices to just one tool.

QUERY BASICS

PeopleSoft's Query program was significantly overhauled in PeopleTools version 7.5, and now provides a convenient point-and-click environment. The features Query provides over a standard SQL tool are that it:

- allows user to look at a list of the fields in each table, instantly recognize keys, and simply click on these fields to generate SQL behind the scenes.
- creates effective-date sub-queries for the user.
- uses delivered row-level security.
- provides elaborate criteria options, including a function that searches through PeopleSoft trees (difficult to do with SQR or COBOL).
- can perform automatic linking of tables with Auto Join feature, which searches for common key fields between two tables.
- will dump output to a printer, file, Microsoft Excel, or Crystal Reports.

The best way to learn about the tool is to use it, so let's step through the process of creating a query that selects a list of all employees and their basic status.

Accessing and Setting Up Query

To access PeopleSoft Query, choose 'Query' in the Go ➤ PeopleTools menu. PeopleSoft launches a separate application. The window that appears shows a list of folders or tables on the left, a blank space on the right (with Fields, Criteria, SQL, and Results tabs), and buttons on the top (see Figure 25-1).

The first step is to choose the table you want to look at. PeopleSoft provides Access Groups, which organize tables into categories that have functional meaning. For example, if you wanted to get information on status, you could expand the HR Access Group, expand another group, and another, and another, hoping to find the right table. You could get a cup of coffee and come back ten minutes later and PeopleSoft will probably still be trying to expand these groups. Each time you expand a group, Query does an elaborate search through all of the PeopleSoft tables. In essence, unless you do not know what table you are look-

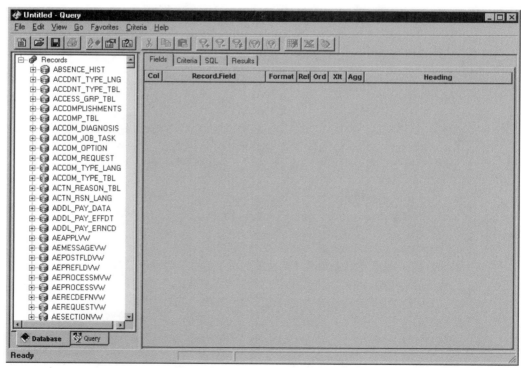

▶ **Figure 25-1**   PeopleSoft Query initial state (without access groups)

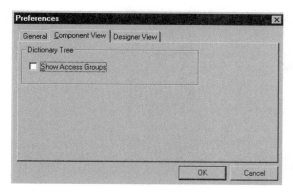

▶ **Figure 25-2** Turning off access groups

ing for, the access groups only provide frustration. It would be faster to look up the table in this book.

Instead, go straight to the View pull-down menu, and choose Preferences (see Figure 25-2).

On the middle tab, Component View, make sure Show Access Groups is unchecked. Then click OK, and now you will see a list of tables, alphabetized to simplify your search. Figure 25-1 shows the list of tables. Scroll down to JOB, double click on it, and you're ready to continue.

> Can't find your table? That is because your system administrator only grants Query access to certain tables. Your personal profile allows you to look at a subset of the available tables in PeopleSoft. Using the Security PeopleTool, an administrator can set up any PeopleSoft table to appear or not appear for you in Query.

Creating a Query

Before continuing, PeopleSoft Query opens a dialogue box to ask you about the PS_JOB table row you are looking for (Figure 25-3). It knows that PS_JOB has an effective date and an effective sequence number as keys. You have the option of choosing the criteria for each key (see Chapter 7 for more information on the PS_JOB table). In most cases, you will want to choose "Effective Date <=," "Current Date," and "Last" effective sequence. This will give you the most recent record as of today. By clicking first, last, or no effective date option, you can just retrieve the first row, last row, or all rows for a given employee.

Once you click OK, the PS_JOB table fields appear on the Query tab, and the Database tab moves to the background. We can always return to it to choose more tables. For now, let's use the Query tab to pick fields for our query. Each field is listed with its field name and description. Fields that are keys have a key

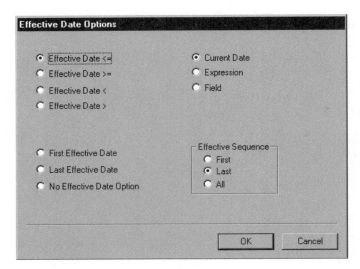

▶ **Figure 25-3** Effective-date
selection in PeopleSoft Query

symbol next to them. Fields that can be validated against control tables have a
"+" expansion button next to them, allowing you to go directly to the related
control table (Figure 25-4).

> The record hierarchy selection at the top of the field list in Figure 25-4 can be
> used to find related tables. PeopleSoft looks at the table you have selected and
> searches for the parent tables as defined in the Application Designer.

Double-click on each of the following fields: EMPLID, EMPL_RCD#,
EFFDT, EMPL_STATUS, ACTION, and ACTION_REASON. Each field
appears on the field tab. Our table is identified by "A," and each field appears
with "A." in front of it, just as in SQL. This alias is automatically assigned.

> To remove a field, right click on it and choose "Select" to remove the check-
> mark next to it (shown in Figure 25-4).

When you click on the lightning bolt button at the top of the screen,
PeopleSoft fetches the result set for the query you just created. In all likelihood,
it will take some time to return. If you are working with a large database, you
may even crash. So, before hitting that lightning bolt, let's specify a single
employee on the criteria tab.

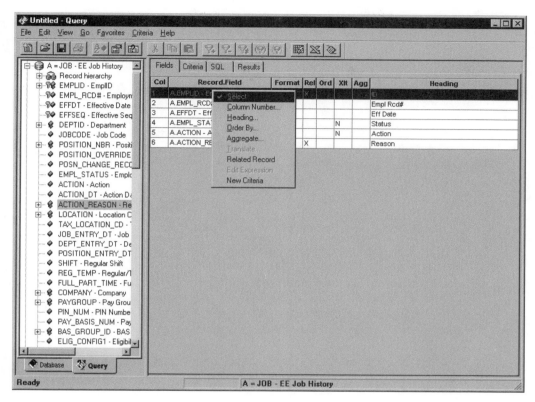

▶ **Figure 25-4**   Removing a field from a PeopleSoft Query

Adding Criteria

Click the criteria tab. The effective date is already here. Although PeopleSoft created it, the effective date statement is still a criterion for the query. Drag the EMPLID field from the left over to the criteria workspace. The field is added as a new criteria item, and you can click on the right side to enter an employee ID. Type in the ID as it is stored in the database; the system is case sensitive.

The criteria tab is extremely flexible. Just as in SQL, you can specify IN clauses or BETWEEN two values, and you can group criteria using AND and OR. To group criteria, use the grouping and ungrouping funnel icons to add or remove parentheses.

Now hit the lightning bolt, and you should get some results. Each column is adjustable by placing your mouse in the title bar in between each column. You can also double-click to expand the column to its largest field value.

When a query shows no signs of life (i.e., says "Fetching Rows" with no response for hours), you should abort the process and notify your system administrator. To do this, you can use the Windows task manger by pressing Control-Alt-Delete together, and canceling the Query application. You can then open Query again and try a query with more criteria. Additional criteria can speed up Query's performance. Also see Appendix B for more information on query performance improvements.

Linking an Additional Table Using Auto Join

The Query tool has an automatic joining feature, which looks at the keys of the tables you are joining and tries to make a match. For example, let's link a description of the action reason field to our query.

First, click on the Database tab at the lower left to return to the table list. The action/action reason description is on the PS_ACTN_REASON_TBL (listed without the PS in Query). Double-click on this table, and the effective date panel appears.

There is a new option on the effective date panel now—to use the effective date from the job table (see Figure 25-5).

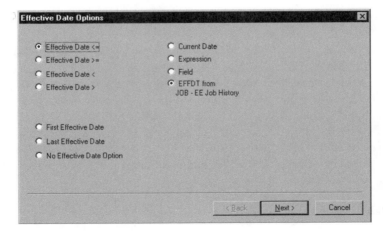

▶ **Figure 25-5** Linking tables by effective date

In other words, if the job table row has an effective date of 11/30/2001, PeopleSoft will find what the description of the corresponding action was as of 11/30/2001. If the description changed after then, the new description would be ignored. We discuss linking tables according to effective date in Chapter 2.

Choose this new option and click the Next button. A new panel shows what Auto Join thinks the join should be. It correctly finds that ACTION and ACTION_REASON are keys on the PS_ACTN_REASON_TBL, and notes that these fields exist on PS_JOB. Click Finish to continue.

Now the Query window lists the additional table as alias 'B.' We can double-click on fields to add them to our query. Double-click on B.DESCR and run the query with the lightning bolt. Figure 25-6 shows the final query.

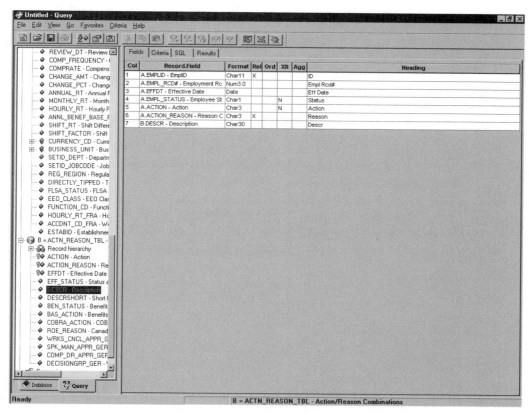

▶ **Figure 25-6**   Final query with fields from two tables

Outputting/Viewing the Query

Generating this query was relatively easy, and we have a row of output (or more, if the employee you chose has more than one employee record number). You have several options for extracting this information:

1. Use copy/paste.
2. Hit the Excel button to dump the result set to a new Excel spreadsheet.
3. Hit the Crystal Reports button to send the result set to a new Crystal Report. Crystal allows you to customize the look of the data and forms a permanent link to your saved PeopleSoft query.
4. Choose Print and print it out (or do a print preview).
5. Run the query somewhere else using the SQL created by PeopleSoft.

This last option utilizes the third tab in the Query window—SQL. If you choose this tab, you will see a complete SQL query, ready to execute in any SQL command environment. With minor modification, it could even be dropped into an SQR program. In a sense, the ability to copy this SQL out of a PeopleSoft query provides flexibility and another great reason to use PeopleSoft Query. When it comes to writing out a SQL statement, Query is the quickest draw. It's tough to type that quickly.

Let's take a closer look at the SQL Query creates to understand just what Query does behind the scenes. The SQL for the query we are using as an example appears below, formatted for legibility. You'll notice that the SQL seems a bit more complex than our request.

```
SELECT
A.EMPLID,
A.EMPL_RCD#,
A.EFFDT,
A.EMPL_STATUS,
A.ACTION,
A.ACTION_REASON
FROM PS_JOB A,
     PS_EMPLMT_SRCH_GBL A1
WHERE A.EMPLID = A1.EMPLID
  AND A.EMPL_RCD# = A1.EMPL_RCD#
  AND A1.OPRCLASS = 'ALLPANLS'
  AND ( A.EFFDT = (SELECT MAX(EFFDT) FROM PS_JOB
                    WHERE A.EMPLID = EMPLID
                      AND A.EMPL_RCD# = EMPL_RCD#
                      AND EFFDT   <= CURRENT DATE)
```

```
AND A.EFFSEQ = (SELECT MAX(EFFSEQ) FROM PS_JOB
                 WHERE A.EMPLID = EMPLID
                   AND A.EMPL_RCD# = EMPL_RCD#
                   AND A.EFFDT   = EFFDT)
AND A.EMPLID = 'BOZO' )
```

The effective date and effective sequence queries are familiar from our discussion of the PS_JOB table in Chapter 7. But the PS_EMPLMT_SRCH_GBL table is a new addition. This is one of several tables that provide security for PeopleSoft. Since one of Query's advantages is that it uses PeopleSoft row-level security, every query must tie to a security table. In this case, the ALLPANLS operator class is executing the query, and if ALLPANLS cannot access PS_JOB according to security, the result set will not be returned.

To take the query and use it in another program, you need to simply remove the security table view and all references to fields related to it. These items are in bold in the query above.

In our discussion of performance issues, the security tables are explored in greater detail. They are actually views of information from several PeopleSoft tables and account for the poor performance of PeopleSoft Query.

ADVANCED QUERY TOPICS

Query provides a frontend to the PeopleSoft database that is more flexible than the delivered panels. One can quickly and easily choose a table and fields, specify an effective date, and link a control table for a description.

There are many queries that in concept are this simple, but in practice require a greater knowledge of Query's functions and limitations. Let's look at some of the additional features (and challenges) that PeopleSoft Query provides.

Aggregating Totals

To aggregate the values in a field (i.e., count, sum, average, or find a minimum or maximum), right-click on the field in the Field tab and choose Aggregate. This will allow you to add the appropriate SQL function to the field. Then, using the Criteria tab, you can indicate criteria for the result of the aggregate.

For example, let's get a count of the number of employees on a leave of absence (EMPL_STATUS is L or P). We choose the PS_JOB table, select EMPLID as the output field, and aggregate EMPLID using the count function. Then we specify the employee statuses we want on the criteria tab, using the 'in list' qualifier, and adding values to the list for L and P. The result is simply a number of employees on leave.

Sometimes it is necessary to add criteria to the actual aggregation clause. For example, if we want to know the employee who has the greatest salary, we could use the maximum aggregate. But what if we want the maximum salary that is under $100,000? Then we need to add criteria to the aggregate, which in SQL occurs in a HAVING clause.

When we create an aggregate function for salary, PeopleSoft offers an additional tab, the Having Criteria tab. This tab works just like the Criteria tab, but only aggregated fields are allowed on it. Turn on the Having Criteria tab by selecting Having under the Criteria menu. To find the maximum salary under $100,000, we place ANNUAL_RT on the Having Criteria tab and specify 'not greater than' $100,000. The resulting SQL contains a HAVING clause at the end.

Finding Distinct

The DISTINCT command is common in many SQL statements. Amy wants to find out a count of how many employees are in the PS_JOB table. She could create an elaborate query, choosing only rows with an employee record number of 1, and the maximum effective date and effective sequence (see Chapter 7 for information on the PS_JOB table). Or she could perform the following SQL:

```
SELECT
COUNT(DISTINCT(EMPLID))
FROM PS_JOB
```

This is easier, but the process for creating such a query in PeopleSoft Query is not readily apparent. PeopleSoft hid the distinct command under the File ➤ Properties menu. Choose the DISTINCT option, and it will apply to the entire query.

Be careful with distinct, since it checks the combination of your selection for distinct occurrences. If you select EMPLID and EFFDT, Query will select all distinct *combinations* of these two fields and will not provide an accurate count of employees.

Custom Sub-Queries

On the Criteria tab you can specify a sub-query, just as in a WHERE clause in SQL. Simply choose a field, such as EFFDT, and then right click in the 'Expression 2' box (on the right side of the criteria item). Choose 'Subquery,' and PeopleSoft takes you to a new, blank query. Create the query, then click 'Return to Parent,' which appears in the Query tab window (where the tables are) at the top. For an example, see the Job Table Status section under Issues, below.

Joining Tables with Unions

Sometimes it is necessary to create a join using a union. A union joins two queries, not two tables. Both of the queries return information in the same format, but both sets of data will be returned as one. For a union, you need two queries that:

- Select the same number of fields
- Select the same order of fields
- Select the same type of fields

For example, you could join a selection of EMPLID and EFFDT with a selection of EMPLID and PAY_END_DT. Whenever the employee ID and date are the same in both selections, one row is returned. Whenever they are different, each unique row is returned.

To perform a union in PeopleSoft Query, choose the Edit ➤ New Union menu item. Query will let you create an entirely new query to tie back to your original query.

Why would you use a union? It is a complex question. In general, a union is useful in a situation where you need to do two separate queries of the same table, but want one set of output. In SQR, you could do one query and then the other.

A union statement is rare, and can often be avoided, if only by doing two queries. An example below of how to retrieve manager information for employees is a good candidate for a union (see Joining on a Field That Could Be Blank).

Using PeopleSoft Trees

The ability to navigate PeopleSoft trees is one of the principal advantages of PeopleSoft Query. On the Criteria tab there are two 'operators' called 'in tree' and 'not in tree.' With these operators you can choose a tree and then choose a node in the tree. If the value is underneath that node, it will be included. Compared to the techniques described in Chapter 11 for navigating the department tree in SQR programs, the 'in tree' function is incredibly simple (although complex behind the scenes). The in tree command is shown in Figure 25-7.

Expressions

PeopleSoft lets you specify nearly every SQL command through expressions. An expression is a field where you can type in whatever you like. Just as in a SQL select statement, you could say SELECT 'HI.' To do this in Query, you need to create an expression and then place the expression on the Fields tab.

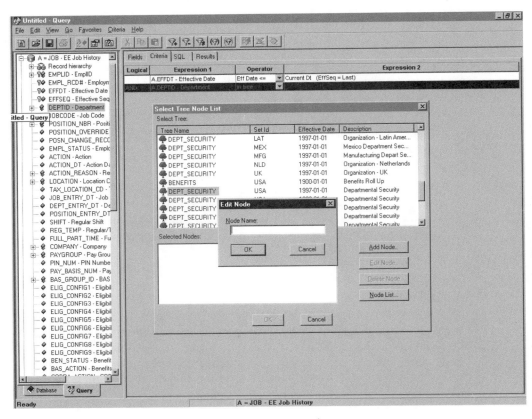

Figure 25-7   Adding a department node for an in-tree search

A more common use is to perform more complex SQL commands. For example, you could list all employees, their salary, and an expression that multiplies their salary by two. In SQL, the expression for the calculated column would be (ANNUAL_RT * 2). In Query, follow these steps:

1. First create a query with the ANNUAL_RT field in it.
2. Go to 'Expressions,' which is in the Query tab on the left, under all of the tables you have chosen.
3. Right-click on 'Expressions' and choose 'New Expression.'
4. Choose the appropriate field type—in this case, a Number.
5. Specify the length you would like. We'll specify 10 integers.
6. Click 'Add Field' to add the field to the expression. You can also

just type it, if you know the alias. In this case, if PS_JOB is the first table you selected, the field would be A.ANNUAL_RT.

7. Type * 2, so the text in the box reads:

```
A.ANNUAL_RT * 2
```

8. Click OK.

9. Don't forget to add the expression to the query! Drag it to the Fields tab in order to add it to the query.

> You can also use an expression as criteria. In the example above, we could drag the expression for double-salary as criteria, specifying that we only want to see employees whose salary when multiplied by two is greater than $100,000.

Prompts/ Parameters

If you are creating a query to be used over and over again, you can tell PeopleSoft to ask for a value, like an as-of date. A prompt can be created like an expression, by right clicking on the Prompts item at the bottom of the table list on the left of the Query window. PeopleSoft offers a list of existing fields you can choose from, and the edits and validations for these fields will automatically apply.

To create an as-of date, we create a new prompt and look up ASOFDATE in the Field pull-down menu. Everything is automatically filled in.

> A note about using parameters. If you will be using a query numerous times, parameters make a lot of sense. Although you could easily create a query that uses the system date every time it runs, consider if you will ever need the ability to run the query for a specific point in time. Perhaps a report needs to be re-executed, and cannot contain new information since a certain date. Even if this is not a requirement, consider instances when you might want to specify a particular date, such as when testing a query. It takes little effort to set up a parameter and can save effort down the line.

Issues (status records, others)

Numerous limitations arise when you try to create a front end for a computer language. The problems we list here are rather permanent, a result of these limitations. Although each PeopleTools release improves Query, it is unlikely these issues will be resolved.

Job Table Status

One of the first things a user is going to do when PeopleSoft is installed is sit down and try to do a query of everyone who is active in a department. It sounds easy, but as we saw in Chapter 7, job table history is difficult to navigate. It is even more difficult in Query, since it requires the customization of sub-queries (i.e., you cannot use Query's automatic effective dating feature).

If we look at an example Query step by step, the issue and its resolution become clearer. First, let's look at an employee's set of PS_JOB data:

```
EMPLID   EFFDT        EMPL_STATUS   ACTION   ACTION_REASON
------   -----------  -----------   ------   -------------
BOZO     10/02/2001   L             PAY      MER
BOZO     09/02/2001   L             LTO      LTD
```

The employee is on long-term disability (LTO/LTD), but has an employee status of 'L.' Since a long-term disability employee is typically not considered active in department headcount reports, the user needs to look at action and action reason. We want employee statuses of 'A,' 'P,' and 'L,' excluding action LTO.

If we create a standard query, selecting these fields off of the PS_JOB table and specifying the most recent effective date and effective sequence, the PAY row will be returned. This does not tell us about the LTD status of the employee. We need to create a query that only retrieves status-related actions. To do this, we must specify criteria within each sub-query. Let's try it:

1. Create a new query with the PS_JOB table and *no effective date option.*
2. Select EMPLID, EFFDT, EMPL_STATUS, ACTION, ACTION_REASON.
3. Add criteria to the query for the EFFDT field. Use the equal-to operand and right-click on the empty Expression 2 box, selecting 'Subquery.'
   a) Select PS_JOB with no effective date option.
   b) Add criteria to link the sub-query back. Set B.EMPLID equal to A.EMPLID (choose A.EMPLID by right-clicking on the empty Expression 2 box and selecting "field.")
   c) Add criteria for the EMPL_RCD# field in the same way (there could be employees with a record number greater than zero).
   d) Now add the status-related criteria. Set ACTION 'not in list' to the non-status-related actions in your database. As delivered, there are numerous actions to exclude. Here let's just exclude 'DTA,' 'PAY,' and 'FSC' for simplicity.

e) Add criteria for the EFFDT field, setting it not greater than an expression. The expression for current date, depending on your database system, is usually SYSDATE. *Do not use the Effdt <= operand, or any effective date operand. This would create another sub-query behind-the-scenes.*

f) Then create an expression for the field we need to select— max(B.EFFDT). Steps for creating an expression are provided in the Expressions section above. Add this expression to the field list.

g) Click 'Return to Parent' at the top of the table list on the left.

4. Add criteria to the query for the EFFSEQ field. Use the Operand subquery again, following steps a) through g) above for the EFFSEQ field. Instead of setting EFFDT to the system date, set C.EFFDT equal to A.EFFDT, since A.EFFDT was already obtained in the first sub-query. And be sure to specify the max(C.EFFSEQ) expression as a number, not a date.

5. Add criteria for EMPL_STATUS that specifies a list of values, and add values 'A,' 'P,' and 'L.' Add criteria for ACTION that sets it not equal to 'LTO.'

Our resulting SQL is shown below:

```
SELECT
A.EMPLID,
A.EFFDT,
A.EMPL_STATUS,
A.ACTION,
A.ACTION_REASON

FROM PS_JOB A,
     PS_EMPLMT_SRCH_GBL A1
WHERE A.EMPLID = A1.EMPLID
  AND A.EMPL_RCD# = A1.EMPL_RCD#
  AND A1.OPRCLASS = 'ALLPANLS'
  AND ( A.EFFDT = (SELECT max( B.EFFDT)
                   FROM PS_JOB B, PS_EMPLMT_SRCH_GBL B1
                 WHERE B.EMPLID = B1.EMPLID
                   AND B.EMPL_RCD# = B1.EMPL_RCD#
                   AND B1.OPRCLASS = 'ALLPANLS'
                   AND ( B.EMPLID = A.EMPLID
                   AND B.EMPL_RCD# = A.EMPL_RCD#
                   AND B.EFFDT <= sysdate
                   AND B.ACTION NOT IN ('DTA','FSC','PAY') ))
  AND A.EFFSEQ = (SELECT max( C.EFFSEQ)
                   FROM PS_JOB C, PS_EMPLMT_SRCH_GBL C1
```

```
                    WHERE C.EMPLID = C1.EMPLID
                       AND C.EMPL_RCD# = C1.EMPL_RCD#
                       AND C1.OPRCLASS = 'ALLPANLS'
                       AND ( C.EMPLID = A.EMPLID
                       AND C.EMPL_RCD# = A.EMPL_RCD#
                       AND C.EFFDT = A.EFFDT
                       AND C.ACTION NOT IN ('DTA','FSC','PAY') ))
          AND A.EMPL_STATUS IN ('A','L','P')
          AND A.ACTION <> 'LTO'
          AND A.EMPLID = 'BOZO' )
```

In summary, this is a simple request and a complex query. We knew this from Chapter 7. When you need to create the SQL with PeopleSoft Query, however, the task turns into a mouse-clicking exercise. It requires end-users to ignore wizards such as the effective-date sub-query creator, which are supposed to help make things easier.

To avoid this long procedure, there are several options that are also described in Chapter 7, such as the modification of the PS_EMPLOYEES table. These modifications render complex status queries obsolete. One may, however, need to perform many of the above steps for other queries, such as queries of benefit election rows.

Job Status and Other Criteria

There is yet another layer, involving the addition of department criteria. This criteria item cannot be simply added to the above example, in neither the main query nor the sub-queries. It must come from another table, where the most recent row *regardless* of action is selected. That is because an example employee could have switched departments:

EMPLID	EFFDT	EMPL_STATUS	ACTION	ACTION_REASON	DEPTID
FRED	07/22/2001	A	DTA	ROG	00012
FRED	01/01/2000	A	HIR	REF	00R32

When we get a list of employees in department 12, Fred should be included. But in order to determine Fred's status, we must look at the action field, which is on a row with a department ID of R32. We have to look at two rows at the same time.

We could link to the PS_JOB table again, but then we would have to go through all of the steps above—again! Making a change to a query that is double the size of the example above would be confusing, and slow.

Instead, if you are using the PS_EMPLOYEES table (described in Chapter 4), you can retrieve the most recent row easily. The employees table always has the most recent row (as long as you have been running the PER099 SQR every night). So, to limit the above example to a department, follow these steps:

1. Take the query from the example above.

2. Add the PS_EMPLOYEES table to it (make sure you are at the parent level).

3. Do not include effective date logic. Query is not smart enough to know that the effective date field is usually used for information only—PER099 will only populate the table with one row per employee ID and employee record number. The logic is not necessary and would slow down the query.

4. Agree to the suggested Auto Join links: EMPLID and EMPL_RCD#.

5. Add criteria specifying D.DEPTID = the department node (in the example, department '00012'). You can also add D.DEPTID to the field list.

The result is a list of employees in a department. The resulting SQL looks like this:

```
SELECT
A.EMPLID,
A.EFFDT,
A.EMPL_STATUS,
A.ACTION,
A.ACTION_REASON,
D.DEPTID

FROM PS_JOB A,
     PS_EMPLMT_SRCH_GBL A1,
     PS_EMPLOYEES D
WHERE A.EMPLID = A1.EMPLID
  AND A.EMPL_RCD# = A1.EMPL_RCD#
  AND A1.OPRCLASS = 'ALLPANLS'
  AND ( A.EFFDT =
     (SELECT max( B.EFFDT)
        FROM PS_JOB B,
             PS_EMPLMT_SRCH_GBL B1
       WHERE B.EMPLID = B1.EMPLID
         AND B.EMPL_RCD# = B1.EMPL_RCD#
         AND B1.OPRCLASS = 'ALLPANLS'
         AND ( B.EMPLID = A.EMPLID
             AND B.EMPL_RCD# = A.EMPL_RCD#
             AND B.EFFDT <= sysdate
             AND B.ACTION NOT IN ('DTA','FSC','PAY')))
  AND A.EFFSEQ =
     (SELECT max( C.EFFSEQ)
        FROM PS_JOB C,
```

```
                    PS_EMPLMT_SRCH_GBL C1
          WHERE  C.EMPLID = C1.EMPLID
            AND  C.EMPL_RCD# = C1.EMPL_RCD#
            AND  C1.OPRCLASS = 'ALLPANLS'
            AND  ( C.EMPLID = A.EMPLID
                   AND  C.EMPL_RCD# = A.EMPL_RCD#
                   AND  C.EFFDT = A.EFFDT
                   AND  C.ACTION NOT IN ('DTA','FSC','PAY')))
    AND A.EMPL_STATUS IN ('A','L','P')
    AND A.ACTION <> 'LTO'
    AND A.EMPLID = D.EMPLID
    AND A.EMPL_RCD# = D.EMPL_RCD#
    AND D.DEPTID = '00012')
```

System Date

In some databases, the system date (current date in Query) contains the time as well as the date. If you are having issues with using the current date (i.e., history rows not appearing or future rows appearing mysteriously), consider that PeopleSoft stores every date with a time of 12:00 a.m.

For example, say today is March 28, 2000 (and it is 4:00 p.m.), and we query the PS_JOB table for all rows equal to today's date. We know there is a March 28 row out there, but it isn't returned. This could be because the database is comparing the 4:00 p.m. time to a 12:00 a.m. time that PeopleSoft stored with the record.

This timestamp is built into the database definition of a date field, but it can be removed, usually with a truncation statement. Refer to your SQL reference manual for your particular database to determine if a timestamp is part of a date, and if there is a truncation statement you can use to remove it. Then you can create an expression that truncates the system date and use the expression in your query instead of the full date and timestamp.

Other Database Commands for Expressions

Depending on the database you are using, there are hundreds of commands that can be used in an SQL statement. Many of these commands are applicable to Query and can be used in expressions.

For example, if you want to translate a PeopleSoft code to a new value, you can create an if/then statement using the DECODE function (again, only in certain databases). Consider the following decode statement:

```
DECODE(A.PAYCHECK_CASHED,'Y','Cashed','N,' 'Outstanding')
```

This statement will print 'Cashed' or 'Outstanding' on the query output, instead of 'Y' or 'N.' It is, in essence, an if/then statement.

Using the Same Table Twice for Different Employees

A common issue arises when users try to get a list of employee names and the name of each employee's department manager. The query needs to get the employee's department, then look up the manager ID on the department table, and tie it back to the personal data table again. PeopleSoft Query will only return a list of the managers—i.e., only employees who manage themselves. Often this means nothing is returned.

The error is caused by the row-level security PeopleSoft places in the SQL. Since Query sees PS_PERSONAL_DATA twice in the query, it assumes it can use the same search table for both. Unfortunately, this forces the SQL to only select employees who match both hits to the PS_PERSONAL_DATA table: the employees who are also managers.

A simpler way to explore this issue is to link the PS_EMPLOYEES table to itself, since all of the fields are in one place (we have removed the other keys, NID_COUNTRY and NATIONAL_ID_TYPE for simplicity, but they should be used for accuracy). The issue is bolded in the SQL below:

```
SELECT
A.EMPLID,
A.MANAGER_ID

FROM PS_EMPLOYEES A,
     PS_EMPLMT_SRCH_GBL A1,
     PS_EMPLOYEES B
WHERE A.EMPLID = A1.EMPLID
  AND A1.OPRCLASS = 'ALLPANLS'
  AND B.EMPLID = A1.EMPLID
  AND (A.MANAGER_ID = B.EMPLID)
```

If we remove the security search record and run the SQL below, we get a list of all employees and their manager ID.

```
SELECT
A.EMPLID,
A.MANAGER_ID

FROM PS_EMPLOYEES A,
     PS_EMPLOYEES B
WHERE (A.MANAGER_ID = B.EMPLID)
```

The only ways to solve this problem is to link PS_EMPLOYEES to a table that uses a different security search table, or shut off row-level security, or use a different query tool. For example, we could link PS_EMPLOYEES to PS_PER-SONAL_DATA. The personal data table uses PS_PERS_SRCH_QRY for security, while the PS_EMPLOYEES table uses PS_EMPLMT_SRCH_GBL. A new query would have the following SQL:

```
SELECT
A.EMPLID,
A.NAME,
B.EMPLID,
B.NAME

FROM PS_EMPLOYEES A,
     PS_PERSONAL_DATA B,
     PS_PERS_SRCH_QRY B1
  WHERE B.EMPLID = B1.EMPLID
    AND B1.OPRCLASS = 'ALLPANLS'
    AND B.EMPLID = A.MANAGER_ID
```

This query will retrieve the correct data because different tables are used.

> When performing a manager ID query, also pay attention to whether the MANAGER_ID field is populated. Often no manager ID is specified, causing employees to drop out of the result set. If no manager ID is specified, the query cannot find a matching row on the second table and drops the employee entirely.

Joining on a Field That Could Be Blank

The manager ID example used above also relates to issue of when a field is sometimes blank. Manger ID is not always filled in for every department (it is not required). When we linked on it in the SQL above, only the employees who have managers specified are listed. What if you want to list all employees, manager or no manager?

We need an outer join—a join that takes the full set from the first table, and matches what it can with the second table. If no value is in the second table, the value is left blank but the value from the first table still appears.

There are two solutions to this issue. If the query is simple, you may be able to use the (+) command to do an outer join. This command depends on the database you are using (this will not work, for example, in a DB2/mainframe environment). The command does not work on sub-queries, so if you need to outer join to a table that requires an effective-date sub-query, you are out of luck. Refer to your database SQL documentation for more information on the use of the (+) command for outer joins.

Simply create an expression and use it as criteria, with the (+) command after the field name. The SQL above would look like this:

```
SELECT
A.EMPLID,
A.MANAGER_ID

FROM PS_EMPLOYEES A,
     PS_EMPLOYEES B
WHERE (A.MANAGER_ID = B.EMPLID (+))
```

The B.EMPLID (+) is an expression. The (+) command indicates that the link should be an outer join.

If this solution does not work for your particular query or database in PeopleSoft Query, you can also create a union between two queries. This involves one query that selects all matches and another that selects all non-matches.

The first query looks like the general query we are running, pulling back only those employees with a manager ID. The second query pulls back everyone who has a MANAGER_ID field value of ' ' (blank). Creating a union between these two data sets brings the entire set back. See the Unions section above for information about how to create a union in PeopleSoft Query.

26

Using SQR with PeopleSoft

PeopleSoft uses Structured Query Reporting (SQR) for most of the delivered code. SQR is also the prevalent tool for customizing PeopleSoft. SQR is a simple language that can be used to perform SQL commands. PeopleSoft provides it to facilitate the creation of 'batch' programs, which perform many transactions at a given time, usually overnight (while data entry is prohibited). A single SQR can be complex enough to turn on and off a deduction for an employee, or simple enough to print a report of employee names and addresses. The capabilities of SQR are limited only by the bounds of the language.

This chapter goes over SQR topics that will help you design a batch environment and decide how to create custom programs of any kind for an implementation. We are using SQR version 4.0.

OTHER REFERENCES

The meaning of SQR commands, and especially the detail of these commands, is not provided in this chapter. SQRIBE, the makers of SQR, provides a language reference that should be sufficient. This chapter goes beyond the command reference to talk about how you will actually use SQR in the PeopleSoft environment.

There are several places you can look for information regarding custom SQR programming:

SQRIBE manuals/command reference. The SQRIBE command reference details every possible command in SQR and provides examples. Although the organization of the manual is poor, all of the necessary facts about SQR are included. This manual is essential for all SQR programmers. Hint: many powerful sub-commands can be found under the 'LET' and 'PRINT' commands.

SQR electronic help file. This is the electronic version of the SQRIBE command reference and comes installed with SQR. It is named 'sqr.hlp.' Often this electronic version is easier to search through, and more convenient than the paper version.

SQL manuals at your implementation. The manual for the platform you are using can provide assistance with complex SQL statements that are embedded in your SQR. Although SQR can be used on many platforms, not all platforms are alike. It is a good idea to have a robust manual detailing the SQL commands for your platform.

PeopleSoft training manuals. PeopleSoft provides a training manual in SQR that provides an example-oriented introduction to the language. There are also thorough descriptions of some of the more common PeopleSoft common modules.

PeopleSoft PeopleBooks. PeopleBooks is primarily a reference dedicated to the online functions of PeopleSoft. This is a great place to do research before beginning a custom SQR. In PeopleBooks you can perform a search on key terms that might identify a delivered program or function that would eliminate the need for a custom SQR program. Often delivered programs can be slightly modified to fulfill a particular requirement.

PeopleSoft online help. PeopleSoft's online forum for technical assistance can provide guidance on difficult SQR issues. There are also several small independent web sites dedicated to discussions of SQR issues. These are good places to look for tips and tricks.

Technical support. Technical support is available from both PeopleSoft and SQRIBE. It is important to determine where an issue resides before choosing which company to contact. PeopleSoft can successfully answer most SQR questions, but SQRIBE is the authority, especially for diagnosing the limitations of the SQR product.

This chapter provides what these references neglect—the interaction between SQR and PeopleSoft. We will look at how the SQR language is configured to work with PeopleSoft and how you can utilize SQR features to get the most from the PeopleSoft database.

WHY SQR?

PeopleSoft is delivered with two robust languages, SQR and COBOL. There is no set rule for using one or the other. Yet each has its own advantages and disadvantages.

Most of the processing-intensive transactions in PeopleSoft occur in COBOL programs. Payroll calculation and benefits administration are written in COBOL. In some technical environments, COBOL may access and process data faster, and COBOL compiles SQL using a limitless and more efficient method than SQR. If the number of SQL statements in a program is high, COBOL may be a faster alternative.

On the other hand, most of the programs in PeopleSoft are written in SQR. PeopleSoft provides a set of common modules for SQRs that can be used for custom programs, too. For users new to computing and programming languages, SQR is easier to understand. Also, SQR facilitates the production of reports since it provides powerful layout tools that would require extra programming in a COBOL program.

In general, SQR provides the following features over common Structured Query Language (SQL). Many of these features can be achieved in COBOL:

- Robust programming commands such as if/then, iterative logic, mathematical and string functions.
- Ability to read and write flat files (rows of data).
- Easy report creation with absolute and relative coordinates for fields, as well as headers and footers.
- Ability to nest SQL statements.
- Ability to group and perform processing when values change in a set (ON-BREAK command).
- Windows, Unix, and MVS compatibility, allowing development in any environment.
- Parameters that can replace SQL, permitting dynamic changes to the function of a single program.
- Modularity allowing common modules to be shared among different programs.

USING SQR WITH PEOPLESOFT

SQR is designed for use with any database anywhere. There is no single component of SQR that is designed specifically for PeopleSoft. PeopleSoft, on the other hand, incorporates SQR often into functional procedures and into PeopleTools. SQR is an integral part of the PeopleSoft package.

Yet SQR is a database tool, not a PeopleSoft tool. It can retrieve data from the database, but it cannot communicate with the online application. Unlike PeopleSoft Query, there is no built-in row-level security in SQR. And when you insert a row of data into a table using SQR, the PeopleCode behind that table is not accessed. The edits, defaults, and validations that are defined in PeopleSoft are not accessible to SQR.

A custom SQR that selects or inserts data into the database should emulate the online application as closely as possible. This means that data must be validated, necessary PeopleCode replicated, and thorough system testing performed. Since SQR and PeopleSoft cannot communicate, sometimes processing must be replicated.

Considering Validations

Whether designing just one SQR or a whole SQR environment, you should consider the effects of different online transactions. Should your program validate fields against a control table as PeopleSoft does, or does PeopleSoft automatically validate the data when it is entered? Even so, is there the possibility that correction mode was used and a value was not validated? Perhaps someone inserted bad data into the database via an SQR (the PeopleSoft database itself has no validation). The level of risk you wish to take should be determined early on.

Since PeopleSoft can be accessed in so many ways, most SQR programs should at least validate all incoming data to the system. Many implementations also validate as much outgoing data as possible. In other words, before creating a file with an employee department ID of '0123,' a SQR should select '0123' from the department table to ensure that the department is valid.

TYPES OF SQRS

There are three basic kinds of SQR programs found in PeopleSoft:

- Batch programs, which do not read or create any files, but manipulate the database.
- Interfaces, which transfer data from a file to the database, or vice versa.

- Reports, which select data from the database, organize it, and print it out.

Batch programs are few and far between, since most delivered batch programs are written in COBOL. The PER099.SQR is a batch program since it selects information from PS_JOB, PS_EMPLOYMENT, and PS_PERSONAL_DATA and places this data in the PS_EMPLOYEES table. No files are involved—the process is self-contained.

PeopleSoft provides numerous interfaces, mostly to the federal government for tax purposes. The interfaces for files that must be sent for federal, state, and local tax data, for the file that must be sent to the bank for direct deposit, and for a file to the general ledger (GL) system, are provided with PeopleSoft. Other interfaces must be custom-built for areas that require the results of PeopleSoft's human resources, payroll, and benefits processes in electronic form.

> PeopleSoft provides an elaborate interface that is much more than an SQR. This program uses multiple custom tables to essentially perform the function of an SQR or a COBOL program. This interface provides payroll data to external systems for processing, when PeopleSoft payroll is not to be implemented. You can find information about this interface under the Payroll Interfaces heading in PeopleSoft's documentation.

There are hundreds of reports delivered with PeopleSoft, which can be easily customized and tailored to your needs. For a comprehensive guide to reports, refer to the PeopleSoft documentation. In many cases a sample of the report is provided; in others it may be difficult to get an idea of what the report looks like or does. Hopefully this chapter will give you a greater understanding for how SQR programs work, enabling you to decipher the function of such 'mystery' SQR reports.

> Several delivered SQR programs are not finished on purpose. The paycheck print program, for instance, must be customized to include signature information. The audit report must be tailored to your implementation's audit controls. Look through the code for comments about customization when confronted with a malfunctioning delivered SQR.

Custom Inbound Interfaces

The inbound interfaces required by many implementations are complex. Often vendors send in deduction and earnings information, such as the election for a 401(k) plan or a special bonus payment for the employee. This data must be entered into the system through the database in bulk due to the volume of the transactions occurring. External systems often perform several functions automatically, such as a change of addresses, direct deposit information, and tracking applicants for hire.

There are some guidelines to keep in mind when building an inbound interface. First, consider how you will validate the integrity of the data. Will you verify each employee ID against the existing database and check each translate value sent against the translate table? More importantly, what does PeopleSoft typically do when the same information is entered online? When you enter an address in PeopleSoft, it places it in several places, updating certain other fields. This occurs in the delivered PeopleCode. Every inbound interface should emulate any essential PeopleCode for every data field and should update every necessary table.

Also consider the timing of your program's run. Earnings information (pay earnings lines) must be entered after paysheets but before payroll calculation. How will you store earnings information if it comes in early, and how will you correct any errors when it comes in late? It is important to build a program for these kinds of inbound transactions that can be manipulated with parameters—and sometimes use temporary custom database tables.

An interface for inbound earnings is delivered with PeopleSoft (PAYUPDT.SQR), but it does not provide several important features. It is an excellent tool, however, for learning about the appropriate tables and values for an earnings interface. For more information on inbound payroll interfaces, see Feeding PeopleSoft in Chapter 16.

Sending Changes Only

A common request made by vendors and other interface recipients is for a 'changes only' file. Many database systems have a date and timestamp automatically included on each row of data. To detect whether something has changed, you can simply query this field for all rows after a specific date.

Unfortunately, this type of field is not provided in PeopleSoft. The date when data is actually entered is rarely stored. Even when the 'entry date' is stored, it can easily become inaccurate.

For example, often it is suggested that many interfaces could send changes to employee information by looking at the ACTION_DT field on the PS_JOB table. This field represents the date the row was entered or changed. A file could easily be created containing only rows with an action date after a specific date.

But once correction mode comes into the picture, the action date loses its meaning. Correction mode allows the user to change the value of a field without updating ACTION_DT. Even when correction mode is banned, often it is a necessary evil for fixing certain mistyped transactions. Once it is used, an interface based on the action date will never work properly. Although a changes-only file is smaller than its counterpart, the full file, the risks of not detecting a change can be significant.

An alternative solution is to use utilities outside of PeopleSoft, such as a custom SQR, to compare an old and a new full file to generate a changes- only file. This method is much safer and is simple to program. In a separate SQR, you can simply compare the value of one entire row to another and then write the rows that differ to a new file.

Another option is to create a version of the PS_EMPLOYEES table that is a day behind the current PS_EMPLOYEES table data. This prior employee data can be compared on a daily basis or at any frequency as long as the employees table update occurs at the same frequency. All changes and corrections can be detected with this method. The restriction is on the frequency you can detect these changes and on the recreation of comparisons at a historical point in time.

Print Versus Write

One of the distinctions between an interface and a report is how they output data. In SQR, you can output data to a file by using a WRITE command. SQR also has a powerful PRINT command, which is used for reports.

Yet in PeopleSoft, a report is actually a file. When SQR opens a new report, it opens a file with a *.lis suffix (or .l01, .l02, etc. for more than one report). The report is written to this text file, which can be opened with any text editor.

Special characters in SQR for font selection and logos obviously won't look right in the text version of a report. But you'll find that not a single PeopleSoft report uses these special characters. All reports are designed to print on nearly any printer, whether mainframe or laser. This means that except for a string of control characters at the beginning of a SQR report output file, the file looks exactly like the finished report.

For example, a delivered deductions-taken report output looks like this:

```
E(0N&l10&l8D&l5E&l66F(s16.66H&k2G                        PeopleSoft
Report ID: PAY001                  DEDUCTIONS REGISTER          Page No. 1
Company  CCB Continental Commerce&Business                      Run Date 10/05/1998
Pay Period End 08/31/1994          On/Off Cycle CONFIRMED       Run Time 19:26:12
Pay Group MO0 Monthly Paygroup
```

Remove the control characters at the front, and the report looks perfect:

```
                                   PeopleSoft
Report ID: PAY001                  DEDUCTIONS REGISTER          Page No. 1
Company  CCB Continental Commerce&Business                      Run Date 10/05/1998
Pay Period End 08/31/1994          On/Off Cycle CONFIRMED       Run Time 19:26:12
Pay Group MO0 Monthly Paygroup
```

Why is this important? Because in SQR, a printed report *is identical to an interface file*. They are created differently and often look different, but they are essentially the same things.

Often this becomes an issue when a mainframe printer is used to print reports, notably form-based reports. For example, the paycheck print program prints paychecks with the information in specific locations. The name is at the top, the check amount at the bottom, etc. In order to print this on a high-volume mainframe printer, a file is necessary. Rather than modify the delivered program to change every print statement to a write statement, spend your time writing a program that strips out the control characters at the top of the delivered report format. Unless the structure of the file must change significantly, it never pays to convert print statements to write statements. Once the leading control characters are removed, a file produced by PRINT and a file produced by WRITE are the same.

BASIC SQR NESTED QUERY

Like COBOL and other languages, a SQR program talks to the database using embedded SQL. An SQL statement is placed within the SQR program, and the SQR engine sends that SQL to the database. SQR also handles the acceptance of a return data set—and this is where SQR provides additional functionality. SQR allows you to nest code, and even other SQL statements, within an SQL statement.

First, let's look at how SQR processes a SELECT statement in a program:

1. SQR encounters a BEGIN-SELECT statement during the initial compile of the SQR program.

2. SQR evaluates the SELECT statement for known syntax issues, erroring out if necessary.

3. The SELECT statement is sent to the database. The database tries to compile it, searching for syntax errors. If an error is found, SQR receives an error, and ceases processing.

4. The compiled SQR is executed.

5. When the select statement is reached, the compiled SELECT statement is executed, and the entire set of data is returned to the SQR. If you selected 9 million rows, 9 million rows go to the SQR in one large package.

6. The SQR looks at your code, and if it finds nested statements, it processes these statements for each line of the return set.

7. SQR goes through every line of the return set until it has no more data to process.

The importance of this sequence should not be underestimated. It tells us that most SQL errors will occur before the statement is even executed. Once the statement runs, it should run error-free. Once data is returned, the database is completely out of the picture. Any subsequent errors are in the SQR.

Laying out the processing steps also makes it easier to understand how nested statements work. How does SQR communicate so intimately with the database? In fact, it just sends the statement and receives the data. Then the action begins.

Let's look at what a nested statement looks like for a 401(k) interface in Table 26-1. This interface is selecting deduction data from paychecks.

▶ **Table 26-1** Sample embedded SELECT in a SQR program

Line #	Code
1	`BEGIN-SELECT ON-ERROR = Process-Error`
2	`PC.SSN`
3	`PC.COMPANY`
4	`PC.NAME`
5	`PC.EMPLID`
6	`DE.PAY_END_DT`
7	`DE.DED_CUR`
8	`DE.DED_CLASS`
9	`DE.PLAN_TYPE`
10	`DE.DEDCD`
11	`ADD 1 TO #records_read`
12	`MOVE &PC.Emplid      TO $emplid       !used by common module`
13	`MOVE &PC.Company     TO $company      !getdedbl.sqc`
14	`MOVE &DE.Ded_Class   TO $dedclass`
15	`MOVE &DE.Plan_Type   TO $plantype`
16	`LET $dedcd           = RTRIM(&DE.Dedcd,' ')`
17	`DO Get-Deduction-Balances           !common module getdedbl`
18	`DO Edit-Validate-Record`
19	`IF $error_found = {no}`
20	`    DO Write-Record`
21	`END-IF`
22	`FROM PS_PAY_DEDUCTION DE,`
23	`PS_PAY_CHECK PC`
24	`WHERE PC.PAY_END_DT      BETWEEN $from_date AND $thru_date`
25	`AND PC.OFF_CYCLE        = {no}`
26	`AND PC.PAYCHECK_STATUS  = {confirmed}`

▶ **Table 26-1** continued

Line #	Code	
27	AND DE.DEDCD	= {401K}
28	AND PC.COMPANY	= DE.COMPANY
29	AND PC.PAYGROUP	= DE.PAYGROUP
30	AND PC.PAY_END_DT	= DE.PAY_END_DT
31	AND PC.OFF_CYCLE	= DE.OFF_CYCLE
32	AND PC.PAGE#	= DE.PAGE#
33	AND PC.LINE#	= DE.LINE#
34	AND PC.SEPCHK	= DE.SEPCHK
35	ORDER BY PC.SSN	
36	END-SELECT	

The SQL statement begins at line 1 and ends at line 36. The SQR compiler, however, knows that lines 11 through 21 are not part of the select statement—they are nested SQR commands (in bold in Table 26-1). It detects this because the first character of each of these lines is a space. To be included in a SQL statement, a line must be fully left-justified (forgetting to indent nested SQR lines is a common debugging frustration).

The select statement is pulling back all of the deductions for 401(k) between two parameter dates (from and through dates). For each row that it brings back, lines 11 through 21 are executed again. The nesting is exactly like a for/next statement in other computer languages.

For each deduction row returned, the following occurs:

1. A records read variable is accumulated (line 11).

2. The values of the selected columns (specified with &) are moved to SQR variables (specified with $ for text, # for numbers) (line 12–15).

3. The deduction code is trimmed, in case it is short and there are spaces after it (line 16). Since the deduction code is used to look up more information later on, it is essential that it not contain trailing spaces.

4. A procedure inside a common module is called. The PeopleSoft-delivered module GETDEDBL.SQC will get the year-to-date balance for the employee for the 401(k) deduction. This involves a select statement against the PS_DEDUCTION_BAL table. Note that this procedure, and hence the select statement, runs for each employee, for each deduction row selected. As a nested SQL, it is called many times. See Appendix C for a list of delivered common modules (line 17).

5. The fields for the output file are validated in a procedure, Edit-Validate-Record. This procedure includes nested SQL to check the value of a company code, for instance, against the PS_COMPANY_TBL (line 18).

6. The Edit-Validate-Record procedure returns a yes or no value if there is an error in the $error_found field. The brackets { } indicate a constant that was defined earlier in the program. {no} is defined as 'N' earlier in the program (line 19).

7. If the record clears, it is written to the file in the Write-Record procedure (line 20–21).

The advantage of nested statements is the ability to process each row individually. This is a conceptually clear method, which also keeps complex coding to a minimum.

In a Query example in Chapter 25, we tried to list employees with manager IDs along with employees who have no manager defined. Although we were able to create a union between two queries to obtain the desired results, the SQL behind it must perform two queries instead of one (to emulate an outer join). In SQR, you could do the first query for all employees, and then for each employee do a query that checks for a manager ID. Not only is the process simpler in SQR, but the coding is easier, too.

UNDERSTANDING DELIVERED SQR PROGRAMS

At different implementations you will often find that SQRs are written with varying standards and levels of explanation. Many PeopleSoft-delivered SQR programs are written using different standards and techniques without any explanation. It is apparent that several people write SQRs at PeopleSoft, and there is no standard format.

As a result, delivered SQRs can be difficult to interpret. PeopleSoft programmers are more likely to use tricks. For example, to get the most recent effective date, some programmers select a large set of data, sort it in descending date order, and then force SQR to break after outputting only the first line. It is difficult to determine if this kind of programming is more or less efficient. One thing, though, is for certain—it is more confusing.

Take a look at the delivered SQR at your implementation. If your PeopleSoft application is stored inside a folder (such as 'psoft'), the delivered SQR will be under psoft\sqr. There are over 1,000 SQR programs in this folder. Many are tax programs, one for each state.

Common Modules

About one third of the delivered SQR programs are actually called SQCs. An SQC is a common module, a piece of SQR code that can be used by any SQR program. A common module is a subroutine that is called by a SQR program. One SQC sets up the printer for output, and another might get the name of a department from the PS_DEPT_TBL. A common module should always be created when you find yourself writing the same code over and over again. With all of the code in just one place, future maintenance is much easier. A common module is exactly the same, in concept, as a copybook in other languages.

PeopleSoft-delivered SQR programs use common modules everywhere. Often you will look at one common module and find that it calls another, and another, and another, until you're several levels deep. It is frustrating, but it facilitates maintenance.

> When building custom programs that use delivered SQCs, pay attention to the SQCs that are included within an SQC. You may be including a module twice, and your program will not compile.

An SQC is simply a piece of a SQR program. When you include an SQC (using the #INCLUDE statement), the SQR compiler takes whatever is in the SQC and pastes it into the SQR program. Let's look at a sample:

```
PRINT 'SQR is '
#INCLUDE posmesge.sqc
PRINT 'The end.'
```

If the posmesge.sqc includes the following code:

```
PRINT 'a great language. '
```

then the output will look like:

```
'SQR is a great language. The end.'
```

This is one way of using a common module. The code is simply placed in the program where the include statement is.

A different method is more common. You will find #INCLUDE statements at the beginning or the end of a program because the common module only contains procedures, which can be called from anywhere in the program. In our sample, to produce the same result, the SQR program would look like this:

```
#INCLUDE posmesge.sqc
PRINT 'SQR is '
DO Positive-Message
PRINT 'The end.'
```

And the posmesge.sqc includes only a procedure:

```
BEGIN-PROCEDURE Positive-Message
    PRINT 'a great language. '
END-PROCEDURE Positive-Message
```

Be sure to look at an SQC carefully to determine what type of module it is—a procedure, or a piece of code to be directly planted into the SQR.

Basic Common Module Calls

There are several delivered common modules that you will see in nearly every delivered SQR. Furthermore, you will want to use some of these modules in your own custom SQR environment. Table 26-2 lists the name of each module, the call you will commonly see, and a short description. A full list of delivered common modules and descriptions can be found in Appendix C.

▶ **Table 26-2**   Common 'common modules' in delivered PeopleSoft SQR

SQC name	Procedure call	Description
curdttim.sqc	Get-Current-DateTime	Get current system date and time.
datemath.sqc	Dtu-Add-Weeks, etc. (many procedures)	Routines for date arithmetic.
datetime.sqc	Init-Datetime (launch first)	Routines to format dates and times.
	Format-Datetime (many others for date format conversions)	
number.sqc	Init-Number (launch first)	Routines to format numbers.
	Format-Number (many others for specific number formats)	
payinit.sqc	Payroll-Report-Initialization	Payroll report initialization and timing routines.
reset.sqc	Reset	Reset printer, prints 'end of report.'
setenv.sqc	No procedure	Define operating system and set #define variables. #includes 'rdbms.sqc' and 'opsys.sqc.' Sets #define date settings.
setup02.sqc (calls 02a)	No procedure	Standard setup section (landscape orientation) for a printer.

Table 26-2 Common 'common modules' in delivered PeopleSoft SQR

SQC name	Procedure call	Description
stdapi.sqc	STDAPI-Init	Process scheduler interface.
stdhdg01.sqc	No procedure	Standard heading #1 for printed reports, contains: report id, run date, run time, report title. There are numerous heading modules, but all of them include heading 01.
validdt.sqc	Validate-Date	Routines to make sure a date value is valid.

When creating custom SQC modules, be sure to use a standard naming convention to avoid the possibility of an upgrade overwriting the module. Often companies use a two-character prefix. An eight-character name should be used to maintain cross-platform compatibility. If your prefix is 'AB' and you are creating a parameter routine, you could name it 'abgetprm,' for example.

SQR and Dates

The latest version of SQR contains some functions for storing and manipulating dates. Unfortunately these date functions can be cumbersome and finicky depending on how you are retrieving date fields.

In previous versions, date handling was not provided by SQR at all. PeopleSoft designed and built several common modules, many of them listed in Table 26-2 above, to handle dates. These modules facilitate the formatting of dates as well as date arithmetic.

Although the new version of SQR can perform many of the same functions as these common modules, the modules are prevalent in delivered SQR code and are often simpler to use. It is wise to keep the use of dates consistent in custom programs, either using the PeopleSoft modules or the SQR functionality.

Running Delivered SQRs

All delivered SQRs can be executed without modification. Many of the SQRs can be accessed through online panels and launched by end-users.

For example, there is a SQR that outputs a list of employee names and addresses. To access this SQR, go to Go ➤ Administer Workforce ➤ Administer Workforce (U.S.) ➤ Report ➤ Employee Home Address Listing. The panel has nothing on it, but if you click on the stop light (without the '!'), the process scheduler window will appear. The process, you can see, is called PER020. Now you can choose where you want the file to go, and click OK to run it.

A SQR can also be run without PeopleSoft's assistance and without the process scheduler. Simply run the SQR engine, sqrw.exe, which is located in the psoft/sqrbinw/ folder. A dialogue box will appear, where you can type in the location of the SQR (psoft/sqr/PER020.sqr), your database username and password, and database name. You should also specify flags for the SQR. Table 26-3 lists all of the necessary flags for executing an SQR, although some of the variables will depend on your system configuration.

▶ **Table 26-3** SQR flags: a brief guide

Flag	Description
-I[directory]	Location of common modules (can specify several locations).
-c	For Windows, tells SQR to open up a window while running so the process can be cancelled.
-keep	Creates an SPF file in addition to text output for reports. An SPF file can be printed on any printer using the SQR print application.
-m[file]	Points to a file that contains parameters/limits for SQR. In PeopleSoft this file is in sqr/allmaxes.max.
-o[file]	Directs screen output to a log file.
-f[file]	Overrides the output directory and filename for reports.

Launching in Windows

There is an easier way to launch an SQR, one that is much more convenient if you are executing an SQR many times. In Windows, create a shortcut that points to the sqrw.exe program. Then right-click on the shortcut, click the shortcut tab, and type in a path, as in Table 26-4.

▶ **Table 26-4** SQR shortcut string (for this example, PeopleSoft is located on drive J)

Description	String (type in as one line)
Location of SQR engine	J:\hr750\sqrbinw\sqrw.exe
Location of SQR program (text file)	J:\psoft\sqr
User ID, password, and database name	adam/password@psdev
Location of common modules	-iJ:\psoft\sqr,J:\psoft\custom\sqr
Open a dialog box while running	-cb
Direct screen output to a log file	-oC:\temp\sqr.log
Create an SPF file for all reports	-keep
Location of limitations file	-mJ:\psoft\sqr\allmaxes.max

When combined, these items are separated by a single space. The complete string looks like this:

```
J:\hr750\sqrbinw\sqrw.exe J:\psoft\sqr\per020
adam/password@psdev -iJ:\psoft\sqr,J:\psoft\custom\sqr -
cb -oC:\temp\sqr.log -keep -mJ:\psoft\sqr\allmaxes.max
```

This string will launch the PER020 program in Windows. The SQR will open up a DOS window, and then close. It will not let you know when it has finished unless the SQR has been programmed to do so by printing output on the screen (using the SHOW or DISPLAY commands). When the process disappears, the program is done, and you can look for the output.

Launching in UNIX

In Unix, you would execute a SQR on the command line, using the SQR command:

```
sqr psoft\sqr\per020 adam/password@psdev -ip-
soft\sqr,psoft\custom\sqr
```

Launching in MVS

In the MVS world, JCL is required to successfully launch a SQR program. Different environmental variables are set within the JCL, and an SQR command line is embedded within the JCL. This command line is passed to the SQR engine at runtime, and follows the same format as the example lines above. PeopleSoft typically provides a JCL template to implementations using an MVS environment.

One important consideration in an MVS environment is the name and location of output files. Since MVS names do not have suffixes, such as *.lis or *.dat, the different files must be sent to pre-created datasets so they do not overwrite one another. The JCL for launching an SQR associates these pre-created datasets to the reports generated by the SQR. The first report produced will be placed in the first dataset named, and so on. The datasets do not need to be defined in the actual SQR, but it is important to pay attention to the order in which reports are created.

Finding the Output

Sometimes it is difficult to figure out whether an SQR program actually ran. The output is nowhere to be found. Look for the Configuration Manager application in psoft\bin\client\winx86\pscfg.exe. Many of the directories are defined in PeopleSoft's Configuration Manager under the SQR tab. Table 26-5 lists the suffixes PeopleSoft uses to identify different files.

▶ **Table 26-5** SQR file suffixes

File	Suffix (name of SQR program +)
Reports	*.lis (for first report), *.l01, *.l02 (for subsequent reports produced by the same program) are automatically placed in the folder where the SQR program resides.
Output file	Can be named within the SQR, usually has the suffix *.dat
Input file	Can be named within the SQR, usually has the suffix *.dat

Delivered Parameter Processing

PeopleSoft delivers a robust set of modules for accepting and processing parameters for SQR programs. It is always a good idea to use parameters in an SQR. Every parameter you add means one less chance that maintenance will need to occur in the future. Of course, you also do not want to have hundreds of confusing parameters. PeopleSoft generally uses date parameters for human resources and benefits and a special suite of payroll parameters for payroll programs (see Chapter 14, table 14-7 for a list). The parameter set is limited yet flexible enough to handle several different types of requests.

When a delivered SQR executes online, it will often ask for parameters directly. For example, a year-end tax report will execute and ask, "Enter a year." The parameter can be entered directly, or alternatively entered right into the command line before execution.

By directly inputting parameters onto the command line, SQR programs can be effectively batch scheduled—an important consideration in a custom environment. Parameters for delivered programs can be stored in a text file and appended onto the command line or stored in a custom table and extracted by a SQR program or script.

To execute a tax report with a quarter and a year parameter, the command line would look like this (parameters in bold):

```
J:\hr750\sqrbinw\sqrw.exe J:\psoft\sqr\per020
adam/password@psdev 3 2000
-iJ:\psoft\sqr,J:\psoft\custom\sqr -cb -oC:\temp\sqr.log
-keep -mJ:\psoft\sqr\allmaxes.max
```

The SQR engine detects parameters because no flag precedes them, and they are separated by a space. SQR will take each parameter and use it to respond to a question asked by the SQR. So when a delivered SQR program runs and asks for a quarter, the SQR engine takes the '3' and types it in, hitting return. Then when the program asks for a year, the engine types in '2000' and hits return, like a player piano.

CUSTOMIZATION

There are several decisions to make when you are creating a custom program in SQR. Will you maintain the same environment that PeopleSoft- delivered SQR programs use, or will you modify the environment to suit the needs of your technical infrastructure? Your custom SQR programs may need to run on a special printer, or be scheduled outside of PeopleSoft, without the delivered process scheduler. This will require some foresight for the design of common modules, parameter settings, and scheduling options. Also consider what types of programs you will be building and whether they will have common elements such as error reports, control reports, and headers or footers.

Common Modules to Build

What is the minimum you need to start an SQR program in PeopleSoft? There are several common modules that should be modified first. They are listed in Table 26-6 below.

▶ **Table 26-6**   Common modules that should be customized

SQC name	Customization
reset.sqc, setup SQCs	If you are using a custom printer (i.e., other than a laser), you will need to change the printer control codes contained in these common modules.
setenv.sqc	Contains numerous constants that must be customized. In particular, prefixes and suffixes must be defined for input and output files.
stdhdg01.sqc	Says 'PeopleSoft, Inc.' at the top; can be customized to contain the name of your company.

Technically, these SQCs do not have to be modified. In most implementations, these SQCs are copied and saved with a different name to facilitate future upgrades. Then delivered programs run with the delivered modules, while custom programs use a special set of modules.

Common modules are useful for basic setup tasks and for special processing. Some suggested custom common modules, useful for most implementations, are listed in Table 26-7. They are listed with a common prefix, in this case 'ps' to identify them as custom modules. This prefix should be changed for your implementation.

▶ **Table 26-7** Suggested custom common modules to build

SQC name	Description

Error Modules

PeopleSoft does not provide extensive error processing. Some sample error module descriptions are listed here as a guide.

pserrdcl.sqc	Declares an error report layout (DECLARE-REPORT and DECLARE-LAYOUT statements)
pserrhdg.sqc	Defines an error report heading (BEGIN-HEADING)
pserror.sqc	Prints errors out on the error report (used to report errors)

Heading/Footer Modules

psftr01.sqc	Your company's privacy footer
pshdg01.sqc	Your company's modified PeopleSoft header. This is a modified version of stdhdg01.sqc. Once this custom SQC is constructed, all of the other stdhdg modules must be customized to refer to the new SQC instead of the old one.

Setup Modules

pslyout2.sqc	Declares a 132-column landscape layout (DECLARE-LAYOUT)
pslyout3.sqc	Declares a 176-column landscape layout (DECLARE-LAYOUT)
pssetenv.sqc	Environment variables (could include any unique #DEFINEs)
pssetup2.sqc	Defines the printer (should be included by pslyout2 and pslyout3)

Table-Accessing Modules

These modules facilitate the retrieval of human resources data. Information about the functional issues requiring these modules can be found in the human resources section of this book.

psstatus.sqc	Returns effdt, action, reason, empl_status for the last status-related JOB table row for an employee ID
pstermdt.sqc	Returns termination date for an EMPLID (the first term record of the most recent term sequence)

Template

Once these modules are defined, a typical SQR template can be used. A sample is shown below. This sample SQR, if executed, would compile but would do nothing. Use is only as a guide for starting a new, custom SQR.

```
!**********************************************************************
!  Author:              Adam Bromwich
!  Specification:       Tax Report
!**********************************************************************
!  Program Function:    Produces an output file of employee tax
!                       dollars withheld for the year.
!**********************************************************************


#INCLUDE 'setenv.sqc'       !set environment

#DEFINE yes        'Y'      !indicator value
#DEFINE no         'N'      !indicator value


!**********************************************************************
!                      BEGIN SETUP SECTION
!**********************************************************************
BEGIN-SETUP
        #INCLUDE 'setup02.sqc'        !Performs declare-printer
END-SETUP

#INCLUDE stdhgh01.sqc     !places a standard header
                                !on the report


!**********************************************************************
!  Main Program
!**********************************************************************
BEGIN-PROGRAM
    MOVE ' Report 01' TO $ReportID      !used on by stdhdg01.sqc
    DO Init-DateTime                    !common module datetime.sqc
    DO Get-Current-DateTime             !common module curdttim.sqc
    DO Init-Number                      !common module number.sqc

    DO Main-Processing                  !execute the main processing
END-PROGRAM

BEGIN-PROCEDURE Main-Processing

(insert code/SQL here)

END-PROCEDURE Main-Processing
!**********************************************************************
!  Common Modules
!**********************************************************************
#INCLUDE 'pserror.sqc'     !Error routine processing
#INCLUDE 'pserrhdg.sqc'    !Error routine headings
#INCLUDE 'curdttim.sqc'    !Retrieve current date and time
#INCLUDE 'datetime.sqc'    !Format date and time
#INCLUDE 'number.sqc'      !Routines for number formatting
```

Let's walk through this template to make every line clear.

After the comment box, the SETENV.SQC common module is included. This common module sets many constants that could be used by subsequent procedures. It should always be included at the very top of the SQR. If SQR encounters a constant that has not been defined yet (i.e., before SQR encounters it), a compiler error will occur.

Two constant declarations are included here as an example. The #DEFINE statement declares a constant value. All constants should be defined at the top of an SQR.

The BEGIN-SETUP paragraph comes first and includes declarations of printers, reports and layouts. Here the printer is defined, and the report and layout are left to SQR's defaults. If you like, you can define a layout (such as landscape, 132 column) and then define reports that use the layout. If your SQR has three reports, you will need to declare each report and specify its layout.

After the setup we include a heading common module. The module has the BEGIN-HEADING statement within it, so we do not need to provide it here.

The main program section is indicated by the BEGIN-PROGRAM heading. You may also see BEGIN-REPORT in some programs. These two headings are identical in meaning; SQR does not distinguish between the two. It is here that the program starts executing. We move a report ID to a variable that is used by the standard header we included earlier.

The next three procedures are located in the common modules included at the end of the SQR. The Init-Datetime procedure is located in the DATETIME.SQC common module. This procedure sets the formatting of the dates to be used in the program. The Get-Current-DateTime procedure is located in the CURDT-TIM.SQC common module. This procedure queries the database for the current date time and stores it in a variable called $AsOfToday. The Init-Number procedure is the same as Init-Datetime but is used for formatting numbers. It is contained in the NUMBER.SQC common module.

Then we call the Main Processing procedure, where SQL and SQR code can be placed. Any number of procedures can be created and called. At the end of the SQR, the common modules that do not require special placement within the SQR are included.

Keep in mind that this template is only an example. It is likely that the SQR programs created at your site will look quite different. This template contains elements that are commonly found in most custom SQRs for PeopleSoft, but these elements are by no means the rule.

Debugging SQR Programs

Debugging an SQR requires a great deal of patience. There is no debugging program provided with SQR, so all debugging must use a trial-and-error method. Some tips:

1. Place SHOW statements in your code to display the values of variables during processing.

2. Place a SHOW *before and inside* an SQL statement, to make sure the statement is executing and returning data.

3. Turn lines of code into comments using the '!' character in order to avoid them.

4. If you are getting hundreds of compiler errors, don't be alarmed. Many compiler errors cause many more additional errors. Just fixing one bug could eliminate half of your compiler errors.

5. Make sure you are running against the correct database, and that the tables you are querying have data in them.

6. If you get a line number back in a compiler error that does not correspond to the SQR, it probably refers to a common module. Since common modules are simply dropped into the SQR program, the system thinks the code is in the SQR program, while the code is really several levels deep in a common module.

7. Make sure common modules are not declared twice and are declared in the right place. When SQR compiles an SQR, it takes the SQCs and places them in the program, then evaluates the code top to bottom. You can easily call a procedure before including an SQC (procedure calls can be anywhere relative to the procedure), but you cannot use a constant before you define it.

8. When defining constants, pay attention to the quotes. A constant can be defined with or without quotes. When it is with quotes, just use the constant. When it is without quotes, use quotes when necessary.

9. You may have accidentally misspelled a variable name. SQR does not require variable declarations, nor can they be forced. If you spell a variable incorrectly, SQR will treat it as a new variable.

10. When all else fails, take out the SQL statement and run it in a database utility. Be sure to add commas between the selected columns, remove any variables, and remove any nested SQR code.

ADVANCED SQR FEATURES

Both functional and technical users of PeopleSoft should know the basic capabilities of SQR. Some of these features are certainly more complex, but they can add flexibility to an SQR program. In general, though, the features described here are as advanced SQR gets and are useful to SQR programmers in particular.

Understanding the Printing Process

One of the most elusive parts of SQR is how reports are declared and printed. Often when more than one report is used in an SQR, information will appear on the wrong report, or the headers will be mixed up. SQR has commands to associate headers with specific reports (FOR-REPORT) and can switch between reports easily (with USE-REPORT). But errors always seem to appear.

Part of the issue is that SQR does not print headers on a page until all of the detail lines on the page are full. Once SQR cannot fit another line on the page, it adds the header and footer and starts a new, blank page (no header or footer). This also occurs when a NEXT-PAGE command is encountered.

This process can be especially confusing when you want to print a piece of information in the header of every report. For example, if you use the $ReportID field in the PeopleSoft standard header, the ID should be a unique value for each report. You must move the new value to this variable right before a page *ends*, not begins. Determining this location requires some extra coding and attention.

Dynamic SQL Clauses

One of the most powerful features in SQR is the ability to create SQL dynamically. Suppose you want to select name and address for one report, but then want name and birthdate for another report. You can use the same SELECT statement for both queries, but set a dynamic variable as one of the columns. By moving 'PD.ADDRESS1' or 'PD.BIRTHDATE' into this dynamic variable, the SQL statement is changed.

Dynamic clauses are very different from regular SQR variables. A dynamic clause can replace SQL, whereas a regular variable can only be used in a WHERE clause. An example:

```
SELECT
PD.NAME
[$second_column]

FROM PS_PERSONAL_DATA PD
WHERE PD.STATE = $state
```

The variable in the brackets [ ] is dynamic, and replaces a line of SQL code. The $state variable is not, and simply contains a value, such as 'PA.'

> In MVS, the brackets are actually slashes /$second_column/. Unfortunately, some delivered SQR programs have dynamic clauses and will need to be manually changed from brackets to slashes.

If the above SQL is inside a procedure, you can call the procedure using $second_column as a parameter. The calling program would have code as follows:

```
MOVE 'PD.ADDRESS1' TO $second_column     !sets the column
DO Get-Personal-Data($second_column)     !calls the SQL
MOVE &PD.ADDRESS1 TO $address1           !stores the result

MOVE 'PD.BIRTHDATE' TO $second_column    !sets the 2nd column
DO Get-Personal-Data($second_column)     !calls the SQL again
MOVE &PD.BIRTHDATE TO $birthdate         !stores the result
```

A similar process can be designed at the program level. Using dynamic SQL, a single program can be designed to retrieve different data for a report or file. The program could accept parameters either on the command line or via ASK statements which obtain user input. The program could use these parameters to retrieve the appropriate data.

Arrays

In most languages, a database array holds data in a three-dimensional arrangement. There are rows and columns, and instances that flow behind them. Think of it like a spreadsheet, then imagine hundreds of spreadsheets on top of one another. To retrieve the value of a cell, you would specify a row, a column, and a level of depth (i.e., get data from arrayname(1,2,3) – depth 1, row 2, column of 3). Figure 26-1 shows a graphical example.

Unfortunately, SQR can only handle two-dimensional arrays. At first glance, it might seem like there is a capability for a third dimension, since a third parameter can be specified. This parameter, however, only multiplies the quantity of a certain column. An array could be defined with a column for 'name,' and then a column called 'paychecks' with an instance of 24. SQR creates an array with 25 columns—one for name, and then 24 paycheck columns. You specify which paycheck column by providing the third parameter. But this third parameter does *not* indicate an additional dimension of data.

Arrays are useful in PeopleSoft for storing the data from certain tables. If you will be looking up hundreds of department descriptions, it could make sense to

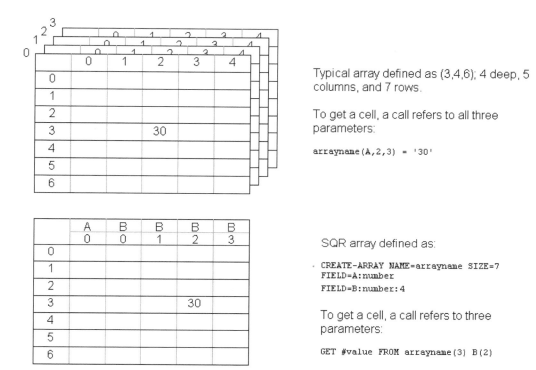

Typical array defined as (3,4,6); 4 deep, 5 columns, and 7 rows.

To get a cell, a call refers to all three parameters:

`arrayname(A,2,3) = '30'`

SQR array defined as:

```
CREATE-ARRAY NAME=arrayname SIZE=7
FIELD=A:number
FIELD=B:number:4
```

To get a cell, a call refers to three parameters:

`GET #value FROM arrayname(3) B(2)`

▶ **Figure 26-1** How SQR arrays differ from typical programming arrays

dump the entire department table into an array and just query the array. The commands for storing and retrieving data from an array are not very refined and often require the use of WHILE loops. Because arrays can be so cumbersome, you should only create them when you must store many values (for counting employees in different categories, for example) or when processing time needs to be improved.

Also, SQR cannot expand arrays if they need to be larger. Users often hit the top limit of an array, so be sure to define the array size as many times the intended size of your data set. There are also limits to the size of an array that are specified by SQR—only 200 fields are allowed, and only 20 arrays can be used in a single program.

Reporting Tables

This Appendix explores each field of the PeopleSoft delivered reporting tables. These tables are discussed in detail in Chapter 4.

A.1 EMPLOYEES

The employees table takes fields from several different tables. Table A-1 associates each field on the PS_EMPLOYEES table to a field on an original PeopleSoft table. When the delivered refresh program PER099 executes, it takes the values from the original PeopleSoft tables and copies them to the PS_EMPLOYEES table.

▶ **Table A-1** Map of employees table: PS_EMPLOYEES

Col.	PS_EMPLOYEES field	Table providing data
1	EMPLID	PS_PERSONAL_DATA
2	EMPL_RCD#	PS_EMPLOYMENT
3	EFFDT	PS_JOB
4	EFFSEQ	PS_JOB
5	NID_COUNTRY	PS_PERS_NID
6	NATIONAL_ID_TYPE	PS_PERS_NID
7	NATIONAL_ID	PS_PERS_NID

▶ **Table A-1**   continued

Col.	PS_EMPLOYEES field	Table providing data
8	NAME	PS_PERSONAL_DATA
9	NAME_PREFIX	PS_PERSONAL_DATA
10	PREFERRED_NAME	PS_NAMES (PREFERRED_NAME)
11	COUNTRY	PS_PERSONAL_DATA
12	ADDRESS1	PS_PERSONAL_DATA
13	ADDRESS2	PS_PERSONAL_DATA
14	ADDRESS3	PS_PERSONAL_DATA
15	ADDRESS4	PS_PERSONAL_DATA
16	CITY	PS_PERSONAL_DATA
17	NUM1	PS_PERSONAL_DATA
18	NUM2	PS_PERSONAL_DATA
19	HOUSE_TYPE	PS_PERSONAL_DATA
20	COUNTY	PS_PERSONAL_DATA
21	STATE	PS_PERSONAL_DATA
22	POSTAL	PS_PERSONAL_DATA
23	GEO_CODE	PS_PERSONAL_DATA
24	IN_CITY_LIMIT	PS_PERSONAL_DATA
25	HOME_PHONE	PS_PERSONAL_DATA (PHONE)
26	PER_STATUS	PS_PERSONAL_DATA
27	ORIG_HIRE_DT	PS_PERSONAL_DATA
28	SEX	PS_PERSONAL_DATA
29	BIRTHDATE	PS_PERSONAL_DATA
30	BIRTHPLACE	PS_PERSONAL_DATA
31	DT_OF_DEATH	PS_PERSONAL_DATA
32	MAR_STATUS	PS_PERSONAL_DATA
33	FORMER_NAME	PS_NAMES (PREFERRED_NAME where NAME_TYPE = 'FR1')
34	ETHNIC_GROUP	PS_DIVERSITY
35	DISABLED	PS_DISABILITY
36	DISABLED_VET	PS_DISABILITY
37	MILITARY_STATUS	PS_PERSONAL_DATA
38	HIGHEST_EDUC_LVL	PS_PERSONAL_DATA

▶ **Table A-1**   continued

Col.	PS_EMPLOYEES field	Table providing data
39	CITIZENSHIP_STATUS	PS_PERSONAL_DATA
40	US_WORK_ELIGIBILTY	PS_PERSONAL_DATA
41	BENEFIT_RCD#	PS_EMPLOYMENT
42	HOME_HOST_CLASS	PS_EMPLOYMENT
43	HIRE_DT	PS_EMPLOYMENT
44	REHIRE_DT	PS_EMPLOYMENT
45	CMPNY_SENIORITY_DT	PS_EMPLOYMENT
46	SERVICE_DT	PS_EMPLOYMENT
47	EXPECTED_RETURN_DT	PS_EMPLOYMENT
48	TERMINATION_DT	PS_EMPLOYMENT
49	LAST_DATE_WORKED	PS_EMPLOYMENT
50	LAST_INCREASE_DT	PS_EMPLOYMENT
51	OWN_5PERCENT_CO	PS_EMPLOYMENT
52	REFERRAL_SOURCE	PS_PERSONAL_DATA
53	BUSINESS_TITLE	PS_EMPLOYMENT
54	FT_STUDENT	PS_PERSONAL_DATA
55	REPORTS_TO	PS_EMPLOYMENT
56	SUPERVISOR_ID	PS_EMPLOYMENT
57	UNION_CD	PS_JOB_LABOR
58	BARG_UNIT	PS_JOB_LABOR
59	UNION_SENIORITY_DT	PS_JOB_LABOR
60	PROBATION_DT	PS_EMPLOYMENT
61	SECURITY_CLEARANCE	PS_EMPLOYMENT
62	WORK_PHONE	PS_EMPLOYMENT
63	BUSINESS_UNIT	PS_JOB
64	DEPTID	PS_JOB
65	JOBCODE	PS_JOB
66	POSITION_NBR	PS_JOB
67	EMPL_STATUS	PS_JOB
68	ACTION	PS_JOB
69	ACTION_DT	PS_JOB

▶ **Table A-1** continued

Col.	PS_EMPLOYEES field	Table providing data
70	ACTION_REASON	PS_JOB
71	LOCATION	PS_JOB
72	JOB_ENTRY_DT	PS_JOB
73	DEPT_ENTRY_DT	PS_JOB
74	POSITION_ENTRY_DT	PS_JOB
75	SHIFT	PS_JOB
76	REG_TEMP	PS_JOB
77	FULL_PART_TIME	PS_JOB
78	FLSA_STATUS	PS_JOB
79	OFFICER_CD	PS_JOB
80	COMPANY	PS_JOB
81	PAYGROUP	PS_JOB
82	EMPL_TYPE	PS_JOB
83	HOLIDAY_SCHEDULE	PS_JOB
84	STD_HOURS	PS_JOB
85	EEO_CLASS	PS_JOB
86	SAL_ADMIN_PLAN	PS_JOB
87	GRADE	PS_JOB
88	GRADE_ENTRY_DT	PS_JOB
89	STEP	PS_JOB
90	STEP_ENTRY_DT	PS_JOB
91	GL_PAY_TYPE	PS_JOB
92	SALARY_MATRIX_CD	PS_JOB
93	RATING_SCALE	PS_JOB
94	REVIEW_RATING	PS_JOB
95	REVIEW_DT	PS_JOB
96	COMP_FREQUENCY	PS_JOB
97	COMPRATE	PS_JOB
98	CHANGE_AMT	PS_JOB
99	CHANGE_PCT	PS_JOB
100	ANNUAL_RT	PS_JOB

▶ **Table A-1** continued

Col.	PS_EMPLOYEES field	Table providing data
101	MONTHLY_RT	PS_JOB
102	HOURLY_RT	PS_JOB
103	ANNL_BENEF_BASE_RT	PS_JOB
104	SHIFT_RT	PS_JOB
105	SHIFT_FACTOR	PS_JOB
106	CURRENCY_CD	PS_JOB
107	JOBTITLE	PS_JOBCODE_TBL (DESCR)
108	JOBTITLE_ABBRV	PS_JOBCODE_TBL (DESCRSHORT)
109	EEO1CODE	PS_JOBCODE_TBL
110	EEO4CODE	PS_JOBCODE_TBL
111	EEO5CODE	PS_JOBCODE_TBL
112	EEO6CODE	PS_JOBCODE_TBL
113	EEO_JOB_GROUP	PS_JOBCODE_TBL
114	JOB_FAMILY	PS_JOBCODE_TBL
115	JOB_KNOWHOW_POINTS	PS_JOBCODE_TBL
116	JOB_ACCNTAB_POINTS	PS_JOBCODE_TBL
117	JOB_PROBSLV_POINTS	PS_JOBCODE_TBL
118	JOB_POINTS_TOTAL	PS_JOBCODE_TBL
119	JOB_KNOWHOW_PCT	PS_JOBCODE_TBL
120	JOB_ACCNTAB_PCT	PS_JOBCODE_TBL
121	JOB_PROBSLV_PCT	PS_JOBCODE_TBL
122	DEPTNAME	PS_DEPT_TBL (DESCR)
123	DEPTNAME_ABBRV	PS_DEPT_TBL (DESCRSHORT)
124	MANAGER_ID	PS_DEPT_TBL
125	EEO4_FUNCTION	PS_DEPT_TBL
126	FROMDATE	as-of date
127	ASOFDATE	as-of date (same as FROMDATE)
128	NAME_AC	PS_PERSONAL_DATA
129	DIRECTLY_TIPPED	PS_JOB

A.1.1 Missing Fields

Since three major tables are included almost in their entirety, the fields that are omitted from the core tables are listed in Tables A-2 through A-4 for reference. Many of these 'forgotten' fields could be required by end-users, such as mail drop and smoker indicator. Refer to the chapter that describes each of these tables in detail for more information on the individual fields.

▶ **Table A-2**   PS_EMPLOYMENT fields not included on PS_EMPLOYEES

Professional experience date	Paycheck location option
Last verification date	SetID
Phone sub-record	Location code
Time reporting location	Mail drop ID
Job reporting required	Paycheck name
Deduction taken	Address sub-record
Deduction subset ID	Payroll system
Paycheck distribution mail option	Benefits system
Paycheck address option	France employment sub-record

▶ **Table A-3**   PS_JOB fields not included on PS_EMPLOYEES

Position data override	Eligibility config. field 8
Position management record	Eligibility config. field 9
Tax location code	Benefits employee status
PIN number	Benefits administration action
Pay basis number	COBRA action
BAS group ID	Employee classification
Eligibility config. field 1	Account code
Eligibility config. field 2	Earnings distribution type
Eligibility config. field 3	Department setID
Eligibility config. field 4	Jobcode setID
Eligibility config. field 5	Regulatory region
Eligibility config. field 6	Germany job sub-record
Eligibility config. field 7	France job sub-record

▶ **Table A-4** PS_PERSONAL_DATA fields not included on PS_EMPLOYEES

Name suffix	Citizenship proof 2
Last name	Smoker
First name	Medicare entitled date
Address other sub-record	Canada personal data sub-record
Age 18 or older	Germany personal data sub-record
Birth Country	France personal data sub-record
Birth State	Japan personal data sub-record
Employee referral ID	UK personal data sub-record
Specific referral source	Alternate character name
Highly compensated last year	Alternate character address
Highly compensated employee	Alternate character address 2
Resume text file	Alternate character address 3
Employee has QDRO indicator	Language code
Person type	Alternate character city
Non-employee training sub-record	Years of work experience
Citizenship proof 1	On demand save now

A.2 BENEFITS_DATA

Table A-5 is a chart showing all of the fields in PS_BENEFITS_DATA and how they map to the base tables. Fields marked "Based on plan type" are common fields used by each plan and are provided by the base tables. The value in these fields depends on the PLAN_TYPE for the row. Other fields are unique to a certain plan table—note that these fields will be empty for other plan types.

▶ **Table A-5** The benefits data table: PS_BENEFITS_DATA

Col.	PS_BENEFITS_DATA field	Table providing data	Intermediary table
1	EMPLID	Based on plan type	PS_BEN_PLAN_DATA
2	EMPL_RCD#	Based on plan type	PS_BEN_PLAN_DATA
3	COBRA_EVENT_ID	Based on plan type	PS_BEN_PLAN_DATA
4	DEPENDENT_BENEF	PS_HEALTH_DEPENDNT	PS_BEN_PLAN_DATA
5	PLAN_TYPE	Based on plan type	PS_BEN_PLAN_DATA

▶ **Table A-5**   continued

Col.	PS_BENEFITS_DATA field	Table providing data	Intermediary table
6	PLAN_TYPE_DESCR	XLATTABLE	PS_BEN_PLAN_DATA
7	EFFDT	Based on plan type	PS_BEN_PLAN_DATA
8	BENEFIT_PLAN	Based on plan type	PS_BEN_PLAN_DATA
9	BEF_PLAN_DESCR	PS_BENEF_PLAN_TBL	PS_BEN_PLAN_DATA
10	PROVIDER	PS_BENEF_PLAN_TBL	PS_BEN_PLAN_DATA
11	PROVIDER_DESCR	PS_PROVIDR_TBL	PS_BEN_PLAN_DATA
12	GROUP#	PS_BENEF_PLAN_TBL	PS_BEN_PLAN_DATA
13	POLICY#	PS_PROV_POLICY_TBL	PS_BEN_PLAN_DATA
14	COVERAGE_ELECT	Based on plan type	PS_BEN_PLAN_DATA
15	COVRG_CD	Based on plan type	PS_BEN_PLAN_DATA
16	COVRG_CODE_DESCR	PS_COVRG_CD_TBL	PS_BEN_PLAN_DATA
17	COVERAGE_BEGIN_DT	Based on plan type	PS_BEN_PLAN_DATA
18	COVERAGE_END_DT	Based on plan type	PS_BEN_PLAN_DATA
19	DEDUCTION_BEGIN_DT	Based on plan type (EFFDT)	PS_BEN_PLAN_DATA
20	DEDUCTION_END_DT	Based on plan type	PS_BEN_PLAN_DATA
21	ENROLLMENT_DT	PS_HEALTH_BENEFIT (calculated)	PS_BEN_PLAN_DATA
22	ANNUAL_PLEDGE	PS_FSA_BENEFIT	PS_BEN_PLAN_DATA
23	FLAT_DED_AMT	PS_SAVINGS_PLAN	PS_BEN_PLAN_DATA
24	PCT_GROSS	PS_SAVINGS_PLAN	PS_BEN_PLAN_DATA
25	FLAT_DED_AMT_ATAX	PS_SAVINGS_PLAN	PS_BEN_PLAN_DATA
26	PCT_GROSS_ATAX	PS_SAVINGS_PLAN	PS_BEN_PLAN_DATA
27	VACN_HOURS	PS_VACATION_BEN	PS_BEN_PLAN_DATA
28	VACN_BUY_FLAT_AMT	PS_VACATION_BEN	PS_BEN_PLAN_DATA
29	VACN_SELL_FLAT_AMT	PS_VACATION_BEN	PS_BEN_PLAN_DATA
30	BENEF_PCT	Based on plan type (beneficiaries only)	PS_BEN_PLAN_DATA
31	FLAT_AMOUNT	Based on plan type (beneficiaries only)	PS_BEN_PLAN_DATA
32	EXCESS	Based on plan type (beneficiaries only)	PS_BEN_PLAN_DATA
33	CONTINGENT	Based on plan type (beneficiaries only)	PS_BEN_PLAN_DATA

▶ **Table A-5**   continued

Col.	PS_BENEFITS_DATA field	Table providing data	Intermediary table
34	DED_CUR	PS_DED_CALC	PS_BEN_PLAN_DATA
35	PAY_END_DT	PS_DED_CALC	PS_BEN_PLAN_DATA
36	CALCULATED_BASE	PS_DED_CALC	PS_BEN_PLAN_DATA
37	BENEFIT_PROGRAM	PS_BEN_PROG_PARTIC	PS_BEN_PLAN_DATA
38	BENEFIT_PROG_DESCR	PS_BEN_DEFN_PGM	PS_BEN_PLAN_DATA
39	COMPANY	PS_JOB	PS_BEN_PLAN_DATA
40	COMPANY_DESCR	PS_COMPANY_TBL	PS_BEN_PLAN_DATA
41	PAYGROUP	PS_JOB	PS_BEN_PLAN_DATA
42	PAYGROUP_DESCR	PS_PAYGROUP_TBL	PS_BEN_PLAN_DATA
43	CURRENCY_CD	PS_BEN_DEFN_PGM	PS_BEN_PLAN_DATA
44	CURRENCY_DESCR	Not populated	PS_BEN_PLAN_DATA
45	NAME	PS_PERSONAL_DATA, PS_DEPENDENT_BENEF	PS_BEN_PER_DATA
46	LAST_NAME	PS_PERSONAL_DATA, PS_DEPENDENT_BENEF	PS_BEN_PER_DATA
47	FIRST_NAME	PS_PERSONAL_DATA, PS_DEPENDENT_BENEF	PS_BEN_PER_DATA
48	NAME_PREFIX	PS_PERSONAL_DATA	PS_BEN_PER_DATA
49	NATIONAL_ID	PS_PERS_NID, PS_DEP_BENEF_NID	PS_BEN_PER_DATA
50	BIRTHDATE	PS_PERSONAL_DATA, PS_DEPENDENT_BENEF	PS_BEN_PER_DATA
51	SEX	PS_PERSONAL_DATA, PS_DEPENDENT_BENEF	PS_BEN_PER_DATA
52	RELATIONSHIP	PS_DEPENDENT_BENEF	PS_BEN_PER_DATA
53	RELATION_DESCR	XLATTABLE	PS_BEN_PER_DATA
54	COUNTRY	PS_PERSONAL_DATA, PS_DEPENDENT_BENEF	PS_BEN_PER_DATA
55	ADDRESS1	PS_PERSONAL_DATA, PS_DEPENDENT_BENEF	PS_BEN_PER_DATA
56	ADDRESS2	PS_PERSONAL_DATA, PS_DEPENDENT_BENEF	PS_BEN_PER_DATA
57	ADDRESS3	PS_PERSONAL_DATA, PS_DEPENDENT_BENEF	PS_BEN_PER_DATA

▶ **Table A-5**   continued

Col.	PS_BENEFITS_DATA field	Table providing data	Intermediary table
58	ADDRESS4	PS_PERSONAL_DATA, PS_DEPENDENT_BENEF	PS_BEN_PER_DATA
59	CITY	PS_PERSONAL_DATA, PS_DEPENDENT_BENEF	PS_BEN_PER_DATA
60	NUM1	PS_PERSONAL_DATA, PS_DEPENDENT_BENEF	PS_BEN_PER_DATA
61	NUM2	PS_PERSONAL_DATA, PS_DEPENDENT_BENEF	PS_BEN_PER_DATA
62	HOUSE_TYPE	PS_PERSONAL_DATA, PS_DEPENDENT_BENEF	PS_BEN_PER_DATA
63	COUNTY	PS_PERSONAL_DATA, PS_DEPENDENT_BENEF	PS_BEN_PER_DATA
64	STATE	PS_PERSONAL_DATA, PS_DEPENDENT_BENEF	PS_BEN_PER_DATA
65	POSTAL	PS_PERSONAL_DATA, PS_DEPENDENT_BENEF	PS_BEN_PER_DATA
66	GEO_CODE	PS_PERSONAL_DATA, PS_DEPENDENT_BENEF	PS_BEN_PER_DATA
67	IN_CITY_LIMIT	PS_PERSONAL_DATA, PS_DEPENDENT_BENEF	PS_BEN_PER_DATA
68	HOME_PHONE	PS_PERSONAL_DATA, PS_DEPENDENT_BENEF	PS_BEN_PER_DATA
69	HLTH_PROVIDER_ID	PS_HEALTH_BENEFIT	PS_BEN_PLAN_DATA
70	PREVIOUSLY_SEEN	PS_HEALTH_BENEFIT	PS_BEN_PLAN_DATA

B

PeopleSoft Query Performance/Fast Security

$$PAY \checkmark$$

$$401K$$

One major advantage of deploying PeopleSoft and a query tool in an organization is the ability for users to create and maintain their own interfaces and reports. Any professional who needs a quick report on a few fields can simply point, click, and print, rather than request a report from an experienced programmer.

A key ingredient to this feature is the response time of the actual query. Users expect a single table with all of the necessary data elements, but they soon find that numerous tables are required for basic reports. When they finally click 'run,' the query screen goes blank and the system requires extraordinary processing time. Even single-table queries, if they involve an aggregate function such as COUNT, can take hours to return. For performance reasons, large implementations (i.e., over 10,000 employees) often cannot use PeopleSoft row-level security as delivered.

One way around the performance issue with PeopleSoft Query is to use reporting tables, such as PS_EMPLOYEES and PS_BENEFITS_DATA. These tables have many data elements, essentially combining several tables into one every night in a batch process. The reporting tables relieve some of the burden on Query.

Even frugal use of tables, however, will not noticeably improve performance unless PeopleSoft's fast security solution is implemented. Fast security is similar to the reporting tables—it too is a nightly batch process that combines many tables into one. Since it combines the security tables, PeopleSoft can look up row-level security elements much faster. Once fast security is in place, users can expect a dramatic improvement in performance. Queries that used to take three hours now take three seconds.

Over the years PeopleSoft has provided more support for fast security, and now provides Application Engine SQL to combine the tables and insert records into a special fast security table. In this appendix we will look closely at this SQL, and go over the other changes to the system that may be required.

B.1 Query Security Overview

B.1.1 Operator Classes

A security administrator takes the employee population and assigns each employee an operator class. The operator class groups individuals into different levels of security access. For example, you could set up an employee class that has access to payroll data and one class that doesn't. Simply assign each user to the appropriate class.

The more operator classes you create, the more complex your security environment becomes. Some implementations assign a unique operator class to every employee. Perhaps one employee should not be able to see another employee. An operator class is created that restricts the access of one employee to see another. Obviously when you create this many operator classes, the performance of the system begins to suffer.

B.1.2 Why Queries Take So Long

The root of the performance issue is in the SQL that is used to look up an employee. Every time a user opens a panel or runs a query, PeopleSoft diligently looks up the user's operator class and checks if the user is allowed to view the data returned. It performs this verification through search views.

A search view contains a join of several security tables. Search views are identified by the naming convention 'SRCH' in the table name. Although there are many search views for different types of data and in different countries, let's focus on the two principal search views:

- PS_EMPLMT_SRCH_GBL
- PS_PERS_SRCH_GLB

These two views look identical, but PeopleSoft has associated them with different panels. When a panel contains an employment record number (EMPL_RCD#), PeopleSoft links it to PS_EMPLMT_SRCH_GBL. If a panel only has an employee ID (EMPLID), it is linked to PS_PERS_SRCH_GBL.

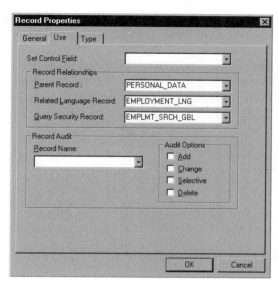

▶ Figure B-1   Record properties
query security record link

This link occurs in the table properties of each table. Figure B-1 shows the PS_EMPLOYMENT table properties (found under File ➤ Object Properties in the Application Designer). The Query Search Record is set to PS_EMPLMT_SRCH_GBL.

With this link established, PeopleSoft knows where to check security when you access the PS_EMPLOYMENT table. If we open the PS_EMPLMT_SRCH_GBL table, and look at the record properties 'Type' tab, we can look directly at the SQL that will run (reformatted below). Let's look at sections of it in detail.

First, the columns the view selects:

```
SELECT
A.EMPLID,
B.EMPL_RCD#,
SEC.OPRID,
SEC.ACCESS_CD,
A.NAME,
A.LAST_NAME_SRCH,
ND.COUNTRY,
ND.NATIONAL_ID_TYPE,
NDT.DESCRSHORT,
ND.NATIONAL_ID

FROM PS_PERSONAL_DATA A,
     PS_JOB B,
     PS_PERS_NID ND,
     PS_NID_TYPE_TBL NDT,
     PS_SCRTY_TBL_DEPT SEC
```

All of the keys one could use to look up an employee are associated with an operator ID and an access code. The name comes from personal data, the Social Security number from the national ID table, and the employee record number from the job table. The national ID description describes the ID as 'SSN,' 'SIN,' etc.

To obtain the security settings for the employee, the department security table is accessed. We will see how it is accessed in the WHERE clauses below. First, though, we get the links between the general employee tables out of the way:

```
WHERE A.EMPLID    = B.EMPLID
  AND A.EMPLID    = ND.EMPLID
  AND ND.COUNTRY = NDT.COUNTRY
  AND ND.NATIONAL_ID_TYPE = NDT.NATIONAL_ID_TYPE
  AND (B.EFFDT >= %CURRENTDATEIN
      OR (B.EFFDT = (SELECT MAX(B2.EFFDT)
                        FROM PS_JOB B2
                        WHERE B.EMPLID     = B2.EMPLID
                          AND B.EMPL_RCD# = B2.EMPL_RCD#
                          AND B2.EFFDT      <= %CURRENTDATEIN)
          AND B.EFFSEQ = (SELECT MAX(B3.EFFSEQ)
                        FROM PS_JOB B3
                        WHERE B.EMPLID     = B3.EMPLID
                          AND B.EMPL_RCD# = B3.EMPL_RCD#
                          AND B.EFFDT     = B3.EFFDT ) ) )
```

The job table selection is standard, but it also ensures that future-dated rows are included. Essentially the query chooses the most recent job table row *or* any rows that are greater than the current date.

```
AND SEC.ACCESS_CD = 'Y'
AND EXISTS (SELECT 'X'
             FROM PSTREENODE SEC3
             WHERE SEC3.SETID     = SEC.SETID
               AND SEC3.SETID     = B.SETID_DEPT
               AND SEC3.TREE_NAME = 'DEPT_SECURITY'
               AND SEC3.EFFDT     = SEC.TREE_EFFDT
               AND SEC3.TREE_NODE = B.DEPTID
               AND SEC3.TREE_NODE_NUM BETWEEN
                   SEC.TREE_NODE_NUM AND SEC.TREE_NODE_NUM_END
               AND NOT EXISTS
                  (SELECT 'X'
                     FROM PS_SCRTY_TBL_DEPT SEC2
                    WHERE SEC.OPRID = SEC2.OPRID
                      AND SEC.SETID = SEC2.SETID
                      AND SEC.TREE_NODE_NUM <> SEC2.TREE_NODE_NUM
                      AND SEC3.TREE_NODE_NUM BETWEEN
                          SEC2.TREE_NODE_NUM AND
                          SEC2.TREE_NODE_NUM_END
                      AND SEC2.TREE_NODE_NUM BETWEEN
                          SEC.TREE_NODE_NUM AND
                          SEC.TREE_NODE_NUM_END ) )
```

The remainder of the query focuses on department security. The access code must be yes (the operator class has access). Then the query looks for all departments that the employee has access to, selecting the operator ID for each (in the SELECT we saw before). The EXISTS clause searches the department security tree for the employee's most recent (or future) department ('B.DEPTID').

Each row on the PS_SCRTY_TBL_DEPT represents a unique operator class, setID, and department ID. Each row also contains a begin and end tree node number (all of the nodes under the department ID). The search view uses these beginning and ending numbers to include all departments the operator class has access to and exclude all of the departments the operator class is not allowed to see.

> The operator ID and operator class fields have different meanings, but PeopleSoft uses them for the same values. An operator ID is the ID you type in to log onto PeopleSoft. Operator classes are also stored in the operator ID field, as you can see on the PS_SCRTY_TBL_DEPT. The PS_EMPLMT_SRCH_GBL view takes the operator ID field from PS_SCRTY_TBL_DEPT and renames it operator class. If there is no operator class for an employee, PeopleSoft defaults to the operator ID, placing the ID value in the operator class field.

The result is a link between the employee and every valid operator class for that employee. The SQL in Table B-1 demonstrates the results.

▶ **Table B-1**   Direct query of employment search view

| The query | ```
SELECT ES.EMPLID,
       ES.OPRCLASS
  FROM PS_EMPLMT_SRCH_GBL ES
 WHERE ES.EMPLID = 'BOZO'
``` |
| Returns the data set | ```
EMPLID   OPRCLASS
------   --------
BOZO     ALLPANLS
BOZO     CLOWNPNL
BOZO     FRA
BOZO     GER
BOZO     USAPANLS
``` |

When a user tries to perform a query on the PS_EMPLOYMENT table, the following occurs:

1. PeopleSoft Query automatically adds the PS_EMPLMT_SRCH_GBL table.
2. The operator class of the user is placed in a WHERE clause and attached to the query.
3. When the SQL executes, only the employees who are associated with that operator class are selected.

For example, if the user is in the 'SOMPANLS' operator class, the employee 'BOZO' would not be returned. Bozo cannot be accessed by users in the 'SOM-PANLS' operator class. But if the operator class is 'GER,' the Query *will* return 'BOZO.'

Unfortunately the steps that actually occur aren't as simple as 1-2-3. The use of the search table really links to a view, which links to many other tables. The SQL above demonstrates how complex the query really is. This SQL must execute for every single row for every single query. In essence, PeopleSoft attaches nine tables to your one table just to determine if you are allowed to see each row.

B.2 THE FAST SECURITY SOLUTION

Since the goal of the complex security view is a list of employees and their operator classes, you can easily create a batch process that creates such a table every night. Some modifications to PeopleSoft are required.

The first step is to populate the delivered fast security table (PS_FAST_SCRTY_1). This can be performed using the Application Engine SQL that is provided, or with a batch program that executes every night. The batch program should delete all of the rows in the fast security table and then load the results of the SQL we described above (with the nine tables) into the table.

Then the appropriate views must be modified. Only the views for the tables that you wish to access need to be modified. The following tables comprise the majority of tables United States implementations will require:

• PERS_SRCH_GBL
• PERS_SRCH_US
• EMPLMT_SRCH_GBL
• EMPLMT_SRCH_US

Here are the basic steps to follow when modifying each view:

1. Copy the security view (i.e., PS_EMPLMT_SRCH_GBL), renaming it in order to save it.
2. Modify the security view, taking out the SQL in the 'Type' tab of the object properties. Replace the SQL with a simple select of the columns in the fast security table PS_FAST_SCRTY_1.
3. Save the view.

Now fast security is active, and queries will run much faster.

There are two versions of fast security. The difference can be detected by looking at the tables provided by PeopleSoft: PS_FAST_SCRTY_1 and PS_FAST_SCRTY_2. Fast security '1' takes the entire security view and places the results in a flat table. Fast security '2' takes only part of the security view and places the results in a flat table (using fewer fields). Version '2' includes the most complex piece of version '1', where department security is determined. Version '2' leaves the key lookup of fields like SSN and NAME to the security view. It takes less time to populate but does not improve performance as much as version '1'. Version '1' performs the entire view.

Fast security '2' does not require any PeopleCode edits, while version '1' should be implemented with two modifications to delivered PeopleCode (see 'PeopleCode Edits' below). Since the key lookup (employee ID, name, SSN) still occurs in the security view in version '2', the effects of changes to the system are recognized immediately. Fast security '2' is slower than version '1' but may be fast enough, depending on the technical environment.

B.2.1 PeopleCode Modifications

There are some additional issues that can be resolved with the addition of PeopleCode. One issue is the procedure of hiring an employee. The record for the employee is created, but it is not replicated into the fast security table until the batch process is executed.

For the PS_EMPLOYEES table, this is not an issue. Users can wait a day before seeing an employee in the PS_EMPLOYEES table. The fast security table, on the other hand, provides access not only to tables in Query but also to *every* PeopleSoft panel. If an employee is hired, and then the operator tries to type in direct deposit information for the employee, PeopleSoft will not recognize the employee ID just assigned. That is because for every panel, PeopleSoft checks the security access to each employee ID against the fast security table. If the employee ID cannot be found, nothing will be returned.

The solution is to add PeopleCode so that when an employee is hired, a row is written out to the fast security table immediately. PeopleSoft will provide the appropriate PeopleCode if you are implementing fast security.

A similar issue develops when a change in department occurs. If an employee changes departments, the related changes in security access do not affect the user until a row is changed in the fast security table. PeopleSoft also provides PeopleCode for department changes.

With these two modifications to PeopleCode, fast security no longer presents real-time issues. Although the modifications to the security views and the addition of two PeopleCode items require modification, the results are astounding. Also, all of the modifications are supported by PeopleSoft and should not present significant issues during upgrades. PeopleSoft has left the security table views alone, despite the addition of new features to PeopleSoft security. For example, a new feature allows a user to be placed under more than one operator class. PeopleSoft provides this feature but requires that the views be manually modified to accommodate it if you wish to use it. This way the tables remain the same and do not present issues for existing users.

PeopleSoft is delivered with many common modules that are used by delivered SQR programs. This Appendix lists each delivered common module and its function. Many of the common modules are of no use at all, but it is important to know the ones that could provide functionality to custom SQR programs.

▶ **Table C-1** Delivered common module descriptions by type

Type	SQC name	Description
API	prcsapi.sqc	Procedure to update the process scheduler request record
API	prcsdef.sqc	Procedure to define the process scheduler variables.
API	prcslng.sqc	Process scheduler API for multiple language use
API	projapi.sqc	API for creating a new project definition
API	stdapi.sqc	Process scheduler interface
Ask	askactn.sqc	Input logic for user-entered actions
Ask	askaod.sqc	Input logic for user-entered as-of date
Ask	askarea.sqc	Get area code from user
Ask	askbu.sqc	Masking logic for user-entered business unit name
Ask	askcalyr.sqc	Input logic for user-entered calendar year
Ask	askcbrpt.sqc	COBRA ask reprint values
Ask	askdept.sqc	Input logic for user-entered department numbers
Ask	askeffdt.sqc	Asks user to enter effective date

▶ **Table C-1** continued

Type	SQC name	Description
Ask	askftd.sqc	Input logic for user-entered from and through dates
Ask	askjbcde.sqc	Input logic for user for salary mass updates by job code
Ask	askldgr.sqc	Masking logic for user-entered ledger group name
Ask	askledg.sqc	Masking logic for user-entered ledger name
Ask	askprd.sqc	Input logic for user-entered period begin/end dates
Ask	askprins.sqc	Input logic for user-entered process instances (PIS)
Ask	askpygrp.sqc	Input logic for user for salary mass updates
Ask	askreqn.sqc	Input logic for user-entered job requisitions
Ask	asksalpl.sqc	Input logic for user for salary plan
Ask	askselct.sqc	Ask-select masking logic for user input. Asks user to enter data, then masks it
Ask	askslpln.sqc	Input logic for user for salary mass updates by salary plan
Ask	asksrvyr.sqc	Input logic for user-entered service years
Ask	askstpin.sqc	Input logic for user for salary step increments
Ask	askvacnt.sqc	Input logic for user-entered vacant position report request
Ask	askxovrd.sqc	Input logic for user-entered exception/override option
Ask	benasof.sqc	Input logic for user-entered as-of date
Ask	benftd.sqc	Input logic for user-entered from/thru dates
Ask	chgasodt.sqc	Request as-of date and update the PSASOFDATE record
Ask	chgftdts.sqc	Request from date and through date
Calculation	car001.sqc	Calculate car & fuel benefit charges
Calculation	datemath.sqc	Routines for date arithmetic
Calculation	datewrk.sqc	Computes days worked
Calculation	eeogroup.sqc	Sex/ethnic group analysis
Calculation	eeogrpuk.sqc	Sex/ethnic group analysis for UK
Calculation	fsadates.sqc	Generates Flexible Spending Account dates (1st and last day of year)
Calculation	sqrtrans.sqc	Translate SQR strings to given language
Calculation	timemath.sqc	SQR time arithmetic procedures
COBRA-specific	cbaskval.sqc	COBRA ask values
COBRA-specific	cbgetval.sqc	Mask run control routines
COBRA-specific	cbraddr.sqc	COBRA address

▶ **Table C-1** continued

Type	SQC name	Description
COBRA-specific	cbrdefs.sqc	COBRA defines
COBRA-specific	cbrdeps.sqc	COBRA enrollment form dependent processing
COBRA-specific	cbrncntl.sqc	Retrieves run control for report parameters needed for benefits reports
Define constants	canrpt.sqc	Sets NID_COUNTRY = 'CAN' for Canada reporting
Define constants	convdef.sqc	Define conversion constants
Define constants	rdbms.sqc	Define database environment constant
Define constants	setenv.sqc	Define operating system and date constants variables. Includes 'rdbms.sqc' and 'opsys.sqc'.
Define constants	stdvar.sqc	Sets payroll national ID type = 'PR'
Define constants	usarpt.sqc	Defines NID_COUNTRY as 'USA' for USA reporting
Formatting	address.sqc	Converts address fields into display address
Formatting	adformat.sqc	Converts address fields using country settings
Formatting	chgampus.sqc	Change an ampersand to an underscore/back space
Formatting	compnum.sqc	Compares two values; SQR does not always correctly compare values; this is the workaround
Formatting	convtab.sqc	Converts a tab-delimited file to comma-delimited
Formatting	currnd.sqc	Currency rounding common module
Formatting	datetime.sqc	Routines to format dates and times
Formatting	eftkana.sqc	Generate Hankaku characters for Japanese EFT files
Formatting	ldadropt.sqc	Load a lookup table with the paycheck address options
Formatting	ldlifcov.sqc	Load a lookup table with the life and AD&D coverage types
Formatting	ldnumlit.sqc	Create array of literals for number-to-words conversion
Formatting	ldnumtrn.sqc	Language-enabled version of ldnumlit.sqc, used in paycheck
Formatting	ldorgsb.sqc	Load array with symbols to represent org. code
Formatting	ldpgmcur.sqc	Load a lookup table with currency code for benefit program
Formatting	ldplntyp.sqc	Load a lookup table with the plan types
Formatting	namenl.sqc	Change format for Dutch name
Formatting	netintrn.sqc	Language-enabled version of netinwds.sqc
Formatting	netinwds.sqc	Convert net pay to words
Formatting	nidformt.sqc	Formats the national ID according to country settings
Formatting	number.sqc	Routines to format numbers

▶ **Table C-1** continued

Type	SQC name	Description
Formatting	ohsutil.sqc	UK data formatting for OHS reports
Formatting	proper.sqc	Capitalizes the first letter of every word in a string
Formatting	rotname1.sqc	Convert name from "last,first,prefix" to "first prefix last"
Formatting	rotname2.sqc	Convert name from "last,first,prefix" to "fi mi prefix last"
Formatting	rotname3.sqc	Convert name from "last,first,prefix" to its 3 components
Formatting	rotname4.sqc	Convert name from "last,first,prefix" to "fi last"
Formatting	rotname5.sqc	Convert from "last suffix,first" to "last first suffix"
Formatting	rotname6.sqc	Convert from "last suffix,first" to "last first mid in"
Formatting	rotname7.sqc	Convert from "Last Suffix,First" to "FIn MidIn Last" (remove suffix from name)
Formatting	rotname8.sqc	Convert from "First MidIn Last Suffix" to "First MidIn Last" (remove title and suffix from name)
Formatting	ukutil.sqc	General United Kingdom formatting routines
Get	bendeps.sqc	Select dependent records
Get	curdttim.sqc	Get current system date and time
Get	cvrgcd.sqc	Retrieves description of a coverage code
Get	getactrs.sqc	Get action reason from the action reason table
Get	getasodt.sqc	Get as-of date from PSASOFDATE record
Get	getbalid.sqc	Get balance ID for calendar year from the installation table
Get	getbennm.sqc	Get the benefit name
Get	getbical.sqc	Get billing calendar
Get	getbunam.sqc	Get the description of a business unit code
Get	getcodta.sqc	Get selected fields from the company table
Get	getcurnm.sqc	Get currency name from the currency table
Get	getcvgcd.sqc	Retrieves coverage code info from COVRG_CD_TBL
Get	getdatcd.sqc	Get year, quarter, and month codes from $asofdate variable
Get	getdedbl.sqc	Get deduction balances
Get	getdednm.sqc	Get deduction name from the deductions table
Get	getdptnm.sqc	Get department name from the department table
Get	getempad.sqc	Get basic personal data for an employee
Get	getempna.sqc	Get the nationality of an employee
Get	getempnm.sqc	Get the person's name from the PS_PERSONAL_DATA record

▶ **Table C-1** continued

Type	SQC name	Description
Get	geternbl.sqc	Get earnings balances
Get	geternnm.sqc	Get earnings name from the earnings table
Get	getestnm.sqc	Get establishment name (used for tips)
Get	getfrmat.sqc	Get format (for diskettes)
Get	getftdts.sqc	Get from date and as-of date from PSASOFDATE record
Get	gethours.sqc	Get hours
Get	getjobtl.sqc	Get job title from the job code table
Get	getlcdta.sqc	Get selected fields from the local tax tables
Get	getlocnm.sqc	Get location name from the location table
Get	getmonnm.sqc	Get month name procedures
Get	getorgsb.sqc	Get symbol for org. code
Get	getpgdta.sqc	Get selected fields from paygroup table
Get	getpgmnm.sqc	Get the name of the current benefit program
Get	getposnm.sqc	Get position name from the position data table
Get	getprvnm.sqc	Get the benefit provider's name
Get	getqtrcd.sqc	Get quarter and month codes from $asofdate
Get	getrplng.sqc	Get the report language
Get	getrptpd.sqc	Retrieve reporting period for benefits reports
Get	getrpttr.sqc	Get reporting period for benefits reports
Get	getsched.sqc	Get benefits administration schedule ID from the user
Get	getschnm.sqc	Get the name of the current benefits administration schedule
Get	getsetid.sqc	Gets the setID for the system
Get	getslgrd.sqc	Get salary grade data from the salary grade table
Get	getstdta.sqc	Get selected fields from the state tax tables
Get	gettxlnm.sqc	Gets the tax location name from the tax location1 table
Get	getunion.sqc	Get union fields from the union table
Get	getweeks.sqc	Get weeks
Get	getwrkcn.sqc	Gets fields from the Works Council table (Germany only)
Get	hrsecty.sqc	Get SQR security flag
Get	readxlat.sqc	Read the translate table for the desired values.
Get	validdt.sqc	Routines to validate date

▶ **Table C-1** continued

Type	SQC name	Description
Heading	stdhdg01.sqc	Standard heading #1 for printed reports, contains: report ID, run date, run time, report title
Heading	stdhdg02.sqc	Standard heading #2 for printed reports, contains company code and company name, includes stdhdg01.sqc
Heading	stdhdg03.sqc	Standard heading #3 for printed reports, contains: as of date, includes stdhdg01.sqc
Heading	stdhdg04.sqc	Standard heading #4 for printed reports, contains: pay period end date, includes stdhdg02.sqc
Heading	stdhdg05.sqc	Standard heading #5 for printed reports, contains: check date and time, includes stdhdg02.sqc
Heading	stdhdg06.sqc	Standard heading #6 for printed reports, contains: paygroup information, includes stdhdg04.sqc
Heading	stdhdg07.sqc	Standard heading #7 for printed reports, contains: department ID and name, includes stdhdg04.sqc
Heading	stdhdg08.sqc	Standard heading #8 for printed reports, contains: period from through dates, includes stdhdg01.sqc
Heading	stdhdg09.sqc	Standard heading #9 for printed reports, contains: asofdate, includes stdhdg02.sqc
Heading	stdhdg10.sqc	Standard heading #10 for printed reports, contains: EMPLID and name, includes stdhdg02.sqc
Heading	stdhdg11.sqc	Standard heading #11 for printed reports, contains: period from through dates, includes stdhdg02.sqc
Heading	stdhdg12.sqc	Standard heading #12 for printed reports, contains: schedule ID, includes stdhdg01.sqc
Heading	stdhdgpi.sqc	Standard heading for printed reports using payinit.sqc, contains payroll information
Heading	stdhdgtr.sqc	Standard heading #1 for printed reports
Heading	stdhtr02.sqc	Standard heading #2 for printed reports
Heading	stdhtr03.sqc	Standard heading #3 for printed reports
Heading	stdhtr04.sqc	Standard heading #4 for printed reports
Heading	stdhtr05.sqc	Standard heading #5 for printed reports
Heading	stdhtr06.sqc	Standard heading #6 for printed reports
Heading	stdhtr07.sqc	Standard heading #7 for printed reports
Heading	stdhtr08.sqc	Standard heading #8 for printed reports
Heading	stdhtr09.sqc	Standard heading #9 for printed reports

▶ **Table C-1**   continued

Type	SQC name	Description
Heading	stdhtr10.sqc	Standard heading #10 for printed reports
Heading	stdhtr11.sqc	Standard heading #11 for printed reports
Heading	stdhtr12.sqc	Standard heading #12 for printed reports
Heading	stdhtrpi.sqc	Standard heading for printed reports using PAYINIT.sqc
Insert	benotr.sqc	Populates tables for PS_BENEFITS_Data
Insert	benpers.sqc	Populates personal data information to benefit tables
Insert	setbuutl.sqc	Inserts rows into the setID table and business unit table
Insert	setidutl.sqc	Inserts rows into the setID table
Pension module	paextrct.sqc	Pension administration benefits value extract
Pension module	pafunctn.sqc	Pension administration functions
Pension module	pagetval.sqc	Masks run control date for pension administration
Pension module	pahdg01.sqc	Pension administration worksheet heading
Pension module	pahdg06c.sqc	Pension administration Social Security worksheet heading
Pension module	paresult.sqc	Reads result tables for pension administration
Pension module	parnctl1.sqc	Retrieve run control parameters for pension administration human resources reports
Pension module	parnctl2.sqc	Retrieve run control parameters for pension administration human resources reports
Pension module	paservce.sqc	Calculates service for pension administration
Pension module	pat08hdg.sqc	Pension administration trustee extract report heading
Pension module	pat09hdg.sqc	Pension administration trustee detail report heading
Pension module	pay300rt.sqc	Retrieves run control parameters from RTRORQST_RUNCTL
Pension module	pay301rt.sqc	Retrieves run control parameters from RTROREPT_RUNCTL
Pension module	pay302rt.sqc	Retrieves run control parameters from RTROSUMM_RUNCTL
Pension module	pay303rt.sqc	Retrieves run control parameters from RTROTERM_RUNCTL
Pension module	paydelrc.sqc	Deletes payroll run control record
PS Financials	fsbegin.sqc	This is the ps/financials standard report driver
PS Financials	fsgetshr.sqc	This procedure will retrieve the correct setID for the set name being shared
PS Financials	fshdg01.sqc	Standard heading #1 for ps/financials reports
PS Financials	fshdg02.sqc	Standard heading #2 for ps/financials reports
PS Financials	fshdg05.sqc	Standard heading #5 for ps/financials reports

▶ **Table C-1** continued

Type	SQC name	Description
PS Financials	fshdg06b.sqc	Standard heading #6 for ps/financials reports
PS Financials	fsldsdta.sqc	Get data from the ledger definition table
PS Financials	fslgrdta.sqc	Get data from the ledger group definition table
PS Financials	fsprcbll.sqc	This is the highest level procedure in the program. It will process the business unit based upon the ask criteria.
Report-specific	askactop.sqc	Get action option for pos002
Report-specific	askap008.sqc	Input logic for user report app008
Report-specific	askap010.sqc	Input logic for user report app010
Report-specific	askcar.sqc	Input logic for p11d reports
Report-specific	askeecrs.sqc	Input logic for user report per101cn
Report-specific	askp034.sqc	Input for per034a - create internal resume
Report-specific	basdep00.sqc	Benefits administration enrollment form dependent processing
Report-specific	ckeyrctl.sqc	Selects run control fields for delivered general ledger interface
Report-specific	ctxflt4.sqc	Generates form flash for Canadian T4 form
Report-specific	ctxflt4a.sqc	Generates form flash for Canadian T4 form
Report-specific	ctxrctl1.sqc	Retrieves run control for report parameters needed for Canadian tax reports
Report-specific	ctxrnctl.sqc	Retrieve data from Canadian process parameters record Canadian tax reports
Report-specific	dddindex.sqc	Audit index
Report-specific	dddtable.sqc	Audit record/SQL table
Report-specific	dddviews.sqc	Audit views
Report-specific	ecbusdoc.sqc	Used when trying to reprocess an inbound data file that was in error
Report-specific	ecin999.sqc	Parses the 999 control records in the flat file. It then validates the control information to make sure further data can be processed
Report-specific	ecmapfld.sqc	No description
Report-specific	ecoutmap.sqc	No description
Report-specific	ecwhere.sqc	Derive where clause
Report-specific	hdg912.sqc	Print headers for tax912xx
Report-specific	hrtrnrpt.sqc	Scenarios for TN010 and TN011 reports
Report-specific	icclrctl.sqc	Run control for calculation

▶ **Table C-1** continued

Type	SQC name	Description
Report-specific	icelhous.sqc	Incentive comp housekeeping routines for elig./calc.
Report-specific	icgbhous.sqc	Incentive comp housekeeping routines
Report-specific	icmemrpt.sqc	Retrieves incentive comp. run control parameters from IC_MEMRP_RUNCTL
Report-specific	icpayint.sqc	Retrieves incentive comp. run control parameters from IC_PYINT_RUNCTL
Report-specific	icround.sqc	Incentive comp rounding rules routine
Report-specific	masschng.sqc	Mass change processing shared procedures
Report-specific	massfile.sqc	Mass change file unload/load procedures
Report-specific	masslayo.sqc	Mass layout #defines
Report-specific	ohs003gr.sqc	Gets common data for the OHS001 and 004 reports (Germany only)
Report-specific	ohs501uk.sqc	Gets health and safety base locations for United Kingdom reports
Report-specific	ohs701bc.sqc	Used for electronic commerce functionality
Report-specific	ohsget.sqc	Masks health and safety record values for health and safety reports
Report-specific	ohsrnctl.sqc	Run control value selection for health and safety reports
Report-specific	opsys.sqc	Operating system environment
Report-specific	pirunctl.sqc	Payroll interface changes report (delivered payroll interface to external payroll system)
Report-specific	progtype.sqc	Procedure to build PeopleCode program type array
Report-specific	prtssaa.sqc	Print data from transmitter record—SSA format
Report-specific	prtssab.sqc	Print data from basic authorization rec—SSA format
Report-specific	prtssae.sqc	Print data from employer record—SSA format
Report-specific	prtssas.sqc	Print data from employee state record(s)—SSA format
Report-specific	rdtap912.sqc	Read tape file for tax912xx
Report-specific	rptsmmca.sqc	Used by TAX810 series of SQRs (quarterly wage listing) as a summary report
Report-specific	rptsmmry.sqc	Print summary information
Report-specific	stgbhous.sqc	Stock administration housekeeping routines
Report-specific	stw2smry.sqc	State w-2 tape summary report heading include
Report-specific	txovrflw.sqc	Utility for splitting tax amounts that overflow fields

▶ **Table C-1**   continued

Type	SQC name	Description
Report-specific	txrnctl1.sqc	Retrieves run control for report parameters needed for tax reports
Report-specific	txrnctl2.sqc	Retrieves run control for report parameters needed for tax reports
Report-specific	w2sort.sqc	Control w2 sort
Report-specific	wlgen.sqc	Wlgen.sqc work list generator
Run control	bngetval.sqc	Masks run control routines
Run control	bnrunctl.sqc	Retrieves run control for report parameters needed for benefits reports
Run control	hrctlfra.sqc	Retrieves parameters for France run control
Run control	hrctlnld.sqc	Retrieves parameters for Netherlands run control
Run control	hrgetfra.sqc	France run control masks
Run control	hrgetnld.sqc	Netherlands run control masks
Run control	hrgetval.sqc	Masks run control value
Run control	hrrnctl1.sqc	Retrieves run control for the parameters of the human resources reports
Run control	hrrnctl2.sqc	Retrieves run control for list of actions
Run control	hrrnctl3.sqc	Retrieves run control for list of job requisitions
Run control	hrrnctl4.sqc	Retrieves run control for list of departments
Run control	payinit.sqc	Payroll report initialization and timing routines
Run control	payrctl2.sqc	Retrieves payroll run control parameters from RC_PAY RECORD
Run control	payrctl3.sqc	Retrieves run control parameters from PS_RC_PAY_UNSHT. Invoked by payroll un-sheet process
Run control	payrnctl.sqc	Retrieves run control for report parameters needed for payroll reports
Run control	pygetval.sqc	Sets defaults for pay run control values
Run control	rdedrctl.sqc	Retrieves run control for report parameters needed for payroll reports which use payinit.sqc
Run control	taxrnctl.sqc	Retrieves data from tax reporting run control record
Run control	tiprnctl.sqc	Gets run control parameters for tips processing run control
Run control	tlgetval.sqc	Gets begin and end dates for time and labor processes
Run control	tlrnctl1.sqc	Gets run control parameters for time and labor processes

▶ **Table C-1** continued

Type	SQC name	Description
SQR setup/utility	chkadvpr.sqc	Check and advice printer settings (including MICR settings)
SQR setup/utility	converr.sqc	SQL error procedure for conversion
SQR setup/utility	eoj.sqc	Perform end of job processing if successful status
SQR setup/utility	reset.sqc	Reset printer, print 'end of report'
SQR setup/utility	setlyo3l.sqc	Landscape layout declaration for reports
SQR setup/utility	setlyo3p.sqc	Portrait layout declaration for reports
SQR setup/utility	setlyout.sqc	Set the layout for the sqr report
SQR setup/utility	setori3l.sqc	Sets layout constants by evaluating paper size (landscape only)
SQR setup/utility	setori3p.sqc	Sets layout constants by evaluating paper size (portrait only)
SQR setup/utility	setprt3.sqc	Sets printer declaration
SQR setup/utility	setup01.sqc	Standard setup section (portrait orientation)
SQR setup/utility	setup01a.sqc	Printer and page-size initialization (portrait)
SQR setup/utility	setup02.sqc	Standard setup section (landscape orientation)
SQR setup/utility	setup02a.sqc	Printer and page-size initialization (landscape)
SQR setup/utility	setup02b.sqc	Printer and page-size initialization
SQR setup/utility	setup02c.sqc	Printer and page-size initialization
SQR setup/utility	setup03.sqc	Printer and page-size initialization
SQR setup/utility	setup03i.sqc	Printer and page-size initialization
SQR setup/utility	setup03l.sqc	Printer and page-size initialization
SQR setup/utility	setup04i.sqc	Printer and page-size initialization
SQR setup/utility	setup04l.sqc	Printer and page-size initialization
SQR setup/utility	setup06.sqc	Setup for extract files
SQR setup/utility	setup07.sqc	Printer and page-size initialization
SQR setup/utility	setup10.sqc	Printer and page-size initialization
SQR setup/utility	setup10a.sqc	Printer and page-size initialization
SQR setup/utility	setup31.sqc	Printer and page-size initialization (portrait)
SQR setup/utility	setup32.sqc	Printer and page-size initialization (landscape)
SQR setup/utility	setupdb.sqc	Database-specific setup
SQR setup/utility	sqlerr.sqc	SQL error-handling procedure
SQR setup/utility	stdinit.sqc	Reports initialization and timing routines

▶ **Table C-1** continued

Type	SQC name	Description
SQR setup/utility	tranctrl.sqc	Supports commit, rollback, etc., across platforms. Can be used in other SQRS by performing a "do commit-transaction" rather than a "commit"
SQR setup/utility	useprntr.sqc	Indicates which printer to use for reports
SQR setup/utility	utils.sqc	Printing utilities (word wrap)
System report	sysauthi.sqc	PS operator authorized item edit report
System report	sysauthp.sqc	Verifies that authorized process group operator exists
System report	sysauths.sqc	PS operator authorized sign on edit report
System report	sysclrls.sqc	Audit of audit tables (verifies data in audit tables is exclusive)
System report	sysdbfld.sqc	PS database field definition edits report
System report	sysecmgr.sqc	Report of EDI maps
System report	syshelpi.sqc	PS help index edits report
System report	syshelpt.sqc	PS help text edits report
System report	sysimpdf.sqc	PS import definition edits report
System report	sysimpfd.sqc	PS import definition field edits report
System report	sysimpxl.sqc	PS import translate edits report
System report	syslang.sqc	Audit report of language tables
System report	sysmenud.sqc	PS menu definition edits report
System report	sysmenui.sqc	PS menu item edits report
System report	sysoprdf.sqc	PS operator-definition edits report
System report	syspcmnm.sqc	PS PeopleCode program manager name report
System report	syspcmpr.sqc	PS PeopleCode program manager report
System report	syspnldf.sqc	PS panel definition field count report
System report	syspnlfd.sqc	PS panel field edits report
System report	syspnlgr.sqc	PS panel group edits report
System report	sysprgnm.sqc	PS PeopleCode program name edits report
System report	sysqrybn.sqc	PS query binds edits report
System report	sysqrycr.sqc	PS query definition criteria edits report
System report	sysqrydf.sqc	PS query definition edits report
System report	sysqryfd.sqc	PS query definition field edits report
System report	sysqryrc.sqc	PS query definition record edits report
System report	sysqrysl.sqc	PS query definition selection edits report

▶ **Table C-1** continued

Type	SQC name	Description
System report	sysrecdf.sqc	PS record definition edits report
System report	sysrecfd.sqc	PS record definition field edits report
System report	systreeb.sqc	PS tree branch edits report
System report	systreed.sqc	PS tree definition edits report
System report	systreel.sqc	PS tree level/node/leaf edits report
System report	systrees.sqc	PS tree structure edits report
System report	sysversn.sqc	PS lock version report
System report	sysviewt.sqc	PS view text edits report
System report	sysxlatt.sqc	PS translate table edits report
Upgrade	updvers.sqc	Common upgrade version lock routines
Upgrade	upg.sqc	Common upgrade defines
Upgrade	upgattr.sqc	Upgrade process—comparison & conflict identification
Upgrade	upgcodes.sqc	Upgrade process—load codes
Upgrade	upghdg01.sqc	Upgrade report standard heading #1
Upgrade	upghdg02.sqc	Upgrade report standard heading #2
Upgrade	upgpr.sqc	Upgrade process—common procedures
Upgrade	upgsetup.sqc	Retrieve parameters from command line

Index

$E tax, 238
$U tax, 238
% wildcard, 11